Education, Ethnicity, Society and Global Change in Asia

In the **World Library of Educationalists** series, international experts compile career-long collections of what they judge to be their finest pieces – extracts from books, key articles, salient research findings, major theoretical and practical contributions – so the world can read them in a single manageable volume. Readers will be able to follow the themes and strands and see how their work contributes to the development of the field.

For more than three decades, Gerard A. Postiglione has witnessed first-hand the globalization of education and society in Hong Kong, China and the wider Asian region. He is a pioneer among Western scholars in the field and his fluency in Chinese has resulted in innovative primary research and fieldwork. He has brought sociological, policy, and comparative perspectives to important educational issues in Asia. His research emphasizes the diversity and complexity of the region, from studies of education and the academic profession during Hong Kong's retrocession, to reform of ethnic minority education and the rise of world class universities in the Chinese mainland, as well as the complexity of mass higher education in an increasingly dynamic Asia. He is one of the researchers most sought-after by international organizations concerned with educational reform in Asia and by major media outlets to inform the public on issues of globalization and higher education.

Gerard was honoured by the Comparative and International Education Society with a Lifetime Contribution Award and Best Book Award for his contribution to the field. In 2016 he was inducted as a Fellow of the American Educational Research Association. This selection of 12 of his most representative papers and chapters documents his scholarship in comparative higher education in Asia.

Gerard A. Postiglione is Chair Professor of Higher Education, former Associate Dean for Research, and Director of the Wah Ching Centre on Education in China, Faculty of Education, The University of Hong Kong.

World Library of Educationalists Series

A full list of titles in this series is available at: www.routledge.com.

Recently published titles:

A Developing Discourse in Music Education
The selected works of Keith Swanwick
Keith Swanwick

Struggles for Equity in Education
The Selected Works of Mel Ainscow
Mel Ainscow

Faith, Mission and Challenge in Catholic Education
The Selected Works of Gerald Grace
Gerald Grace

From Practice to Praxis: A reflexive turn
The Selected Works of Susan Groundwater-Smith
Susan Groundwater-Smith

Learning, Development and Education: From learning theory to education and practice
The Selected Works of Knud Illeris
Knud Illeris

(Post)Critical Methodologies: The Science Possible After the Critiques
The Selected Works of Patti Lather
Patti Lather

Education, Ethnicity, Society and Global Change in Asia
The Selected Works of Gerard A. Postiglione
Gerard A. Postiglione

Leading Learning/Learning Leading: A Retrospective on a Life's Work
The Selected Works of Robert J. Starratt
Robert J. Starratt

Education, Ethnicity, Society and Global Change in Asia
The Selected Works of
Gerard A. Postiglione

Gerard A. Postiglione

LONDON AND NEW YORK

First published 2017
by Routledge
2 Park Square, Milton Park, Abingdon, Oxon OX14 4RN

and by Routledge
711 Third Avenue, New York, NY 10017

Routledge is an imprint of the Taylor & Francis Group, an informa business

© 2017 Gerard A. Postiglione

The right of Gerard A. Postiglione to be identified as author of this work has been asserted by him in accordance with sections 77 and 78 of the Copyright, Designs and Patents Act 1988.

All rights reserved. No part of this book may be reprinted or reproduced or utilised in any form or by any electronic, mechanical, or other means, now known or hereafter invented, including photocopying and recording, or in any information storage or retrieval system, without permission in writing from the publishers.

Trademark notice: Product or corporate names may be trademarks or registered trademarks, and are used only for identification and explanation without intent to infringe.

British Library Cataloguing-in-Publication Data
A catalogue record for this book is available from the British Library

Library of Congress Cataloging-in-Publication Data
Names: Postiglione, Gerard A., 1951- author.
Title: Education, ethnicity, society and global change in Asia:
the selected works of Gerard A. Postiglione.
Description: Abingdon, Oxon; New York, NY: Routledge, [2017] |
Series: World library of educationalists series | Includes bibliographical references and index.
Identifiers: LCCN 2016053631 | ISBN 9781138234338 (hbk) |
ISBN 9781315307237 (ebk)
Subjects: LCSH: Educational sociology—Asia. | Educational change—Asia. | Education and globalization—Asia. | Educational sociology—China. | Educational sociology—China. | Education and globalization—China. | Educational sociology—China—Hong Kong. | Educational sociology—China—Hong Kong. | Education and globalization—China—Hong Kong.
Classification: LCC LC191.8.A785 P67 | DDC 370.950—dc23
LC record available at https://lccn.loc.gov/2016053631

ISBN: 978-1-138-23433-8 (hbk)
ISBN: 978-1-315-30723-7 (ebk)

Typeset in Galliard
by codeMantra

To Li-fang, Ashley, and Rosie

Contents

Acknowledgements	ix
Introduction: contexts, processes, and institutions	1

PART I
Contexts: society and education   11

1	From Capitalism to Socialism? Hong Kong education within a transitional society	13
2	Education: China	35
3	Contexts and reforms in East Asian education—making the move from periphery to core	49

PART II
Cultural processes: pluralism and assimilation   67

4	The education of ethnic minority groups in China	69
5	Ethnic minority identity and educational outcomes in a Rising China	82
6	Making Tibetans in China: the educational challenges of harmonious multiculturalism	94
7	Dislocated education: the case of Tibet	114

PART III
Institutions: universities under globalization   143

8 Maintaining global engagement in the face of national integration in Hong Kong   145

9 Anchoring globalization in Hong Kong's research universities: network agents, institutional arrangements, and brain circulation   161

10 The rise of research universities: the Hong Kong University of Science and Technology   186

11 Research universities for national rejuvenation and global influence: China's search for a balanced model   217

12 Global recession and higher education in eastern Asia: China, Mongolia and Vietnam   235

Index   265

Acknowledgements

I would like to thank The University of Chicago Press, Routledge Press, ABC-CLIO Inc, Elsevier Publishing Company, The University of Chicago Press, the World Bank and Springer Press for allowing me to reprint my articles.
The chapters were reprinted from:

Part I: Contexts: society and education

From Capitalism to Socialism? Hong Kong Education within A Transitional Society, *Comparative Education Review*, Vol. 35, No. 4, 1991, pp. 627–49.

Education, in X. Zang (ed.) *Understanding Chinese Society*, London: Routledge Press, 2011, pp. 83–98.

Contexts and Reform in East Asian Education – Making the Move from periphery to Core, with Jason Tan, in G. Postiglione, G. and J. Tan, *Going to School in East Asia*, Westport: Greenwood Press, 2007, pp. 1–19.

Part II: Cultural processes: pluralism and assimilation

Education of Ethnic Groups in China, *The Routledge International Companion to Multicultural Education*, James Banks, ed., New York and London: Routledge Press, 2009, pp. 501–11.

Ethnic Identity and Educational Outcomes in China, International Encyclopedia of Education, in Peterson, Baker, McGaw (eds). *International Encyclopedia of Education*, Oxford: Elsevier, 2010, pp. 616–22.

Making Tibetans in China: Educational Challenges for Harmonious Multiculturalism, *Educational Review*, Vol. 60. No. 1, 2008, pp. 1–20.

Dislocated Education: The Case of Tibet, *Comparative Education Review*, Vol. 53, No. 4, 2009, pp. 483–512.

Part III: Institutions: universities under globalization

The Academic Profession in Hong Kong: Maintaining Global Engagement in the Face of National Integration, *Comparative Education Review*, Vol. 42, No. 1, 1998, pp. 30–45.

Anchoring Globalization in Hong Kong's Research Universities: Network Agents, Institutional Arrangements and Brain Circulation, *Studies in Higher Education*, Vol. 38, No. 3, 2013, pp. 345–66.

The Rise of Research Universities: The Case of the Hong Kong University of Science and Technology, in P. Altbach and J. Salmi, eds. *The Road to Academic Excellence: Emerging Research Universities in Developing and Transition Countries*, Washington DC: The World Bank, 2011, pp. 63–100.

Research universities for national rejuvenation and global influence: China's search for a balanced model, *Higher Education*, Vol. 70, No. 2, 2015, pp. 235–50.

Global Recession and Higher Education in Eastern Asia: China, Mongolia and Vietnam, *Higher Education*, Vol. 62, No. 6, 2011, pp. 789–814.

Introduction
Contexts, processes, and institutions

During my 35 years in Asia, three topics shaped my research on education and are reflected in the selections chosen for this volume: social context, ethnicity, and globalization. The selected works in this volume are divided into three thematic sections: Contexts: society and education; Processes: pluralism and assimilation; and, Institutions: universities and globalization. These themes address three questions: What social forces determine the form and content of education systems? What do state schools do to ethnic minority students and how do they respond? Why do universities align with or resist globalization? The selections also reflect three shifts over 35 years. My early years were spent studying Hong Kong as it approached its reunion with the Chinese mainland, and I also began to study education in China and its Asian neighbors. My middle years were occupied with fieldwork in ethnic regions of western China. In later years my focus shifted toward globalization and how it shapes universities in Hong Kong, the Chinese mainland, and Asia. The rest of this chapter will introduce the selected works in each of the three thematic sections.

I. Contexts: society and education

This section analyzes education and society from three different theoretical perspectives: socialist transition, competing social demands, and world systems.

The first article, entitled "From Capitalism to Socialism?" was published in *Comparative Education Review,* and anticipated Hong Kong's reunion with China. It was composed while on sabbatical at Stanford University, when there was intensive study of socio-political transition in the third world (Carnoy and Samoff 1990). At the time, socialist states were beginning to assume the trappings of capitalism. Socialist China was weary of capitalism but ready to integrate capitalist Hong Kong into the nationalist framework (Postiglione 1991). Deng Xiaoping had not yet taken his 1992 Southern Tour which reinvigorated the country's market economy and kick started its economic boom. Although published eight years before Hong Kong's reunion with China, this article has an interpretation that still rings true 20 years after the reunion, though changes since 2016 have begun to chart a new course for this special administrative region of China.

2   *Introduction*

The second selection introduces China's education system for the second edition of *Understanding Chinese Society* (Zang 2011, 2016). After providing a brief historical background, this extract takes a straightforward Weberian approach. It does so by explaining the form and content of education as a result of a market of demands for practical skills, status culture, and social control. These three demands operate simultaneously, but each takes precedence in different historical circumstances. In times of rapid economic growth, the demand for practical skills exerts the most influence, emphasizes relevant knowledge in the school curriculum, and prepares students for the labor market. In times of political strife, the demand of the state for social control takes precedence with an added emphasis on patriotism in the school curriculum. In more prosperous times as the urban middle class grows and gains influence, there is a demand on education for status culture to differentiate middle class children with prestigious certification and academic degrees. The market of social demands is recalibrated year by year according to how fast the economy grows, how much the urban middle class gains influence, and how much the state exerts control to ensure social stability. Case studies can be found in *Education and Social Change in China: Inequality in a Market Economy*, a collection of fieldwork papers that contrast the education of rural, ethnic minority, urban migrants and urban middle class students (Postiglione, 2006).

The final selection, entitled " Contexts and Reform in East Asian Education – Making the Move from Periphery to Core," was composed with Jason Tan, a past student and professor of the Singapore National Institute of Education. It contains an overview of education in East and Southeast Asia (Postiglione and Tan 2007). Originally written as an introduction to an 18-chapter volume, this abridged selection argues that Asia has been moving from the periphery to the core of the world system. While venerating world systems theory, this extract also gives it a decent burial in light of new economic circumstances and geopolitical realities. South Korea, Japan, and China, including Hong Kong and Taiwan, helped make world systems theory obsolete. Yet, this is less apparent in much of Southeast Asia. This selection points out how each country, in its own way, adapted to economic globalization and what this means for student life. The manner in which different socio-political systems adapt is selective, sometimes more democratic, and sometimes more autocratic. Meanwhile, intra-regional cooperation in education has grown amid the new regional environment of financial interdependence.

II. Processes: pluralism and assimilation

Having spent the first 28 years of life amid the ethnic diversity of New York City, I became attracted to the study of China's ethnic minorities – the subject of the selections in this section. China's 110 million ethnic minority population is relatively under researched. What happens when people of different ethnic groups come together? Does education promote assimilation, pluralism, or something in between?

The first selection, "Education of Ethnic Groups in China," introduces the study of China's ethnic minority education, including policies and related literature in order to raise the question of whether or not multiculturalism is an option. It poses the Western concept of multiculturalism against that popularized by Fei Xiaotong (Fei, 1989). Fei's *duoyuan yiti geju*, which may be rendered as "pluralism within the organic configuration of the Chinese nationality," or, in short, "pluralism within unity," gives recognition to the reality of China as a multiethnic state. However, it takes an historically situated assimilationist stance. In order to capture the reality of multiethnic socialization in such a large and diverse country, the selection poses a central research question: To what extent do schools in China create an atmosphere that has positive institutional norms toward diverse cultural groups. In fact, state policy accords prominence to the cultural characteristics of ethnic minority regions. Yet, in practice, ethnic minority cultures are often viewed by much of the citizenry as backward.

The second selection, "Ethnic Identity and Educational Outcomes in China," looks at ethnic identity by placing an emphasis on how identity is constructed by students within state schools. It does this by reviewing case studies of my past doctoral students who published books about how Tibetan, Uyghur, Mongol, Naxi and Korean students in China construct their ethnic and national identities within their school experience. While constructed through state schooling, these identities are rooted in the distinct ethnic ideological themes of each group. Moreover, China's interethnic relations have been pushed toward an era of critical pluralism by the intensification of market reforms and rapid urbanization. Where enlightened policies and practices in education produce greater interethnic understanding, critical pluralism leads to a harmonious multiculturalism. However, in other cases, critical pluralism leads to plural monoculturalisms when policies and practices in education inadequately alleviate interethnic misunderstanding and conflict, and where ethnic minority cultures resist national integration. In short, education policies and practices can play a pivotal role in determining the possibility of promoting harmony or separatism.

The third and fourth selections resulted from a decade of studying education in the Tibetan Autonomous Region (TAR) of China. At the time, doing fieldwork in the TAR was a unique experience. The warmth and cultural intelligence of Tibetan people are legendary. The challenge was to uncover the truth in an atmosphere in which the Chinese state and international media were engaged with each other in a war of symbolic violence. It is easy enough to cherry pick data that aligns neatly with a particular interpretation. It was obvious from the start of the research that the truth lay somewhere in between two poles. My access to Tibetan areas of China outside of the TAR was helped by my engagement as a consultant with international development agencies, such as the Asian Development Bank and the United Nations Development Programme. My research focused on bread and butter issues in rural and nomadic areas such as school finance, student dropouts, bilingual education, boarding schools, and teacher quality.

4   *Introduction*

The third selection, "Making Tibetans in China: Educational Challenges for Harmonious Multiculturalism," is an abridged introduction to 50th anniversary of the journal *Educational Review*, part of a collection of studies by scholars of Tibetan education. The article reviews policies and realities in semi-rural and nomadic regions of the TAR (Postiglione, Jiao, Gyatsola 2005, 2006). These policies aimed to provide basic subsidies for items like food, lodging at school, and cloth (for clothes and blankets), as well as inland schools (which admit students to boarding schools throughout the country for their secondary education). This article delves into the issue of state schooling versus Tibetan culture. This issue is often viewed through the lens of education as a civilizing institution. Useful as it might be, this lens lacks an emphasis on student agency. Schooling also contains space where ethnic minority students construct their identities. They do it in ways that are not always prescribed by the state, in ways that are rooted in their ethnic ideological themes which give meaning to their everyday lives within and outside of school (Luo 2016, Yang 2017).

The fourth selection, "Dislocated Education: The Case of Tibet," was the lead article for an issue of the *Comparative Education Review*. It examined a specific and sometimes controversial policy: education for ethnic minorities in boarding schools far away from their home communities. A similar policy was used unsuccessfully in three Western countries. Many scholars, present company included, have a fixed notion of schools in which minority students are plucked from their ethnic homelands and schooled in mainstream national culture far from home. There is good reason for such a viewpoint since Americans, Australians, and Canadians imposed such practices on native peoples with devastating results. This was less the case in the so-called Tibet inland (*neidi*) schools – boarding schools in major Chinese cities for graduates of primary school (most of who were Tibetans) from the TAR. Anglo-Christian cultures of America, Australia and Canada established boarding schools to eliminate native cultures to which they had no affinity. This contrasts with the case of Chinese and Tibetans who shared a Buddhist tradition, as well as adjunct geographies, for a thousand years. While Tibet *neidi* schools made ample use of the opportunity to inculcate patriotism to the Chinese state above any regional or ethnic allegiance, they also tolerated and even celebrated selected aspects of Tibetan culture. These schools inadvertently deepened ethnic identity by situating Tibetan students within Chinese cities. This particular selection uses Ogbu's folk theory of success to explain how such a policy could be sustained for so many years with the support of Tibetan parents who were initially apprehensive but became convinced that *neidi* schools would lead to good jobs for their children when they return to Tibet (Ogbu 1987). The flip side is that these schools take the best students away from local secondary schools, and return many of them as teachers who are less fluent in Tibetan and without native fluency in Chinese. Since the research was carried out, the policy changed and become more focused on older students – those entering senior high school (Zhu 2007).

The works in this section followed publication of *China's National Minority Education: Culture, Schooling and Development*, a collection of research papers by a group of noted overseas specialists (Postiglione 1999). Taken together, that research and the selections in this volume cast some doubt on straight line assimilation theory and bring out the complexity of China's ethnic minority education, especially the stunning diversity across groups and regions. The debate in China continues about the policy, initiated at the establishment of the PRC, which designates large parts of the country as ethnic autonomous areas. Some scholars contend that this policy has deepened ethnic divisions rather than promoted national unity. Nevertheless, when compared internationally, China has been a relatively stable multiethnic nation considering the size of its minority population and the vast area they occupy – including half of the land and ninety percent of the border shared with 14 countries. There is no simple template for understanding China's ethnic intergroup relations. Critical pluralism as a theory of ethnic intergroup processes in China opens the way for regions to respond on the basis of different demands at different times with implications for what form of multicultural education is practiced. There is a need for further research to assess the extent to which educational policies support social equality, enliven the economy for local benefit, sustain a concerted cultivation of ethnic cultures, and offer opportunities for national inclusion.

III. Institutions: academies, universities and globalization

This section contains five articles about the institution of higher education, including research universities and the larger systems of which they are a part. The selections cover Hong Kong, the Chinese mainland and the adjoining region. There is an overriding interest in how globalization, particularly global networks and economic forces, shapes the rise of Asian universities.

The first article, "The Academic Profession in Hong Kong: Maintaining Global Engagement in the Face of National Integration," was published in *Comparative Education Review* shortly after Hong Kong's retrocession to Chinese sovereignty. Universities on the Chinese mainland had not yet experienced a period of institutional consolidation that would raise the average enrolment of a university from a few thousand to ten or twenty thousand students. Access to higher education in the Chinese mainland was only four percent in 1995, rising to 20 percent by 2005 and 40 percent by 2017. Hong Kong also expanded its enrolments in university degree places from eight to 16 percent between 1989 and 2000, and enrolment in all forms of postsecondary education reached 60 percent by 2015. Unlike in the Chinese mainland where only about fifteen percent of academic staff possessed a doctorate, most university academics in Hong Kong were hired with a doctorate. This first article cites the Hong Kong professoriate's key challenge: to maintain its professional autonomy and academic freedom, both of which have been challenged on occasion since 1997. Data in the article came from the first international survey of the academic profession, a study coordinated by the Carnegie Foundation for the Advancement of Teaching. In comparative terms, Hong Kong academics were among the most internationally collaborative in their research, and deeply concerned about institutional governance. As of this writing, there is still nowhere in Asia where academic freedom is more highly protected by institutional heads. Nevertheless, as the first sentence of the last paragraph of the first selection states: "The main challenge for Hong Kong's professoriate is to maintain its globalism while fostering the rapid expansion of academic exchange with universities in China" (Postiglione 1998: 45)

The second selection, "Anchoring Globalization in Hong Kong's Research Universities: Network Agents, Institutional Arrangements and Brain Circulation," explains how a society with seven million people and an economy that only allocates 0.7 percent of its GDP to research and development, can have more highly ranked research universities than any other city in the world. Known for its entrepreneurial prowess, global trade, and competitive business practices, Hong Kong evolved to become a center for the translation and diffusion of knowledge. Under its mini-constitution, making it a system distinct from that in the Chinese mainland, Hong Kong kept its universities closely integrated into global research networks, while benefitting from the economic and cultural rise of the rest of the country. An enabling environment of institutional governance, bilingual and cross cultural competency, and academic freedom helps ensure that it can anchor globalization in beneficial ways. Open borders and communication infrastructure drive a global reception and dissemination of scientific knowledge. In short, Hong Kong's exceptionalism depends also on the ability of its universities to anchor globalization.

The third selection, "The Rise of Research Universities," is a case study by invitation of the World Bank. It explains the unprecedented rise of the Hong Kong University of Science and Technology (HKUST), which became a leading international university within ten years of its establishment. This study became part of a collection about the challenge for middle-income and developing countries—as well as some industrial nations, to build and sustain successful research universities. That challenge includes how to participate effectively in the global knowledge networks on an equal basis (Altbach and Salmi 2011). HKUST capitalized on the advantages long enjoyed by Hong Kong's premier university, the University of Hong Kong. Yet, HKUST also had the advantage of unique timing. It joined the fold of research universities at a period of rapid expansion in higher education, when the Hong Kong Research Council was being established, and when Hong Kong's economy was able to provide the highest academic salaries in the world. In anticipation of Hong Kong's return to China, HKUST attracted outstanding overseas Chinese scientists and scholars, many already distinguished at top tier American universities. HKUST was also able to focus heavily on the fields of science and technology and emphasize the commercialization of scientific discoveries with expertise in its business faculty. Students were required to take liberal arts courses, a curriculum reform that was unique at the time in Hong Kong's universities.

The fourth selection, "Research Universities for National Rejuvenation and Global Influence: China's Search for a Balanced Model," arose from an invitation to guest edit a special issue of the journal, *Higher Education*, about the rise of Asia's research universities. This research was driven by an emergent discourse – that globalization will shift from Westernization or Easternization. The question became: Can a Chinese university model develop and eventually become a force in international higher education? The Chinese model has its roots in the academies of the Tang and Song Dynasties. The PRC regime that leads the world's second largest economy is promoting national rejuvenation and a "China Dream". Since culture follows power, China began its soft power initiative that included building Confucian Institutes around the world. In May of 1998 I was present at a speech by China's president in which he told an international audience that China would build world class universities. I wondered about the long-term implications of this for Hong Kong's universities. How were Hong Kong's universities to integrate with counterparts in the rest of China when they were at opposite end of the continuum with respect to institutional governance and academic culture? With data from the Changing Academic Profession project, an international study of 19 countries, it became clear that there were key differences in university governance and academic culture between the systems in Hong Kong and the Chinese mainland.

Despite the differences in academic governance with leading Western systems, China's universities will continue to rise in the global rankings and their international influence will grow. While Hong Kong's top universities have an academic profession with an international profile unsurpassed anywhere else, China's top universities are also riveted on internationalization by providing preferential policies to attract returning talent home from overseas, as well as by permitting foreign universities to run degree programs and set up campuses.

Nevertheless, China's universities embody a precarious balance. On the domestic side they must respond to the rising demand for greater access to higher education, the demands of the new urban middle class for high status degrees and credentials, the demand of the industrial elite for relevant knowledge and skills, and the demand of the state for social stability. Meanwhile, the aspiration "to go global" necessitates a difficult juggle. That juggle comprises a deepening internationalization, an increase in institutional autonomy, and a growing concern by government about a loss of national sovereignty in education.

Research for the fifth and final selection in this book was invited by the Asian Development Bank, and considers the inevitable. Global and regional economic shocks will occur every decade or two. In 1998, Asia experienced a regional economic crisis that had a significant effect on higher education by pushing universities toward public-private partnerships in order to survive. A decade later, Asia was rocked by a global economic recession. Vulnerable populations throughout Asia could no longer afford to pay for their children's higher education. The global economic recession also threatened to stifle national initiatives for building knowledge economies by making it more difficult to attract talented scientists and teachers who could offer quality instruction and conduct world standard research.

This final selection, "Global Recession and Higher Education in Eastern Asia: China, Mongolia and Vietnam," published in the journal *Higher Education*, looks at how higher education systems in three Asian countries handled economic shocks. With an open and exposed economy, Mongolia had to moderate its strategic plans for higher education, though it has since moved back on track. Vietnam focused on widening its pathways to technical and professional higher education with an emphasis on science and technology. Although China has a larger population than both Mongolia and Vietnam, it managed to limit its exposure to external shocks. China handled the earlier Asian economic crisis of the late 1990s by expanding higher education in order to keep youth out of a tight labor market for four more years until the crisis subsided. It also viewed the crisis as an opportunity to stimulate the domestic economy through consumption by a growing number of single-child urban middle class households who were very willing to transfer a chunk of income for the opportunity to acquire a university education for their children. It behooves Asian universities to anticipate future economic shocks and take advantage of them in ways that encourage intra-regional cooperation, and push university systems toward innovative ways to protect vulnerable populations.

Conclusion

The selections in this book hardly do justice to the complexity of education in Asia, a region arrayed with political systems that take different approaches to principles and practices of democracy and equality. Some economies relied on excavation and low skill manufacturing. All aim to expand their service economies with high tech manufacturing. Asia is no longer on the periphery of the world system. If anything, it is becoming the core again, with China returning to the position it held for 17 Centuries as the world's GDP leader. In short, contexts, processes, and institutions can help explain how this dynamic region approaches educational reform.

As this collection illustrates, cultural values and historical experiences still constitute a context for debate about educational reform, especially as societies grapple with overlapping philosophies, rapid social change, new methods of learning and assessment, and new management practices. Those who look back at the era straddling the 20th and 21st Centuries will have to untangle themes such as globalization, decentralization, and privatization as they wove their way into a landscape of educational reform, with results that defy simple generalizations. Educational reforms in Asia will continue to address new challenges. However, the results already include some striking accomplishments.

Students in Singapore, South Korea, Shanghai, and Hong Kong nearly lead the world in mathematics and science achievement. Asian students overwhelmingly populate prestigious graduate schools of science and engineering at leading

American universities. Asia's top-tier research universities have indeed risen. According to the Times Higher Education, almost one-eighth (24) of the world's top 200 are Asian universities, most with Confucian heritages. This could rise to one-quarter by 2050 (Postiglione, 2015). But world class universities are not enough if systems of higher education remain relatively weak. Moreover, Asian higher education is highly vulnerable to global economic trends.

I have been privileged to be a scholar in residence for 35 years in Asia. Looking back, I am also humbled by the work of many colleagues who have explained Asia far better than I have. Finally, any errors in this text are my responsibility alone.

References

Altbach, P.A. and Salmi, J. eds. (2011). *The Road to Academic Excellence: Emerging Research Universities in Developing and Transition Countries.* Washington DC: The World Bank, 2011, pp. 63–100.

Carnoy, M. and Samoff, J. eds. (1990). *Education and Social Transition in the Third World.* Princeton: Princeton University Press.

Fei, X. (1989). *Zhonghua Minzu de Duoyuan Yiti Geju (Pluralism-unity structure of the Chinese nation).* Beijing Daxue Xuebao. (Journal of Peking University) (4). pp. 1–19. (in Chinese).

Luo, J. (2016). *Social Structuration in Tibetan Society: Education, Society and Spirituality.* New York: Rowman and Littlefield.

Ogbu, J. (1987). Variability in Minority School Performance. *Anthropology and Education Quarterly.* (18): 312–34.

Postiglione, G.A. ed. (1991). *Education and Society in Hong Kong: Toward One Country and Two Systems.* New York: M.E. Sharpe.

Postiglione, G.A. (1998). The Academic Profession in Hong Kong: Maintaining Global Engagement in the Face of National Integration. *Comparative Education Review.* 42(1): 45.

Postiglione, G.A. (2006). *Education and Social Change in China: Inequality in a Market Economy.* New York: M.E. Sharpe.

Postiglione, G.A. and Tan, J.E.T. (2007). *Going to School in East Asia*, Westport: Greenwood Press.

Yang, M. (2017). *Learning to be Tibetan: The Construction of Ethnic Minority Identity at Minzu University.* New York: Rowman and Littlefield.

Zang, X. (2011, 2016). *Understanding Chinese Society*, London: Routledge Press.

Zhu, Z. (2007). *State Schooling and Ethnic Identity: The Politics of a Tibetan Neidi School.* New York: Rowman and Littlefield.

Part I
Contexts
Society and education

1 From Capitalism to Socialism? Hong Kong Education within a Transitional Society

Contrary to events in Eastern Europe, where socialist societies are assuming the trappings of capitalism, Hong Kong is impelled to accommodate a socialist metropole. China's decision to shun the 1989 global socialist transformations resulted in a more hardline stance toward Hong Kong's future. In 1997 the British will retreat from their colony, after a period in which the territory grew from a desolate outpost in the South China Sea to one of the world's largest financial and commercial centers. As Hong Kong confronts an uncertain future—a transfer of sovereignty to the People's Republic of China—education may become a vehicle for negotiating social transition as well as an instrument to resist decolonization.

For several years there has been a swell of local scholarship on the approaching "yiguo, liangzhi" (one-country, two-system) arrangement.[1] However, literature on the implications of the transition for education is virtually nonexistent.[2] This article identifies some of the major implications of the 1997 return of sovereignty for selected aspects of the educational policy process. I examine three potential policy orientations—capitalism, socialism, and patriotism—and consider the potential of education to reconcile or heighten the contradictions between these orientations within a "one-country, two-system" arrangement.

Education in Transition Societies

Education and Hong Kong's Future

With the formal signing of the *Sino-British Declaration on the Question of Hong Kong* in 1985, the predominant vision of Hong Kong society toward its future was one of continued stability and prosperity within a framework that would permit a great degree of autonomy under the mother country's sovereignty. Until June 1989, conditions existed for the realization of that vision and were to be reflected in the Basic Law of the post-1997 Special Administrative Region (SAR) government. After June 4, 1989, the Basic Law Drafting Committee temporarily suspended work; the conditions for the fulfillment of the post-1997 vision had indeed changed.[3] Accordingly, society's expectations toward education also began to change as the problem of reconciling capitalism, socialism, and patriotism became more pronounced. Hundreds of thousands of secondary and postsecondary school students, teachers, and administrators joined demonstrations to express their sentiments on political events in China.[4] Education department officials ignored enforcement of the long-standing ban on politics in schools, and school principals and teachers wrestled with how to react to students' political poster displays and their participation in territory-wide demonstrations.[5] Many months after the suppression of the democracy movement in Beijing, Hong Kong remained in a severe confidence crisis as cooperation between the British and Chinese governments became strained.

Educational Policy Intervention Points within the Transfer of Power

Such events added a new dimension to the already unusual nature of Hong Kong's decolonization process. Power has gradually shifted to the local elite and the new middle class, yet most power still resides with the British government. Hong Kong's people still look to the British government to press for a speedier democratization although Beijing denies its appropriateness. The local elite assert that Hong Kong is not a colony in the classical sense yet express concern that in 1997 the mother country may gain the same amount of influence wielded by the British in the territory's affairs, including education. Some refer to the transfer of sovereignty as the replacement of one hegemonic force with another because the territory's future degree of autonomy will not be determined by the colonial metropole or even by the people of the territory itself but rather by the Beijing government. Confidence in the Sino-British Agreement on Hong Kong's future will be won or lost within a plural society that favors decolonization and supports Chinese sovereignty yet remains apprehensive in the face of Beijing's interference in Hong Kong's affairs. The degree to which decolonization is occurring as opposed to the replacement of one force by another is a complex question whose answer awaits the outcome of struggles over representative government in Hong Kong, and the direction of future events in China, including a change of governments. The precise nature and characteristics of Hong Kong as a transitional society are inseparable from the evolution of these factors during the crucial run-up to 1997.

Educational policy intervenes by shaping the thinking of the generation that will lead Hong Kong after 1997; it influences the selection criteria for recruitment into important positions within the transitional Government Civil Service; it maintains a highly skilled labor force in the face of the large-scale emigration of talented people; it determines to some extent the degree of cultural penetration; it influences socialization processes that build an identity essential for reuniting people in Hong Kong with the rest of China; and, finally, it bolsters or restrains the general process of democratization in the society.

Hong Kong's economy has long contributed to nation building in China. It continues to do so, and for this reason it will not be dismantled for at least fifty years after the return of sovereignty in 1997. Hong Kong's political system has made no such direct contribution.[6] Its future political system will be defined by the Basic Law, promulgated by China's National People's Congress, and will be strictly limited by the boundaries of the new SAR.[7] This is not to suggest a separation between the economic and political spheres; it is only that economics and politics cannot be separated in understanding Hong Kong's development. A secluded bureaucratic polity has existed alongside an atomistic Chinese society to provide a positive noninterventionism within the economic sphere, thus allowing capitalism to operate virtually unfettered by popular influence.[8] This, coupled with government control over land sale, and the availability of low-wage labor—the latter made possible through government subsidized housing and inexpensive food and clothing from China—explain the tremendous success of the domestic economy.[9]

Education in Hong Kong has not yet veered from its colonial setting. Except for minor revisions to the content of some textbooks, schooling continues to introduce children to a sociopolitical system that has remained almost unchanged for over 140 years.[10] Moreover, China has no explicit nation-building education strategy for Hong Kong after 1997. Nevertheless, education is increasingly considered a key institution in the transitional period. Plans for the expansion of higher education and the introduction of civics education are just two examples.[11] Also, without a military to strengthen a particular brand of patriotic socialization, education may assume a more important ideological function.

Informing the Study of Education in Transitional Societies

Although Hong Kong little resembles most transitional societies, educational similarities do exist.[12] In colonial to postcolonial transitional settings, preindependence education may remain largely unchanged except for schools' specific role in affirming national identity. Educational policy changes are directed more at the content of education than at the system's form or structure. Social studies, history, and language curriculum may be revised, for instance. Colonial social structures may remain almost intact through the early postcolonial period, with the colonial power vacuum being filled by a national bourgeoisie. Hong Kong will retain its economic system, and the local bourgeoisie is already replacing the colonial elite. Nevertheless, the continued emigration of large numbers of the local bourgeoisie prior to 1997 could result in totally new circumstances. One scenario depicts an ever-increasing infusion of Beijing-sponsored capital coupled with new immigrants from China—born and educated under socialism—actively replacing the present bourgeoisie with a new "socialist bourgeoisie." This would have a measurable influence on the cultural ethos of Hong Kong schools.[13] Another scenario depicts increasing internalization of many spheres of the territory, including education, as a way to discourage Beijing's explicit interference after 1997.

The conditions of education where socialist transition is under way are unique.[14] Here, changes in education are complete and comprehensive, taking in the system's form, structure, and philosophical foundations. Socialist transition theory may have limited relevance to Hong Kong's initial phase. While socialist transition is viewed as a reality within the context of the "one-country, two-system" policy, such a shift will require at least 50 years. Most Hong Kong residents consider such a situation far too remote for concern at present. Nevertheless, today's primary school children will be at the helm of socialist transition in 2047. Moreover, given that the 2047 transition, not unlike the 1997 transition, will need a ten-year preparation period before the actual conversion, the education system might well begin to consider how it should prepare students. Furthermore, there are indications that a socialist bourgeoisie may gain influence in government departments such as the police. Here, the recruitment ban on graduates from the so-called leftist or patriotic secondary schools has been lifted, as it has in government-run postsecondary teacher training colleges.[15] The leftist secondary schools are also poised to join the government's proposed direct subsidy scheme for private schools, a scheme many consider elitist. These schools rejected the formal curriculum in the 1960s and early 1970s, when the Cultural Revolution spilled over into Hong Kong, and were excluded from the colonial education system until recently.[16] The government has also established a Provisional Council of Academic Accreditation that will consider the standing of educational qualifications from China (including Taiwan) as they relate to Hong Kong's occupational structure.[17] The increasing emigration of talented members of the Hong Kong work force and the 1 percent unemployment rate have compounded the importance of the Council's work. Finally, before June 4, 1989, the American Chamber of Commerce and the Institute of International Education in Hong Kong were addressing the problem of getting students from the People's Republic of China to return home after completing their degree studies in the United States. They had proposed that these students be recruited to firms in Hong Kong as an intermediary step toward their eventual return, a measure that could supply much-needed highly skilled labor for Hong Kong.[18] Such moves are important elements in Hong Kong's transition.

Hong Kong informs the study of education within transitional societies by adding such new dimensions as the expansion of externally sponsored national socialist capital, the increasing numbers of immigrants born and raised under socialism, and the further integration of leftist elements into government organs and the occupational structure. At the same time, liberal groups are expanding in the territory, some even advocating the downfall of the Beijing government or communism itself.[19] These four elements become even more important when viewed against the background of Hong Kong's evolving cultural ethos and the dual identities, Chineseness and "Hongkongeseness."[20] As a Chinese society with a long history of colonial rule, Hong Kong possesses structural features distinguishable from those of both traditional and modern China. This has fostered an ethos that represents "at once a departure from dominant Chinese values and a continuation of Chinese heritage."[21] The dual nature of the ethos is visibly a postwar phenomenon and has been particularly salient with the advent of the 1997 issue and the younger generation's rise to prominence. Furthermore, the sharp value differences in these two identities become more distinct as they are situated within selected types of schools. These types differ on such important cultural, social, and political features as the medium of instruction (English or Chinese), the school's political leaning (in support of Beijing or Taipei), their connection with various clansmen and provincial associations in China, and their social class composition.[22] The plurality of Hong Kong schools has existed and flourished alongside a highly centralized educational policy-making bureaucracy. This bureaucratic polity has enjoyed a high degree of insulation as part of a government not directly representative of the people. Nevertheless, through a variety of formal and informal consultative channels, the educational policy process maintained a threshold level of legitimacy within the Chinese community, even though schools with stronger ties to the colonial elite enjoyed greater influence.

Educational Policy Options and the Resolution of Contradictions

There are three broad policy options or orientations relating to school politics and educational policy in Hong Kong's transitional period. Each deals differently with reconciling emerging problems. The first and most likely option, in the short run, would maintain the status quo consensus-bound consultative policy process. The second option hinges on increased democratization of the society. This would bring the pluralism of Hong Kong schools more into the forefront of the policy process, resulting in a less consensus-bound, and a more conflict-prone, policy process. The third option would reflect the replacement of the influence of one metropole by another. This option would see the shoring up of traditional consultative mechanisms for insuring legitimacy of the educational policy process, with greater influence exerted by those individual schools and groups of schools having or building closer ties with mainland institutions.

These characteristics and potential options provide a background to view the potential role of education in Hong Kong in solving complex problems emerging from the transfer of sovereignty from Britain to China. Their positioning will determine whether educational policy will work toward reconciling or heightening the contradictions between capitalism, socialism, and patriotism. The degree to which educational policy does either will depend not only on the positioning of these unique characteristics and the dual identities reflected in the cultural ethos of Hong Kong but also on how selected contextual features bear on the educational policy process.

The Sino-British Declaration and the Educational Policy Process

The Sino-British Declaration in 1985 provided a blueprint for the territory's future. Although the agreement furnishes little detail aside from declaring the return of sovereignty over Hong Kong to China, it nevertheless permits Hong Kong to maintain its capitalist modes of production along with the general lifestyle of its people. "Gong Ren Zhi Gong," Hong Kong people running Hong

18   *Contexts*

Kong, is a basic tenet of the document. The Sino-British Declaration contains a brief provision concerning education that is similar to that found in the Draft Basic Law.

> The Hong Kong Special Administrative Region Government shall on its own decide policies in the field of culture, education, science, and technology, including policies regarding the education system and its administration, the language of instruction, the allocation of funds, the examination system, the system of academic rewards and the recognition of educational and technological qualifications. Institutions of all kind, including those run by religious and community organizations, may retain their autonomy. They may continue to recruit staff and use teaching materials from outside the Hong Kong Special Administrative Region. Students shall enjoy freedom of choice of education and freedom to pursue their education outside the Special Administrative Region.[23]

This statement, and that in the Draft Basic Law, places educational control with the SAR government. Many groups in Hong Kong doubt this government will be autonomous and representative, especially in the wake of the military crackdown on the democracy movement in China. Nevertheless, in 1997 the People's Republic of China will inherit a government-education relationship that is, in one way, similar to its own. In both societies, educational policy is the province of a small group of elites. The government of Hong Kong is not directly elected by its people; yet it has steadily increased its role in shaping the course of education over the last two decades.[24] Despite these considerations, the educational provisions of the Joint Declaration and the Basic Law, in themselves, give little hint as to which of the three educational policy orientations will be favored.

Maintaining Legitimacy within the Policy Process

The key feature of educational policy in Hong Kong in regard to transitional processes is the maintenance of legitimacy. Colonial societies carry an inherent suspicion toward government and an opposition to its policies. The Hong Kong government has skillfully minimized this problem by building an extensive consultative network. Having the chance to be heard by government increases the satisfaction of groups and thereby yields a threshold level of legitimacy for its policies. This occurs within a system possessing a marked degree of pluralism under a centralized, nonrepresentative structure of territory-wide educational governance.

Under the Education Ordinance, the Director of Education controls all government schools and supervises all other kindergarten, primary, and secondary schools in the territory.[25] He also supervises postsecondary institutions except universities and polytechnics. The ordinance provides the director with broad-ranging powers over the life and practice of schooling, staff and pupils, and particularly the appearance of anything political in schools. Most of the schools are publicly funded but privately operated; each has an unpaid management committee and supervisor appointed by the sponsoring body. In most cases, committee members are lay persons who are not involved with policymaking or day-to-day school affairs. The supervisor has considerable legal responsibility and usually works closely with the school head in policy and personnel decisions. The principal has absolute power over the staff and pupils. The education department appoints heads of government schools, and sponsoring agencies name those of other schools. According to the government's Code of Aid, all aided schools are funded according to the same formula, regardless of location, sponsorship, or prestige. Schools in the small private sector are mainly financed by fees paid by the students' parents.

Educational policy in Hong Kong falls somewhere between a centralized and a decentralized system. More accurately, decision making and policy are part of the centralized system, yet a broad and complex consultative process has evolved since the late 1970s. Although the education system is modeled on that of the United Kingdom in its structure, organization, admission and examination regulations, and curriculum, it is not a duplicate of that or any other educational system. Traditionally, a colonial elite that is less representative of the people than the existing powers has shaped educational policy. As the education system expanded in the 1960s and 1970s, the policy process became more complex with the flowering of a variety of education associations, unions, and pressure groups, all entering into the consultative process.

In general, the highest decision maker is the governor in council. Four committees advise the governor on educational matters: the Board of Education concerns itself with education from kindergarten to sixth form, the Universities and Polytechnics Grants Committee is responsible for funding and development of university education, and the Vocational Training Council is responsible for technical education. Insufficient coordination led to the founding of a fourth committee, the Education Commission, composed of appointed members of the community and representatives from the other three committees. It provides the governor consolidated advice on overall development of the education system.[26]

The legitimacy of the educational policy process is increasingly tied to committee membership. The most controversial issue concerned Szeto Wah, president of the Hong Kong Professional Teachers Union and one of the few elected (rather than appointed) members of the Hong Kong Legislative Council.[27] As a long-time critic of the Government Education Department and a liberal member of the Legislative Council, which opposes many of the Beijing Government's policies toward Hong Kong, Szeto was not appointed to the Education Commission even though he enjoyed broad support among both the rank and file of the teaching profession and large sectors of the community. This became a major challenge to the government's legitimacy in matters of educational policy. Other characteristics of the transitional period further threaten that legitimacy and heighten contradictions facing Hong Kong. Furthermore, these characteristics determine whether policy orientations will incline toward the colonial status quo consultative or nonconsultative, the emergent conflict-prone democratic, or new restructured consultative patterns of formulating educational policy.

Contextual Processes and Educational Policy

Educational policy changes in Hong Kong's history have occurred within the context of a minimally integrated sociopolitical system: a British-controlled autonomous bureaucratic polity has existed alongside an atomistic Chinese society.[28] The government was largely secluded from Chinese society until the latter part of the 1980s. However, more activism by Chinese society, particularly in struggles for more representative government, is bringing a new sociopolitical context to educational policy issues.

Decolonization

A local British economist once described Hong Kong as "a part of China that happens, for the time being, to be administered by someone else."[29] This statement does little to alter the fact that Hong Kong is still a colonial society, even though decolonization has already begun. The first section of Hong Kong was obtained by the British as a result of the First Opium War (1840–42). Through the Sino-British treaties of 1842, 1860, and 1898, the area of what is today known as Hong Kong was ceded or leased to the British,[30] although the People's Republic of China refuses to recognize these treaties. Nevertheless, negotiations have been completed for recovery of the territory. Initial indications are that the colonial elite will be replaced by an elected and appointed group of local residents of Chinese descent. It is not yet clear how and to what degree the new leadership will represent Beijing's interests. At present, the Xinhua News Agency, Beijing's official representative in Hong Kong, already exerts considerable influence.

Educational issues during decolonization were long a serious problem in former British colonies. History shows that events leading to drastic changes in tertiary education have been repeated again and again in different British colonies, such as India, Kenya, and Malaysia. Political observers and educational reformers suggest that, in the past, Britain used education as a powerful tool to keep control over its colonies after decolonization. The elite education system allowed the British government to continue to influence those who received tertiary education and would subsequently become community leaders. This was to insure a favorable relationship with the territory after British withdrawal.[31]

Decolonization is leading to a fundamental change in Hong Kong's educational policy process. This has been most clearly exemplified in a controversial proposal for the standardization of university education into a three- rather than four-year scheme.[32] Although not part of any colonial conspiracy, the Hong Kong Education Commission appears to be working toward insuring a continuation of the three-year British system, while many sectors of the education community pressure the commission to bring the University of Hong Kong into line with universities in China, the United States, and elsewhere. The commission also proposed a second scheme that would allow increased government subsidies to elite schooling. The major result of the first proposal was to pressure the Chinese University of Hong Kong to cut its academic program from four to three years. At the same time, it prevented the University of Hong Kong from implementing a planned conversion to a four-year scheme. Although gaining approval in the Legislative Council, the debates surrounding approval and the narrow margin of victory for the measure made it clear that the education community was split over which model university education should adopt.

This growing activism manifested itself after the 1988 release of the Education Commission's Report Number Three, which contained the controversial proposals. At one time, 4,000 university students, more than one-quarter of Hong Kong's total university student population, marched on the government to protest the plan. The proposal also had resource implications, thus uniting secondary school principals who received government subsidies for the upper year of their secondary schools. This upper year would have been eliminated if a four-year university structure prevailed. The major educational groups were divided over this issue.[33] This split marked a significant change from the past consensus-bound politics of education to a more conflict-prone, yet democratic, debate among various sectors of the education community and helped to advance the second plan even though the result was a marginal victory for the status quo. However, owing partly to this controversy, the government decided to bypass the consultative process in its next major educational policy venture.

What makes this issue a manifestation of the decolonization process is that the Hong Kong government, having traditionally avoided such legitimacy-threatening confrontation, instead opted to break away from the means it used in the past to avoid confrontation and create consensus. As Cheng notes, it had so often in the past dealt with such situations by "putting the issue to rational scrutiny or resorting to powerful third party arbitration. Instead, members of the Educational Commission came out in defense of its proposals, thus intensifying government-citizen antagonisms."[34] There have been other examples as well. Since 1989, important policies have been announced with little or no consultation among relevant groups.[35] The government appears less concerned about its legitimacy in educational matters, without apparent reason. Its legitimacy is more, rather than less, vulnerable as 1997 approaches. Its efforts to short-circuit the traditional consultative process may be naively calculated to avoid any political instability during the last phase of colonialsm.

The issue of truncating the Chinese University program from four to three years was not new.[36] Although it had been argued before, the context of the deliberations surrounding the latest debate was different. The Sino-British declaration added strength to the case for bringing Hong Kong University education into line with that in China. At one time, opposition groups even appealed, albeit unsuccessfully, to China's quasi ambassador in Hong Kong, to support the four-year structure since it coincided with that in China. The result of this case does not so much signify an abandonment of the Chinese character of the

Chinese University of Hong Kong, and an embrace of colonial values, as an acknowledgement that groups in Hong Kong are prepared to exercise their right, as spelled out in the Joint Declaration, to resist following the model of education in China.

Democratization

"Power, both administrative and executive is in the hands of civil servants who are in law primarily responsible, through the governor, to the United Kingdom."[37] Until 1985 the people of Hong Kong could neither appoint these public servants to office nor remove them. Nevertheless, government officials and others often proclaim that Hong Kong is essentially democratic. Until 1980, the only major body even partly elected was the Urban Council, whose main functions are municipal (e.g., street cleaning, control of hawkers, public libraries). As late as the mid-1970s, only 10 percent of the adult population was entitled by education to vote in its elections, and in 1969, for example, only 0.05 percent bothered to do so. In 1983, a district administration scheme was set up in order to permit some forms of public consultation and participation. A portion of the membership of these district boards is elected in the same way as a portion of the members of the Urban Council. At the end of 1983, there were 904,916 registered electors representing only 32 percent of the total potential electorate. Moreover, voter turnout was sparse. In urban regions, for instance, only 250,000 of the potential electorate of 708,119 were registered to vote, and of this group only 35 percent actually cast ballots. The first concrete effort to permit election to a governing body that wields any real power and influence took place in 1985. This breathtaking reform allowed indirect election of a small section of the recently enlarged Legislative Council. The election involved only 1 percent of the population, and of the 1 percent only 50,000 bothered to vote. The most recent popular elections for the district board showed a disappointing 17 percent of the eligible population participating.[38] A government green paper on representative government was published in 1987 and contained several graduated options ranging from a continuation of the status quo to a "one man, one vote" system of electing a majority of the legislature before 1997.[39] The Beijing government viewed this document as potentially interfering with the smooth transfer of sovereignty since the Basic Law Drafting Committee, established by the 1985 Sino-British agreement, was also to take up the issue of representative government and had not yet reported to the National People's Congress. At that time, a large sector of the general public considered it wise that Hong Kong avoid confrontation with Beijing over this issue. However, the 1989 suppression of the democracy movement in China fueled calls for speeding up the pace of political reform in Hong Kong. This resulted in a tremendous surge of support for direct elections of all legislative councillors before 1997.

The schools have never been a force in democratizing Hong Kong; if anything, they hindered the process. Until the late 1980s, the school curriculum virtually ignored raising political consciousness. The planned return of sovereignty changed that to some degree, leading to minor modifications of the school curriculum.[40]

Such curriculum changes also provided much-needed legitimacy to a colonial government often accused of dragging its feet in introducing opportunities for representative government. In this sense, the curriculum appears to the populace as an instrument to bolster attempts at expanded representative government.

After 1985, the year of the signing of the Joint Declaration, the number and range of school curriculum topics dealing with political awareness increased. Although this may be associated in any society with a general trend toward more affluence and a growing middle class, it derived at least equally from the expected return of sovereignty in 1997. For example, civics education made its appearance during this time. Implementation was difficult due to a political apathy spawned over many decades. Yet this constituted the most direct attempt to influence the curriculum with regard to Hong Kong's future. Nevertheless, activities that encourage political involvement are minimized. Government guidelines emphasize political tranquility: "In light of Hong Kong's recent political development, evolution should be the watch-word and the emphasis in this guide will be on civic education as a politically socializing force for promoting stability and responsibility," and "Democracy means different things to different people. ... So education for democracy per se would be difficult to interpret."[41]

These curriculum changes are occurring against a backdrop of important changes in the political culture of Hong Kong. The sociopolitical landscape has been gradually transformed away from its traditionally apolitical orientation. Rapid economic growth, expanded educational opportunity, and a younger population have led to a decline of traditional institutions and social customs. Social and economic issues have been pushed into the political arena, and this has led to demands for more government action. After a long period in which a secluded bureaucracy existed apart from the Chinese society, there have been new efforts to formalize government-people relationships. An increasing number of people hold that the government is responsible for the solutions to their personal and family problems. The people of Hong Kong are fast adopting an active, and even interventionist, conception of government, and they would like the government to measure up to their expectations. Moreover, it is apparent that the people of Hong Kong are becoming more favorably disposed toward political activism of many kinds as the growth of political pressure groups demonstrates. A prominent Hong Kong political scientist notes that "tactics which involve a quantum of confrontation or violence are increasingly rated as effective means to compel the government to give in."[42] This is no small change. Local structures are still inadequate for social and political participation, including areas of education decision making. Nevertheless, curriculum changes, coupled with the general move toward more political activity within schools and teachers' increasingly activist role in grass roots politics, point to a shift away from status quo policy options that limit schools from taking a more visible role in territory-wide educational policy processes.

Localization

Localization, a process in which local people are increasingly given priority in appointments to high-level posts in government and industry, was never taken as a serious objective until the signing of the Joint Declaration on Hong Kong's future in 1985. Before then, recruitment to upper-level government posts clearly favored expatriates. Political scientist Myron Mushkat expressed this view just prior to the Sino-British Joint Declaration:

> A more subtle explanation for the extent of expatriate recruitment is that it dovetails with the higher objectives of "colonial control." Hong Kong, after all, is a British dependent territory and in order to fulfil its role with a measure of effectiveness the United Kingdom must have at its disposal reliable mechanisms for providing societal direction. The presence of a fairly large number of Britons in key policy making posts may thus be construed as a factor which facilitates "colonial management." One could argue, however, that this legitimate objective no longer requires the balancing of each local appointment with an expatriate one and that a ratio more favourable to the local component need not detract from the U.K's grip over Hong Kong.[43]

The Hong Kong government adopted localization of the civil service as official policy as early as 1947, but expatriates continued to hold a significant number of high-level positions as late as the mid-1980s.[44] Expatriate officers comprised almost one-half of all directorate officers and almost one-third of those at the top of the Master Pay Scale.[45]

According to the Sino-British Declaration on Hong Kong, after 1997, "The government and legislature of the Hong Kong Special Administrative Region shall be composed of local inhabitants."[46] Furthermore, while foreign nationals may be employed by the future Hong Kong civil service, they may not hold posts as heads of major government departments, including the police department, nor as deputy heads of some of those departments.[47] In his study of government planning in respect to localization policy, John Burns concluded in 1987 that "it indicates a failure of the government's policy of localization over the years. Coherent plans to localize problem grades and departments are urgently needed. Hong Kong must develop a confident, forward looking civil service for the years up to and beyond 1997. Much needs to be done."[48]

Since that time, however, the government appointed the first nonexpatriate as director of education.[49] Local Hong Kong Chinese are increasingly appointed to top posts in other government departments as well. Nevertheless, because of the great exodus following the Sino-British agreement, the pace of localization, particularly in the middle-level civil service, has slowed. In an effort to stall the exodus of key individuals, the British government is proposing to make available 50,000 "insurance" passports, carrying the right of abode in the United Kingdom, and is encouraging other nations with large interests in Hong Kong to do the same.[50] This will confound the educational policy process by building stronger loyalties to the United Kingdom on the part of educational policymakers even after 1997. China has already asserted that it will not recognize the overseas passports of local residents of Chinese descent and will undoubtedly develop countermeasures throughout the transitional period for what it sees as illegitimate means to limit its sovereignty.

Educational policy has been increasingly fashioned toward the recruitment of native Hong Kongese into the civil service. Because an explicit English language facility is necessary to succeed on linguistically based civil service examinations, the policy process reflects colonial support of elite schools and the preservation of the University of Hong Kong as a wholly English-medium institution.

This process has also favored a large Anglo-Chinese system of secondary schools. By the early 1980s, these schools peaked, surpassing the number of Chinese medium schools by nine to one.[51] Although the official medium of instruction in the Anglo-Chinese schools was English, a different reality prevailed in most schools. The limited number of competent English-speaking teachers led to many variations in the quality of language instruction. Even when competent English-speaking teachers were available, many students were not able to learn through this medium. Parents, however, resisted educationalists' pleas to reconsider Anglo-Chinese schools. The Education Department eventually took steps to increase the number of schools in the Chinese sector by providing incentives for those questionable Anglo-Chinese schools to convert to Chinese-medium instruction. This resulted in an increase in the number of Chinese-medium secondary schools and a corresponding influence on the ethos of many Hong Kong secondary schools.

The medium of instruction in most secondary schools in Hong Kong is still officially English, a fact of educational life that places a tremendous burden on students, especially since most have little contact with native English speakers. The effects of this practice on culture and identity interest researchers more than parents—most of whom continue to opt for as much English-medium education as possible.[52] Thus, children attending elite English-medium schools have an advantage in gaining government civil service posts.

This pattern may be further reinforced by a new set of language policy proposals that would make entrance into English-language secondary education dependent on an examination administered after primary six.[53] The stated aim is to improve competency in at least one language and eliminate the use of "Chinglish," a mixture of English and Chinese. In reality, however, the proposal will further extend elitist elements in the educational system and further restrict access to the University of Hong Kong and thus government civil service positions.[54]

However, all past government-initiated language proposals have fallen short of implementation. The medium-of-instruction controversy dates back to the end of World War II, the government forever being in the bind of either eliminating parental choice in medium of instruction on the one hand, or eliminating good sound educational practice on the other. Some accuse the government of being halfhearted, as has been the case with *Putonghua* (Mandarin, the official idiom of China) teaching. In this respect the Education Commission never went beyond recommending that the schools be encouraged to teach *Putonghua* either before or after hours or as an extracurricular activity, and only two schools use it as a medium of instruction.[55] Some researchers, like Robert Baur and Herbert Pierson, are confident that *Putonghua* will replace English and Cantonese to become the language of power and the official language of government and that everyone will be required to learn it.[56]

Growing business opportunities in the China trade and investment area along with the expanding interactions between China and Hong Kong have added to a new groundswell favoring Chinese mother tongue schooling over English-medium schooling. In fact, the battle to preserve Hong Kong's status as an English-speaking territory is far from won. At the same time, many educationists in China criticize Hong Kong's return to Chinese mother tongue education. This is because Hong Kong Chinese consider Cantonese, rather than *Putonghua*, as their mother tongue.[57] The majority of Hong Kong educators strongly resist Mandarin as a teaching medium. This exemplifies again how the dual identity of Hong Kong's cultural ethos manifests itself within educational issues even as it impinges on localization and recruitment into the government civil service. Thus, school language policy and the extent to which individuals can function competently in *Putonghua*, Cantonese, and English may easily influence the legitimacy of emerging political leaders and the orientation of educational policy.

The Structuralization of Social Classes

There is a high degree of inequality in Hong Kong. While the average citizen enjoys the third highest living standard in Asia, half a million people live without running water or legal electricity.[58] The inequality of income distribution in Hong Kong is staggering. Such levels of disparity, in the case of most societies, could generate class conflict and industrial hostilities. However, when industry, trade, and commerce are prosperous and the labor market is active, workers' wages in Hong Kong are still much better than those of their counterparts on the mainland. The Gini coefficient, which measures income inequality in a population, fell from 0.49 in 1961 to 0.43 in 1971 and remained about the same in 1981. This was still considerably higher than what was observed in the United states (0.25), Taiwan and Korea (0.3), and Singapore (0.4).[59] Forty percent of the population is engaged in manufacturing, 22 percent in government and science occupations, 16 percent in commerce, and 5 percent in agriculture. In 1976, 51.6 percent of the population comprised the working class (all manual employees), 36.5 percent the new middle class (nonmanual employees), and 11.9 percent the capitalist class (all employers and self-employed persons).[60] The working class has had no political power in the legislature despite the fact that its political orientation and ideological identifications run the gambit from extreme right (in support of Taiwan) to extreme left (in support of the People's Republic of China).[61] Except for 1952, 1967, and 1984, when there were street riots, the territory has been stable, with little overt social unrest or conflict since the end of World War II. Signs indicate, however, that a politically conscious middle class is emerging and assuming a more active role in organizing community political affairs. It is gaining more control over the education system and insuring that its children inherit their middle-class status. A future concern with regard to China's regaining sovereignty over Hong Kong is not so much its willingness to tolerate capitalism as much as its tolerance of the great gaps that exist among social classes in Hong Kong.

Access to opportunity and life chances has increasingly been placed within the domain of formal education. Chinese tradition holds education in high esteem, and the idea of having a scholarly examination system as a key determinant for access to high positions, especially in government, is not new.[62] However, the character of the school selection process in Hong Kong is brutal. Even though education is compulsory (and free) until age fifteen, less than 6 percent enter postsecondary university-level education in Hong Kong. Equity within this system is questionable, and as in other industrial societies, the meritocratic ideology (anyone who is capable and works hard in school, regardless of social class, can achieve success), has remained quite durable.

Research in Hong Kong has consistently confirmed what has been all too evident in the Western developed nations: that family background, however measured, is the best predictor of school achievement.[63] School factors also play a large role. In this regard, there is great disparity among schools, as confirmed in a recent report by a visiting panel: "There are striking variations indeed. Hong Kong has some of the best schools in the world in terms of student attainment. ... most of the schools however, leave something to be desired. Facilities, teacher qualifications, examination results and other indicators of quality rank low. Students are allocated to these school for various reasons, including their test performance and lack of opportunity owing to the educational and economic status of their parents."[64]

Little has been done to relieve inequality, and if, as expected in the early 1990s, the economy goes through a period of crisis, the gap between the social classes could increase. If so, the schools will likely become an arena of social class conflict.

Interdependence

There has been a growing interdependence, both economically and politically, between Hong Kong and the People's Republic of China. China is well justified in its assertion that it is responsible for the economic success of Hong Kong. Through immigration, it provides the indispensable manpower needed to fuel Hong Kong's industrialization. China also subsidizes a large percentage of Hong Kong's foodstuffs and provides relatively inexpensive clothing. Moreover, the mainland provides the colony with 35 percent of its water supply. Hong Kong remains a useful contact point with the West for China. The most common explanation for China's position with respect to Hong Kong has been and remains mutual advantage. This is not to suggest that it would be unwilling to sacrifice some level of mutual economic advantage for sovereignty. China has the military power to overrun Hong Kong in a few hours. Alternatively, it can use its supporters in Hong Kong to destabilize it.

The points of interdependence between China and Hong Kong are unique to ideologically opposed economic systems. Hong Kong is the largest market for China's exports, while China has become the second largest export market for Hong Kong.[65] In short, Hong Kong is a major source of China's investment capital and will continue to play a major role in financing China's modernization. By 1980 China's net foreign exchange earnings from Hong Kong had already reached U.S. $6.9 billion, representing 36.5 percent of China's total foreign exchange for that period.[66]

Economic interdependence has not been followed by educational or academic interdependence. There is virtually no structural interdependency between the two educational systems. Few formal institutional agreements have been signed between universities in Hong Kong and universities in other parts of China. The number and diversity of these universities would make it difficult to choose only a few with which to engage in formal arrangements. Yet formal agreements with many could easily become overwhelming given the small size of Hong Kong's only two universities. Informal exchanges allow links to be maintained with the majority of higher educational institutions in China. Thus, formal academic exchanges and research projects are conducted through faculty or academic department agreements, although each university sets aside funds that members of departments and faculties can use in academic exchanges.

In the 1980s, academic exchanges, albeit imbalanced in favor of science and engineering, increased between Hong Kong and the rest of China.[67] Early exchanges brought university staff together but resulted in little substantive cooperative work. The later phase moved toward joint cooperative projects between departments or faculties of different institutions, including those facilitated by the World Bank and other international agencies. There are also foundations within Hong Kong that encourage and sponsor faculty exchanges between universities.[68] Student exchanges in both directions have also increased. Special scholarships have permitted an increasing number of Hong Kong students to study at China's leading universities, although the number dropped after June 4, 1989 (postgraduate enrollment decreased by 75 percent). Key point universities in China such as Beijing University and Qinghua University offer full scholarships to Hong Kong students. This complements the already large number of Hong Kong students attending universities in South China in close proximity to Hong Kong. More students from China are enrolled in graduate rather than undergraduate programs in Hong Kong's two universities, and the numbers have steadily increased.

Hong Kong's interdependence extends beyond China. As an international trading center it has developed economic interdependence, including student flows, with many other nations. Many of the university staff in Hong Kong earned their credentials outside of Hong Kong or the rest of China. Furthermore, Hong Kong students presently earning postsecondary degrees outside of

Hong Kong number at least 35,000—more than double those studying at the territory's two universities.[69]

Given the strengthening of ties with universities in other parts of China, where academic freedom is often limited, Hong Kong's universities have expressed surprisingly little concern over academic freedom, even after the crackdown on universities in China following the Tiananmen incident. At the moment, the tenure system in Hong Kong's universities protects the critical scholar. However, many non-tenure-track three-year renewable contracts are offered to new recruits. Such terms potentially make critical scholars more vulnerable. Unlike Hong Kong's journalists, who have steadfastly battled the forces that threaten their future openness, the universities have yet to elevate this issue to the forefront. However, the universities have seldom been openly critical of government policy, whether of Hong Kong or China. On the only occasion when both universities challenged the government's Educational Commision on the length of university education, the commission's decision prevailed.

Although interdependence with the rest of China has a tremendous potential to influence educational policy in Hong Kong, as yet it has not. The extent of Beijing's influence will be determined either by mediation through an essentially democratic educational policy process or by exertion through a restructured consultative system designed to align educational developments with mainland interests. Even if in the unlikely event that Beijing makes a determined effort to leave Hong Kong educational politics in its present form, local leaders would be hard-pressed to pick up where the colonials left off without establishing a new source of legitimacy.

Education, Culture, and Identity

Traditional Chinese society was perpetuated by a state-dominated social order. In colonial Hong Kong, such a social order has existed for a hundred and fifty years. Although it has undergone changes in the last two decades, the basic nature of the political order has remained unscathed, albeit different in many ways from that of traditional Chinese society and of mainland China.

The nature of governance in Hong Kong includes such elements as authoritarianism, benign and enlightened rule, separate but blurred public and private spheres, and the rule of law. As Lau Siu Kai and Kuan Hsin Chi state: "The establishment of colonial rule in Hong Kong was based until several decades ago on military force. In the long span of colonial rule, subtle versions of the doctrine of the economic prowess and cultural superiority of the white people, and the civilizing mission of the colonizer, had occasionally emerged to justify colonial dominance. Still, there has not been an elaborate, systematic theory, explicitly articulated, to buttress the legitimacy of authority in Hong Kong."[70]

Confucianism, for instance, disappeared from the content of Hong Kong civil service examinations. This deprived the residual Confucian presence of instrumental value, relegating it to cultural backwaters. The Confucian influence lingers, but this is contingent more on the natural influence of social customs and family socialization than on any institutional underpinning such as schooling.

Hong Kong Chinese society differs from traditional and modern Chinese society in a number of ways: its high degree of modernization, industrialization, and urbanization; its dominance by market forces; the erosion of tradition; the adapted changes in the family and other primary and quasi-primary social structures; the lack of a moralizing elite; and the dominance of an economic elite. Furthermore, the values embodied in the Hong Kong Chinese elites differ from their counterparts in China. Their moral status is shaky, and they lack a sense of cultural or moral mission.

Hong Kong's history has left the school system with the task of resolving the tensions that result from a long colonial period. Dora Choi Po-King considers the strains between cultural tradition and modern education as manifest in the identity crisis of Hong Kong students. She explains, in part, the source of this tension in the 1970s: "The post-war generation was, therefore, bombarded with Western cultural influence both in and outside the school. Yet they were constantly reminded of their Chinese cultural heritage, and they did acquire a national cultural identity which was, however, never substantiated by any concrete ties, nor even candid discussion of relevant political developments. Caught in this ambiguous situation, the Hong Kong-born post-war generation met with a severe crisis of cultural identity."[71]

Local scholars raise questions as to the implications of the reincorporation of Hong Kong in 1997, especially as it relates to the apparent tension in the cultural identity of Hong Kong students. They identify the educational challenge of 1997 as socialization into a "one-country, two-system" society. Hong Kong educational policy will be beset with a major dilemma, that of building an education system that can reconcile the ideological contradiction between capitalism, socialism, and patriotism.

Notes

1 See John Burns and Ian Scott, *The Hong Kong Civil Service and Its Future* (Hong Kong: Oxford University Press, 1988); Joseph Y. S. Cheng, ed., *Hong Kong in Transition* (Hong Kong: Oxford University Press, 1986); Christopher Howe, "Growth, Public Policy, and Hong Kong's Relationship with the People's Republic of China," *China Quarterly*, no. 95 (1983), pp. 512–33; Y. C. Jao, Leung Chi-keung, Peter Wesley-Smith, and Wong Siu-lun, *Hong Kong and 1997: Strategies for the Future* (Hong Kong: University of Hong Kong, Center of Asian Studies, 1985); Lau Siu Kai and Kuan Hsin-chi, "The Changing Political Culture of the Hong Kong Chinese," in Cheng, ed., pp. 26–51; Gerard Postiglione, "The Structuring of Ethnicity in Hong Kong," *International Journal of Intercultural Relations* 12 (1988): 247–67; Lucian W. Pye, "The International Position of Hong Kong," *China Quarterly*, no. 95 (September 1983), pp. 456–68; A. J. Youngson, ed., *China and Hong Kong: The Economic Nexus* (Hong Kong: Oxford University Press, 1983); Ian Scott, *Political Change and the Crisis of Legitimacy in Hong Kong* (Hong Kong: Oxford University Press, 1989); Albert H. Yee, *A People Misruled: Hong Kong and the Chinese Stepping Stone Syndrome* (Hong Kong: Associated Press International, 1989); Myron Mushkat,

Hong Kong: The Challenge of Transformation (Hong Kong: University of Hong Kong, Center of Asian Studies, 1989).

2 Paul Morris, "The Effects on the School Curriculum of Hong Kong's Return to Chinese Sovereignty in *1997*," *Journal of Curriculum Studies* 20, no. 6 (November-December 1988): 509–28; and Gerard A. Postiglione, ed., *Education and Society in Hong Kong: Toward One Country and Two Systems* (Armonk, N.Y.: M. E. Sharpe, in press).

3 Among the first to resign from the Basic Law Drafting Committee were the outspoken liberal legislative councillors Lee Chu Ming and Szeto Wah. The editor of the Ming Bao daily newspaper, Louis Cha, who formerly had supported the Beijing government, also resigned after June 4, 1989.

4 See "World Marches for China," *Hong Kong Standard* (May 29, 1989), p. 1; and "Xianggang Shubaiwanren zaishangjie zhichi xueyun," *Wen Hui Bao* (May 29, 1989), p. 1.

5 See *South China Morning Post*, "Call to End Politics Ban in Schools" (June 7, 1989). On June 16, 1989, the University of Hong Kong Faculty of Education conducted a territory-wide meeting of school teachers and principals in which accounts of student activism were discussed. Most students were involved in territory-wide demonstrations; however, many students had organized speeches, political poster displays, letter writing, and student assemblies within school.

6 However, in its early history Hong Kong at times became the base for launching radical activities that contributed to nation building in China, e.g., Sun Yixian's anti-Manzhou uprisings.

7 See *The Draft Basic Law of the Hong Kong Special Administrative Region of the People's Republic of China* (Hong Kong: Consultative Committee of the Basic Law, April 1988).

8 See Lau Siu Kai, *Society and Politics in Hong Kong* (Hong Kong: Chinese University of Hong Kong Press, 1982).

9 See Manuel Castells, *The Shek Kip Mei Syndrome: Public Housing and Economic Development in Hong Kong* (Hong Kong: Center of Urban Studies and Urban Planning, January 1986).

10 See Lau.

11 "Tertiary Doors Will Open to More Students," *South China Morning Post: Year in Review* (January 14, 1990); and "Academic Hits Out at Crisis Intervention," *South China Morning Post* (November 5, 1989).

12 See Philip G. Altbach and Gail P. Kelly, eds., *Education and Colonialism* (New York: Longman, 1978), pp. 1–52.

13 See Lau and Kuan (n. 1 above).

14 See Martin Carnoy, *The State and Political Theory* (Princeton, N.J.: Princeton University Press, 1985).

15 "Leftist School Leavers Gain Acceptance," *South China Morning Post* (October 2, 1989); what distinguishes these so-called patriotic, leftist, or pro-China schools is that they have traditionally supported the Beijing government's policies. During the Cultural Revolution, for instance, they rejected the formal curriculum of the Hong Kong education department. These schools have the strongest links with those in mainland China.

16 See "Pro-China Schools in Subsidy Bid," *South China Morning Post* (October 8, 1989).

17 See "Provisional Hong Kong Council for Academic Accreditation," in *Hong Kong 1989* (Hong Kong: Government Printer, 1989).

18 See *Returning to Hong Kong: The Hong Kong Employment Guide for 1990 Graduates of Overseas Universities* (Hong Kong: American Chamber of Commerce, with the Institute of International Education, 1990).

32 *Contexts*

19 See Stanley Leung, "Mind Your Own Business Ji Tells Hong Kong," *South China Morning Post* (June 23, 1989), p. 1.
20 See Lau and Kuan.
21 Ibid., p. 187.
22 See *Xianggong jiaoyu shouce* (Xianggong: Shangwu shuguan, 1988); also, Huo Guoqiang, *Xianggong zhongxue gailan* (Xianggong: Xianggong zhonghua jidujiao qingnianhui, 1988).
23 *Sino-British Declaration on the Question of Hong Kong*, initialed text, Xinhua News Agency, Hong Kong branch (September 26, 1984). See also these Chinese sources on the subject of the "one-country, two-system" policy: for instance, Zhao Qiu Yi, *Yi Guo Liang Zhi Gai Lun* (Jilin: Jilin Daxue Chubanshe, 1988); Zhao Xiao Wang, Deng Yun, and ZhouBing Yin, *Yi Ge Guo Jia Liang Zhong Zhi Du* (Tianjin: Jie Fang Jun Chubanshe, 1989); *Xianggong Wenti Wenjian: Xuanji* (Beijing: People's Press Renmin Chubanshe, 1985); *Xianggong Jiaoyu Mian Mianguan* (Guangzhou: Guangdong Renmin Chubanshe, 1988); and Lei Qiang, Wu Fu Guang, Zhong Guang, and Zheng Tain Xiang, *Xianggong Gaodeng Jiaoyu* (Guangzhou: Guangdong Gaodeng Jiaoyu Chubanshe, 1988).
24 See, e.g., *The Hong Kong Education System* (Hong Kong: Education Department, 1981); also, for an earlier historical account, see Anthony Sweeting, *Education in Hong Kong, Pre-1841 to 1941: Fact and Opinion* (Hong Kong: Hong Kong University Press, 1990); and Bernard Hung-kay Luk, "Chinese Culture in the Hong Kong Curriculum" (paper presented at the annual conference of the Comparative and International Education Society, Cambridge, Mass., March 31, 1989).
25 See Bernard Hung-kay Luk, "Education," in *The Other Hong Kong Report*, ed. T. L. Tsim and B. H. K. Luk (Hong Kong: Chinese University Press, 1989).
26 See Visiting Panel, *A Perspective on Education in Hong Kong* (Hong Kong: Government Printer, 1982).
27 See Luk, "Education," p. 178.
28 See Lau (n. 8 above).
29 Youngson, ed. (n. 1 above), p. 1.
30 Gregor Benton, *The Hong Kong Crisis* (London: Pluto, 1983), p. 4.
31 See Frank Choi, "Education Report Criticized for Promoting Elitist System," *Hong Kong Standard* (October 25, 1988).
32 See *Education Commission Report No. 3* (Hong Kong: Education Department, 1988).
33 See, e.g., "Split Over Educational Reforms," *South China Morning Post* (October 27, 1988).
34 Cheng Kai Ming, "Educational Policy-making in Hong Kong: The Changing Legitimacy," in Postiglione, ed. (n. 2 above).
35 Vicky Wong, "Academic Hits Out at Crisis Intervention," *South China Morning; Post* (November 5, 1989).
36 A. E. Sweeting, "The Cat among the Pigeons, ECR3 and the Universities" (University of Hong Kong, Department of Curriculum Studies, 1988, typescript).
37 John Rear, "One Brand of Politics," in *Hong Kong: The Industrial Economy*, ed. K. Hopkins (Hong Kong: Oxford University Press, 1971), p. 55.
38 Norman Miners, *The Governance and Politics of Hong Kong*, 4th ed. (Hong Kong: Oxford University Press, 1986).
39 See *Green Paper: The 1987 Review of Developments in Representative Government* (Hong Kong: Government Printer, May 1989).
40 Morris (n. 2 above), p. 514.
41 See *Guidelines on Civic Education in Schools* (Hong Kong: Education Department, 1985), pp. 8–9.
42 See Joseph Cheng, "The Changing Political Culture of the Hong Kong Chinese," in Cheng, ed. (n. 1 above), pp. 37–38.

43 Myron Mushkat, *The Making of the Hong Kong Administrative Class* (Hong Kong: University of Hong Kong, Center of Asian Studies, 1982), p. 60.
44 See Civil Service Branch, "Civil Service Personnel Statistics, 1986" (Hong Kong: Civil Service Branch, Government Secretariat, 1986, mimeographed), pp. 11–12.
45 Ibid.
46 *A Draft Agreement between the Government of the United Kingdom of Great Britain and Northern Ireland and the Government of the People's Republic of China on the Future of Hong Kong* (Hong Kong: Government Printer, 1984), p. 17.
47 Ibid.
48 John Burns, "Succession Planning and Localization," in Burns and Scott (n. 1 above), p. 105.
49 Michael Leung became the director of education.
50 Ronald Skeldon, "Emigration and the Future of Hong Kong," *Pacific Affairs* 63, no. 4 (Winter 1990–91): 500–524.
51 See *Report of the Working Group Set Up to Review Language Improvement Measures* (Hong Kong: Education Department, 1985).
52 See John Gibbons, "The Issue of the Language of Instruction in the Lower Forms of Hong Kong Secondary Schools," *Journal of Multilingual and Multicultural Development*, no. 3 (1982), pp. 117–28.
53 See *Report of the Working Group Set Up to Review Language Improvement Measures* (Hong Kong: Education Department, 1985).
54 "Jiaoyu shiqu tigong jihui xiaoyong fenliu jiaoxue tuzeng fenhua maodun" *Jingji Ribao*, Hong Kong (November 24, 1989); and "Zhongchan jieji zinu jiaoyu yaoqiu zendzhuan shangxuewei mianliu xianggong rencai," *Xin Bao*, Hong Kong (November 27, 1989).
55 See Ora Kwo, "Language Studies in a Changing Political and Economic Context: The Teaching of Putonghua in Hong Kong Schools" (paper presented at the First Hong Kong Conference on Language and Society, Hong Kong, April 1988).
56 Herbert Pierson, "Language Attitudes and Use in Hong Kong: A Case for Putonghua" (paper presented at the First Hong Kong Conference on Language and Society, Hong Kong, April 1988); also, Robert Bauer, "The Hong Kong Cantonese Speech Community" (University of Hong Kong, Center of Asian Studies, 1984, typescript).
57 S. W. Wai, "Secondary Schools Favor Teaching through Chinese," *South China Morning Post* (November 12, 1986), p. 3.
58 See Benton (n. 30 above), p. 19.
59 Lee M. K., "Emerging Patterns of Social Conflict in Hong Kong Society," in *Hong Kong in the 1980s*, ed. Joseph Y. S. Cheng (Hong Kong: Summerson Eastern, 1982), p. 25.
60 *Hong Kong Census* (Hong Kong: Government Printer, 1976).
61 Lau (n. 8 above), p. 4.
62 See Max Weber, *The Religion of China* (New York: Free Press, 1951); J. M. Menzel, *The Chinese Civil Service* (Boston: D. C. Heath, 1963); and E. A. Kracke, "Religion, Family and Individual in the Chinese Examination System," in *Chinese Thoughts and Social Institutions,* ed. John K. Fairbank (Chicago: University of Chicago Press, 1957).
63 See Allan Brimer and Patrick Griffen, *A Study of Mathematics Achievement in Hong Kong* (Hong Kong: University of Hong Kong, Center of Asian Studies, 1985); R. E. Mitchell, *Pupil, Parent and School: A Hong Kong Study* (Taipei: Orient Culture Service, 1972); Pedro Ng, "Access to Educational Opportunity: The Case of Kwun Tong" (Hong Kong: Chinese University of Hong Kong Social Research Centre, 1975); and David Post and Pong Suet Ling, "Socio-economic Indicators and Higher Education Access in Hong Kong" (paper presented at the Comparative and International Education Society Annual Meeting, Cambridge, Mass., March 31, 1989).

64 Visiting Panel (n. 26 above), p. 58.
65 See Lau Pui-king, "Economic Relations between Hong Kong and China," in Cheng, ed. (n. 1 above), pp. 235–67.
66 See Jao Y. C., "Hong Kong's Role in Financing China's Modernization," in Youngson, ed. (n. 1 above), pp. 12–76.
67 Bai Jie Rui, *Jinggong Xueshu Jiaoliu Xiankuang Yu Qiandan* (Xianggong: Jinggong Xueshu Jiaoliu Zhongxin, 1985).
68 The Peihua Foundation and the Beijing-Hong Kong Academic Exchange Center are examples.
69 Jay Henderson, "Hong Kong Students Flood U.S.," *South China Morning Post* (April 27, 1986), p. 19.
70 Lau and Kuan (n. 1 above), p. 19.
71 Choi Po King, "Cultural Identity and Colonial Rule: The Hong Kong-China Connection" (paper presented at the Chinese University of Hong Kong, Conference on Chinese Cultural Tradition and Contemporary Modern Education, November 7, 1988), p. 31.

2 Education: China

Contemporary education in Chinese society has become more of a priority for both families and government for different reasons. Families view it as a path to social mobility and are willing to spend a large portion of the household budget for it. For government, education is socialization into the national identity and a means to strengthen the nation and build a knowledge economy. Compared to other developing countries, China has made rapid progress in implementing nine years of basic education, senior secondary academic and vocational schools, and a system of mass higher education. According to the National Outline for Medium- and Long-term Education Reform and Development 2010–2020, the average years of schooling for the working age population will reach 11.2 years by 2020 (from 9.6 years in 2010). By 2030, the access rate to higher education will reach 40 percent. Education has become central to making the country globally competitive by providing human capital that will drive its transition from middle- to high-income nation (Outline 2010). This chapter starts with a brief history of education, to be followed by a discussion of contemporary primary and secondary schools, higher education, the rural-urban divide, and education for ethnic minority groups in China.

A brief history

As a social institution, schools generally promote continuity more than change. For most of China's history, education has been a conservative force, as Confucianism emphasized the diligent study of moral principles underlying the social order (Elman and Woodside 1994, Lee 2000). For over a thousand years, Confucian orthodoxy was the basis of an examination system (*keju*) that determined merit and the path to officialdom for men. This examination system did make possible a certain equality of opportunity among men, although the advantages were still in favour of those families who had wealth and power (Chang 1963). While it created a pool of highly educated men, it was superimposed upon a mostly illiterate population.

After the defeat of China in the Opium Wars in 1840, the Qing Dynasty began to consider initiating educational reforms in the name of modernization. By 1905 the imperial examination system was abolished. A Ministry of Education was established that used Japan's education system as a model for modernization. Western missionaries also established schools and universities, and a small number of Chinese students began to study overseas. After the collapse of the Qing Dynasty and the establishment of the Republic of China in 1911, the new government permitted co-education, sought to remove classical learning from primary school, emphasized the learning of mathematics and science, and made lower primary education compulsory. The New Culture Movement of 1919 replaced the classical written language with a Beijing-based vernacular called Mandarin that became the national language. Some contend that the visit of educational philosopher John Dewey in 1919 influenced the establishment of a new school system based on the American 6–3–3 pattern.

Throughout the effort to reform and modernize the new nation, debates continued about the best way to modernize while retaining the essence of Chinese education. This became less of an issue as Communist Party Chairman Mao Zedong heralded the establishment of the People's Republic of China in 1949. Radical Marxism and Mao Zedong thought reached a peak during the Cultural Revolution of 1966–76, a time of class struggle and political upheavals that led to the closure of schools and universities for two years. A hyper-politicized definition of educational success prevailed until 1976.

When Deng Xiaoping led China into an era of economic reform and opening to the outside world in 1978, academic standards were reintroduced along with a national college and university entrance examination (*gaokao*) (Pepper 1996). Deng espoused that 'science and technology are the key to modernization and education is the means to develop science and technology' (Gu 2001: 112). Since Deng's administration, China has popularized basic education, shown the world that Shanghai secondary school students come first over those in 60 countries in science and mathematics, provided access to higher education for more students than any other country in the world, and built several world-class universities.

However, while the economic reforms brought about much prosperity, they also led to vast inequalities that began to be reproduced in the education system. The legitimacy of an education system depends to a great extent on the promise of social mobility and a better future (Postiglione 2006). The most formidable domestic challenge for the state is to ensure that education responds to a diverse population: to rural as well as urban families, to rural migrants as well as urban middle class, to ethnic minorities as well as poor rural Han Chinese, to girls as well as boys, to those with learning disabilities as well as those who are intellectually gifted. While China has succeeded in the impressive achievement of providing nine years of basic education to more than 95 per cent of the school age population in a country of over a billion people, it is also haunted by educational inequality. The richest 10 per cent of society was 23 times richer than the poorest 10 per cent in 2007, an increase since 1998, when it was only 7.3 times (Jia 2010). While this might create upheavals in many other societies, relative stability has been maintained by China's rapid economic growth and a cultural heritage with a preference for harmonious social development. As economic indicators rise for a nation of one-child families, quality of life has become a priority and education is expected to make sure it is achieved.

Unsurprisingly, there has been a rapid expansion of educational opportunities for all social groups in the post-1979 era. The state has continued to popularize basic education and literacy for all, expand secondary and tertiary vocational-technical education for job skills in a burgeoning labour market, and increase university enrolments to strengthen the knowledge economy. The demand from the new middle class in an increasingly urbanized society was met by a highly differentiated system of educational credentials leading to elite urban schools and top-tier universities, both domestic and foreign. Women and ethnic minorities began to gain greater access to more social and educational opportunities (Postiglione 2009a). The demand of the state for education as social control was met through the preparation of high-calibre leaders who were able to reconcile communist precepts with market economics (Law 2006).

Managing domestic demands continues to be increasingly difficult and complex. China's education system is shaped by a shifting market of demands from different sectors of the population. Rural parents pay more and more for their children's education and demand that it will lead to a good job (Xie and Postiglione 2015). Meanwhile, employers demand that graduates have relevant knowledge and skills for supporting industrial upgrading. An increasingly influential urban middle class demands that education bring with it a cultural capital and social status that places their children in an advantaged position. This has fuelled shadow education (e.g. cram schools and supplementary coaching for examinations) and opportunities to study abroad as early as junior secondary school. Meanwhile, rural migrant children struggle to obtain meaningful access to urban schools. Other 'left behind' rural children are cared for by grandparents and school services in villages and towns as their parents migrate to cities for work. Finally, the state continues to demand that education be an engine for economic growth but also an instrument to prepare leaders, integrate ethnic minorities, promote ideological socialization, and maintain social stability.

These overlapping demands for practical skills, status culture and social control compete at different times for influence over educational reforms. Each demand takes precedence in different circumstances and at different times. Such a market of multiple demands is recalibrated year by year according to how much the economy grows, how much social dissatisfaction arises, and how quickly the urban middle class prospers. Changes in society determine the pecking order of these demands. In times of rapid economic growth, the demand for practical skills is a top priority. In times of internal strife, the demand of the state for social control takes precedence. As the middle class expands, the demand for education to confer status culture grows. Reforms in the structure and content of education are influenced by a combination of the three demands. It is also influenced by how well the legal system can temper market forces that obstruct equity and social justice in education.

Equally important, the expansion of educational opportunities in China has to reconcile multiple polarities: foster high-quality learning not only in schools of the prosperous east but also in the poorer west; ensure social stability but not stifle innovation and creativity; preserve aspects of cultural heritage while adhering to the ideological precepts of a socialist market economy; promote mainstream cultural capital while sustaining the cultural vitality of an ethnic minority population a hundred million strong; learn from the outside world to spur high-level scientific and technological progress but temper the younger generation's attraction to aspects of globalization viewed by the government as hostile to national interests; and remain committed to a market economy while providing fair educational opportunities.

Even though China has shifted away from a planned economy and toward a market economy, the central government still sets out national plans and directs local authorities to design implementation strategies. For education, there are usually five-years plans, though occasionally they may introduce a longer-term initiative. One example is the National Outline for Medium- and Long-term Education Reform and Development, 2010–2020, which aligns with interlocking plans for science and technology (2006–2020) and talent development (2010–2020). Such plans provide a macroscopic framework. While the local authorities are expected to follow them closely, there is enough flexibility to refute the idea of a strictly top-down authoritarian system. Localities sometimes find creative ways to circumvent central policies. This is especially true if educational policies from the central government appear unsuitable for local conditions due to financial or cultural reasons, as in the case with some ethnic minority regions. Rather than confront higher authorities, localities often find alternative means of making progress. Non-adherence to central policies may result in trouble for local officials if results are unimpressive or directly contradictory to central policies. But by instituting experiments and alternative adaptations of a policy in ways that improve education, local governments can influence subsequent policy deliberations at the central level.

Primary and secondary schools in today's China

The main school subjects are mathematics and Chinese language and literature, science, geography, history and moral education. Secondary school students in the city of Shanghai scored above their counterparts in 60 countries on an international evaluation of mathematics and science achievement. However, students in many other parts of China are far less competitive. For all children in China, learning English is a requirement from grade three of primary school. At the end of nine years of basic education (six years of primary and three years of junior secondary education), an examination determines the future path for students who continue on in school (Cheng 2000). About half of all students are tracked into the vocational/technical path, while the rest attend senior secondary school in preparation for the national entrance examination for college and university. Vocational schools struggle with funding constraints, teacher quality issues, facilities and equipment, and alignment of training with labour market needs, especially in less developed parts of the country. However, the Ministry of Education has made it a priority to improve senior secondary and tertiary vocational-technical education by building school-industry partnerships. The requirements of gifted and special needs students were not addressed until about 1985. There are an increasing number of special schools, and vocational training schools that have been established for special needs students. The concept of inclusive education has become a regular part of the discourse on educational reform.

In many ethnic minority areas there are nationality schools (*minzu xuexiao*) in which the commonly used written script (Uyghur, Tibetan, Mongolian, or Korean, etc.) may be used as the medium of instruction. In cases where a minority only has an oral language in common use, a phonetic script is devised, and the medium of instruction can be in that mother tongue for the first year or two of primary school, after which the medium of instruction switches to Chinese. The medium of instruction is a complex issue and varies across ethnic autonomous regions (Postiglione 2009a; Postiglione and Beckett 2011).

After completing the compulsory nine years of education, students who wish to continue to senior secondary school normally pay for further education. Although most primary and secondary schools in urban China are state run, the private school movement has gradually gained momentum. Private (*minban*) schools have proved that they can also provide a high-quality education, sometimes superior to that in state-run urban schools, though this is more the case in primary and secondary education than in tertiary education.

The government has encouraged the private school movement, partly because it is unwilling to risk increased government funding in an entrenched school system in which bureaucracy and corruption often place educational progress at risk. Instead, it has looked to social forces (*shehui liliang*), including non-government groups and individuals, to take a lead in establishing and running private schools. While good government schools may survive, some less successful government schools have become converted to the private mode of finance and management to make them more competitive (Hu et al. 2009). By the mid-1990s, a growing number of urban students began to attend the growing number of private schools, including pre-schools, primary and secondary schools, as well as colleges and universities (Lin 1999). In 2003, the government also promulgated a Private Education Promotion Law (2003).

In short, Chinese society is learning to adapt to a transformative education system. Markets have come to matter as much as Marxism in educational provision. Parents are paying more for their children to receive a quality education and access to a college or university that leads to a job after graduation. China has managed to push enrolment rates for primary and secondary schooling to levels above many other developing countries, despite the fact that it only allocates a relatively small proportion of its Gross Domestic Product to education, finally reaching 4 per cent by 2011.

The rural-urban divide

There is generally a significant difference between rural and urban education. For example, it is notable that while girls outperform boys in urban regions, the opposite is true in rural areas of the country. Before the school finance reform of 2007, less than a quarter of the funds for education went to rural areas, even though more than half of the national population was considered rural. China's new market economy has continued to favour the urban middle class, leaving the rural poor, rural migrants, ethnic minorities and rural girls with poorer access to education and higher drop-out rates.

The rural-urban gap is also reflected in the structure of the education system. More urban than rural students have access to three years of preschool (the final year of which is kindergarten). Preschools emphasize basic training as well as the writing of Chinese characters, games, dance and singing, and promote values such as kindness and beauty. Most rural students do not have the opportunity to attend preschool, although the government has made the expansion of rural preschool education a high priority since 2011. Approximately 20 per cent of preschool-age children do not get a year of preschool education. About 40 per cent attend no preschool at all. These national figures mask urban-regional disparities. A 2008 Survey showed that 56 per cent of rural children aged four to six attended no preschool education (Rural Education Action Programme, 2008). Even in a major city like Shanghai, only about 60 per cent of migrant children aged three to five are in preschool. As a consequence, rather than take their children with them, many migrant parents leave their children behind. These become the so-called left-behind children (*liushou ertong*).

At age six, urban children begin six years of primary school, which is usually located in their neighbourhood. For many Chinese children the school day is long and arduous with a lot of homework – on top of household responsibilities, especially for girls. The story of Guo Guo, a senior secondary school student from Chongqing city, is typical (Muyi 2005; Yang 2006). She awakes about 6:30 a.m. and eats a piece of bread on her way to school. After the regular school day she begins her evening school class at 4:40 p.m. Her father delivers her dinner to her at school, after which Guo Guo begins her second evening school class at 6:30 p.m. After evening school she arrives home to do her daily homework assignment, which she completes by 1:00 a.m., then gets to sleep not much before 2:00 a.m. In some rural and pastoral areas, students may not begin school until they are eight years old if the school is far from home and roads are unsafe for small children. This situation is beginning to change as village schools are consolidated at town and county level and rural students are bussed to central schools. In such cases, an increasing number of students board at school.

Fewer girls attend school in rural areas and may also drop out of school earlier than boys (Ross 2006). There has been an effort to correct the impression in society that a boy is more valuable than a girl. The sex ratio has improved from the 2000 census figure of 117 boys to 100 girls to the 2010 census figure of between 103 and 107 boys to 100 girls. The encouraging news is that female illiteracy has been slashed from 31 per cent in 1990 to 13 per cent in 2000 and 7 per cent in 2012 (National Bureau of Statistics 2013). Boys and girls attend primary school in near equal numbers nationally, but rural girls have a lower attendance and higher dropout rate.

In the past it was common for many rural village children to attend a two-or three-year primary school in their village, then move on to board at a full six-year primary school in the township to complete their primary education. Those going on to junior secondary school would board at the school in the county, far from their home village. After nine years of basic education, about a quarter to two-thirds of students attend senior secondary vocational-technical school. In some rural areas, vocational-technical education begins as early as junior senior secondary school. In order to make better use of scarce resources, many village schools have been closed. Many rural migrants have taken their children to urban areas for schooling, or left them behind (*liushou ertong*) with relatives and friends in their villages. Children of migrants have diminished educational opportunities. New national guidelines have been proposed to eliminate this problem.

There are other issues related to education in rural areas. A nine-year cycle of compulsory education is guaranteed by law. However, it is not unusual for there to be supplementary fees, especially in rural areas. Indeed, as educational costs rise, many poor households find it increasingly difficult to cover the costs (Kong 2010). Some rural counties struggled to fund nine-year compulsory education. Until late 2005, many children in poor rural counties were required to pay for their schoolbooks. However, since 2007, governments at central and local levels have instituted measures to prevent schools from charging exorbitant fees. Financial reforms in education have improved the free provision of school textbooks and injected funds to assist schools in poorer rural regions (Lou and Ross 2008). The situation has gradually been eliminated in which many rural areas lack the basic conditions necessary for education, including desks, and teaching aids like chalk. School facilities have been improved nationwide. However, the Sichuan earthquake of 2008 demonstrated the poor quality of school building construction.

Teacher qualifications and salaries are on the rise but often not enough to keep good teachers in rural areas. Some remote areas have qualified teachers, new schools, adequate facilities and even libraries, while others endure shortages of all of them. Achieving a more balanced development remains an elusive priority and drop-out trends have been a major problem in rural areas. For example, in a study of three poor counties in Southwest China, Ding (2012) found there were 214 persons in the seventh grade in 2007, 152 in eighth grade in 2008, and 104 in ninth grade in 2009. In this case, more than half dropped out. Although this is not a typical case, and Ding even called it an extreme case, it does demonstrate that high drop-out rates still exist in some localities. Such a situation could be viewed as troubling since attendance is very high in urban schools. Ding concludes that the government's 2007 policy of free compulsory education and living expenses subsidies for boarding school students resulted in a decline of the drop-out rates. This does not mean that merely increasing funding is the answer to improvements in education.

Rural girls have constituted a high proportion of the drop-outs. Municipalities like Beijing and Shanghai, and east coast provinces like Zhejiang and Jiangsu have lower drop-out rates for girls (Ross 2006). Urban families with their only child being a girl are more likely to give as much attention to ensuring a good education as if she were a boy. While 16 provinces in eastern China had virtually full enrolment, the Northwest and Southwest have struggled to catch up. However, the statistics on school attendance and enrolment do not always match the reality because there is pressure on local officials to reach targets set by the central authorities. This can result in a sugar coating of educational statistics. However, such statistics are increasingly being challenged. A study in 2005 contended that enrolment figures were exaggerated. Students were encouraged to attend on the day that attendance figures were tallied by school inspectors (Ma 2005; Zhu 2005).

The Chinese government set aside 15 billion yuan for rural education in order to reduce educational inequality between rural and urban areas. The *Decision of the State Council to Further Strengthen Education in Rural Areas* has proposed to achieve the 'two basics' (literacy and basic education) and improve the educational quality in 372 rural western counties in China. By 2007 all poor students were exempted from miscellaneous fees and textbook charges, and would receive lodging allowances for boarding at school.

Finally, migrant children's education, which is related to the rural-urban divide, has become a major challenge to continued urbanization of the country. There were 35.81 million migrant children aged 0–17 in 2010, and 69.73 million left-behind children aged 0–17. This amounts to almost one in every four children – over 100 million in total (National Bureau of Statistics of China 2013). Migrant children do not have the same educational rights as urban children. Migrant schools, though not always legal, are sometimes the only option for migrant children. Yet these schools are often closed down for not meeting the basic building standards of space and safety.

Public primary and junior secondary schools are supposed to take the major responsibility to educate migrant children and their enrolment rates should reach the local level. Migrant children are supposed to be charged the same amount for school fees as children of permanent urban residents. Even when they are able to attend school, their parents' lack of an urban household registration document means children must return to their hometown once they wish to attend senior secondary school.

Finally, poor nutrition for children in rural areas is directly linked to educational achievement. Nutritional deficiency in early childhood substantially hinders cognitive development, leading to poor educational performance. Making early childhood education compulsory is one way of monitoring nutritional indicators. Survey data in rural areas shows that stunting and nutritional deficiencies affect more than 20 per cent of children in poor rural counties (Hannum et al. 2012).

Education and ethnic minority groups

Another major dimension of educational inequalities is the gap in schooling between Han Chinese and ethnic minority groups in China. Only ten countries in the world have total populations that surpass that of China's ethnic minorities. The 55 officially designated minority groups live in 116 ethnic autonomous areas, which cover half the country and 90 per cent of the border region. In minority areas, the state has to ensure education promotes access and equity, economic development, cultural autonomy as set out in the constitution, and national unity. The education of ethnic minorities has thus become a key sector of China's education system (Zhu 2007; Chen 2008; Gao 2008; Yu 2008; Zhao 2010). The Ministry of Education has a division dealing directly with their educational policy and practices. The State Ethnic Affairs Commission also has a division of minority education that oversees many of the ethnic (*minzu*) colleges in China.

It is impossible to conceptualize China's ethnic minorities as a single entity due to cultural, regional and developmental differences. However, the government's unified set of ethnic minority education policies is intended to be implemented flexibly so as to take account of the unique situation in each ethnic minority region. Ethnic autonomous regions became authorized to develop their own educational programmes, including levels and kinds of schools, curriculum content and languages of instruction. Special funds for minority education were increased, and a portion of the annual budget for ethnic minority areas could be used for education. Funds for teacher training increased and various types of in-service training have been set up. Schools can be established according to the characteristics of the ethnic minorities and their regions. In rural, frontier and cold mountainous regions, boarding schools were arranged and stipends provided for students. Special emphasis in education could be placed on ethnic minority language, culture and historical traditions. Several major universities have special remedial classes for minority students with preparatory programmes in the first year. University admission standards for minority students have been lowered or points added to ethnic minority students' examination scores to make admission easier to attain.

There are some issues related to educational policies for ethnic minorities in China. Through state educational institutions, ethnic minority culture becomes transmitted, celebrated, transmuted, truncated, or in some cases eliminated. Formal education can become an instrument to broaden cultural sophistication beyond the ethnic community, or it can radically intensify ethnic identities and inequalities in cultural capital. In the case of China, the diversity that exists among its ethnic minority population is only partially reflected in the content of school textbooks, even though minority languages are emphasized in many regions.

In addition, multi-ethnic diversity is salient in propaganda but not highly encouraged in state education. Ethnic cultures are celebrated at national events, but cultural diversity in schools and society is carefully managed. It is prescribed within the context of the ruling ideology of 'ethnic plurality within the unity of the Chinese nation' and within the government's 'harmonious society' campaign. The debate over cultural preservation, ethnic autonomy and state schooling has remained complex (Postiglione 1999).

Schools can shape ethnic identity through the values they transmit. Making ethnic minorities into Chinese citizens is an educational task, which has remained a work in progress. Culturally meaningful access to mainstream schools, colleges and universities has remained a major challenge for improving the quality of ethnic minority community life in China.

Furthermore, most minority groups have trailed Han Chinese in educational attainment. The notion of cultural backwardness has continued to be part of popular discourse about ethnic minorities, and has often been cited in China as the principal reason for educational inequalities between Han Chinese and ethnic minority groups. Cultural backwardness however is not a good argument since about ten of China's 55 minority groups have education levels above the national average. There is a key question on the extent to which school norms recognize and encourage diverse cultural groups and create a learning environment that reflects the ethnic diversity of the nation. The extent to which schools in China create an atmosphere that has positive institutional norms towards diverse cultural groups is limited by notions of cultural backwardness. In some cases, mainstream education has led to a loss of self-esteem and interest in education, particularly in the case of Tibetans, and is reflected in drop-out rates (Nyima 1997, 2000).

China's higher education

Beginning in 1998, China's higher education system experienced an unprecedented expansion (Postiglione 2005, 2009b). As universities became increasingly viewed as instruments of national competition, more students attended higher education in China than anywhere in the world (Levin 2010). Between 1999 and 2004, enrolments nearly quadrupled. In 1999, enrolment in higher education stood at 1.6 million, and in 2004, enrolment was 4.473 million. According to the 2007 Ministry of Education statistics, in 1990, less than 4 per cent of the 18–22 age group was enrolled in higher education, compared to 22 per cent in 2005. In 2014, there were seven million college and university graduates. However, less than half had located a job by the time of graduation, prompting a major effort to find ways to address this problem.

The decision to begin a rapid expansion in 1998 was in response to several factors. The successful policy of basic education had pushed more and more students toward higher levels of the education system. The Asian financial crisis had slowed the economy and the government's decision to expand higher education was a way to keep more students out of the labour market until the economy picked up again. It was also a way to get families to spend more of their savings so as to stimulate the economy in the aftermath of the Asian economic crisis. Education is the fastest growing focus of consumer spending by urban residents. This spending is increasing at an average rate of about 20 per cent annually. An average of 10 per cent of savings goes to education, which is higher than the 7 per cent put aside for housing. Finally, the expansion of higher education was a way for China to strengthen its knowledge economy amid economic globalization.

China has the world's second largest economy, yet its universities produce fewer independent thinkers than its competitors. As China loses its labour cost advantage, maintaining the country's economic ascent will depend on boosting the quality of its higher education system. Generating new products and services, as well as building a civil society, will require universities to foster creative and innovative thinking, in addition to carrying out cutting-edge research. China's higher education system has expanded to widen student access, but there is a need to reform university governance and better align university teaching to the needs of the workplace.

The National Outline for Medium- and Long-term Education Reform and Development 2010–2020 calls for less bureaucratic control of universities and more institutional autonomy. Universities are to be governed by the institutions themselves. Student admission is no longer to be determined solely by the national college and university examination. The universities will aim to make their admission criteria more diverse, with an emphasis on whole-person development. As the massification of higher education continues apace into the future, China's colleges and universities will become more of a leading force in the larger education system and, as has been the case in other countries, a major driver of the democratization of Chinese society.

Rising unemployment of university graduates, something not seen before China embarked on mass higher education, has created an inflationary spiral that will have to be addressed sooner or later. China has to rapidly expand but also privatize much of its higher education system, raise the quality of undergraduate education while broadening the curriculum for more liberal thinking, provide jobs for seven million graduates annually, and keep a lid on various forms of academic corruption.

The globalization of the Chinese economy is compelling universities to adapt and compete like never before. With the phasing out of a planned economy, Chinese higher education moved towards reforms similar to those in other parts of the world, including a proliferation of non-government-supported institutions of higher education. Private (*minban*) colleges and universities were entering the scene for the first time since 1949, and their numbers were increasing rapidly. By 2006 they numbered 318 with 1,467,000 students (Hu et al. 2009). Some universities even established independent colleges on their own campuses to compete with private colleges and universities. These independent colleges admitted students with lower scores and charged them higher fees than regular students. However, for both *minban* and independent colleges, quality remains a problem. The main accomplishment of private higher education has been to improve access to higher education for more students.

China is making great efforts to establish several world-class universities that can stand alongside leading universities such as Harvard and Yale, Oxford and Cambridge. To do so, China launched two programmes in higher education known as Project 211 and Project 985. These two plans selected a group of top universities and provided very generous financial support for them to upgrade their standards of teaching and research. Peking and Tsinghua universities, both located in Beijing, and Fudan and Jiaotong universities in Shanghai enjoy some of the highest reputations in the country. However, China's efforts to build world-class universities are heavily influenced by global university ranking systems developed in the West. Although it tries to catch up with top universities in the USA and the UK, many Chinese scholars argue that China should not neglect its own historical tradition of academies to develop its full potential and become an internationally influential part of the higher-education landscape (Hayhoe 1995; Yang 2013).

Conclusion

China's education system is confronting many challenges. It has to unite a vast multi-ethnic country by managing increased diversity and providing every student with an education that will open their opportunities and pathways to the national mainstream of knowledge and skills, employment and wealth. It has to both raise the quality of education and reduce the uneven balance in access and equity across regions and groups. This will be complicated by the changing demographic profile. Since the beginning of the economic reforms in 1979, there has been a gradual decline in the number of children by about a third. Those 14 years of age or under declined from 360 million in 1975 to less than 250 million in 2010. As the population ages and fewer young people enter the workforce to support an increasingly older national demographic, the education system has to go into overdrive. The number of students with an education has to increase but this will be unhelpful if young people are unable to adapt to an increasingly high-tech world in which the low-level jobs that have supported China's rise are gradually eliminated. The rapid expansion of higher education can make Chinese society more prosperous and stable but only if it aligns with changes in society and the economy.

Bibliography

Chang, Chung-Li (1963) 'Merit vs. Money', in Johanna M. Menzel (ed.), *The Chinese Civil Service*, Lexington, MA: D.C. Heath and Company, pp. 22–27.

Chen, Yangbin (2008) *Muslim Uyghur Students in a Chinese Boarding School*, New York: Lexington Press.

Cheng, K.M. (2000) 'Understanding basic education policies in China: what ethnographic research can tell', in Heidi Ross and Judith Liu (eds), *Education in China: The Ethnographic Eye*, New York: Garland Press, pp. 29–50.

Ding, Y.Q. (2012) 'The problem with access to compulsory education in China and the effects of the policy of direct subsidy to students', *Chinese Education and Society* 45 (1): 13–21.

Elman, Benjamin A. and Alexander Woodside (1994) *Education and Society in Late Imperial China, 1600–1900*, Berkeley: University of California Press.

Gao, Fang (2008) 'What it means to be a "model minority"?', *Asian Ethnicity* 9(1): 55–67.

Gu, M.Y. (2001) *Education in China and Abroad: Perspectives from a Lifetime in Comparative Education*, Hong Kong: Comparative Education Research Centre.

Hannum, E.C., J.H. Liu and E. Frongillo, (2012) 'Poverty, food insecurity and nutritional deprivation in rural China', available online at http://repository.upenn.edu/cgi/viewcontent.cgi?article=1039&context=gansu_papers [accessed 11 February 2015].

Hayhoe, R. (1995) *China's Universities, 1895–1995*, London: Routledge.

Hu Wei, Xie Ximei and Chai Chunqing (2009) 'The development of private schools in China', in Yang Dongping, Chai Chunqing and Zhu Yinian (eds), *The China Education Development Yearbook*, Leiden: Brill Press, pp. 289–294.

Jia, Chen (2010) 'Country's wealth divide past warning level', *China Daily*, available online at www.chinadaily.com.cn/china/2010-05/12/content_9837073.htm [accessed 25 February 2011].

Kong, P. (2010) 'To walk out: Rural parents' views on education', *China: An International Journal* 8(2): 360–373.

Law, Wing-Wah (2006) 'Citizenship, citizenship education, and the state in China in a global age', *Cambridge Journal of Education* 36(4): 597–628.

Lee, Thomas H.C. (2000) *Education in Traditional China: A History*, Leiden: Brill.

Levin, Richard (2010) 'The rise of Asia's universities', The Royal Society, London, availabel online at http://opac.yale.edu/president/message.aspx?id=91 [accessed 2 February 2011].

Li, Chunling (forthcoming) 'Socio-political change and inequality of educational opportunities', *Chinese Education and Society*.

Lin, Jing (1999) *Social Transformation and Private Education in China*, New York: Praeger.

Lou, Jingjing and Heidi Ross (2008) 'The road to free and compulsory education', *Chinese Education and Society* 41(1): 408.

Ma, Josephine (2005) 'Many rural children cheated of their right to schooling', *South China Morning Post*, 15 January, p. 4.

Muyi (2005) 'The story of Guo Guo', *Renmin Ribao* (People's Daily), 25 November.

National Bureau of Statistics of China (2013) 'What Census Data Can Tell Us About Children in China: Facts and Figures 2013', available online at www.unicef.cn/en/uploadfile/2013/1216/20131216111141945.pdf [accessed 8 March 2015].

Outline (2010) *Outline of China's National Plan for Medium and Long-term Education Reform and Development (2010–2020)*, available online at www.moe.edu.cn/publicfiles/business/htmlfiles/moe/s3501/index.html [accessed 11 February 2015].

Nyima, Baden (1997) 'The way out for Tibetan education', *Chinese Education and Society* 30(4): 7–20.

Nyima, Baden (2000) *Wenming de kunhuo: Zangzu de jiaoyu zhilu* (The puzzle of civilization: The way out for Tibetan education), Chengdu: Sichuan Education Press.

Pepper, Suzanne (1996) *Radicalism and Educational Reform in Twentieth-Century China: The Search for an Ideal Development Model*, Cambridge: Cambridge University Press.

Postiglione, Gerard A. (ed.) (1999). *China's National Minority Education: Culture, Schooling and Development*, London: Routledge.

Postiglione, Gerard A. (2005) 'Higher education in China', *Harvard China Review*, (Spring): 138–143.

Postiglione, Gerard A. (2006) *Education and Social Change in China*, New York: M.E. Sharpe.

Postiglione, Gerard A. (2009a) 'Education of ethnic groups in China', in James Banks (ed.), *The Routledge International Companion to Multicultural Education*, London: Routledge, pp. 501–511.

Postiglione, Gerard A. (2009b) 'Higher education since 1949', *Encyclopedia of Modern China, Vol. 1,* Detroit, MI: Charles Scribner's Sons, pp. 482–486.
Postiglione, Gerard and Gulbahar Beckett (2011) *China's National Minority Language Education,* London: Routledge.
Private Education Promotion Law (2003), available online at http://baike.baidu.com/view/129889.htm.
Ross, Heidi (2006) 'Challenging the gendered dimensions of schooling', in Gerard Postiglione (ed.), *Education and Social Change in China,* New York: M.E. Sharpe, pp. 25–50.
WangYan (2009) 'Confucian institutes and international promotion of the Chinese language', in Yang Dongping, Chai Chunqing and Zhu Yinian (eds), *The China Education Development Yearbook,* Leiden and Boston, MA: Brill Press, pp. 289–294.
Watkins, David and John Biggs (eds) (1996) *The Chinese Learner: Cultural, Psychological and Contextual Influences,* Melbourne: Australian Council of Educational Research.
Xie, A.L. and G.A. Postiglione (2015) 'Guanxi and school success: An ethnographic inquiry of parental involvement in rural China', *British Journal of Sociology of Education,* available online at www.tandfonline.com/doi/pdf/10.1080/01425692.2014.1001061 [accessed 16 March 2015].
Xinhua (2007) 'China warned of risks of imbalanced sex ratio', *China Daily,* available online at www.chinadaily.com.cn/china/2007-8/24/content_6055339.htm [accessed 25 February 2011].
Yang, D.P. (ed.) (2006) *Jiaoyu lanpishu: 2005 Zhongguo jiaoyu fazhang baogao* (Blue Book on Education: The Development Report on China's Education, 2005), Beijing: Shehui kexue wenxian chubanshe.
Yang, R. (2013) 'Indigenizing the Western concept of the university: Chinese experience', *Asia Pacific Education Review* 14(1): 85–92.
Yu, Haibo (2008) *Schooling and Identity among the Naxi,* New York: Lexington Press.
Zhao, Zhenzhou (2010) *Am I Privileged? Minority Mongol Students and Cultural Recognition in Chinese Universities,* New York: Lexington Press.
ZhuQingshi (2005) 'Jiaoyu gongping jishu zhidu baozhang' (Educational equality news institutional guarantees), *Zhongguo qingnianbao* (China Youth News), available online at www.news.ustc.edu.cn.
Zhu, Zhiyong (2007) *State Schooling and Ethnic Identity: The Politics of a Tibetan Neidi School in China,* New York: Lexington Press.

Films/documentaries

Education, Education, Why Poverty? (2013), www.youtube.com/watch?v=BP61LwODTnY
Yige buneng shao (Not one less) (2011), www.youtube.com/watch?v=9wtN6fgjNCc.
Children of Blessing (2007), directed by Teng Xing, Minzu University, Beijing, 14 May, www.youtube.com/watch?v=m9ZgpSt84cw.

3 Contexts and reforms in East Asian education—making the move from periphery to core

There may be a good deal of truth to the well-known stereotype about East Asian education (Tu, 1996). School children in Singapore and Hong Kong nearly lead the world in mathematics and science achievement (USDOE, 1999, 2007; OECD, 2000, 2004; Ruzzi, 2005; Thao Le and Li Shi, 2006). Those in the northeast Asian powerhouse economies of Japan and South Korea are also near the top of the international rankings, and mainland China is rising quickly. Asian students overwhelmingly populate prestigious graduate schools of science and engineering at leading American universities (Johnson, 1993; Nash, 1994; Li, 2006). In short, the school systems of China (including the Mainland, Hong Kong, and Taiwan), Japan, South Korea, and Singapore have already demonstrated the potential to challenge national school systems in other parts of the world. Malaysia and Thailand may not be far behind and fresh attention is being focused on schooling in the vast island nations of Indonesia and Philippines, as well as the transitional economies of Vietnam, Laos, and Cambodia. Though not all countries fit the East Asian stereotype, nonetheless, many are central players in a region that also includes such diverse countries as Brunei, Mongolia, Myanmar, North Korea, and the newest member of the United Nations Timor Leste. As East Asia continues to consolidate itself within the major regional divisions of the global economy, the education systems of these countries will increase their regional cooperation and interactions (Fung et al., 2000).

Despite the stereotype, education and social development across East Asia has been highly uneven, with each country's sociocultural context contributing differentially to its academic results. Moreover, the massification of schooling has placed added pressure on schools to not only address social development needs but also to promote the capacity for innovative thinking within the volatile global environment of competitive market economies (Suarez-Orozco and Qin-Hilliard, 2004). While the educational achievements of some nations are highly notable and may be attributed to traditional values, the lack of academic success in other countries has as much to do with the sociocultural context as with traditional values (Cummings, 2003). In each case, it is necessary to consider the way a country weathered colonialism before it strengthened statehood amid new international alliances. Even with the diverse religious and ideological orientations, and rapid sociopolitical transitions, East Asian societies, with few exceptions, are noted for executive-led government, consensus-driven management styles, and gradual but steady struggles to democratize within slowly incubating civil societies (Renders, 2004; Watson, 2004). Perspectives on cultural values and the historical experiences with colonialism still constitute the context and core of much debate about school reform, especially as countries grapple with overlapping educational philosophies, rapid curriculum change, newly promoted learning methods, bilingual teaching demands, intensified assessment procedures, and school-based management practices (Cookson et al., 1992; Cummings, 2003). Meanwhile, macroscopic themes such as globalization, decentralization, and privatization continue to weave their way into a landscape of discourse on school reform, with results across the region that defy simple generalizations (Mok, 2004; Bjork, 2006).

How East Asian countries reconcile their historical transitions with the contemporary challenges of educational reform within rapidly changing global conditions remains a formidable area for exploration (Thomas and Postlethwaite, 1983; Tan and Mingat, 1992; Morris and Sweeting, 1995; Cummings and Altbach, 1997; Fung et al., 2000; Mok, 2006). Moreover, school policies and practices are seldom, if ever, autonomous from their sociocultural contexts. In the case of higher education, the sociocultural context is also driven by a world system in which some Asian nations, with their national flagship universities, aspire to move from periphery to core (Postiglione and Mak, 1997; Postiglione, 2006b).

It is apt to begin this introduction with East Asia's rising giant (Guthrie, 2006). Contemporary China carries the heavy burden of being the oldest continuing civilization on the planet bent on re-attaining the global status it once held (Hayhoe, 1992). China has the largest school population in the world, with educational practices that are firmly grounded in long held Confucian values. Although China's consciousness of itself as a multiethnic state has become more prominent, its most valued cultural capital is that anchored in the heritage of the majority Han Chinese (Mackerras, 1994, 1995). Its economic rise has meant more funding for education. However, the proportion of GDP for education has remained far below that in other developing countries. Meanwhile, the growing attention that accompanies its economic rise is matched by a growing global interest in its cultural traditions, including the ideal of the Chinese learner (Watkins and Biggs, 1996, 2001). China's educational values and traditional practices span the millennia and have left a deep impression on other regional systems. These not only include the Chinese societies of Hong Kong, Macao, and Taiwan but also Japan, Korea, and Vietnam. The international significance of China's educational values and practices cannot be underestimated, as testified to by the new soft power that has come with the establishment of over 100 Confucian institutes around the world (Yang, 2007).

In a world in which schooling is considered to be an equalizer, Chinese cling to the belief that diligent study can overcome social obstacles such as family background, religion, gender, and ethnicity. This idea can be traced back as far as Confucius, who argued that "In education, there should be no distinction of classes" (有教无类) (Legge, 1970). This formed the basis for the imperial examination system with its roots in the Song Dynasty over a thousand years ago. In a study of the Qing Dynasty, the noted historian Chang Cheng-Li (1963) pointed out that: "The examination system did indeed make possible a certain 'equality of opportunity,' but the advantages were heavily in favor of those who had wealth and influence." This view has as much relevance today as it had during the Qing era. Schooling in the socialist market economy of China has become increasingly dependent on household wealth and family income. One of the greatest challenges since the dismantling of the imperial examination system in 1905 has been to establish an education system able to reconcile the essence of Chinese culture with the ways of the outside world. Semi-colonialism left its mark on China and contributed to an ideological battle that lasted beyond the Chinese civil war. Chairman Mao Zedong saw schools as a bulwark against colonialism, capitalism, and dependency, as well as a means to ensure social equality among the masses. Despite the tumultuous years of the Cultural Revolution, China's education system came to be seen by the World Bank as a model for the developing world (Pepper, 1996). The reform and opening of China to the outside world that began in the late 1970s radically changed the direction of schooling (Postiglione and Lee, 1995). Economic reforms that made way for market forces created a larger role for schools in social stratification systems. Fee paying education became the norm and once more, private schools for the middle class families became a reality. Ballooning social inequalities place more pressure on schools to provide quality schooling for all, including the children within China's 100 million ethnic minority population (Postiglione, 1999, 2006a). Schools are viewed as playing a key role in restoring China to its historical position as a leading nation, but Chinese have retained the idea that education provides fair and equal opportunity based on merit with diligence and hard work being the key determinants of success.

Small but mighty, Hong Kong has always been a part of China except for 155 years of colonial rule (Postiglione and Tang, 1997). In 1997, it became a Special Administrative Region of China with a great deal of autonomy in most spheres, including education. Hong Kong has not escaped historical traditions superimposed upon a colonial social-cultural landscape. Hong Kong moved from privately resourced schools to a public school system with management by a diverse collection of organizations, especially during the 1970s when nine-year compulsory education was made compulsory (Sweeting, 1990, 2004). Meanwhile, its postsecondary system, including a growing number of universities with high levels of institutional autonomy, correspondingly expanded and diversified. The continuities, as identified by Law (2007), are "educational developments in response to changing economic and/or sociopolitical needs; a struggle among concerns about access, efficiency, equity, quality, and catering for diverse learning needs; struggles among nongovernment actors in sponsoring and managing public schools; and the controversy of using English or Chinese as the medium of instruction." As an immigrant society under colonial rule, Hong Kong was conservative of many Chinese traditions, but added an overlay of Westernized, largely British school system features (Postiglione, 1991; Zheng et al., 2001). Law remarks on the fragility of mutual trust among education stakeholders in Hong Kong, something that might have roots in the colonial era. While Hong Kong maintains the distinction of being ranked at the top of the world in mathematics achievement, it struggles with how to maintain that status while moving toward promotion of innovative learning styles of the kind it believes can ensure its 21st century survival without natural resources and heavy manufacturing. Its close neighbor Macao, even tinier and wed to a casino-driven tourist economy, has similar baggage from its three hundred-plus-year colonial period under the Portuguese that was severed in 1999. Hong Kong and Macao are the last regions of East Asia in the 20th century to have shed the colonial title. Each was dynastic sovereign territory until foreign settlements became established. In both cases, Chinese schools continued to exist amid colonial governance. Ironically, the retrocession of territorial sovereignty led to a more determined effort to emphasize Western style school reforms, largely due to determined efforts to cultivate problem solvers and innovative thinkers to support a rising economy within the global community. To this day, Hong Kong remains in denial about its educational inequalities, even while its Gird coefficient is one of the highest in the world. Although technically not in Northeast Asia, Hong Kong is included here because it is part of China. Yet, it is a significant integrative economy of Southeast Asia, where it shares a colonial heritage with Singapore and Malaysia, something that has influenced the structure of its school system to this day, including the medium of instruction.

Taiwan continues to be affected by the unsettled cross-straits relationship with the Chinese mainland, but has a common historical tradition influenced by Confucian values. As Chou and Ho (Chapter 15) note, these include political authoritarianism, the family, examinations, saving habits, local organization, and social networks. Within this configuration of enduring values is the belief that education involves, above all else, hard work and effort. Chinese students were expected to be diligent, persistent, and cultivated. The tumultuous development path taken by Taiwan as it moved from an authoritarian to democratic sociopolitical system of governance did ripple into the arena of school reform and can be seen in debates over many issues ranging from the medium of instruction, the interpretation of Taiwan history and identity, and the degree of managerial autonomy for schools. The policy agenda in more recent times has been deeply affected by the twin ideologies of globalization and localization. Like other East Asian societies with a Confucian heritage, Taiwan has tried to reconcile its traditional stress on examinations with new thinking about what constitutes meaningful learning. Yet, family resources continue to reinforce the school's role as a selection agency with cram school fees becoming a fixed expenditure of Taiwan families. Chou points out that gender equity in access to higher education has steadily increased, but the proportion of indigenous peoples gaining access to higher education is barely half of that within the mainstream population.

Japan continues to be the most successful economy and education system in East Asia. As early as 1905, China used Japan's school system as a model for its early development as a republic. Akira Arimoto reminds us that even before the Meiji restoration, a period associated with the establishment of a modern Japanese education system, the common people of the Tokugawa Era gave education a great deal of attention. Its temples for children's education were effective and literacy rates exceeded those in Western countries. The Meiji restoration's system of compulsory education actually confronted resistance and low enrollment rates in many rural areas. In this sense, Arimoto (Chapter 7) echoes other scholars of Japanese education that "the Tokugawa era became the foundation for modern Japanese education beyond the Meiji Restoration." Eventually, Meiji schooling became viewed as a modern selection system for upward social mobility and tilted Japan's schooling from ascription-based to achievement-based selection. Japan has become, as Arimoto calls it, a degree-o-cratic society with its accompanying educational pathology. Japan is one of the few East Asian countries not colonized, but its education system experienced a major transition from its pre to postwar periods. The postwar educational system was restructured by an education basic law with detailed provisions, for equal opportunity, including for male and female students; compulsory schooling for all; cooperation among school, family, and the community; education for nation-building; religious education; and responsibilities for national and local governments. Japan has demonstrated an uncanny talent for borrowing and adapting knowledge. Centuries of interactions with neighbors, including China and Korea, show a fundamental pattern of placing a high value on mastering and imitation, foreign knowledge and techniques. The parts of this process include imitation, examination, criticism, and innovation. The optimism in Japan is wed to the challenges of mastering this process of which education is a part. Looking ahead, there is a renewed emphasis in schools for building patriotism.

Like Japan, Korea has long ago been highly influenced by its neighboring lands (Fairbank et al., 1989). The cultural influence of China's Tang Dynasty remains evident in language and culture. In a different sense, the colonial period of Japanese occupation is also not easily forgotten or forgiven. Globalization has brought South Korea closer to its traditional neighbors while the North Korean regime remains a question mark, despite some signs of a reform orientation after many years of isolation. After 35 years of Japanese colonial rule, Korea had to dig itself out of the devastation of the Korean War at mid-century that split it in two and resulted in two divergent paths of development that continue to the present. The South Korean peninsula placed its national focus on universal education to overcome mass illiteracy, lasting into the 1970s, after which it moved rapidly into expansion of secondary education to meet the human resource needs of its rapidly developing economy. Amid periodic political turmoil, the public demand for greater education opportunities, including in higher education, led to an expansion that made South Korea virtually the first universal system of higher education in East Asia. Choi (Chapter 14) notes Koreans' positive outlook and unwavering faith in academic credentials. Since the turn of the century, South Korea has been riveted on the educational challenges of the global economy. Korean education is most impressive at the primary and secondary level and least at the tertiary level. South Korea has achieved an extraordinary transformation to become one of the most highly schooled countries in the world. Its elementary and secondary students score high in mathematics and science on international tests and the gender gap has narrowed. Teachers are generally well trained and indicators like dropout rates and school violence are relatively low. University education is subject to extreme competition and low quality. Efforts, including intensive internationalization, are under way in an effort to build world-class universities. An obsession with education created rapid expansion and contributed to both national development and social problems. The linking of educational credentials to the traditional values of Confucian scholars limited the attraction of vocational–technical education. Intense pressure for educational attainment created a competitive entrance examination system. The result was enormous pressure on students and a financial burden on families, as well as a stifled reform effort to promote innovative education. Those unhappy with the system found alternatives in the expanding study-abroad trend. This further intensified social stratification with English-speaking Koreans in an advantaged position.

Meanwhile North Korea continues to inch forward at a snail's pace in educational reform. However, the passion for education in the North is no less intense. With an ideology of self-reliance and self-identity, communism remains a determinate force. Three quarters of the way through the 20th century, the North had achieved universal basic education. Nevertheless, social background played a large part in determining opportunity. Party members and urban residents retain a distinct advantage over others. As Reed and Kim (Chapter 11) make clear, the striking feature of education in the Democratic People's Republic of Korea (DPRK) is its isolation within a political system virtually bereft of international interface. Most of the economy remains state run, as are schools. However, Reed believes the DPRK is gradually emerging from its isolation with possibly profound implications for education. While globalization is opposed, computer literacy and information technology are heavily promoted, along with foreign language instruction. Without the Soviet Union as the main trusted partner, past practices learned from them are disappearing. Educational differentiation is more apparent. Advanced middle school is a kind of key or magnet school. UNESCO developed a plan with the DPRK ministry that set out goals for all levels of education with a focus on infrastructure and teacher training. As Reed concludes, "Education in North Korea has been remarkably successful in addressing the basic literacy needs of the people. However, the educational system clearly reflects the inflexibility of the political system that it serves."

Mongolia's position in Northeast Asia contrasts sharply with that of North Korea. Though ruled by the communist party for many decades, it is far more reformist than North Korea. The breakup of the Soviet Union affected Mongolia more than North Korea, especially for the school system. Unlike the Koreans who borrowed heavily from China's Tang Dynasty, the Mongols ruled China during the Yuan Dynasty. When Genghis Khan conquered the known world, including Korea, about 800 years ago, he was illiterate. Yet, the record keeping necessitated by his conquests did convince him of the value of education. When Kublai Khan conquered China and established the Yuan Dynasty, he took significant measures to support education, something which also aided Mongol governance of China. Mongol adoption of Tibetan Buddhism lasted through the end of the Yuan dynasty and into its colonization by China's last imperial dynasty. By the start of the 20th century, Mongolia had thousands of monastery schools. When it gained its independence in 1921, virtually all schools were attached to monasteries. As the Soviet influence increased, monasteries eventually became to be viewed as destabilizing and a Soviet-sponsored school system became institutionalized. By the time the Soviet influence waned in 1989, Mongolians were strapped with a Cyrillic alphabet. Efforts to bring back Mongolian script with the help of China, which had retained it in Inner Mongolia, were unsuccessful. While the ex-Soviet republics tried various approaches to decentralization of education, Mongolia turned out to be the most successful. Beginning in the 1990s, a series of international development agencies began a series of education projects in Mongolia and donor support remains strong. The focus has turned to sustaining reform and improving school quality and access. As John C. Weidman, Regsuren Bat-Erdene and Erika Bat-Erdene (Chapter 10) note: "The foundation is strong but much remains to be done."

These northeastern members of the East Asia community of school systems have generally been heavily influenced by China at some point in their history. However, the countries of Southeast Asia differ in this respect. With the exception of Vietnam where Confucianism took hold as early as the 10th century, the rest of the region was only close to China through trade. Unparalleled diversity has made it virtually impossible to offer a concise overview of Southeast Asian education. However, economic globalization may be changing that to some degree. Across the region, long entrenched but differing cultural traditions interweave with colonial heritage, multiethnic and religious states, liberal democratic tendencies and socialist regimes in transition (Brown, 1994; SarDesai, 1994; McCloud, 1995). Nevertheless, there are some pronounced patterns across systems. Beginning with national roots and colonial experiences, the education systems in Singapore and Hong Kong, share an affinity with Chinese intellectual values and, with Malaysia, also share a British colonial heritage. Yet, all have taken on more standardized aspects of global education systems as they aspire to be internationally competitive. While education in Vietnam shares a Chinese heritage with Hong Kong and Singapore, it also has its own indigenous tradition with an overlay of colonial French and Soviet-Russian themes. Indonesia completely shed Dutch colonial influence, where Islam has remained a salient factor in development. Thailand was never colonized, though the debates about future direction wrestle with the issue of globalization and how to emphasize local wisdom in education. The Christian influence on Philippine education remains a salient historical theme as is its American colonial heritage. Meanwhile, Southeast Asian education can hardly escape the increasing effect of its neighboring giants, China and India.

In Vietnam, postcolonial educational expansion has been repeated (Pham, 1988). A state socialist welfare regime developed from the 1940s and 1950s in northern Vietnam, and later on a national basis after the reunification of the entire country in 1975 (Dang, 1997). London (Chapter 18) points out how Vietnam's Communist Party promoted mass education as a basic right of citizenship, and centralized educational governance. Despite these measures, inequalities continued to exist in terms of provision at the regional level, in terms of scope and quality, and access across different population segments. In reality, the provision of social services privileged the political elite and urban-based state-sector workers over all others. While the gradual collapse of the planned economy and the transition to a market economy that began in the 1980s has meant greater investments in mass education and improvements in education access, new inequalities in enrollment and financing have emerged as a result of the unequal distribution of the fruits of economic expansion. Clear differences have emerged between the principles and institutions of the state socialist and Marxist Leninist regimes in terms of education finance. A greater proportion of the burden of education finance has been shifted from the state onto households. This increased household responsibility has in turn fuelled the development and reproduction of inequalities of access to upper secondary education.

The Philippines is atypical of Southeast Asian nations in having a Spanish and American colonial past, in addition to being the only Asian nation with a Roman Catholic majority. Spanish colonization over the course of 333 years left a lasting legacy of religious education and the foundations of higher education. Various religious orders such as the Augustinians, the Franciscans, the Jesuits, and the Dominicans established parish schools to teach Christian doctrine. The Spanish period also saw the establishment of a few colleges such as the Colegio de Santo Tomas, later to become the University of Santo Tomas. The beginnings of a national public school system were inaugurated by the passing of a royal decree in 1863. By the end of the 19th century, the Philippines had a higher literacy level than some European nations. The Americans, who ruled for almost 50 years, further entrenched a national public school system with the passing of the Education Act of 1901. The first quarter of the 20th century completed the template that contemporary Philippine education continues to follow. Another key legacy was the use of the English language as a medium of instruction in a multilingual country that lacked a lingua franca at the time. Despite several attempts over the 1990s to institute reforms such as decentralization of education governance, and improving efficiency and equity of education services, implementation has been patchy. Torralba, Dumol and Manzon (Chapter 12) attribute the patchiness to a lack of political will, political instability, excessive political interference by various parties, and economic constraints.

Singapore presents an interesting case of a city-state with a government that firmly believes in keeping a tight rein on the national education system. The first two postindependence decades were spent centralizing authority over a hitherto disparate set of parallel systems operating in different language media under British colonial rule. Various measures taken included standardizing such aspects as subject curricula, national examinations, teacher qualifications, and eventually making the English language the primary medium of instruction in all schools. The focus began shifting in the mid-1980s toward encouraging more diversity in educational pathways and curricula. These measures included the introduction of independent schools and autonomous schools. Nevertheless, as Tan (Chapter 13) notes, the strong hand of the state remained in order to steer the education system in the direction of supporting national economic development plans and fostering social cohesion (Tan, 2004). From the mid-1990s a series of large-scale educational reforms such as Thinking Schools, Learning Nation and National Education were launched to meet the perceived needs of the knowledge economy while at the same time fostering social cohesion in a culturally diverse society. There is currently official recognition and support for fundamental changes in teaching and learning. However, the success of undertaking such changes in schools that have been largely driven by traditional notions of examination success remains patchy.

Like Singapore, Malaysia was colonized by Great Britain before gaining political independence. The two countries share a common dilemma of how to integrate an ethnically, linguistically, religiously and culturally diverse populace. Their approaches to this dilemma have diverged considerably over the past four decades. Following ethnic clashes in 1969, the Malaysian government introduced affirmative action policies in employment and education to redress the socioeconomic disparities between the native bumiputera majority and the non-bumiputera ethnic minorities. For instance, bumiputeras received, and continue to receive, preferential treatment in scholarship awards and entry to higher education. In addition, the Malay language was institutionalized as the predominant medium of instruction in national schools. In his chapter, Loo (Chapter 9) points out that although Malaysia has made advances in providing universal access to education, the policy of affirmative action remains highly emotive and controversial. There are allegations that the policy has proved ethnically divisive, and has downplayed individual merit in favor of ethnic affiliation. Furthermore, the national school system has failed as an instrument of national integration. The majority of ethnic Chinese, who constitute about a quarter of the total population, enroll their children in Chinese-medium primary schools, while the vast majority of bumiputera children are enrolled in the national schools. In recent years, the English language has been reinstated as the medium of instruction for mathematics and science in order to boost national economic competitiveness.

Another Southeast Asian country with a British colonial past is Brunei, a tiny oil-rich Malay-Islamic monarchy. Prior to the attainment of full political sovereignty in 1984, there were essentially three parallel education systems: a secular government system, an Islamic system, and a system of Arabic schools. These schools continue to exist currently, in addition to independent schools. Like Singapore, Brunei's government continues to retain British colonial influence in the form of the General Certificate of Education Ordinary and Advanced Level examinations. Tight government control comes in the form of the Melayu Islam Beraja (Malay Islamic Monarchy) national ideology, which is perpetuated through the schools. Upex (Chapter 2) points out several major problems facing Brunei's economy, such as an overdependence on petroleum industry, a bloated public sector, and a mismatch between educational qualifications and labor market needs. The generous welfare system (locally nicknamed Shellfare) is beginning to show cracks due to rapid population increases and internal spending problems. The chapter points out a key dilemma facing Brunei education: reconciling the need to modernize and prepare a skilled knowledgeable workforce with the current emphasis on feudalism and institutionalized religion. Other urgent areas of need include changing the top-down management approach, improving teacher professionalism and morale, and changing the examination-oriented mode of teaching and learning.

Indonesia, like Brunei, has a majority Muslim population. In fact, it has the world's largest Muslim population, even while remaining an officially secular state. Dutch colonialism maintained a centralized and elitist schooling system, with limited opportunities for the poor, rural, or non-European populations. Independence in 1945 brought about a determination to maintain centralized governance in order to hold together a large culturally diverse population spread over 6,000 islands. The government under President Sukarno faced the onerous task of overcoming a massive illiteracy problem while lacking any lingua franca for effective communication. Also lacking were financial resources, physical infrastructure, and trained teachers. Christano and Cummings (Chapter 6) explain that the primary task facing schools was to foster a uniquely Indonesian identity through the use of a common lingua franca, Bahasa Indonesia, and the propagation of the national ideology *Pancasila*. Sukarno's successor, Suharto, continued the policy of having education serve a key nation-building function. The first major step toward loosening tight centralized control of schools nationwide came with the promulgation of regulations in 1994 authorizing local governments to incorporate local content in the official curriculum. The fall of President Suharto in 1998 and his replacement by Habibie initiated one of the most sweeping reforms in Indonesia's history, namely, transforming the country into a decentralized state. This policy thrust was extended to education as well, with the central government's role being restricted to establishing national education policies and defining guidelines for minimum education standards. Individual districts began shifting toward a school-based management system that allowed local schools greater management autonomy.

Timor Leste, the newest nation in Southeast Asia, has had a turbulent political history for the past few decades. This includes 24 years of Indonesian occupation after the withdrawal of the Portuguese colonial government in 1974, and the subsequent violence leading to the eventual withdrawal of Indonesian forces. Under the Portuguese, education provision was conducted in Portuguese mainly in Catholic schools. In addition, the education of women was minimal. Berlie (Chapter 17) asserts that education has been a traditionally neglected sector, and hence the new post-Indonesian government faces an uphill task in reconstructing the schooling system and building teacher capacity. Besides widespread illiteracy, policymakers face the arduous task of choosing a politically acceptable medium of instruction from among Portuguese, English, Bahasa Indonesia, and various indigenous languages. Many Timorese teachers at the primary level have only a senior secondary education, and the situation is worse in rural and remote areas. Despite the best efforts of the government, with the assistance of various international organizations such as the World Bank, UNICEF, and UNESCO, the massive infrastructural and financial issues facing education in Timor Leste persist.

Like Timor Leste, Cambodia shares a recent turbulent political past and is a country engaged in the task of national reconciliation and reconstruction. French colonization began in 1863 and was marked by the introduction of a modern secular education system that served to produce male French-speaking civil servants for the colonial administration. In the 20th century, the colonial government modernized the traditional wat schools and expanded educational access outside the urban areas. A Franco-Cambodian education system operated on a 3+3+4 model with French as the medium of instruction. However, no university existed during this period. Furthermore, because monks teaching in traditional wat schools were not supposed to have contact with female students, girls' participation in modern education was limited. After the end of French colonialism in 1953, the incoming government began expanding enrollments, but all these gains were almost completely lost after 1970 during the period of the Khmer Republic under Lon Nol, the devastating Khmer Rouge rule from 1975 to 1979, and the Vietnamese occupation in the 1980s. In particular, the Khmer Rouge regarded education of the prewar period as being totally irrelevant to individual or national needs, and viewed educated people such as students, teachers, and professors as dangerous and untrustworthy. Many school buildings were destroyed and many educated Cambodians were killed. Since the 1980s, the task of reconstruction has been proceeding, in large part due to the largesse of development assistance agencies. Educational enrollments have increased at primary, secondary, and higher education levels. In this respect, Sopheak and Clayton (Chapter 3) give particular attention to the education of girls and use this as a prism with which to see the historical transformation of schooling in Cambodia.

Laos shares a French colonial heritage with Cambodia and Vietnam. The French colonial authorities preserved the traditional wat schools, which they viewed as a means of preserving traditional religion and culture. Lessons in secular schools were conducted mainly in French. Similar to these two other former French colonies, the various postindependence governments began expanding educational access. The Royal Lao government announced in 1951 that primary education would be compulsory and would be conducted in the Lao language, while secondary education would continue in French. However, secondary enrollments continued to be rather limited. Schooling under the Pathet Lao from the mid-1950s was focused on Marxist-Leninist revolutionary propaganda, and on socializing the non-Lao ethnic minorities into good socialists. The advent of the Lao People's Democratic Republic in 1975 meant that education was to play a major socializing role for national integration and nationalism in a socialist country. Educational access improved tremendously, especially in rural areas. However, educational quality remained rather low, mainly because of a lack of textbooks and skilled teachers. The introduction of the New Economic Mechanism in 1985 meant the reorientation of the education system toward meeting the needs of the free labor market, even while attempting to produce loyal revolutionary socialist citizens. Manynooch Faming (Chapter 8) shows that particular attention was paid to the schooling of non-Lao ethnic minorities in order to integrate and "civilize" them.

Thailand presents an interesting case of a country that has never been formally colonized. In traditional Thai society, centers of learning were houses, temples and the palace rather than schools. Houses prepared children with practical work-oriented skills, temples focused on moral education and ethics, while the palace provided education in governmental ethics. Nevertheless, European ideals of schooling began permeating Thai society in the last quarter of the 19th century, with the formal establishment of the first royal school in 1871 and the first public school in 1884. Over the course of 60 years, schools were established all over the country and a supervisory system put in place to oversee the expansion of schooling. The introduction of democratic institutions in 1932 led to greater attention being paid to equal educational opportunities and expansion of enrollments. Compulsory education was expanded to seven years after World War II, and women's educational opportunities improved. However, as Paitoon Sinlarat (Chapter 16) explains, schooling was largely conducted along the lines of a "one-size-fits-all" model and became increasingly irrelevant to individual and economic needs. The 1999 National Education Act attempted to encourage greater decentralization of management and to promote the idea that learning could take place not only in schools, but also in alternative venues such as homes, community bodies, and other social institutions.

Explanatory frameworks and the continued relevance of core–periphery

How much is hegemony and how much is self-determination in East Asian education? Is center–periphery still relevant to the analysis of its education systems? (Amos et al., 2002). This is especially apparent in higher education with the quest for world-class universities by China, Korea, and Japan. East Asian higher education systems are closely tied to global markets and follow what sometimes appears to be dependent pattern of adaptions driven by Western developed economics (Altbach, 1981, 1997, 2004; Altbach and Selvaratnam, 1989; Altbach and Umakoshi, 2004). Yet, there is also a significant amount of resistance. As East Asian countries adapt to ways that help embed economic globalization within their national landscape, the manner in which the adaptation occurs is more selective, open, and democratic than before. Moreover, while global communication with core (center) university systems has been more open and transparent, the system is closed to direct intervention from the outside, making hegemony a less plausible explanation for the manner in which the system is reacting within the new global environment of financial interdependency (Chapman and Austin, 2002).

One does not have to travel far in the region to hear calls to build world-class universities coming from vice-chancellors, ministries of education, and national leaders. Japan, South Korea, and China are particularly prominent in this respect (Min, 2003; Rosen, 2004; Park, 2005). These three countries' national flagship universities are reaching for the gold standard, and the Southeast Asian university systems cannot escape the implications for their own development. As a block, East Asia may be pivotal to the global shift in the center–periphery equation. The region has some of the fastest growing economies in the world with certain linguistic attributes that set it apart.

While the discourse of center and periphery is still relevant to the analysis of university systems, the analytical frameworks from which it has arisen may or may not be. Theories of globalization have done little so far except to provide a thematic framework for the rapid and interdependent changes that increasingly characterize social life. Efforts to analyze the theoretical underpinnings of globalization inevitably return to the well of world-systems theory, neo-Marxism, and institutionalism, where there is also evidence of eclectically combined theoretical elements that derive from one or more of these. Although not theories of globalization, they address transnational structuring. Taken together, world-systems theory and neo-institutionalism help point us in the direction of an answer to the central question about East Asian education: How much is hegemony and how much is self-determination?

With China's rise from the status of a poor developing country to an economy which causes global reverberations, dependency theory seems less relevant than it did in the past. New circumstances and geopolitical realities give the impression that these perspectives are obsolete. While colonialism and dependency have shaped the past, the present appears to be less affected by them, though these ideologies still lurk in the background as shadows of the past and cautions for the future. China, Japan, and South Korea on their own, and the Southeast Asian countries united under the Association of Southeast Asian Nations (ASEAN), have become more emergent in the global knowledge production system and international economic power structure. While the global center has moved toward the United States since the collapse of the bipolar world, a discourse on empire has gained attention, with growing global criticism of foreign interventions and apprehension about what agencies such as the World Bank and International Monetary Fund have done with global inequality.

What kinds of framework can be used to provide explanations of global processes in education, especially higher education, and to make them more congruent with what is actually happening, not only in Northeast Asia but also Southeast Asia, a geographical cluster of countries with smaller populations, diverse cultures, and more island-based and peninsular economies, and which have developed more slowly than their Northeast Asian neighbors? China's own experience in the periphery has made it a flag bearer at times for developing countries, even though its own position in the center–periphery system has clearly changed. Meanwhile, Japan has worked to take on the role of a regional development agency and, by doing so, hopes to distance itself from its widely remembered historical aspirations from the first half of the previous century. South Korea has attained mass higher education faster than any country in the world. With the predominance of center–periphery approaches and their hegemony in discourse and policy, it is imperative to refocus on their explanatory value, especially in light of the changes in global development. Market liberalization has been epitomized in Asia as a contemporary form of civilization that it must catch up with in order to survive. Its switch from opponent to reluctant or willing supporter has had much to do with the end of the Cold War, continued pressure on regimes to deliver on domestic development promises, and the success in the 1980s of the four Asian Tigers (Singapore, Taiwan, Hong Kong, and South Korea). The enforcement of catch-up strategies in higher education enhances our understanding of the new international system, with burgeoning student populations, knowledge-economy discourse, reforms in governance, border-crossing academic programs, overseas study patterns, and new trade in educational services. Proper analysis of the international relations of higher education economies and human capital systems requires grounding in external realities that determine overarching domestic processes of state power and economic reproduction. In general, then, it appears that center–periphery explanations may lose some explanatory value, as part of the process of global transition.

Without a focus on social stratification and educational inequality within East Asian countries, new explanatory frameworks would be severely constrained (Kerchkoff, 2001; Meyer, 2001). New forms of growing inequalities on both domestic and international levels that are being reproduced through compulsory education and the massification of higher education remain the major challenge for any new framework of analysis. However, new economic power in Asia and its deepening global economic integration raise new questions.

There is an increasing need to come to terms with the resilience of poverty and how it finds its way into education in the form of a plurality of reasons for student dropout patterns: economic, informational, social, and cultural handicaps that hamper adjustment to modern learning environments. The major indicator of this phenomenon in East Asia is the new privatization that reaches beyond traditional domestic formats and places profit alongside education. However, the grossly abused privatization discourse does not necessarily entail a move beyond the center–periphery platforms associated with promises of national progress. This is actually part of an international process that pulls East Asian education back into a position that keeps center–periphery platforms relevant. In short, private education has the potential to be part of an exploitative relationship in which core nations are collaborators. Even while the discourse in Asia calls for rejection of selected Western value positions, it has been slower at developing newer analytical categories for schooling-state development experience.

Alternative strategies of development infer rival analytical categories which one can use to frame how the new wealth/elite classes in East Asian capitalist countries maintain state regimes. Thus, any new understanding of relations between states and markets in East Asian education can be realized only through the study of alternative strategies of market capitalist development (ASIHL, 1998, Dumlao-Valisno, 2001; Varghese, 2001). Studies of existing paradigms of dependency, neo-colonialism, and postmodernism are bound to be limiting in certain respects, especially when they focus on the structure of schooling as an incontrovertible and fundamental expression of the essence of national development.

There is a methodological imperative to approach the study of schooling as part of an historical process whose dynamics are internal to it. In the coming decades, East Asia will continue along the path of massification in basic, senior secondary, and tertiary education and its top universities will become more influential both within the national scene and as a symbol of their nations' unique intellectual contribution to the global knowledge economy. In this sense, they are already pushing the limits of the center–periphery equation. But they are not there yet. Much could happen in the coming years to determine whether or not East Asian education will break loose of the limits of core–periphery frameworks.

References

Altbach, P.G. (1981). "The university as center and periphery," *Teachers College Record*, 82(4): 601–621.
—— (1997). *Comparative Higher Education: Knowledge, the University, and Development*. Boston: Center for International Higher Education.
—— (2004). *Asian Universities: Historical Perspectives and Contemporary Challenges*. Baltimore, MD: Johns Hopkins University Press.
Altbach, P.G. and Selvaratnam, V. (1989). *From Dependence to Autonomy: The Development of Asian Universities*. Amsterdam: Kluwer Academic Publishers.
Altbach, P.G. and Umakoshi, Tow (2004). *Asian Universities: Historical perspectives and Contemporary Challenges*. Baltimore, MD: Johns Hopkins University Press.
Amos, K., Keiner, E., Proske, M., and Olaf-Radtke, F. (2002). "Globalisation: Autonomy of education under siege? Shifting boundaries between politics, economy and education," *European Educational Research Journal*, 1(2): 193–213.
ASIHL (Association for Southeast Asian Institutions of Higher Learning) (1998). New Trends in Higher Education: Market Mechanisms in Higher Education Toward the 21st Century. Proceedings, Universitas Indonesia. Jakarta, 22–23, July.
Bjork, Christopher (2006). *Educational Decentralization: Asian Experiences Conceptual Contributions*. Netherlands: Springer Press.
Brown, David (1994). *The State and Ethnic Politics in Southeast Asia*. London: Routledge and Kegan Paul.
Chang Cheng-Li (1963). "Merit and money," in Johanna M. Menzel (ed.), *The Chinese Civil Service: Careers Open to Talent*, pp. 22–27. Boston, MA: D.C. Heath Co.
Chapman, D. and Austin, A. (eds.) (2002). *Higher Education in the Developing World: Changing Contexts and Institutional Responses*. Westport, CT: Greenwood Press.
Cookson, Peter, Sadovnik, Alan, and Semel, Susan (1992). *The International Handbook of Educational Reform*. Westport, CT: Greenwood Press.
Cummings, William K. (2003). *The Institutions of Education: A Comparative Study of Education Development in the Six Core Nations*. Oxford: Symposium Books.

Cummings, William K. and Altbach, Philip G. (1997). *The Challenge of East Asian Education: Implications for America.* Albany, NY: State University of New York.

Dang, Ba Lam (1997). "Vietnam," in G. Postiglione (ed.), *Asian Higher Education,* pp. 359–372. Westport, CT: Greenwood Press.

Dumlao-Valisno, Mona (2001). "A note on the economic crisis and higher education in the Philippines," in *Impact of the Economic Crisis on Higher Education in East Asia,* pp. 147–155. Paris: UNESCO (IIEP).

Fairbank, John K., Reischauer, Edwin O., and Craig, Albert M. (1989). *East Asia: Traditions and Transformations.* Boston, MA: Houghton Mifflin.

Fung, Alex C.W., Pefianco, Erlinda C., and Teather, David B. (2000). "Challenges in the New Millennium," *Journal of Southeast Asian Education,* 1(1). Bangkok: SEAMO.

Guthrie, Doug (2006). *China and Globalization: The Social, Economic and Political Transformation of Chinese Society.* New York: Routledge.

Hayhoe, Ruth (1992). *Education and Modernization: The Chinese Experience.* New York: Pergammon Press.

Henders, Susan J. (ed.) (2004). *Democratization and Identity: Regimes and Ethnicity in East and Southeast Asia.* Lanham, MD: Lexington Press.

Johnson, J.M. (1993). *Human Resources for Science and Technology: The Asian Region (Surveys of Science Resources Series, Special Report, NCF 93–103).* Washington DC: National Science Foundation.

Kerckhoff, Alan (2001). "Educational stratification in comparative perspective," *Sociology of Education,* Extra Issue. Sociology at the Dawn of the 21st Century, 3–18.

Komolmas, Prathip M. (1998). "Thailand: New trends in higher education toward the 21st century," in *New Trends in Higher Education: Market Mechanisms in Higher Education Toward the 21st Century,* pp. 111–125. Jakarta: The Association of National Science Foundation.

Lê, Thao and Shi, Li (2006). Chinese-background Students' Learning Approaches, AARE, Adelaide November, 27, Accessed on April 20, 2007 from http://www.aare.edu.au/06pap/le06370.pdf.

Legge, James (Translated) (1970). *The Four Books; Confucian Analects,* Chapter: XXVIII, p. 357. Taipei: Culture Book Company.

Li, Cheng (ed.) (2005). *Bridging Minds across the Pacific: U.S.-China Educational Exchanges,* 1978–2003. New York: Lexington Books.

Li, Mei (2006) "Beyond push and pull factors: An economic and sociological analysis on mainland Chinese students' outflow to Hong Kong and Macau for higher education." Doctoral dissertation, The University of Hong Kong.

Mackerras, Colin (1994). *China's Minorities: Integration and Modernization in the 20th Century.* Hong Kong: Oxford University Press.

────── (1995). *China's Minority Cultures: Identities and Integration Since 1912.* New York: Longman and St. Martin's Press.

McCloud, Donald G. (1995). *Southeast Asia: Tradition and Modernity in the Contemporary World.* Boulder, CO: Westview.

Meyer, John (2001). "Reflections: The worldwide commitment to educational equality," *Sociology of Education,* Extra Issue. Sociology at the Dawn of the 21st Century, 154–158.

Min, Weifang (2004). "Chinese higher education: The legacy of the past and the context of the future," in Philip G. Altbach (ed.), *Asian Universities: Historical Perspectives and Contemporary Challenges,* pp. 53–83. Baltimore, MD: Johns Hopkins Press.

Mok, Ka Ho (ed.) (2004). *Centralization and Decentralization: Educational Reform and Changing Governance Chinese Societies.* Hong Kong: Comparative Education Research Center and Kluwer Press.

────── (2006). *Education Reform and Education Policy in East Asia*. London: Routledge.
Morris, Paul and Sweeting, Anthony (eds.) (1995). *Education and Development in East Asia*. New York: Garland Press.
Nash, M.J. (1994). "Tigers in the lab: Asian-born, U.S.-trained researchers are headed home to challenge the technological supremacy of the West," *Time* (International Edition), November 21, pp. 48–49.
OECD (2000). Knowledge and Skills for Life: First Results from the Organization for Economic Cooperation and Development (OECD), Programme for International Student Assessment (PISA), 2000. OECD Publications, 2, rue Andre-Pascal, 75775 Paris Cedex 16, France. Accessed on January 12, 2007 from http://www.SourceOECD.org.
OECD (2004). Learning for Tomorrow's World—First Results from PISA (Programme for International Student Assessment), 2003, Accessed on January 12, 2007 from http://www.oecd.org/document/55/0,2340,en_32252351_32236173_33917303_1_1_1_1,00.html.
Park, Kyung-Jae (2005). "Policies and strategies to meet the challenges of Internationalization of Higher Education," Paper read at the Third Regional Follow-up Committee for the 1998 World Conference on Higher Education in Asia and the Pacific, Seoul, Korea, July 5, 2005.
Pepper, Suzanne (1996). *Radicalism and Educational Reform in 20th Century China: The Search for an Ideal Development Model*. New York: Cambridge University Press.
Pham, Minh Hac (1988). *Vietnam's Education: The Current Position and Future Prospects*. Hanoi: Gioi Publishers.
Postiglione, Gerard A. (ed.) (1991). *Education and Society in Hong Kong: Toward Country and Two Systems*. New York: M.E. Sharpe.
────── (1999). *China's National Minority Education: Culture, Schooling and Development*. New York: Falmer Press.
────── (2005). "Higher education in China: Perils and promises for a new century," in *Harvard China Review*, Spring: 138–143.
────── (2006a). *Education and Social Change in China: Inequality in a Market Economy*. New York: M.E. Sharpe.
────── (2006b). "Finance and governance in Southeast Asian higher education," in Joaquin Tnes and Francisco Lopez-Segrera (eds), *Higher Education in the World, 2006: The Financing of Universities*, pp. 187–192. New York: Palgrave.
Postiglione, Gerard A. and Lee, Wing On (1995). *Social Change and Educational Development: Mainland China, Taiwan and Hong Kong*. Hong Kong: Center of Asian Studies.
Postiglione, Gerard A. and Mak, G.C.L. (1997). *Asian Higher Education*. Westport, CT: Greenwood Press.
Postiglione, Gerard A. and Tang, J.T.H. (eds) (1997). *Hong Kong's Reunion with China: The Global Dimensions*. New York: M.E. Sharpe.
Rosen, Stanley (2004). Beida Reforms, a special issue of the journal *Chinese Education and Society*, 37(6), November-December, New York: M.E. Sharpe.
Ruzzi, Betsy Brown (2005). *International Education Tests: An Overview, New Commission on the Skills for the American Work Force*, National Center on Education and Economy (April). Accessed on January 22, 2007 from http://www.skillscommission.org/pdf/Staff%20Papers/International%20Tests.pdf.
SarDesai, D.R. (1994). *Southeast Asia: Past and Present*. 3rd edn. Boulder, CO: Westview Press.
Sinlarat, P. (2004). "Thai universities: Past, present, and future," in P.G. Altbach (ed.), *Asian Universities: Historical Perspectives and Contemporary Challenges*, pp. 201–220. Baltimore, MD: Johns Hopkins University Press.

Suárez-Orozco, Marcelo M. and Qin-Hilliard, Desirée Baolian (eds) (2004). *Globalization: Culture and Education in the New Millennium.* Berkeley, CA: University of California Press.

Sweeting, A.E. (1990). *Education in Hong Kong: Pre 1841 to 1941.* Hong Kong: Hong Kong University Press.

—— (2004). *Education in Hong Kong: 1941–2001.* Hong Kong: Hong Kong University Press.

Tan, J."Singapore: Small nation, big plans," in in P.G. Altbach (ed.), *Asian Universities: Historical Perspectives and Contemporary Challenges*, pp. 175–200. Baltimore, MD: Johns Hopkins University Press.

Tan, Jee-Peng and Mingat, Alain (1992). *Education in Asia: A Comparative Study of Cost and Financing.* Washington, DC: The World Bank.

Tu, Wei-Ming (ed.) (1996). *Confucian Traditions in East Asian Modernity: Moral Education and Economic Culture in Japan and the Four Mini-Dragons.* Cambridge, 114A: Harvard University Press.

UNESCO (2004). UNESCO Institute for Statistics. Accessed on January 12, 2007 from http://www.uis.unesco.org/profiles/EN/EDU/countryProfile_en.aspx?code=40313.

USDOE (1999). "Highlights from TIMMS, overview and key findings across grade levels," *The Third International Mathematics and Science Study*, National Center Department of Education, NCES 1999–081. Accessed on February 4, 2007 from http://nces.ed.gov/pubs99/1999081.pdf.

—— (2007). *International Comparisons in Education: Trends in International Mathematics and Science Study.* Washington, DC: National Center for Education Science, National Center for Educational Statistics, U.S. Department of Education.

Varghese, N.V. (2001). Impact of the Economic Crisis on Higher Education in East Asia. Paris: UNESCO (IIEP)

Watkins, David A. and Biggs, John B. (eds) (1996). *The Chinese Learner: Cultural, Psychological and Contextual Influences.* Hong Kong: Hong Kong University Press.

—— (2001). *Teaching the Chinese Learner: Psychological and Pedagogical Perspectives.* Hong Kong: Hong Kong University Press.

Watson, James (2004). "Globalization in Asia: Anthropological perspectives," in Marcelo Suárez-Orozco and Desiree Baolian Qin-Hilliard, (eds.), *Globalization: Culture and Education in the New Millennium*, pp. 141–172. Berkeley, CA: University of California Press.

Yang, Rui (2007). "China's soft power projection in higher education," *International Higher Education* (46): 24.

Zhang, Victor, Law, Kwok-keung and Wong, Siu-lun (2001). "The Crisis of Governance in Hong Kong," in S.K. Lau, M.K. Lee, P.S. Wan, and S.L. Wong (eds.), *Indicators of Social Development: Hong Kong 1999*, pp. 1–32. Hong Kong: Institute of Asia-Pacific Studies, Chinese University of Hong Kong Press.

Part II
Cultural processes
Pluralism and assimilation

Part II

4 The education of ethnic minority groups in China

Only 10 countries in the world have total populations that surpass that of the ethnic minority population of China. Most ethnic minorities live within China's designated ethnic minority autonomous regions which cover half the country and provide minority residents with preferential educational policies. Like other multiethnic states, China faces a number of educational challenges: first, ensuring educational access and equity for its 56 officially designated ethnic groups; second, ensuring education that promotes the economic development of its 155 ethnic minority autonomous areas; third, ensuring that schools, colleges, and universities in ethnic minority regions function in accordance with the principle of cultural autonomy as set out in the Chinese constitution; and, fourth, ensuring that education builds interethnic unity. By the start of the 21st century, basic education was popularized in nearly 90% of China's populated regions, including its ethnic minority regions (Ministry of Education, 2006; Xia, Ha, & Abadu, 1999). However, those in remote areas still received only a few years of schooling. At the other end of the system, China's rapidly expanding system of higher education, the largest system in the world, has increased ethnic minority opportunity, yet minority access to the top universities remains a major challenge.

This is not to say that multiethnic diversity is strongly encouraged in schools, only that it is increasingly salient in society and more recognized than in previous decades. While ethnic minority culture is often celebrated by the state at national events, ethnic diversity in schools and society is carefully managed. The current leadership prescribes Chinese ethnicity within the context of its "harmonious society" campaign, and China's ethnicity is viewed as a plurality within the organic unity of the Chinese nation.

Therefore pluralism is as important as harmony in conceptualizing ethnic intergroup processes in China (Gladney, 1991; Mackerras, 1994, 1995). It has been the source of much cultural vitality throughout China's history, though not as conflict free as portrayed, as in imperial times during the Mongol and Manchu eras when intergroup processes included both harmonious acculturation and conflict prone impact integration (Dikotter, 1992). It is helpful to understand the background themes that guide ideology about ethnic minorities in China. For much of its history, China was a highly pluralistic area of the world and guided by a culturalist tradition that assimilated many groups into its cultural center. At about the time of the incursions of the Western powers into China in the 19th century, this began to change, and by the 20th century China began to adopt the policies of the former USSR. This amounted to a more politicized set of themes which led to the establishment of nationality autonomous regions. There are a number of scholars in China who now suggest that China drew upon that characteristically culturalist position so as to strengthen national identity among its ethnic minorities (Ma, 2007a, 2007b). In fact, ethnic minority education policies and practices since the founding of the People's Republic of China have paralleled the changing political climate.

After the revolution in 1949, the government worked with ethnic minority elites to integrate diverse territories into the national fabric (Dreyer, 1976). Ethnic minority groups were identified and minority languages were recognized and supported. However, political campaigns that stressed class struggle resulted in less generous policies toward ethnic minority cultural vitality. The Cultural Revolution wrought havoc on the cultural traditions of ethnic minorities. This was followed by a national effort to redress past wrongs, and was accompanied by a resurgence of ethnicity. Since 1978, China's economic reforms and its opening to the outside world have contributed to a critical pluralism in education in which national patriotism and ethnic minority cultural autonomy have to keep pace with market forces and globalization.

As schools work to situate the autonomy of ethnic minority cultural transmission within the national context, the practical challenge is how to make schooling work in ways that bring ethnic minority culture into the national and global or international spheres with the least amount of dislocation to ethnic communities and national unity. The debate over cultural preservation, ethnic autonomy, and state schooling remains complex in China. Schools shape ethnic identity through the values they transmit. Making ethnic minorities into Chinese citizens is an educational task which remains a work in progress. This task cannot remain disconnected from strategies for the improvement of the learning environment and academic achievement of ethnic minorities.

While there may be a variety of perspectives about why minority educational achievement levels are far behind those in the rest of the country, culturally meaningful access to mainstream national education remains the main challenge for improving the quality of ethnic minority community life in China. The notion of cultural backwardness continues to adhere to popular discourse about ethnic minorities, and it is often cited in China as the principal reason for educational underachievement (Harrell, 2001). This notion is not unique to China and was also used by Western nations to stress their cultural superiority, most notably by the British for over a century to the Irish, who they insisted were in need of being civilized, even though Ireland became richer per capita than any other nation in Europe. In fact, about 10 of China's 55 official ethnic minority groups have education levels above the national average. Some, like Chinese Koreans, have earned the status of *youxiu minzu*, a notion similar to a model minority elsewhere.

Thus, a key question concerns the extent to which school norms recognize and encourage diverse cultural groups and create a learning environment that reflects the ethnic diversity of the nation (Banks, 1994). With these themes in mind, this chapter will review the basic situation and policies, research literature, case studies, and debates about China's ethnic minority education.

Basic situation

Ethnic minorities in China are referred to as *shaoshu minzu*, formerly rendered as "national minorities" but more recently as "ethnic minorities" (Bilik, 2000). Their population increases faster than that of the majority Han because of a relaxed birth control policy in the sparsely populated minority areas, but also an increased willingness to acknowledge ethnic minority roots, owing in no small part to the preferential policies in family planning, employment, and education. The largest ethnic minority has more than 15 million members and the smallest only about 2,000. While they account for less than 10% of the population, their land contains substantial mineral deposits, forest reserves, and most of the animals that supply milk, meat, and wool. In all, there are 155 nationality autonomous areas (5 autonomous regions, 30 autonomous prefectures, and 120 autonomous counties, including three autonomous banners). The main ethnic group in each of these autonomous areas does not usually (about one-third of the time) account for more than half of its population. The law on ethnic regional autonomy adopted in May 1984 includes provisions for autonomous organizations, rights of self-government organizations, help from higher level organizations, training and assignment of cadres, specialists, and skilled workers among the minority peoples, and the strengthening and developing of socialist relations among ethnic groups (Heberer, 1989).

It is virtually impossible to conceptualize China's ethnic minorities as a single entity, owing to cultural, regional, and developmental differences. However, the government's unified set of ethnic minority education policies is intended to be implemented flexibly so as to take account of the unique situation in each ethnic minority region. Ethnic minorities can be differentiated according to many criteria. These include: population size; the nature of the identification of the group; the size, location, and terrain of the region they occupy; the proportion of members of the minority group that inhabit an autonomous province, prefecture, or county; their proximity to and relations with other ethnic groups, including the Han; whether the neighboring Han were migrants or indigenous residents of the region; whether the ethnic minorities are rural or urban groups, agricultural or pastoral groups, border or inland groups, or concentrated or dispersed groups; having a strong religious tradition or none; having a written or spoken language or both; having members of their ethnic group also living across the Chinese border in other countries, either as ethnic minorities or as the major nationality; and, finally, whether they have had a separate tradition of foreign relations with peoples of another region of the world (Zhou, E., 1984).

The educational policies adopted for ethnic minorities since 1979 include the establishment of the Department of Ethnic Minority Education under the State Ministry of Education (which became the State Education Commission from 1985 to 1998), with corresponding organizations and appointments made at the provincial (*minzu jiaoyu chu*), prefecture (*minzu jiaoyu ke*), and county levels (*minzu jiaoyu gu*). Ethnic autonomous regions became authorized to develop their own educational programs, including levels and kinds of schools, curriculum content, and languages of instruction. Special funds for minority education were increased, and a portion of the annual budget for ethnic minority areas could be used for education. Funds for teacher training increased, and various types of in-service training have been set up. Schools can be established according to the characteristics of the ethnic minorities and their regions; in pastoral, frontier, and cold mountainous regions, boarding schools were arranged and stipends provided for students. Special emphasis in education could be placed on ethnic minority language, culture, and historical traditions. Higher education expanded, and cooperation increased between frontier universities and those in the interior. There are 13 designated ethnic minority colleges and universities which have taken on an increasing number of majority Han students in recent years, amid a debate about mainstreaming of ethnic minorities in higher education. Several major universities have special remedial classes for minority students, with preparatory programs in the first year. University admission standards for minority students have been lowered or points added to ethnic minority students' examination scores to make admission easier to attain. Directional admission and work assignments after graduation were arranged so as to build links between ethnic minority areas and the rest of the country.

Of all of the areas of Chinese education, the gaps between policy and practice are probably no more in evidence than in ethnic minority education. In particular, gender disparities persist between the advanced coastal areas and the poor and remote areas of northwest and southwest China where most ethnic minorities reside. Girls constitute 70% of the school-age children under 11 years old who are not in school. They also constitute 75% of the dropouts from primary school. Nine municipalities and provinces had already reached 100% universalization of 9-year compulsory education in 1998, whereas seven provinces and ethnic minority autonomous regions remained below 60% (World Bank, 2004).

Concepts and policies

While China as a nation reacts to the countervailing demands of internationalism, patriotism, and communalism, its education system has to respond to a shifting market of demands. These may include: the demand of individuals for relevant knowledge and practical skills in an increasingly market-oriented economy; the demand of the middle class, ethnic minorities, and other social groups for status culture; and the demand of the state and the national bureaucracy for social control, rationalization, and patriotism. At certain times the state's demands take prominence and exert a strong influence on representations of ethnic minority culture in schooling. At other times, ethnic minority groups demand an improved delivery of practical skills that can aid economic development, even if at some expense to cultural preservation. Whatever the case, the demands of ethnic minority groups for schools to elevate the status of their culture within the national framework are ubiquitous. At times, ethnic minorities see schools as an embodiment of future prosperity but distant from their values and the traditions of their communities. Still, their degree of participation depends to a large extent on the extent to which schooling leads to improved living standards, especially for those minority groups that live in poorer regions of western China.

The Chinese leadership's assumptions about ethnic intergroup processes manifest themselves in the structure and content of schooling, and much can be learned about China by studying how it schools its ethnic minorities, represents their ethnic heritage, socializes them into a national identity, structures their educational opportunities, and links their schooling to economic development.

Social context has a profound influence, especially during the shift from a socialist planned economy (pre-1978) to a market-oriented economy (post-1978) that is more open to the outside world. At the start of the reform period, the Chinese anthropologist Fei Xiaoteng's theory, known as ethnic pluralism within the organic configuration of the Chinese nation, guided much ethnic minority policy (Fei, 1980, 1986, 1991). Since then, market forces have penetrated virtually all ethnic minority communities. This has increased the degree of interethnic contact, especially in the marketplace, and has led to a stage of critical pluralism in which patterns of ethnic interaction enter a tipping point between interethnic conflict and interethnic harmony. It is here that state schools are expected to play a major role in nudging China toward the latter and strengthening a sense of common Chinese nationality, thereby moving China along the path of harmonious multiculturalism.

State schools serve a conservative function by defining and reproducing a national culture that bolsters the social, political, and economic status quo. China's state schools conserve a particular brand of national culture (*zhonghua minzu wenhua*), and are supervised by an authoritarian state weary of outside cultural influences, especially from the West and separatist forces in China's two far western provinces of Xinjiang and Tibet. State schooling is also charged with the responsibility to conserve ethnic minority cultures within a national context in which Han Chinese cultural capital remains dominant.

The Chinese state's approach to ethnic minority education, although highly centralized, has a great deal of flexibility at the local level. Yet the extent to which schools in China create an atmosphere that has positive institutional norms toward diverse cultural groups is limited by notions of cultural backwardness. State education policy accords importance to the special cultural characteristics of ethnic minority regions. However, there is a divide between the national curriculum and ethnic minority community knowledge and values. More research is needed on this issue (Postiglione, 1999).

Research literature

Research literature in English on ethnic minority education access and underachievement in China has moved ahead rapidly, beginning in the 1980s and 1990s. The focus has been on multiple factors, including language and religion, cultural transmission and household finance, migration, social stratification, and employment (Hannum, 2002; Iredale, Bilik, Su, Guo, & Hoy, 2001; Lee, C. J., 1986). Stites (1999), Lam (2005), and Zhou, M. L., and Sun (2004) examined China's efforts to develop a viable bilingual policy for the education for ethnic minorities.

With respect to religion, Mackerras (1999) pointed out that state school systems adhere to the principle of secularity, but there are signs of religious revival as a reaction to it. Gladney (1999) examined Chinese Muslims and how religious education and state education provide different representations of minority culture (Yi, 2005b). Sautman (1999) examined preferential access to higher education for ethnic minorities and noted that China is ahead of most countries in the policies and practices of preferential treatment in higher education, but there is also a growing debate about the negative effects of preferential treatment policies.

The question of Chinese education as a civilizing mission is addressed in research by Harrell and Erzi (1999) through their study of the Yi minority, who feel that acculturation cannot and should not lead to assimilation. Several similar studies were conducted in China's multiethnic province of Yunnan and nearby Guizhou, including Hansen (1999), who stresses the negative effects of the popular perception about cultural backwardness on the Dai minority. Trueba and Zou (1994) concluded that Miao students' strong sense of belonging to a minority, together with the social support they receive from teachers, administrators, and peers, allows them to surmount obstacles to achieving success in school and university. Lee, M. J. B. (2001) pointed out that oppositional identities noted in Ogbu's research (1978, 1981) in the United States do not exist among the ethnic minorities she studied in Yunnan. Also in Yunnan, Tsung (2003) noted the difficulties of basic education conducted in multiple ethnic minority languages. Yu (2008) studied identities of Yunnan Naxi students, who are permitted more curriculum knowledge about their cultural heritage and who outperform most other minorities, and Cheung (2003) analyzed Christianity's role in the education and identity of rural Miao. Also in the south of China, Nam (1996) examined cultural capital as a key element in the academic achievement of the Yao of Guangdong.

Gao (2007, 2008) studied a Korean Chinese school and examined how the model minority stereotype affects the situation of ethnic Korean children in China. Chen (2004, 2008) found that Uyghur minority students bound for universities develop ways to access social capital from their classmate networks to help them adapt to senior secondary schooling in Chinese cities. Zhao (in press) focused specifically on how little universities recognize the cultural distinctiveness of ethnic Mongols at the major universities of China, while Clothey (2003) found how language tracks in a state-sponsored ethnic minority university influence the strength of ethnic identity.

Palden Nyima's research noted how mainstream education leads to a loss of self-esteem and interest in education, particularly in the case of Tibetans, and is reflected in dropout rates (1997, 2000). Upton's research demonstrated how Tibetan language schooling had a major influence on the surrounding community in its role as a training ground for the elite (1999). Bass (1998) provided an overview of educational policies and development in Tibet since 1950, noting that the basis of the Tibetan Autonomous Region (TAR) educational policy is the state's measures to improve educational access for ethnic minorities in China. Zhang, Fu, and Jiao (2008) note that teaching and learning in Tibet University remain relatively conservative because of remoteness, economics, and traditions in monastery education, as well as people's sense of culture preservation.

At the other end of the education system, Bass (2008) points out that the theme of cultural backwardness remains salient. Seeberg (2006, 2008) provides empirical research to explain the struggle of Tibetan girls for education, while noting how they have become part of new social networks that both bind them to their traditional place and create new space for their educational empowerment. Bangsbo (2008) conveys the perspectives of nomadic households about the irrelevance of some school learning to daily life, and the lack of available jobs upon graduation. The Qinghai-based scholar Wang, S. Y. (2007) noted the inadequacies of current educational reforms for improving Tibetans' economic survival in a market economy. His 2007 study argued that the present school education failed to equip the Tibetan student in market participation. His study, citing others' research, also found that, across Tibetan regions, Tibetan-owned businesses were estimated as only about 20% of total businesses. This figure could reflect the serious competition in seeking employment by the Tibetan graduates in their home areas. Wang's study concluded that the issue of the language of instruction was one of the key factors that affected the quality of secondary education and further hindered Tibetan students from market participation. Yi's (2005a) research demonstrates how schools in Qinghai can limit Tibetan students' chances of acquiring the kinds of cultural capital that could enable them to progress, and instead cause them to become academic under-achievers. Wang, C. J., and Zhou (2003) point out the effects of state preferential policies and dislocated boarding schools.

Other research discusses Chinese minority education underachievement in different contexts (Postiglione, 1992a, 1992b, 2000; Postiglione, Teng, & Ai, 1995). Chapman, Chen, and Postiglione (2000) study measures aimed at improving teacher education for ethnic minority regions. With particular reference to Tibet, studies have focused on factors that contribute to school dropouts and measures implemented to raise attendance levels in village and township primary schools in semi-rural and semi-nomadic communities (Postiglione, 1997a, 1997b, 2007; Postiglione, Jiao, & Gyatso, 2005, 2006). The ability of households to access networks of social relationships that stretch from village to county to city is useful for increased educational rewards and becomes a determinant of upward mobility (Postiglione, 2006). The measures that improved school participation rates were qualified teachers, household financial incentives, and curriculum relevance. Studies of elite government secondary schools for Tibetans in urban China examined where the opportunities to attend university would be increased (Postiglione, Zhu, & Jiao, 2004; Zhu, 2007). Students who graduate from the boarding schools for Tibetans that are established in Chinese cities generally feel that they learned to become more independent and self-reliant than their counterparts who stayed in Tibet. However, they report a deterioration of Tibetan language skills and lack of knowledge about their historical and cultural background (Postiglione, Jiao, & Manlaji, 2007).

There has been an increasing amount of research in Chinese on ethnic minority education since the mid-1980s by Chinese scholars (Ha & Teng, 2001; Teng, 2002). The study of ethnic minorities in China has been traditionally dominated by the Nationalities Research Institute of the Chinese Academy of Social Science and Central University of Nationalities, both of which were heavily influenced by the work of China's most noted anthropologist, Fei Xiaoteng. Anthropology departments, especially at Zhongshan and Yunnan universities, have also been engaged in the study of ethnic minorities for many years. The study of ethnic minorities' education was not a busy field of study until the 1990s, when Teng Xing of the Central University of Nationalities established a research institute for ethnic minority education, assumed the editorship of the *Journal of Research on Ethnic Minority Education* (*Minzu Jiaoyu Yanjiu*), and spent a Fulbright year studying educational anthropology with Professor John Ogbu at the University of California, Los Angeles. Yet, in recent years, sociology departments, like the one at Peking University led by Ma Rong, have also been taking a role in the study of ethnic minority education. Finally, overseas Chinese students and scholars in America, where ethnicity is well developed as a field, are increasingly focusing their research on ethnicity and education. This group also includes an increasing number of ethnic minority scholars.

Such research partially represents the growing vitality of the sociological study of ethnic minority education in China and the many emerging issues and debates. Nevertheless, they provide a sense of the complex nature of the field as a function of the tremendous diversity of China's ethnic minority communities. It is less probable that research by Chinese sociologists of education will contribute to a one-size-fits-all formula for ethnic minority educational policy. However, through empirical studies, they are bringing more clarity and attention to the educational challenges and dilemmas confronting ethnic minority communities.

The amount and type of research on ethnic minority education in China are a function of the way it is organized. At the national level, the Department of Ethnic Minority Education of the State Education Commission conducts policy-related research, usually commissioned as part of the national 5-year plan. The National Association for Ethnic Minority Education Research organizes conferences attended by scholars and officials on specific themes. The Central University of Nationalities' Institute of Ethnic Minority Educational Research is the only research institute that specializes in research on ethnic minority education. Other units of the Central University of Nationalities and the Chinese Academy of Social Science's Institute of Nationalities Research produce research on ethnic minorities, including education topics. Research is also conducted by other units at the national level, including universities and research institutes (i.e. the National Institute of Educational Research, Beijing Normal University's Institute of Educational Research, and Shanghai Academy of Educational Science's Human Resource Development Institute). Among the journals that publish specifically on minority education are the *Journal of Research on Ethnic Minority Education* (*Minzu Jiaoyu Yanjiu*) and *China's Ethnic Minority Education* (*Zhongguo Minzu Jiaoyu*). Research on ethnic minority education also occasionally appears in other national level journals dealing with minority research, including *Nationalities Research* (*Minzu Yanjiu*) and *Ethnic Unity* (*Minzu Tuanjie*). Other ethnic minority educational research may appear in national level journals such as *Educational Research* (*Jiaoyu Yanjiu*), *Sociological Research* (*Shehui Xue Yanjiu*), and similar journals. The education commissions of ethnic autonomous regions also publish journals, such as *Education in Tibet* (*Xizang Jiaoyu*) or *Education in Xinjiang* (*Xinjiang Jiaoyu*). Finally, the ethnic minority institutes, known as nationalities colleges and universities (*minzu xueyuan, minzu daxue*), and other tertiary level institutions in minority regions also publish journals containing material on ethnic minority education.

Toward harmonious multiculturalism in China

Ethnic identity in China is still an official category defined by the state and placed on all identity cards. Through state educational institutions, ethnic minority culture becomes transmitted, celebrated, transmuted, truncated, or in some cases eliminated. For example, the language of instruction may send a message to students about their ethnic identity within mainstream society, as well as become an aid or obstacle to gaining equal footing in the job market after graduation. Formal education can become an instrument to broaden cultural sophistication beyond the ethnic community or it can radically intensify ethnic identities and inequalities in cultural capital. In the case of China, the diversity that exists among its ethnic minority population is only partially reflected in the content of school textbooks, even though minority languages are emphasized in many regions. Under the government's new curriculum reforms, schooling could come to more accurately reflect the cultural diversity that characterizes China's ethnic minorities and increase understanding among ethnic groups nationwide, as well as make state schools much more attractive to ethnic communities, thereby promoting a harmonious multiculturalism for a more unified nation (Postiglione, 2008).

References

Bangsbo, E. (2008). Schooling for knowledge and cultural survival: Tibetan community schools in nomadic herding areas. *Educational Review, 60(1),* 69–84.
Banks, J. A. (1994). *Multiethnic education: Theory and practice* (3rd ed.). Boston: Allyn & Bacon.

78 Cultural processes

Bass, C. (1998). *Education in Tibet*. London: Zed Press.

Bass, C. (2008). Tibetan primary curriculum and its role in nation building. *Educational Review, 60*(1), 39–50.

Bilik, N. (2000). *Xiandai beijingxia de zuqun jiangou* [The structuring of contemporary ethnicity]. Kunming, China: Yunnan Education Press.

Chapman, D., Chen, X. Y., & Postiglione, G. A. (2000). Is pre-service teacher training worth the money? A study of ethnic minority regions in China. *Comparative Education Review, 44*(3), 300–327.

Chen, Y. B. (2004). *Uyghur students in a Chinese boarding school: Social recapitalisation as a response to ethnic integration*. Unpublished doctoral dissertation, University of Hong Kong, Hong Kong.

Chen, Y. B. (2008). *Muslim Uyghur students in a Chinese boarding school: Social recapitalization as a response to ethnic integration*. New York: Lexington Press.

Cheung, W. C. (2003, January). *Narrating ethnic identities: A comparative study of education and ethnic identity construction of a minority group*. Paper presented at the meeting on Chinese Education, Chinese University of Hong Kong, Hong Kong.

Clothey, R. (2003, March). *A study of the ethnic identity of students at the Central University of Nationalities*. Paper presented at the annual meeting of the Comparative and International Education Society, New Orleans, LA.

Dikotter, F. (1992). *The discourse on race in modern China*. Hong Kong: Hong Kong University Press.

Dreyer, J. T. (1976). *China's forty millions: Minority nationalities and national integration in the PRC*. Cambridge, MA: Harvard University Press.

Fei, X. T. (1980). Ethnic identification in China. *Social Sciences in China, 1*, 97–107.

Fei, X. T. (1986). Zhonghua minzu de duoyuan yiti geju [Plurality within the organic unity of the Chinese nation]. *Beijing Daxue Xuebao* [Journal of Beijing University], *4*, 1–19.

Fei, X. T. (1991). *Zhonghua minzu yanjiu xin tance* [New explorations in China's ethnic studies]. Beijing: Chinese Academy of Social Sciences.

Gao, F. (2007). "Koreanness" as a cultural capital: Ethnic educational aspirations of Korean families in Northeast China. In D. A. Bryant, F. Gao, B. B. Hennig, & W. K. Lam (Eds.), *Research Studies in Education* (Vol. 5, pp. 211–220). Hong Kong: University of Hong Kong Faculty of Education Press.

Gao, F. (2008). What it means to be a "model minority": Voices of ethnic Koreans in northeast China. *Asian Ethnicity, 9*, 55–67.

Gladney, D. C. (1991). *Muslim Chinese: Ethnic nationalism in the People's Republic*. Cambridge, MA: Council of East Asian Studies and Fellows of Harvard University.

Gladney, D. C. (1999). Making Muslims in China: Education, Islamicization and representation. In G. Postiglione (Ed.), *China's national minority education: Culture, schooling, and development* (pp. 55–94). New York: Falmer Press.

Ha, J., & Teng, X. (2001). *Minzu jiaoyu xue tonglun* [A general survey of ethnic minority education]. Beijing, China: Jiaoyu kexue press [Educational Science Publishing House].

Hannum, E. (2002). Educational stratification by ethnicity in China: Enrollment and attainment in the early reform years. *Demography, 39*(1), 95–117.

Hansen, M. H. (1999). *Lessons in being Chinese: Minority education and ethnic identity in southwest China*. Seattle: University of Washington Press.

Harrell, S. (2001). *Ways of being ethnic in southwest China*. Seattle: University of Washington Press.

Harrell, S., & Erzi, M. (1999). Folk theories of success: Where Han aren't always the best. In G. Postiglione (Ed.), *China's national minority education: Culture, schooling, and development* (pp. 213–242). New York: Falmer Press.

Heberer, T. (1989). *China and its national minorities: Autonomy or assimilation.* New York: M. E. Sharpe.

Iredale, R., Bilik, N., Su, W., Guo, F., & Hoy, C. (Eds.). (2001). *Contemporary minority migration, education and ethnicity.* Cheltenham, UK & Northampton, MA: Edward Elgar.

Lam, A. (2005). *Language education in China.* Hong Kong: Hong Kong University Press.

Lee, C. J. (1986). *China's Korean minority: The politics of ethnic education.* Boulder, CO: Westview Press.

Lee, M. J. B. (2001). *Ethnicity, education and empowerment: How minority students in southwest China construct identities.* Aldershot, UK: Ashgate Press.

Ma, R. (2007a). Bilingual education for China's ethnic minorities. *Chinese Education and Society,* 40(2), 9–25.

Ma, R. (2007b, November 2). *A new perspective in guiding ethnic relations in the 21st century: "De-politicization" of ethnicity.* Paper read at the Beijing Forum, Beijing, China.

Mackerras, C. (1994). *China's minorities: Integration and modernisation in the 21st century.* Hong Kong: Oxford University Press.

Mackerras, C. (1995). *China's minority cultures: Identities and integration since 1912.* New York: St. Martin's Press.

Mackerras, C. (1999). Religion and the education of China's minorities. In G. Postiglione (Ed.), *China's national minority education: Culture, schooling, and development* (pp. 23–54). New York: Falmer Press.

Ministry of Education (2006). *Zhongguo jiaoyu tongji nianjian 2005* [Statistics on education in China 2005]. Beijing, China: People's Education Press.

Nam, Y. (1996). *A comparative study of Pai Yao and Han Chinese junior secondary school dropouts in Liannan Yao Autonomous County, Guangdong Province, the People's Republic of China.* Unpublished doctoral dissertation, University of Hong Kong, Hong Kong.

Nyima, P. (1997). The way out for Tibetan education. *Chinese Education and Society,* 30(4), 7–20.

Nyima, P. (2000). *Wenming de kunhuo: Zangzu de jiaoyu zhilu* [The puzzle of civilization: The way out for Tibetan education]. Chengdu, China: Sichuan Education Press.

Ogbu, J. (1978). *Minority education and caste: The American system in cross-cultural perspective.* New York: Academic Press.

Ogbu, J. (1981). Education, clientage, and social mobility: Caste and social change in the United States and Nigeria. In G. Berreman (Ed.), *Social inequality: Comparative and developmental approaches* (pp. 277–300). New York: Academic Press.

Postiglione, G. (1992a). China's national minorities and educational change. *Journal of Contemporary Asia,* 22(1), 20–44.

Postiglione, G. (1992b). The implications of modernization for the education of China's national minorities. In R. Hayhoe (Ed.), *Education and modernization: The Chinese experience* (pp. 307–336). New York: Pergamon Press.

Postiglione, G. (Ed.). (1997a). The schooling of Tibetans [Special issue]. *Chinese Education and Society,* 30(4).

80 Cultural processes

Postiglione, G. (Ed.). (1997b). The schooling of Tibetans [Special issue]. *Chinese Education and Society*, 30(5).

Postiglione, G. (Ed.). (1999). *China's national minority education: Culture, schooling, and development.* New York: Falmer Press.

Postiglione, G. (2000) National minority regions: Studying school discontinuation. In J. Liu (Ed.), *The ethnographic eye: Interpretive research on education in China* (pp. 51–71). New York: Falmer Press.

Postiglione, G. (Ed.). (2006). *Education and social change in China: Inequality in a market economy.* New York: M. E. Sharpe.

Postiglione, G. (2007). School access in rural Tibet. In E. Hannum & A. Park (Eds.), *Education and reform in China* (pp. 93–116). New York: Routledge.

Postiglione, G. (2008). Making Tibetans in China: The educational challenges of harmonious multiculturalism. *Educational Review*, 60(1), 1–20.

Postiglione, G., Jiao, B., & Gyatso, S. (2005). Education in rural Tibet: Development, problems, and adaptations. *China: An International Journal*, 3(1), 1–23.

Postiglione, G., Jiao, B., & Gyatso, S. (2006). Household perspectives on school attendance in rural Tibet. *Educational Review*, 58(3), 317–337.

Postiglione, G., Jiao, B., & Manlaji. (2007). Language in Tibetan education: The case of the Neidiban. In A. W. Feng (Ed.), *Bilingual education in China: Practices, policies and concepts* (pp. 49–71). New York: Multilingual Matters.

Postiglione, G., Teng, X., & Ai, Y. (1995). Basic education and school discontinuation in national minority border areas of China. In G. Postiglione & W. O. Lee (Eds.), *Social change and educational development: Mainland China, Taiwan and Hong Kong* (pp. 186–206). Hong Kong: Centre of Asian Studies.

Postiglione, G., Zhu, Z. Y., & Jiao, B. (2004). From ethnic segregation to impact integration: State schooling and identity construction for rural Tibetans. *Asian Ethnicity*, 5(2), 195–217.

Sautman, B. (1999). Expanding access to higher education for China's national minorities: Policies of preferential admissions. In G. Postiglione (Ed.), *China's national minority education: Culture, schooling, and development* (pp. 173–211). New York: Falmer Press.

Seeberg, V. (2006). Tibetan girls' education: Challenging prevailing theory. In G. Postiglione (Ed.), *Education and social change in China: Inequality in a market economy* (pp. 75–110). New York: M. E. Sharpe.

Seeberg, V. (2008). Girls first! Conditions for promoting education in Tibetan areas of China. *Educational Review*, 60(1), 51–68.

Stites, R. (1999). Writing cultural boundaries: National minority language policy, literacy planning, and bilingual education. In G. Postiglione (Ed.), *China's national minority education: Culture, schooling, and development* (pp. 95–130). New York: Falmer Press.

Teng, X. (2002). *Zuqun, wenhua yu jiaoyu.* [Ethnicity, culture, and education]. Beijing, China: Minzu Press. Trueba, H., & Zou, Y. (1994). *Power in education: The case of Miao university students and its significance for American culture.* Washington, DC: Falmer Press.

Tsung, L. (2003, January). *Language policy and minority education in China: The case of the Yi, Naxi, Dai and Tibetan schools in Yunnan.* Paper presented at the Meeting on Chinese Educational Research, Chinese University of Hong Kong, Hong Kong.

Upton, J. (1999). The development of modern school based language education in the PRC. In G. Postiglione (Ed.), *China's national minority education: Culture, schooling, and development* (pp. 281–342). New York: Falmer Press.

Wang, C. J., & Zhou, Q. H. (2003). Minority education in China: From state preferential policies to dislocated Tibetan schools. *Educational Studies*, 29(1), 85–104.
Wang, S. Y. (2007). The failure of education in preparing Tibetans for market participation. *Asian Ethnicity*, 8(2), 131–148.
World Bank. (2004). *Basic education in poor/minority areas*. Retrieved December 24, 2007, from www.worldbank.org.cn/English/content/683u1148366.shtml.
Xia, Z., Ha, J. X., & Abadu, W. (1999). Xizang Zizhiqu Minzu Jiaoyu 50 Nian [50 years of ethnic education in the Tibetan Autonomous Region]. *Zhongguo minzu jiaoyu 50 nian* [50 years of ethnic education in China] (pp. 45–74). Beijing, China: Hongqi Chubanshe [Red Flag Press].
Yi, L. (2005a). Choosing between ethnic and Chinese citizenship: The educational trajectories of Tibetan minority children in northwest China. In V. L. Fong & R. Murphy (Eds.), *Chinese citizenship: Views from the margins* (pp. 41–67). London & New York: Routledge.
Yi, L. (2005b). Muslim narratives of schooling, social mobility and cultural difference: A case study in multi-ethnic northwest China. *Japanese Journal of Political Science*, 6(1), 1–28.
Yu, H. B. (2008). *Schooling and identity among the Naxi*. Unpublished doctoral dissertation, University of Hong Kong, Hong Kong.
Zhang, L. F., Fu, H., & Jiao, B. (2008). Accounting for Tibetan university students' and teachers' intellectual styles. *Educational Review*, 60(1), 21–37.
Zhao, Z. Z. (in press). *Am I privileged? Minority Mongol students and cultural recognition in Chinese universities*. New York: Lexington Press.
Zhou, E. (1984). Guanyu woguo minzu zhengce de jige wenti [A few questions concerning our country's nationality policy]. In Zhou Enlai (Ed.), *Zhou Enlai xuanji* [Selected works of Zhou Enlai] (Vol. 2, pp. 247–271). Beijing, China: People's Press.
Zhou, M. L., & Sun, H. K. (Eds.). (2004). *Language policy in the People's Republic of China: Theory and practice since 1949*. Norwell, MA: Kluwer Academic Press.
Zhu, Z. Y. (2007). *State schooling and ethnic identity: The politics of a Tibetan neidi school in China*. New York: Lexington Press.

5 Ethnic Minority Identity and Educational Outcomes in a Rising China

Introduction

Despite China's meteoric rise, little international scholarly attention has focused on its 110 million ethnic minority population who occupy half of China's land mass and 90% of its border regions (Gladney, 1991; Harrell, 2001; Mackerras, 1994, 1995). China's centuries of experience with ethnic intergroup processes and how it navigates its global economic integration in an increasingly multicultural world add up to a Chinese ethnicity on the move, and one with potentially far-reaching international implications. Already, there is an apparent clash of East–West cultural perspectives on the plight of Tibetans in China.

China presents itself as a multiethnic state but promotes cultural assimilation (Heberer, 1989). Educational institutions in ethnic minority regions become civilizing agencies to transmit mainstream Han Chinese cultural capital. The aspiration to become an economic power, and also to restore its status as one of the world's great civilizations – especially following the nineteenth-century humiliations at the hands of the Western powers – drives national ethnicity. While its economic rise is a promising start for this restoration, China remains highly sensitive about the presentation of its twenty-first-century civilization to the larger global community.

Thus, reconciling ethnic minority cultures within the vision of its national civilization is a major undertaking. China is moving with trepidation toward embracing a Western-style multiculturalism. Yet, it is aware that many of its overseas families – still considered patriotic and Chinese by blood – have become integrated into Western multicultural countries. Unlike the United States with a large population of voluntary migrants, China is a land of indigenous minorities who are not likely to migrate and therefore more akin in this respect to Native Americans (Ogbu, 1978). While several of China's ethnic minority groups sustained their own slave societies into the early twentieth century, these differed in key respects from the slave experience of African Americans. The American government's concern with a Hawaii separatist movement pales in comparison with China's intense focus on its territorial unity – still a major theme in its ethnic minority discourse and foreign policy. For these and other reasons, the Chinese education makes national unity a central focus. With most of its overseas students and future leaders having studied in the United States, China has come to view the United States as a nation that has successfully used education to build a staunchly patriotic nation. (Like the United States in earlier times, China has used the term nationalities to refer to what is now rendered in English as ethnic groups (the term, in Chinese, for nationalities (*minzu*) and ethnic groups is the same), although there has been a growing popularity among Chinese anthropologists (Bilik, 2000) to use the word *zucun* for ethnic group.)

This article argues that China contributes to the global picture of ethnicity by having sustained the longest history of state-sponsored preferential treatment policies in education, and the manner in which it uses education to navigate its current phase of critical pluralism within its emergent global integration.

Ethnic Minority Education Policy

Most – though not all – of China's ethnic minorities occupy western regions of the country which are poorer and more remote than China's prosperous east-coast urban areas. Many ethnic minority families have only just entered their first generation of literacy and schooling. Moreover, since most ethnic minorities live in concentrated communities called autonomous regions, their educational opportunities are far lower than what would be available to those in China's prosperous cities such as Shanghai, Beijing, and Guangzhou. In fact, China's pace of economic development has exacerbated, rather than alleviated, social inequality. According to the Gini coefficient – which is used to measure the degree of inequality within a country – China's Gini coefficient of 0.47 makes it the most unequal country in Asia following Nepal. Nevertheless, of the 55 officially designated ethnic minorities of China, several groups (i.e., Koreans, Tatars, Daur, Russian, Xibe, Bai, and others) have educational achievement levels near or above the national average. It is also notable that socialist China had much earlier instituted a set of comprehensive preferential treatment policies that are still in effect.

These preferential policies provide subsides for minority schools, bilingual education, school textbooks in minority languages, curriculum reforms, ethnic minority teachers training, and boarding schools. In higher education, the most notable policies are those that provide preferential access to college and university through both admission quotas and points added to scores on the national entrance examinations, as well as remedial classes during the first year of college and university (Xia *et al.*, 1999).

These policies are widely believed to ensure educational opportunities for economically and educationally underserved ethnic minorities, especially under the increasing impact of marketization. While these policies have been successful in reducing inequalities by raising the numbers of ethnic minorities attending school and university, most ethnic minority groups still have lower rates of access and educational achievement, especially at university level.

The Sociology of Ethnic Minority Education in China

Research on ethnic minority-education underachievement in China has moved ahead in recent years. The focus has been on multiple factors – ranging from language and religion, cultural transmission and family background, migration,

84 *Cultural processes*

and politics (Iredale *et al.*, 2001; Hannum, 2002; Lee, 1986, 2001; Stites, 1999; Lam, 2005; Zhou and Sun, 2004; Mackerras, 1999; Gladney, 1999; Lin, 2005b; Harrell and Ma, 1999; Hansen, 1999; Tsung, 2003; Nam, 1996; Yu, 2009; Cheung, 2003; Chen, 2004). While there are several works that focus on university students, most focus on ethnic identity in provincial or special universities (Lee, 2001; Trueba and Zou, 1994; Clothey, 2003) rather than ethnic minority access to and achievement at China's top universities (Sautman, 1999). There is also a growing literature on specific groups. For example, in the case of Tibetans, literature has increased in recent years (Nyima, 1997, 2000; Upton, 1999; Bass, 1998, 2008; Zhang *et al.*, 2008; Seeberg, 2006, 2008; Bangsbo, 2008; Wang, 2007; Yi, 2005; Wang and Zhou, 2003). While the literature on ethnic minority achievement in education is multidimensional, most of it is focused on school rather than university access (Chapman *et al.*, 2000).

Among mainland-based Chinese sociologists and anthropologists, the literature has also grown rapidly. For example, Teng Xing established a research institute for ethnic minority education at the Central University of Nationalities and edits its *Journal of Research on Ethnic Minority Education* (*Minzu jiaoyu yanjiu*) (Teng, 2002). More recently, in a special issue of *Chinese Education and Society*, Ma (2007) has examined one of the stickier issues in the sociology of ethnic minority education – bilingual education and sees an increase in support for Chinese as the medium of instruction in ethnic minority schools. While he favors giving ethnic minority parents a choice of either native language or Chinese as medium of instruction, a market economy prods parents to choose the language of the job market, irrespective of the educational benefit. Zhao (2007) has examined the ethnic minority cultural dimension and concludes that minority culture is marginalized at universities. Zhu (2007) explores how minority students in state boarding schools construct ethnic identities and the specific modes used by individual students. Qian (2007) examined how the hidden curriculum creates discontinuities within cultural traditions and ethnic identities. Ba (2007) – a member of the Yugur ethnic minority of Gansu province – studied how schools disseminate both ethnic minority and modern culture, and argues that there is an estrangement and disjuncture between the culture of the classroom and the community – a result of the choice to absorb the national plan of instruction. Finally, Wang (2008) examined how the children of rural migrants from minority regions who try to settle in Beijing experience double discrimination – as migrants and as ethnic minorities – as they strive for urban membership.

Case Studies

Recent case studies have improved understanding of the processes at work in China's minority education. Although the 1990s saw an increase in the amount of useful quantitative data available, it was unable to capture detailed processes at work as minority students construct meanings and identities from state schooling or to explain why minority children have higher dropout rates. The following section contains the case studies of the education of minorities like Tibetans,

Uyghurs, Mongols, Naxis, and Koreans in China. While the themes of these studies are about national integration, ethnic and national identity, and cultural recognition, a common concern in all of these studies is equal opportunity in educational access and achievement.

Zhu (2007) studied the challenge to Chinese education posed by Tibet. Tibetans have had a written language for over 1500 years – one that is in common use across a territory as large as the continental United States. Despite a rich cultural heritage, Tibet has the lowest educational levels of any provincial level entity in China. Doubtless, this has something to do with poverty and remote geographical location. Therefore, schools and classes for Tibetan students were relocated to Chinese cities beginning in 1985 where better school facilities and trained teachers could be used to foster talent to drive Tibet's economic development. In the first year, one-quarter of all primary school graduates were sent to relocated schools in China for 4 years of junior secondary education and 3 years of senior secondary or vocational education. Zhu provides a grounded view of what actually happens in these schools through the eyes of Tibetan students. He also illustrates the contestation over the meaning of Tibetan culture, who defines it, and how students innovate in constructing their identities around that definition. While the school attempted to assign a desired identity in accordance with the state ideologies, the Tibetan students were able to assert a Tibetan identity expressed through the representation of Tibetan culture, as well as influenced by their experiences on and off their school campus.

Chen (2008) examined how Uyghur students in the so-called Xinjiang Classes (Chinese boarding schools located outside of the home province of Xinjiang), respond to the school goal of ethnic integration. Guided by the theoretical framework of social capital analysis, the study's findings suggest that Uyghur students' response to the goal of ethnic integration can be viewed within a series of analytical levels, including the history of the Uyghurs within China, the Xinjiang boarding schools as a formal organization, Uyghur students' social networks, communal norms and sanctions, and Uyghur students' social actions in the Xinjiang Classes. The study finds that the Uyghur students have created bonding social capital within the social practice of their ethnic norms and sanctions. Their social practice draws ethnic boundaries and demonstrates resistance to the school goal of ethnic integration. The students have also created a linking social capital to tap into the resources of peers, as well as staff and teachers, that improves their academic performance and helps them adapt to life in the boarding school. Nonetheless, they lack bridging social capital which connects them with students and teachers of other ethnic groups, thus making the goal of ethnic integration more difficult to achieve. The study explains the Uyghur students' responses as a form of social recapitalization. While boarding-school life limits the acquisition of social capital from their families and communities in Xinjiang, they develop new forms of social capital among ethnic peers on campus to help facilitate their academic success.

Zhao (2009) examined ethnic minority cultural recognition at universities through a multicase study focused on the Mongol undergraduate students' experiences and perceptions. She examines the institutional obstacles to cultural recognition in higher education – despite the state and university discourses of equal access to learning through preferential admission policies. Zhao reports on three particular institutions: the Inner Mongolia Normal University (governed by a Mongol nationality autonomous region), Beijing Normal University (governed by the State Ministry of Education), and the Central China University of Nationalities (governed by the State Ethnic Affairs Commission). Zhao expresses doubts on the extent to which the universities recognize Mongol culture. She asserts that Mongols are a "decorated culture," marginalized within the context of university life and few Mongol students speak Mongol language on campus. She also notes the complex layering of identity between *minkaomin* and *minkaohan* students – the former who enter university by taking the examination in their native language and the latter who take it in Chinese. Not unexpectedly, Inner Mongolia Normal University gives more attention to Mongol culture than Beijing Normal University because the former is within the Inner Mongol Autonomous Region. However, even in the Central China University of Nationalities, ethnic culture is marginalized. Zhao acknowledges that preferential admission policies help Mongol students, but concludes that the lack of cultural recognition on the part of universities limits meaningful access to higher education in China for its ethnic minorities, thereby sustaining their patterns of underachievement.

Yu (2009) studied state schooling and Naxi minority-identity construction. She examined Naxi secondary school students' experience, as well as the role played by Naxi intellectuals', as an asset in student-identity resurgence since the 1980s. The changing roles of school, community, and family in the identity construction suggest that Naxi students retain a strong Naxi identity, by inheriting the knowledge, values, and worldview of their ethnic group, while also managing to fit into mainstream culture. Three forces affect identity construction of the Naxi students: the state and the school; Naxi intellectuals; and socialization in the family and community. As an institution of the state, the school conveys national ideology and instills a sense of ethnic unity and an understanding of the culture of the Chinese nation. While the school takes an active role in ethnic identity construction of the Naxi students, Naxi intellectuals – through their research publications – respond to policies and activities so as to revitalize Naxi culture. The Naxi process of identity construction is characterized by a relatively harmonious and creative engagement with ethnic and national identity. Two factors contributed to this harmonious identity construction. First, since the late 1970s, the identity of ethnic minority groups has been gaining strength and recognition in China, while – at the same time – market forces have been creating assimilationist pressures. The minorities have taken steps to revive the use of their native languages, and to demand that their native cultures are taught in the public schools. Second, the Naxi already have a long historical tradition of integrating well into Han Chinese culture. Their traditional education is heavily influenced by Confucianism and interactions over several hundred years with Han Chinese. The study contributes to an understanding of why Naxi students adapt generally better than many other ethnic minority groups in China to state schooling.

Gao (2008) studied ethnic Koreans in China, a group widely recognized as a model minority primarily for their academic success rates which are above the national average in China. This research examines how Korean elementary-school students construct meaning out of the model minority stereotype in the context of their school and home experience, and how the meaning construction impacts their educational aspirations and strategies in peer networks. Through comparative analysis, Gao notes that, in a variety of cultural contexts, ethnic Koreans survive as a distinct group that participates in the mainstream without being completely assimilated. Koreans in China and the United States are believed to pull themselves up by their cultural predispositions. This research points to the continued need to modify the model minority stereotype that tends to essentialize ethnic Koreans as a homogeneous group with academic attitudes and success. Research results argue that the model minority stereotype may reinforce the cultural deficiency argument about the academic failure of backward minorities, silence the disadvantages suffered by ethnic Koreans, and lead to no active intervention to remedy them.

China's Ethnic Pluralism

Thus, pluralism is as important as harmony in conceptualizing ethnic intergroup processes in China, and has been the source of much cultural vitality throughout China's history. Yet, this pluralism has not been free of ethnic conflict as in imperial times during the Mongol and Manchu Eras when intergroup processes included both harmonious acculturation and conflict-prone impact integration (Dikotter, 1992).

It is helpful to understand the background themes that guide education of ethnic minorities in China (Dreyer, 1976; Fei, 1980). For much of its history, China was a highly pluralistic society in the world and guided by a culturalist tradition that assimilated many groups into its cultural center. At about the time of the incursions of the Western powers into China in the nineteenth century, this began to change, and, by the twentieth century, China began to adopt the policies of former USSR. This amounted to a more politicized set of themes which led to the establishment of national autonomous regions. There are a number of scholars in China who now suggest that China should draw upon that characteristically culturalist position so as to strengthen national identity among its ethnic minorities (Ma, 2007a, 2007b). In fact, ethnic minority-education policies and practices since the founding of the People's Republic of China have paralleled the changing political climate.

Following the revolution in 1949, the government worked with ethnic minority elites to integrate diverse territories into the national fabric (Dreyer, 1976). Ethnic minority groups were identified and minority languages were recognized and supported. However, political campaigns that stressed class struggle resulted in less generous policies toward cultural vitality of the ethnic minority. The

Cultural Revolution wrought havoc on cultural traditions of ethnic minorities. This was followed by a national effort to redress past wrongs, and accompanied by a resurgence of ethnicity. Since 1978, China's economic reforms and its opening to the outside world have greatly increased the interactions between different ethnic communities. This has contributed to a critical pluralism in education in which national patriotism and ethnic minority cultural autonomy have to keep pace with market forces and globalization.

The decision of the Chinese leader Deng Xiaoping in December of 1978 to launch economic reforms and open China to the outside world continues to have major implications for ethnic minority education. In China's new market economy, competition has become part of the national ethos – making preferential policies for minorities less popular among the majority ethnic group. Moreover, as restrictions on population movement are lifted to fuel the labor market for increased economic growth, both ethnic minorities and Han Chinese migrate to urban areas where they increasingly interact and compete. Many Han Chinese also migrate westward to ethnic minority autonomous areas for work and, often, outcompete local ethnic minorities for jobs. This is especially true for jobs in national infrastructure projects linked to the central government's western development project. The same is true for many small-scale businesses that serve the growing population of Han Chinese from other parts of the country.

Within the ethnic minority autonomous regions, interethnic interaction and competition for jobs has increased. The resulting increase in inter-ethnic animosities is viewed as part of the reason for the government's nationwide harmonious society campaign. (While this campaign focuses on ethnic minority regions and minority–Han relations, it is also related to growing urban labor, urban migration for jobs, rising costs in rural areas, relocation of households due to urban development, and other social problems.)

The underlying theory of ethnic relations in China since the launching of the economic reforms and the opening to the outside world is Fei Xiaotong's *duoyuan yiti geju*, also rendered in English as plurality within the unity of the Chinese nation (Fei, 1986, 1991). This assimilationist theory has floundered in the arena of globalization and market forces. Rather than move China's ethnic minorities toward cultural assimilation, economic globalization and state schooling have also made ethnicity more salient and intensified ethnic identities.

As the reform period unfolded, China's ethnicity entered a period of critical pluralism. This phase of increased interethnic contact, resurgence, and saliency of ethnic identity occurred along with discontinuance of the job-allocation system, market competition for jobs, compulsory mass schooling that stresses a unified national identity, and telecommunications that make it easier for remote ethnic communities to sustain and extend ethnic solidarity. The increasingly critical nature of ethnic pluralism has placed Chinese ethnicity at a crossroad. Ethnic intergroup antagonisms and misunderstandings can foster a nation of plural monoculturalisms in which ethnic groups emphasize their cultural identities above those of the nation and limit their potential to take on a multiple role in national development. The other direction for Chinese ethnicity is toward a harmonious multiculturalism. This would coincide more closely with the state's campaign for a harmonious society. However, the Chinese state has been unwilling to fully embrace multiculturalism. How educational institutions handle the current phase of critical pluralism may determine whether it generates a national society of plural monoculturalism or harmonious multiculturalism (Sen, 2006). If China is to head in the direction of harmonious multiculturalism – in which conflictual tendencies that characterize interethnic relations are viewed as positive opportunities for building increased mutual understanding, then education has a role in transmitting multiculturalism in three ways: first, by making the curriculum of state schools more relevant to the cultural vitality of ethnic communities; second, by stressing multiculturalism and critical thinking skills; and, third, not only by sustaining preferential treatment policies that increase access to higher education but also increasing ethnic minority cultural recognition on campus so as to foster more meaningful access and academic success.

Conclusion

Ethnic diversity in China rivals that of anywhere else in the world and is the source of much of the nation's vitality. This not only includes diverse cultural traditions and practices, but also the differing social, economic, and political statuses. While the majority Han Chinese culture and Confucian education heritage exert a significant influence on East Asia and beyond, the cultural traditions and practices of China's ethnic minorities are not widely recognized in China's school curriculum. Nevertheless, they are in the family and community through linguistic, religious, and social practices. Religion is central to the lives of most of China's minorities and the Chinese constitution guarantees freedom of religion (Mackerras, 1994, 1995). However, there is a strict separation between schools and religious institutions. All but two of China's 55 officially designated ethnic minority groups have their own languages. Some have more than one, and at least 21 ethnic minority languages are used in schools, either taught as a subject or used as a medium of instruction. Since 90% of China's border regions are occupied by ethnic minorities, schooling is expected to ensure that national identity is strengthened enough to ensure social stability, especially in the case of Tibet and Xinjiang where the government has identified separatist movements. Therefore, educational policies are challenged to strike a balance between local and national interests so that the dual construction of ethnic and national identities can take place simultaneously.

See also: Affirmative Action and Higher Education in Brazil; The Education of Indigenous Students; The History of Education: Race and Education.

Bibliography

Ba, Z. (2007). A socio-anthropological analysis of the function of Yugur-nationality schools. *Chinese Education and Society* 40(2), 77–88.
Bangsbo, E. (2008). Schooling for knowledge and cultural survival: Tibetan community schools in nomadic herding areas. *Educational Review* 60(1), 69–84.
Bass, C. (1998). *Education in Tibet: Policy and Practice Sine 1950.* London: Zed Books.

Bass, C. (2008). Tibetan primary curriculum and its role in nation building. *Educational Review* 60(1), 39–50.

Bilik, N. (2000). *Xiandai beijingxia de zuqun jiangou (The Structuring of Contemporary Ethnicity)*. Kunming: Yunnan Education Press.

Chapman, D., Chen, X., and Postiglione, G. A. (2000). Is pre-service teacher training worth the money: A study of ethnic minority regions in China. *Comparative Education Review* 44(3), 300–327.

Chen, Y. (2004). *Uyghur Students in a Chinese Boarding School: Social Recapitalisation as a Response to Ethnic Integration*. Unpublished doctoral dissertation, University of Hong Kong.

Chen, Y. (2008). *Muslim Uyghur Students in a Chinese Boarding School: Social Recapitalization as a Response to Ethnic Integration*. New York: Lexington Press.

Cheung, W. C. (2003). Narrating ethnic identities: A comparative study of education and ethnic identity construction of a minority group. *Paper Presented at the Meeting on Chinese Education*, Chinese University of Hong Kong.

Clothey, R. (2003). A study of the ethnic identity of students at the central university of nationalities. *Paper Presented at the Annual Meeting of the Comparative and International Education Society*, New Orleans, LA.

Dikotter, F. (1992). *The Discourse on Race in Modern China*. Hong Kong: Hong Kong University Press.

Dreyer, J. T (1976). *China's Forty Millions: Minority Nationalities and National Integration in the PRC*. Cambridge, MA: Harvard University Press.

Fei, X. (1980). Ethnic identification in China. *Social Sciences in China* 1, 97–107.

Fei, X. (1986). Zhonghua minzu de duoyuan yiti geju (Plurality within the organic unity of the Chinese nation). *Beijing Daxue Xuebao (Journal of Beijing University)* 4, 1–19.

Fei, X. (1991). *Zhonghua minzu yanjiu xin tance (New Explorations in China's Ethnic Studies)*. Beijing: Chinese Academy of Social Sciences.

Gao, F. (2008). What it means to be a "model minority"? Voices of ethnic Koreans in Northeast China. *Asian Ethnicity* 9, 55–67.

Gladney, D. C. (1991). *Muslim Chinese: Ethnic Nationalism in the People's Republic*. Cambridge, MA: The Council of East Asian Studies and Fellows of Harvard University.

Gladney, D. C. (1999). Making Muslims in China, education: Islamicization and representation. In Postiglione, G. (ed.) *China's National Minority Education: Culture, Schooling and Development*, pp. 55–94. New York: Falmer Press.

Hannum, E. (2002). Educational stratification by ethnicity in China: Enrollment and attainment in the early reform years. *Demography* 39(1), 95–117.

Hansen, M. (1999). *Lessons in Being Chinese: Minority Education and Ethnic Identity in Southwest China*. Seattle, WA: University of Washington Press.

Harrell, S. (2001). *Ways of Being Ethnic in Southwest China*. Seattle, WA: University of Washington Press.

Harrell, S. and Ma, E. (1999). Folk theories of success: Where Han aren't always the best. In Postiglione, G. (ed.) *China's National Minority Education: Culture, Schooling, and Development*, pp. 213–242. New York: Falmer Press.

Heberer, T. (1989). *China and Its National Minorities: Autonomy or Assimilation*. New York: M. E. Sharpe.

Iredale, R., Bilik, N., Su, W., Guo, F., and Hoy, C. (eds.) (2001). *Contemporary Minority Migration, Education and Ethnicity*. Cheltenham: Edward Elgar.

Lam, A. (2005). *Language Education in China*. Hong Kong: Hong Kong University Press.

Lee, C. J. (1986). *China's Korean Minority: The Politics of Ethnic Education*. Boulder, CO: Westview Press.

Lee, M. J. B. (2001). *Ethnicity, Education and Empowerment: How Minority Students in Southwest China Construct Identities*. Aldershot: Ashgate Press.

Ma, R. (2007a). Bilingual education for China's ethnic minorities. *Chinese Education and Society* 40(2), 9–25.

Ma, R. (2007b). *A New Perspective in Guiding Ethnic Relations in the 21st Century: "De-politicization" of Ethnicity*. Paper read at the Beijing Forum, Beijing, China.

Mackerras, C. (1994). *China's Minorities: Integration and Modernisation in the 21st Century*. Hong Kong: Oxford University Press.

Mackerras, C. (1995). *China's Minority Cultures: Identities and Integration Since 1912*. New York: St. Martin's Press.

Mackerras, C. (1999). Religion and the education of China's minorities. In Postiglione, G. (ed.) *China's National Minority Education: Culture, Schooling and Development*, pp. 23–54. New York: Falmer Press.

Nam, Y. (1996). *A Comparative Study of Pai Yao and Han Chinese Junior Secondary School Dropouts in Liannan Yao Autonomous County, Guangdong Province, the People's Republic of China*. Unpublished doctoral dissertation, University of Hong Kong.

Nyima, P. (1997). The way out for Tibetan education. *Chinese Education and Society* 30(4), 7–20.

Nyima, P. (2000). *Wenming de kunhuo: Zangzu de jiaoyu zhilu* [The puzzle of Civilization: The Way Out for Tibetan Education]. Chengdu, China: Sichuan Education Press.

Ogbu, J. (1978). *Minority Education and Caste: The American System in Cross-Cultural Perspective*. New York: Academic Press.

Qian, M. (2007). Discontinuity and reconstruction: The hidden curriculum in schoolroom instruction in ethnic minority areas. *Chinese Education and Society* 40(2), 60–76.

Sautman, B. (1999). Expanding access to higher education for China's national minorities: Policies of preferential admissions. In Postiglione, G. (ed.) *China's National Minority Education: Culture, Schooling and Development*, pp. 173–211. New York: Falmer Press.

Seeberg, V. (2006). Tibetan girls' education: Challenging prevailing theory. In Postiglione, G. (ed.) *Education and Social Change in China: Inequality in a Market Economy*, pp. 75–110. New York: M. E. Sharpe.

Seeberg, V. (2008). Girls first! Conditions for promoting education in Tibetan areas of China. *Educational Review* 60(1), 51–68.

Sen, A. (2006). *Identity and Violence: The Illusion of Destiny*. New York: W. W. Norton.

Stites, R. (1999). Writing cultural boundaries: National minority language policy, literacy planning, and bilingual education. In Postiglione, G. (ed.) *China's National Minority Education: Culture, Schooling and Development*, pp. 95–130. New York: Falmer Press.

Teng, X. (2002). *Zuqun, wenhua yu jiaoyu (Ethnicity, Culture, and Education)*. Beijing: Minzu Press.

Trueba, H. and Zou, Y. (1994). *Power in Education: The Case of Miao University Students and Its Significance for American Culture*. Washington, DC: Falmer Press.

Tsung, L. (2003). Language policy and minority education in China: The case of the Yi, Naxi, Dai and Tibetan schools in Yunnan. *Paper Presented at the Meeting on Chinese Educational Research*, Chinese University of Hong Kong.

Upton, J. (1999). The development of modern school based language education in the PRC. In Postiglione, G. (ed.) *China's National Minority Education: Culture, Schooling, and Development*, pp. 281–342. New York: Falmer Press.

Wang, C. and Zhou, Q. (2003). Minority education in China: From state preferential policies to dislocated Tibetan schools. *Educational Studies* 29(1), 85–104.

Wang, L. J. (2008). *Ethnic Migrants, Social Networks and Educational Access: Membership Capitalization in Beijing.* Doctoral dissertation, The University of Hong Kong.

Wang, S. (2007). The failure of education in preparing Tibetans for market participation. *Asian Ethnicity* 8(2), 131–148.

Xia, Z., Ha, J., and Wushuer, A. (1999). *Xizang Zizhiqu Minzu Jiaoyu 50 Nian* (50 years of ethnic education in the Tibetan Autonomous Region), *Zhongguo minzu jiaoyu 50 nian* (50 Years of Ethnic Education in China). Beijing: Hongqi Chubanshe (Red Flag Press).

Yi, L. (2005). Choosing between ethnic and Chinese citizenship: The educational trajectories of Tibetan minority children in northwest China. In Fong, V. L. and Murphy, R. (eds.) *Chinese Citizenship: Views from the Margins*, pp. 41–67. London: Routledge.

Yi, L. (2008). *Cultural Exclusion in China: State Education, Social Mobility and Cultural Difference.* London and New York: Routledge.

Yu, H. (2008). *Schooling and Identity among the Naxi.* Unpublished doctoral dissertation, University of Hong Kong.

Yu, H. B. (2009). *Identity and Schooling Among the Naxi: Becoming Chinese with Naxi Identity.* New York: Lexington Press.

Zhang, L., Fu, H., and Jiao, B. (2008). Accounting for Tibetan university students' and teachers' intellectual styles. *Educational Review* 60(1), 21–37.

Zhao, Z. (2007). Ethnic Mongol students and cultural recognition: Case studies of three Chinese universities. *Chinese Education and Society* 40(2), 26–37.

Zhao, Z. (2009). *Am I privileged?: Minority Mongol Students and Cultural Recognition in Chinese Universities.* New York: Lexington Press.

Zhao, Z. Z. (2009). *Minority Mongol Students and Cultural Recognition in Chinese Universities.* New York: Lexington.

Zhou, M. and Sun, H. (eds.) (2004). *Language Policy in the People's Republic of China: Theory and Practice Since 1949.* Norwell, MA: Kluwer Academic Press.

Zhu, Z. (2007). *State Schooling and Ethnic Identity: The Politics of a Tibetan Neidi School in China.* New York: Lexington Press.

Further Reading

Clothey, R. (2005). China's policies for minority nationalities in higher education: Negotiating national values and ethnic identities. *Comparative Education Review* 49(3), 389–409.

Harrell, S. and Ma, E. (1999). Folk theories of success: Where Han aren't always the best. In Postiglione, G. (ed.) *China's National Minority Education: Culture, Schooling and Development*, pp. 213–242. New York: Falmer Press.

Nyima, P. (2000). *Wenming de kunhuo: Zangzu de jiaoyu zhilu* (The puzzle of civilisation: the way out for Tibetan education). Chengdu: Sichuan Education Press.

Postiglione, G. A. (1992a). China's national minorities and educational change. *Journal of Contemporary Asia* 22(1), 20–44.

Postiglione, G. A. (1992b). The implications of modernization for the education of China's national minorities. In Hayhoe, R. (ed.) *Education and Modernization: The Chinese Experience*, pp. 307–336. New York: Pergamon Press.

Postiglione, G. A. (ed.) (1997a). Special Issues: The Schooling of Tibetans. *Chinese Education and Society* 30(4), 3–6.

Postiglione, G. A. (ed.) (1997b). *Special Issues: The Schooling of Tibetans*. *Chinese Education and Society* 30(5), 3–6.

Postiglione, G. A. (ed.) (1999). *China's National Minority Education: Culture, Schooling and Development*. New York: Falmer Press.

Postiglione, G. A. (ed.) (2001). *Special Issue: Bilingual Education in China*. *Chinese Education and Society* 34(2).

Postiglione, G. A. (ed.) (2006). *Education and Social Change in China: Inequality in a Market Economy*. New York: M. E. Sharpe.

Postiglione, G. A. (2007). School access in rural Tibet. In Hannum, E. and Park, A. (eds.) *Education and Reform in China*, pp. 93–116. New York: Routledge.

Postiglione, G. A. (2008). Making Tibetans in China: The challenges of harmonious Multiculturalism. *Educational Review* 60(1), 1–20.

Postiglione, G. A. (2009). Dislocated Education: The Case of Tibet, *Comparative Education Review* 53(4), 483–512.

Postiglione, G. A. and Jiao, B. (2010). Tibet's Relocated Schools: Popularization Reconsidered, with Ben Jiao, *Asian Survey*.

Postiglione, G. A., Jiao, B., and Gyatso, S. (2005). Education in rural Tibet: Development, problems, and adaptations. *China: An International Journal* 3(1), 1–23.

Postiglione, G. A., Jiao, B., and Gyatso, S. (2006). Household perspectives on school attendance in rural Tibet. *Educational Review* 58(3), 317–337.

Postiglione, G. A., Jiao, B., and Manlaji (2007). Language in Tibetan education: The case of the Neidiban. In Feng, A. W. (ed.) *Bilingual Education in China: Practices, Policies and Concepts*, pp. 49–71. New York: Multilingual Matters.

Postiglione, G. A., Teng, X., and Ai, Y. (1995). Basic education and school discontinuation in national minority border areas of China. In Postiglione, G. and Lee, W. O. (eds.) *Social Change and Educational Development: Mainland China, Taiwan and Hong Kong*, pp. 186–206. Hong Kong: Centre of Asian Studies.

Postiglione, G. A., Zhu, Z., and Jiao, B. (2004). From ethnic segregation to impact integration: State schooling and identity construction for rural Tibetans. *Asian Ethnicity* 5(2), 195–217.

Yi, L. (2005a). Choosing between ethnic and Chinese citizenship: The educational trajectories of Tibetan minority children in northwest China. In Fong, V. L. and Murphy, R. (eds.) *Chinese Citizenship: Views from the Margins*, pp. 41–67. London: Routledge.

Zhou, E. (1983). Guanyu woguo minzu zhengce jige wenti (A few questions concerning our country's nationality policy). In Gansu Sheng Minzu Yanjiusuo (Gansu Province Institute of Minority Nationality Studies) (eds.) *Zhongguo minzu guanxishi lunwen xuanji* (*The Historical Relations among China's National Minorities*), pp. 1–23. Gansu: Gansu Minzu Press.

6 Making Tibetans in China

The educational challenges of harmonious multiculturalism

Introduction

Tibet is required by China to have an education system that popularizes basic education, and also socializes Chinese citizens into a political discourse consonant with the state programme to build a harmonious society (Wu 1995, 1999; Wang and Lou 2007).[1] The extent to which this so called civilizing mission occurs is reflected in enrolment rates, school curriculum, the medium of instruction, and preferential treatment policies. Yet, the success or failure of this major effort hinges to a great extent upon how much and how many Tibetan households become persuaded by the logic of modern state schooling and the value of schools for survival within an expansive market economy (Postiglione, Ben Jiao and Gyatso 2006). New patterns of population mobility, increased flows of information from outside Tibet, and rapid economic change have had a profound effect on the transmission and replication of traditional culture. Views differ about the way this transmission process has been managed and directed (Dorjee and Giles 2005; Sautman and Dreyer 2005).[2] Nevertheless, the expansion of educational opportunities has made Tibetans more like Chinese, though no less Tibetan, as ethnic identities are remodelled by state schooling and responded to by local communities.[3]

Regardless of the cultural transformations taking place in Tibet, the analysis of the education system, policies, programmes, problems and practices inevitably has to be based on the realities of students, households, schools, teachers and communities.

This paper argues that while enrolment rates continue to rise, most schooling produces mixed results, or worse, in terms of providing a quality learning environment that can propel academic achievement to a level comparable with the national average, as well as foster a harmonious multiculturalism that can sustain Tibet's social and economic development. Until then, the potential of education to help Tibetans labour effectively in the TAR and across China will remain severely limited.

The urgency of basic education for all

Although the TAR is one of the most remote regions of China, the prosperity of the mainland and the central government's intention to make the TAR economically prosperous, culturally visible, nationally integrated, and politically secure, have led to steadily rising living standards for many Tibetans (Goldstein et al. 2003; Sautman and Dreyer 2005). Yet, like elsewhere in China, development is unbalanced across localities, and education has had to compete with other investments viewed by local authorities as more able to provide a quicker rate of return (Wu, Ciren and Junmei 2006). Moreover, improvements in school access are behind the rest of the country (N.A. 2006). Contemporary Tibet's main educational policies are set within the context of a socialist state adapting to market economics, while permitting a special status for Tibet's educational needs (Geng and Wang 1989; Wu 1999). Education initiatives have greatly increased the number of children that receive a basic education (N.A. 2005). However, a comprehensive focus on student learning, innovative and critical thinking skills, as well as school based curriculum development and school development planning are still a long way off.[4] While gains in school enrolment will continue in the coming years, formidable challenges remain wedged between the dual axis of economic development and cultural conservation.

Nomadic regions present the greatest challenge because of their remoteness and poverty levels. This is true of places like Nyerong, a 5000 metre high nomadic county in northern Tibet where households move from winter to summer pastures. The harsh weather (−32°C is common in winter) necessitates using yak dung to heat classrooms most of the year.[5] When the first community schools were established, the enrolment rate was 2%, rising to 11% in 1980. By 2007, most children attended school and 6 years of basic education is becoming the norm. This has been accomplished by consolidating nearly all of the village schools into seven township schools, led by a county seat primary and junior secondary school. Unqualified teachers were discontinued. Most qualified teachers are imported from other areas of Tibet, and 60 to 70% of them had attended boarding schools in urban China. Many students travel long distances and most live at school, a handicap for households that rely on children to tend herds of yak or sheep. By 2009, the county aims to reach 9 years of universal education and transit everyone to Chinese medium instruction in junior secondary school, despite a 99.9% Tibetan population.

Tibetans are challenged to adapt their cultural heritage so as to capitalize upon the national administration of schooling for their economic and social development (Postiglione 2007). One example of the conundrum faced in Tibetan education during the shift to a market economy concerns language education and the medium of school instruction. Although most primary schools still use Tibetan as a medium of instruction, Chinese is the language of secondary school and the ticket to nonfarm sector employment. This causes high dropout rates in junior secondary school, especially in poor rural and nomadic areas, and sharply decreases the learning potential of many students. Yet, there is an unmistakable vision that long-term survival entails gaining competency in three completely different languages: Tibetan, as the native language; Chinese, as the national language; and English as the international language. In the short term, competition for jobs in the non-farm sector has already led to a questioning of current language education policy. Rural and nomadic households generally see basic education as providing useful literacy in Tibetan, but little technical skill for competition in the non-farm labour market (Wang 2007).

Popularizing basic education in rural and nomadic regions of Tibet is a daunting task, even though major infrastructural developments have led to increased optimism. The Tibetan plateau has become more easily accessible by road, rail, and air, and telecommunication infrastructure has brought Tibet closer to the rest of China, as well as to the global village. On the one hand, schools have to develop the talents, expertise, values and leadership skills of all Tibetans so as to promote and sustain an adaptable, innovative, and globally conscious community. On the other hand, for most schools in Tibet, poverty dictates that the first priority is to ensure students' basic nutrition needs, health and safety, and in many cases, living accommodations, even before allocating resources to enhance the classroom learning environment. In short, the basic rudiments of basic education still require immediate attention.

Tibetans continue to face the question of how schools can become vibrant institutions within their communities, integrated with their values and traditions, yet functional to the household economy and a rise in their living standards. Cognizance among Tibetans about sustaining their natural and cultural resources is ubiquitous. Tibet's devoutly religious population and internationally popularized cultural traditions are legendary. Trilingual capacity, limited as it is to a tiny (but growing) number of young intellectuals, is impressive nonetheless, especially given that Tibetan, Chinese, and English are vastly different languages. As institutions of selective social and cultural reproduction, the complex role played by Tibetan schools will come to have a significant impact on the aspirations of a new generation of Tibetan youth.

Historical antecedents and education targets

Tibet's early period within the People's Republic of China saw the establishment of a government primary school in Lhasa in 1951 (Zhou 2002) at a time when the Seventeen Point agreement set out to maintain the spoken and written language in school education (Sino-Tibetan Agreement 1951). Beijing assumed responsibility for the management of Tibet in 1951. Monasteries remained the principal educational institutions until the fourteenth Dalai Lama fled during the uprising of 1959. He remains in exile (Goldstein 1989, 1997). Children of some elite families went for study in Beijing, while others studied in India (Mackerras 1994, 1995). After 1959 schools in Tibet began to pattern themselves after those in the rest of China (Nyima 1997, 2000; Mackerras 1999). During the Great Leap period, basic education was expanded rapidly though community (*minban*) schools. China's TAR was formally established in 1965, and land became redistributed and administered by People's Communes (Grunfeld 1996; Xia, Ha, and Abadu 1999). The Cultural Revolution wrought havoc and destruction on monasteries and schools, followed by an admission of errors by government. By 1978, with a loosening of restrictions on religion, many children studied at monasteries. Communes were abandoned in 1984[6] and the quality of schools improved, making them more attractive. However, as the household become the unit of production, children laboured more at home and attendance rates dropped (Bass 1998, 215). School enrolment rates stagnated before rising significantly in the 1990s, albeit accompanied by offsetting dropout rates at the upper grades of primary school (Xia, Ha and Abadu 1999).

Literacy rates and school access in Tibetan regions of China have continued to rise year by year. School and classroom conditions are far better than they were a decade ago.[7] The quality of teachers has inched ahead and more Tibetans are being admitted into secondary school and university. Yet, educational progress in Tibet has been far slower, and not nearly as impressive as in the rest of China, where the popularization of 9 years of compulsory education has been hailed internationally as a major success (Postiglione 2006). It would seem, then, that the basic education in Tibet should move into the fast lane of increased access. Yet, with only 7 years remaining for China to meet its international commitment to "Education for All", Tibet could be the spoiler unless its educational development shifts into overdrive between now and 2015 (UNESCO 2000).

Efforts have been focused on providing 3 years of education in pastoral/nomadic areas, 6 years in agricultural and semi-agricultural areas and 9 years in cities. By the end of the century there were over 800 primary schools enrolling more than 300,000 students and almost 80% of children were said to be entering school. The 94 high schools only enrolled about 40,000 and 13 technical schools enrolled about 3000 students. Teaching quality was upgraded to where about 70% of primary and junior secondary school teachers were said to be qualified to teach (Zhou 2002). By 2005, 68 counties were said to have achieved 6 years of basic education and 40 counties achieved 9 years (Ma 2005). More recent sources put the number of primary schools at 890 with an enrolment rate of 96% for school age children, and an increasing number of counties universalizing 9 years of compulsory education (i.e. 46 of 73 counties) (Zheng 2007).

Achieving these targets required a significant financial outlay. However, even if access targets, as measured by enrolment rates, move to within reach, meaningful access to high quality learning environments for all Tibetans will remain elusive for years to come.[8] Above all, quality education for Tibetans necessitates a serious effort and intensive focus on how Tibetans actually learn best.

Preferential education policies for Tibet

Aside from the huge financial outlay for basic education, school access targets in China's ethnic minority regions could not be achieved without additional policies designed for implementation in ethnic minority regions (Ha and Teng 2001). This is especially the case with respect to the TAR which promulgates its own specific educational measures to attain enrolment targets (TAR ERI 1999). For example, some county authorities instituted a system for school attendance reward points to be converted by households to cash at the end of the year (Postiglione, Ben Jiao and Gyatso 2006). Also, a small part of teacher salaries are withheld in some areas as an incentive for them to sustain attendance and promotion rates.

Such short-term measures vary from county to county but some policies are consistently applied throughout the TAR, including the three guarantees (*sanbao*), bilingual education, and the *neidi* Tibet schools (*Xizang neidiban*).[9]

The three guarantees

The "three guarantees" is specifically directed at enrolment rates in primary schools (Tongzhi 1994).[10] It includes measures designed to relieve families of costs associated with schooling. It makes provision for food, at least a tea drink during the daytime for children who live beyond 2 kilometres from school and tsampa (barley flour) and other foods for those who board at school. It also includes providing clothes, school wear in some cases, and a blanket at boarding school. The third guarantee is living quarters, since geography necessitates that most rural and nomadic children be accommodated at school beginning in upper primary and junior secondary school. On its own, the three guarantees are only partially effective, though probably more so than the non-attendance fines, something most poor households cannot afford to pay. The attendance reward point system is sometimes used to supplement the three guarantees and the compulsory education fine. Local officials often plead with village and township parents to send at least one or more children to school.[11] When attendance rates are low at junior secondary school, county officials sometimes visit schools to interview household heads at the school about their children's nonattendance. Rural and semi-nomadic households are often under great strain to arrange grazing for their livestock and to ensure that their livestock remain within particular areas or risk sanctions. Some communities have tried a rotating system of joint household responsibility for grazing livestock so that more children could attend school, with mixed success. In short, the three guarantees is an essential policy. But, without other measures, it is only partially effective in popularizing basic education.

Other problems with the three guarantees include the quality of accommodation[s] and food. Poor construction of dormitory buildings raises safety concerns and winter conditions make it difficult for those schools without electricity to provide light for evening study.[12] Food provisions are usually meagre and require households to supplement what schools provide. Research in western regions of China by Hannum and others points to the importance of health and nutrition for both attendance and learning quality (Yu and Hannum 2006).[13] Another minor measure accommodates the demands of the harvest seasons, as a head of a township primary school explained: "In the busy spring and winter seasons, we use a '*xunhuo*' measure, which means that the school is called off and students are sent home to help with planting or harvesting. However, this period cannot go beyond seven days."[14] In recent years as the price of winter fungus has sky-rocketed throughout China, school attendance in many Tibetan areas has dropped. Winter fungus is sold as a medical herb and is harvested in late spring/early summer. Many children leave school for up to a month.[15] A school head in a nomadic region remarked in June of 2007 that all children had been absent during the previous month to gather winter fungus with their families, but they would be back at school soon in order to sit for the region wide examination for placement to secondary school.

The extent and manner in which the three guarantees are implemented remains a subject in need of further study. Although there has been increased transparency about the use of funds, with some schools displaying the accounting details on a centrally located bulletin board, the extent to which it can offset household hardships varies from place to place. Nevertheless, it remains an indispensable measure, especially within the scheme of other development and infrastructural costs. It is not unusual in interviews with some village or township heads that topics relating to land and livestock, herding and health care, generate much more enthusiasm than those relating to education. When questions about schools, teaching methods, and learning materials arise, interest levels plateau. Officials follow directives from above but from their purview, there are many pressing nonschool related matters in their day to day administrative business. The school is often the only visible physical structure of state presence in a village and its function in the eyes of household heads may vary. Promotion of children to a far away county secondary school is viewed as worthwhile by some families, but many see the small yields and counterproductive aspects because children may return without knowledge and skills relevant to rural life or become detrimentally influenced by urban youth.

Also, the length of junior secondary school for rural and nomadic areas has been 4 years instead of the standard 3 years, since students must spend a remedial year improving their Chinese in preparation for the switch to Chinese medium instruction. This unpopular measure of attending for an extra year is being discontinued. In some cases, promotion to junior secondary school may lead to placement in a *neidi* or dislocated secondary schools – a Chinese style boarding school in an urban centre far from Tibet. Being tracked into the *neidi* school requires a high examination score but is an attractive proposition from the point of view of an increasing number of parents because it virtually guarantees a good jobs upon return to Tibet, (though local TAR secondary school heads are not always in favour of *neidi* schools since they draw away the best talent from Tibet).

Ethnic identity issues are naturally less salient in poor rural and nomadic areas where there is little exposure as yet to other ethnic groups and school instruction is conducted in Tibetan. Moreover, the struggles of day to day life in most households, struggles similar to life among poor rural and nomadic people anywhere on the globe, take priority over questions of ethnic identity. This changes slightly when children enter junior secondary school, where Chinese is the medium of instruction and students have several non-Tibetan teachers.

Medium of instruction

The medium of instruction policy for Tibet remains a key issue. It relates closely to both learning capacity and ethnic identity (Postiglione 1999, 2001; Zhou and Fishman 2003; Zhou and Sun 2004). Unlike many indigenous ethnic minorities in the developing world, Tibetans have had a highly sophisticated written script for over a thousand years (Chodag 1988; N.A. 2005). Originated during the reign of Songsten Gampo in the sixth century, this script was developed over the next fourteen centuries in an area that came to extend as wide as the continental US (Goldstein 1989; Iredale et al. 2001). As compulsory state schooling has taken hold in Tibetan communities, medium of instruction policy has become a focus of some debate, as it is also in other parts of China's ethnic minority regions (Yu 1995; Stites 1999; Zheng 2002; Lam 2005). This is even more relevant to Tibetan secondary schooling, since most primary schooling in the TAR is still conducted through Tibetan (N.A. 2005). The next decade will be important because it may come to mark the first time that all children in Tibet are exposed to state schooling for 6 years. Therefore, as the focus moves from school access to learning quality, the medium of instruction will probably remain the most critical issue facing the education of Tibetans in China. There are many multilingual places in the world where the medium of instruction becomes an emotive and politicized issue and the same is the case for Tibetan regions (Nyima 1997; Bass 1998; Upton 1999). As Upton has noted few Tibetans advocate not learning any Chinese. Most agree that Chinese is needed to ensure survival in a market economy since it broadens access to non-farm occupation. Dual track education (Tibetan and Chinese) is generally available in the urban areas, but after the primary school grade three, there is a shift toward Chinese as the medium of instruction, with only language and literature courses taught in the Tibetan language (Postiglione 1997; Pingcuo 2005).

From an educational point of view, unless a student has achieved a threshold level of competency in the second language, its use as a medium of instruction can severely limit the potential for academic success and can lead to other deleterious effects noted by sociologists of education. While many parents may be in favour of Chinese as a medium of instruction due to its currency in the job market, they may not be aware of the countless studies showing that students do not learn well unless they have achieved a level of competency in the second language so as to be able to learn school subjects effectively (Baker 2001; Street 2001). In short, learning should take priority in schooling and while the national language must be studied, it is the responsibility of the school that students learn in the most efficient manner, whether that is in the national language or the language of Tibet (Dai et al. 1997; Zhou 2000). Moreover, students may have a sufficient level of competency in Chinese for effective learning, but unless their teachers are able to teach competently through Chinese, student learning will be affected. In many nomadic counties, there is a shortage of Chinese language specialists, in which case teachers of other subjects who are unqualified as language teachers, will take on the role of teaching Chinese as a subject.[16] In short, the notably low achievement level in education for Tibetans has a great deal to do with the language policy. School achievement statistics for Tibet are not always listed in tables with other provinces due to the significant gap. This keeps Tibetans labelled as bottom achievers in China, with the unintended effect of strengthening Tibetan identity.

While TAR secondary schools use Chinese as the medium of instruction, many secondary schools in Qinghai province, bordering the TAR, use Tibetan for school subjects (science, math, history, etc.) up through senior middle school. Experiments in the TAR that use Tibetan as the language of instruction for science and mathematics subjects have yielded successful results. There are advocates of Tibetan as a language of science and modernity, as well as a means of raising achievement scores since students will learn more efficiently and then can perform better on college and university entrance examinations. This is fraught with some risk however, as proponents of Tibetan medium instruction may be labelled as separatists. China has done a great deal to produce school textbooks in ethnic minority languages, including Tibetan and about 21 other languages. The five province/region Tibetan learning materials leadership group has facilitated the production of Tibetan language learning resources and has visited other countries to learn about how bilingual education is undertaken elsewhere. However, the Tibetan language school textbooks in mathematics, science and other subjects are often direct translations of Chinese language materials. Moreover, the updating of Tibetan language textbooks is slow and costly. Meanwhile, Tibetan medium of instruction is often viewed as a hindrance to advancement as TAR secondary school graduates soon discover when they have to compete for jobs with the thousands of TAR students returning with good grasp of Chinese from 7 years at *neidi* schools. The *neidi* schools add more complexity to the issue of language education as well shall see later.

Dislocated education

The third major policy with significant implications for rural education in the TAR is the *neidi xizang ban* (inland Tibet secondary schools and classes) or dislocated schools, which send primary school graduates to secondary schools across China (Postiglione, Zhu and Ben Jiao 2004; Zhu 2007). These schools are special for several reasons: first, they take the best and brightest away from Tibet's education system and send them to cities across China for up to 7 years. Second, the graduates return to Tibet for government jobs ranging from school teachers to government officials. Third, given that few Chinese have learned to speak Tibetan, and few Tibetans have lived in China, these bilingual youth are well suited to be cultural middlemen/women between Tibet and the rest of China. The form and content of their education represents the kind that the state would like to be the norm for Tibetans, and the increasing demand on the part of parents for these schools ensures that the *neidi* education policy will continue indefinitely, despite its stratifying effect upon Tibetan society. While school resources and the quality of teachers in Tibet continue to improve, top students are removed in large numbers and sent to study in China.

The call for Chinese cities to establish schools and classes for Tibetans began in 1981 by Central government leaders Hu Qili and Tian Jiyun.[17] Beijing, Lanzhou and Chengdu established such schools in 1985, and were followed by Shanghai, Tianjin, Liaoning, Hebei, Henan, Shandong, Jiangsu, Shanxi,

Hubei, Chongqing, Anhui, Shanxi, Hunan, Zhejiang, Jiangxi and Yunnan; in all 16 provinces and cities had them by September 1986, with the financial responsibility shared by the TAR and host city. In 1990 President Jiang Zemin declared that these schools help Tibetans to understand the motherland, and broaden their view of the world, echoing Hu Qili's statement in 1986 that *neidi* schools be a 10 to 20 year strategy. The Tibet *neidi* schools policy was viewed as so successful that in 1999, it was extended to cover students from another far western provincial level entity – the Xinjiang Uyghur Nationality Autonomous Region (Chen 2005).

From 1985 to 2005, more than 25,000 primary graduates were selected and sent to study in these schools to study in secondary schools in different provinces and municipalities of China in 20 provinces and municipal cities (Pingcuo 2005). In 2006, there are 28 junior and senior middle schools and teacher training schools which have inland Tibetan classes. More than 90 universities or post-secondary institutions have admitted Tibetan students. In the first 20 years, the Central government has invested 180.5 million RMB and regional governments have invested 500 million RMB into these inland Tibetan class projects (N.A. 2007).[18] It should also be noted that the provinces and municipalities of China send thousands of teachers and educational officials to Tibet. However, most stay for a few years at most, find life at county level an adjustment, and view students as being slower and more difficult to teach than those in China.

In the early years of the *neidi* school policy, most schools were junior secondary schools.[19] These schools had a 4 year programme that included a preparatory year for improving Chinese language skills before embarking on the national standard 3 year junior secondary school curriculum. The schools also contract a teacher from Tibet to teach Tibetan language and literature. In later years, some schools expanded to include senior secondary school. Others converted from a junior to senior secondary school and recruited from *neidi* junior secondary schools. In the early years, most graduates of the junior secondary schools returned to Tibet for summer and then went back to China for 3 years of specially arranged vocational technical education before returning to Tibet. However, over the years, more and more junior secondary school graduates went on to senior secondary schools in China before they returned to Tibet. This transition to academic senior secondary schooling has opened the door for Tibetans to enter universities in China. However, many enter with the aid of preferential policies, that specifically make places available to Tibet *neidi* school graduates. While most students enter *neidi* schools at 11 years old; if they remain there for 7 years of secondary schooling and then go on to university, including a remedial year, this means that many Tibetan students spend 11 or 12 years in China with only about three summer visits home.

Most schools, if not classes, are ethnically segregated.[20] Tibetan students do not study with students of Han or other ethnic groups, unless they happen to be from Tibet, and only a tiny number are, usually of mixed marriages. There is some organized contact in sports and cultural events with Chinese students from urban schools in the vicinity. Tibetan New Year is observed with special foods and visits from Tibetan leaders.

Not unlike boarding schools for children in other parts of the world, the schools place a great emphasis on discipline, with a teacher being assigned for dormitory work.[21] Students are not permitted to leave the grounds except for a few supervised hours shopping on a Sunday. All teachers (except one or two Tibetan teachers for Tibetan language and literature courses) are local Han Chinese. Few if any have visited Tibet. The campus usually has symbols of Tibet, including murals, ceramics, statues, photos, etc. Dormitory rooms have phones and children can call home but the cost is not covered by the school. The cell phone phenomenon is new and will probably increase contact with parents, though reception in many rural and nomadic areas of Tibet is still not possible.

Of primary school graduates who enrol in *neidi* education, about three quarters come from Tibetan medium schools and the rest from Chinese medium schools. According to Zhou (2003), 16% of the TAR population is urban and many of their residents are either bilingual or have achieved bi-literacy in Tibetan and Chinese. The other 84% of the population are rural or nomadic, and hence are usually only speakers of Tibetan. By 1999, more than 95% of the primary schools in the TAR were using Tibetan as the medium of instruction. However, only 13% of secondary school students and 5% of senior secondary school students were attending classes that use Tibetan as the medium of instruction.

While the early cohorts were dominated by urban children of cadre families, the authorities aimed to shift enrolments in favour of children from rural and nomadic families. However, the ratio of rural and nomadic children still does not reflect that in the general population. Students are selected on the basis of examinations, according to quotas set for each region of Tibet. Host *neidi* schools are paired with specific districts in Tibet for student selection. The study programme, curriculum, subject teachers and fees are handled by each *neidi* school. Over time, more *neidi* schools were added, selection quotas were modified, and rural and nomadic student enrolments increased. Partnerships between the host *neidi* city and TAR districts were adjusted, and students who scored below the cut-off could be recruited as self-paying students. Eventually, the cost of air and/or train fares from Tibet to the *neidi* school were passed on from government to household. Finally, the proportion of students attending regular senior secondary *neidi* schools and going on to college and university rose with massification of higher education.

My research based on oral histories of *neidi* school graduates makes it clear that these dislocated Chinese boarding schools do not conform to the stereotype of institutions to unmake ethnic minorities (Spack 2002). While there is a strict separation between religious and the state education, the schools themselves have not been used to de-culturate by prohibiting the use of native language and the erasure of students' cultural memories. Tibetan families are not coerced to send their children to the *neidi* schools. Moreover, many families whose children fail to score high enough to gain entrance to these schools will pay the extra fee to get them admitted. Still others send their children to the growing number of private (*minban*) secondary schools in China, Chengdu in particular.

The stated mission of the *neidi* schools is not explicitly to civilize the Tibetans. However, Tibetan culture, though celebrated throughout China, especially in its popular media, is defined by the state schools. Unlike many other twentieth century boarding schools for indigenous peoples in other countries, the *neidi* schools for Tibetan students offer classes about ethnic language, and literature. Moreover, the school environment recognizes Tibetan culture through its many representations of art and architecture, music and observance of Tibetan holidays. Behaviour is not controlled through corporal punishment and it is not used if students speak Tibetan while inside or outside of the school. Nearly all students speak of the close relationship they had with their Han Chinese teachers. Discipline rather than fear is the norm shaping behaviour, though the schools also make use of ample reference to moral and political education curriculum, school rituals and teacher modelling to shape behaviour. Communication with students' Tibetan home is not cut-off by school authorities. Parents are permitted to visit and a small but growing number do visit the schools, though for most the travel costs are prohibitive.[22]

From the perspective of most students attending the *neidi* schools, adjustment was relatively rapid though climatic and food changes required some adaptation time. Many were in awe of the contrast in economic conditions between Tibet and the urban China. A major challenge for them was Chinese medium instruction, for which most experienced difficulty. It was common instructional practice to require students to keep a diary in Chinese about their daily activities. At the same time, students also study Tibetan language and literature as a school subject at junior secondary school level. Among students, the use of Tibetan on campus is complicated by the Tibetan regional dialects. At junior secondary school, students from different dialect areas often use the majority dialect, usually the Lhasa dialect. After their Chinese improves, especially at senior secondary level, more Chinese is used among students for communication. English is also a required subject in the curriculum. However, the greater emphasis on the study of Chinese and other subjects outweighed the study of Tibetan and English. Attention to the study of Tibetan wanes in senior secondary school as students prepared for the national entrance examination for college and university.

Students who graduate from the Chinese boarding schools generally feel that they learned to become more independent and self-reliant than their counterparts who stayed in Tibet. They also remark positively about teaching methods used. Their employers, many of whom are school heads, comment positively about the capabilities of the *neidi* school graduates, even while being ambivalent about the inland school policy. School heads perceived the *neidi* schools as drawing the best students away from their schools and returning them as teachers who could not teach effectively through Tibetan. *Neidi* school graduates' Chinese language skills were naturally better than their counterparts. However, culturally, students do say that they generally needed months or years to readapt to Tibet, after which they felt no cultural gap between themselves and other Tibetans. Among the cohorts we interviewed, all wanted to return to Tibet after graduation. Of those interviewed, only a few expressed a wish to remain in China, though these few also returned to Tibet. Some considered further education and would be willing to return to China for such study. Nevertheless, staying in China for work was not an option. The intention of the *neidi* school policy is that students return to help Tibet's development. However, enforcement of this policy would be difficult. Many students return to be with their families but many also return because to remain in China would require employment opportunities for them that do not exist, as well as a supportive Tibetan community. Thus, the only way to remain in urban China is to attend university. The irony is that while Tibetans are competing for jobs in Tibet with outsiders (*waidi ren*) from other provinces, they are not prepared to compete for viable jobs in Chinese cities where they are educated. Considering the difficulty of competing for jobs with the migrants coming to Tibet from other parts of China, finding viable employment in Chinese cities, despite having spent up to 7 years there, was not an option. Moreover, the disintegration of the centrally planned job allocation system in favour of market forces has left an increasing number of graduates without jobs. Yet, the high demand for school teachers in rural and nomadic area primary schools of Tibet has virtually guaranteed jobs to *neidi* school graduates. School teaching and security jobs remain among the last protected areas of the guaranteed job allocation system, something which also helps the popularity of the *neidi* schools.

Remaining in China for several years of work after completing studies there could be considered akin to what Chinese students do after completing their studies overseas, where few Tibetans get to go due partly to their triple language burden. Arrangements could be made for Tibetans to return to China for work experience with a salary, or even to teach at a *neidi ban* school after graduation from university. However, these *neidi* graduates are viewed as playing a key role in Tibet for skills transmission, political stability, and as cultural middlemen. Therefore, there is little incentive at present for such arrangements.[23]

The result of the *neidi* school policy has also been the deterioration of Tibetan language skills among the graduates (Postiglione, Ben Jiao and Manlaji 2007). After returning to Tibet, not all need to use Tibetan as a working language, but those who work in the countryside or teach at school do face challenges to be effective. The *neidi* school graduates realize the importance of Tibetan language and literature in their work environment and in their understanding of their native culture. Most expressed regret about not learning Tibetan well, and not knowing enough about Tibetan culture and history. Schools in the TAR may not have done much better in teaching about Tibetan history and culture, yet the Tibetan language skills of their students were far superior. *Neidi* school students undoubtedly had a greater sensitivity, having lived and studied for several years within a Chinese boarding school that emphasized the language and cultural heritage of Han China.

In short, the *neidi* school policy, which indirectly reinforces a Tibetan identity, does not yet foster the confidence necessary for graduates to compete successfully in a market economy for work outside of Tibetan communities in China or elsewhere. Within Tibet, a *neidi* school education does lead them to government posts and teaching positions in schools. Moreover, their work units comment quite positively on their performance, except in the area of Tibetan language skills which are seldom, if ever, outstanding. They are more comfortable than other TAR graduates in a multicultural environment, having not only first hand experience living and studying in urban China, but also having contact with classmates from different regions of Tibet. They express an independence, self-reliance, and leadership capability that elaborates their Tibetan identity and makes them more able to adapt to multiple roles and situations. In this sense, the *neidi* schools have the potential to promote a harmonious multiculturalism in Tibet. Yet, this is undercut by their perceived inadequate knowledge of Tibetan language and cultural heritage.

With half of China's land mass composed of ethnic minority autonomous regions, the role of education in fostering cross-cultural understandings for harmonious ethnic intergroup relations can hardly be underestimated. This underlines the importance of not only access to school but also to more multicultural curriculum that will keep China from being a plurality of separate cultures that are inward looking.

Neidi school graduates need not only be provided with preferential treatment to enter universities in China but also encouraged to study overseas in greater numbers with their Han Chinese counterparts. Moreover, those in Tibet who fail to enter *neidi* schools need to be given opportunities to study for at least some period of time in other parts of China, including the Special Administrative Regions of Hong Kong and Macao, in order to broaden their understanding of China and the world. This approach resonates with China's emergent global influence. This will also work to moderate the social stratification resulting from the structured inequality in Tibet's education system with *neidi* school graduates' self-paying elite status among graduates of TAR schools.

Education, harmonious society and Tibetan civilization

The heart of the matter of education for Tibetans lies in the improvement of access to quality education for sustainable development of social, cultural, and economic resources. At the very least, quality education is about learning how to read, write, and communicate; how to perceive, plan, act, and innovate; how to think critically and creatively; how to learn how to learn, how to be confident, engaged, and effectively committed to community development. It means developing a disposition conducive to making the community more effectively integrated into the larger regional, national, and global scene. In short, addressing the challenge of providing access to a quality education for Tibetans may well be inseparable from how to mobilize the community around the transmission of relevant knowledge and skills, while building capacity for adapting new knowledge to a rapidly changing environment. In order to move ahead in Tibet, the student has to move from the periphery to the core of the classroom equation.

The issue of Tibetan cultural vitality has been considered from many perspectives and remains an area of concern. Therefore, improving access to quality education would also include being sensitive to how Tibetan children change and adapt themselves to school, how values are defined and transmitted, what educational/learning environments are provided for ethnic identity construction, and how governance models in Tibetan regions support the localization of selected parts of the school curriculum. For Tibetans to capitalize upon increased educational opportunity, it may be necessary to bring school curriculum closer to community needs, strengthen the capacity of teachers to develop school based curriculum, involve more stakeholders in school governance, and make learning more Tibetan in character by exposing the myth of Tibetan cultural backwardness.

Anyone doing research on ethnic minority education in China cannot help being exposed to this notion of cultural backwardness as the principal reason for under-achievement in education (Harrell 2001). This is a curious point anywhere in the world and has been alluded to in other cultural contexts by Amartya Sen, specifically in a reference to the nineteenth century British view of poverty in Ireland:

> While poverty in Britain was typically attributed to economic changes and fluctuations, Irish poverty was widely viewed in England as being caused by laziness, indifference and ineptitude, so that Britain's mission was not seen as one "to alleviate Irish distress but to civilize her people and to lead them to feel and act like human beings."
>
> (Sen 2006, 105)

That Ireland is now richer in per capita income than nearly every country in Europe pushes the imagination about Tibet's future, especially given its geographical location where it can increasingly benefit from the rise of the two emergent global economic giants.

Nevertheless, the scholarship on civilizing discourse can place too much stress on the correspondence between state mission and cultural outcomes. More emphasis could be placed instead on the responses to the civilizing mission, as well as context factors including the shift from a planned to a market economy, generational changes, expanding information access in Tibet, and China's economic globalization. The civilizing mission has for half a century been a layer of discourse but it has not diminished Tibetan identity. Pluralism is as important as harmony in conceptualizing ethnic intergroup processes in Tibet. It has been the source of much cultural vitality throughout China's history, though not as conflict free as portrayed, as in the case of the Mongol and Manchu Eras when intergroup processes included both harmonious acculturation and conflict prone impact integration. One educational issue, then, is how to situate the autonomy of Tibetan cultural transmission within the national context. The practical challenge is how to make schooling work in a way that brings Tibetan culture into

108 *Cultural processes*

the national and global/international spheres with the least amount of dislocation as the larger community benefits from not only its economic resources but equally from its autonomous cultural perspectives.

Cultural diversity in China rivals that anywhere else in the world. This is not to say that multi-ethnic diversity is strongly encouraged, only that is it increasingly salient and widely recognized. While ethnic minority culture is celebrated, ethnic diversity is managed. The "harmonious society" campaign prescribes Chinese ethnicity as "plurality within the organic unity of the Chinese nation" (*duoyuan yiti geju*) (Fei 1986).[24] Yet, there is no question that a more open attitude toward education for cultural diversity has taken place in some ethnic minority areas of China (Yu 2007). Given that Tibet is the most remote and ethnically homogenous of China's five major provincial level autonomous regions, future developments could have national implications for the way that ethnic intergroup processes are conceptualized in a more globally integrated China. The debate over cultural preservation, ethnic autonomy, and state schooling remains complex. As Appiah points out in his work on the ethics of identity, "We must help children to make themselves: and we have to do so according to our values because children do not begin with values of their own" (Appiah 2005, 137). Making Tibetans within China is an educational task that remains a work in progress. This debate cannot remain disconnected from strategies for the improvement of the learning environment and academic achievement of Tibetans. In searching for reasons why Tibetan educational achievement levels are far behind those in the rest of the country, a variety of perspectives are available but new thinking about a well resourced and community driven learning environment for schools is a natural step forward.

Acknowledgements

This paper acknowledges the financial support of the Hong Kong Research Grants Council under grants project codes: HKU 7191/02H and HKU 7194/98H. Appreciation goes to the Wah Ching Centre of Research on Education in China, which I had the honour of directing at the University of Hong Kong for many years. I also express appreciation to the Centre of Contemporary Tibet Studies of the Tibet Academy of Social Science. In particular, thanks to Ngawang Tsering, Ben Jiao and Sonam Gyatso. I am grateful to Professor Melvyn C. Goldstein for his inspirational scholarship and insights about Tibetan culture and history; his suggestions on research methodology have been greatly appreciated. Any errors in this manuscript are mine alone.

Notes

1. In this paper, by Tibet it is meant the Tibetan Autonomous Region (TAR) of the People's Republic of China. The TAR is often referred to as "political Tibet", as distinguished from "ethnic Tibet", a much larger region that includes not only the TAR but also the Tibetan areas of the four adjacent Chinese provinces of Qinghai, Sichuan, Yunnan, and Gansu.

2 This may explain why much empirical research appearing in English is often by Tibetans themselves, or by long-term foreign experts in development projects who have lived and worked in Tibetan regions for a decade or more.
3 The other two officially designated ethnic groups in Tibet are the Moinba and Luoba, though there is some debate as to how they differ from Tibetans.
4 Field notes from visits to rural and nomadic schools from 1997 to 2007.
5 Field notes 26 August 2007; even the county seat school does not have a modern heating system.
6 To this day, one commune still exists in the TAR.
7 Field notes from visits to rural and nomadic schools from 1997 to 2007.
8 At the moment, the education discourse is dominated by the school for jobs paradigm. However, the urgent educational challenge also lies with access to relevant knowledge, integrated community development, cultural vitality, economic alternatives, and more recently, environmental preservation.
9 There has been a great deal of confusion about the translation of *Xizang neidiban* from Chinese to English. The government's former translation of "Tibet Inland Schools and Classes" could give the impression that these schools and classes are held within Tibet. A more recent government translation is Hinterland Schools. In actuality, the *Xizang neidiban* are largely located in major Chinese cities and are basically Chinese Boarding Schools, thus the more English translation would be dislocated schools.
10 The three guarantees, a policy that was discontinued for a short time in the 1990s, still constitutes a major pillar of educational reform in Tibet. Without it, rates would drop drastically.
11 For example, I was at Sokang school on 1 and 2 September 2001 when Penam county and local officials, 12 in all, met 100 Mag villagers, one household head at a time, to discuss why all of their children were not attending school.
12 Field notes from visits to rural and nomadic boarding schools.
13 In the 1990s, I visited many schools without electricity of any kind, but remote schools increasingly have light bulbs for classrooms, the main educational technology aside from a blackboard that is sometimes bereft of chalk. A wood or coal stove in the middle of the classroom is not uncommon.
14 Rural school head, Penam county, May, 1999.
15 Field notes, 15 June 2007.
16 Interview with county education official and secondary school head, 26 August 2007.
17 The leaders usually address the national meetings concerning Tibet development and education, of which there are three types. One type is initiated by the Secretariat of Central Committee of the Communist Party of China. It is called the "Tibet Work Forum", and has been convened four times in 1980, 1984, 1994 and 2001, respectively. The second type is organized by the State Council of China. It is called "The Second Support to Tibet Conference" held in 1987 and focuses on education. The third type is convened by the Education Ministry and conducted by the State Council of China. In 1993 this forum was named "Support Education in Tibet". All of these emphasize the importance of education in the development of Tibet and propose strategies on education. See F.T. Ying (1984).
18 "Concerning Attaining the Target of the Formation of Interior Region Tibetan Schools and Classes for Cultivating Talented Students", Central Government Document Number 22 of 1984; and, "Circular Concerning Attaining the Central Implementation Target of Cultivating Tibetan Talent in the Interior Regions", Document Number 25 of 1984.
19 At least 18 of the schools were junior secondary schools, though only three (Beijing, Chengdu and Tianjin) had junior and senior secondary levels.
20 The majority of the Tibetan students attend segregated classes in *neidi* schools, though there has been some experimentation. Small numbers of academically superior

students were sent to neighbouring schools to study in integrated classes with Han Chinese students. While this is viewed as a positive step toward mainstreaming, it is also seen by neidiban school heads as draining off the best talent from the *neidi* school (which in turn takes top students away from TAR schools).
21 Some Tibetan teachers of language and language and literature, and some management personnel were also sent to the neidiban.
22 Field notes from fieldwork visits to three schools in Beijing, Chengdu and Wuhan.
23 The case is different for the inland (*neidi*) school students from Xinjiang since Uygurs have well established networks based on trading and religious links with other Muslim minorities, especially Hui who have an urban presence throughout China.
24 There are various translations, including "plurality and unity within the configuration of the Chinese nationality". In general, however, this is considered by many scholars as a straight-line assimilation theory.

References

Appiah, K.A. 2005. *The ethnics of identity*. Princeton, NJ: Princeton University Press.
Baker, C. 2001. *Foundations of bilingual education and bilingualism*. 3rd ed. Buffalo, NY: Multilingual Matters.
Bass, C. 1998. *Education in Tibet: policy and practice since 1950*. London: Zed Books.
Chen, Y.B. 2005. *Uyghur students in a Chinese boarding school: social recapitalisation as a response to ethnic integration*. PhD diss., Faculty of Education, University of Hong Kong.
Chodag, Tiley. 1988. *Tibet: the land and people*. Beijing: New World Press.
Dai, Q.J., X. Teng, X.Q. Guan, and Y. Dong. 1997. *Zhongguo shaoshu minzu shuangyu jiaoyu gailun* [Introduction to bilingual education for China's minorities]. Liaoning: Nationalities Press.
Dorjee, Tenzin, and H. Giles. 2005. Cultural identity in Tibetan diasporas. *Journal of Multilingual and Multicultural Development* 26, no. 2: 138–57.
Fei, X.T. 1986. Zhonghua minzu de duoyuan yiti geju [Plurality within the organic unity of the Chinese nation] *Beijing daxue xuebao* [*Journal of Beijing University*] 4: 1–19.
Geng, J.S., and X.H. Wang, eds. 1989. *Xizang jiaoyu yanjiu* [Research on education in Tibet]. Beijing: Zhongyang minzu xueyuan chubanshe [China Nationalities Institute Press].
Goldstein, M.C. 1989. *A history of modern Tibet, 1913–1951: the demise of the Lamaist state*. Berkeley, CA: University of California Press.
———. 1997. *The snow lion and the dragon: China, Tibet, and the Dalai Lama*. Los Angeles, CA: University of California Press.
Goldstein, M.C., Ben Jiao, C.M. Beall, and Phuntsog Tsering. 2003. Development and change in rural Tibet: problems and adaptations. *Asian Survey* 43, no. 5: 758–79.
Grunfeld, T. 1996. *The making of modern Tibet*. East Gate rev. ed. New York: M.E. Sharpe.
Ha, J., and X. Teng. 2001. *Minzu jiaoyu xue tonglun* [A general survey of ethnic minority education]. Beijing: Jiaoyu kexue chubanshe [Educational Science Publishing House].
Harrell, S. 2001. *Ways of being ethnic in southwest China*. Seattle, WA: University of Washington Press.
Iredale, R., N. Bilik, W. Su, F. Guo, and C. Hoy, eds. 2001. *Contemporary minority migration, education and ethnicity*, 139. Cheltenham: Edward Elgar.

Lam, A. 2005. *Language education in China*. Hong Kong: Hong Kong University Press.
Ma, E.J. 2005. Zhonggong Xizang zizhichu jiaoyu gongzuo weiyuanhui 2005 gongzuo baogao [Work meeting report on education in the Tibetan Autonomous Region of China 2005]. *Xizang jiaoyu* [*Tibet education*] 12: 3–6.
Mackerras, Colin. 1994. *China's minorities: integration and modernisation in the 21st century*. Hong Kong: Oxford University Press.
———. 1995. *China's minority cultures: identities and integration since 1912*. New York: St Martin's Press.
Mackerras, C. 1999. Religion and the education of China's minorities. In *China's national minority education: culture, schooling and development*, ed. G. Postiglione, 23–54. New York: Falmer Press.
Mac Pherson, S., and Dawa Bhuti. 2007. Multilingualism in diaspora networks: The case of Tibetan female youths in Toronto, Canada. Paper presented at the annual meeting of the American Educational Research Association, April, in Chicago, IL.
N.A. 2005. Xizang shuangyu jiaoyu qingkuang [The bilingual education situation in Tibet]. In *Yuyong wenzi gongzuo jianbao* [*Language planning and administration work newsletter*], 151. http://202.205.177.129/moe-dept/yuyong/jianbao/151.htm.
———. 2006. *Zhongguo jiaoyu tongji nianjian 2005* [*Statistics on education in China*]. Beijing: People's Education Press.
———. 2007. Fourteen thousand talents were nurtured by the inland Tibetan classes in the past 20 years. *Xizang* ribao [*Tibet Daily*]. January 29.
Nyima, Palden (Nima, Baden). 1997. The way out for Tibetan education. *Chinese Education and Society* 30, no. 4: 7–20.
Nyima, Palden. 2000. *Wenming de kunhuo: Zangzu de jiaoyu zhilu* [*The puzzle of civilisation: the way out for Tibetan education*]. Chengdu: Sichuan Education Press.
Pingcuo, Xiangba. 2005. *Xizang zizhiqu jiaoyu zhi* [*Education annals of the Tibetan Autonomous Region*]. Beijing: China Tibetology Press.
Postiglione, G. ed. 1997. The schooling of Tibetans (I) & (II). *Chinese Education and Society* 30, nos. 4–5.
———. ed. 1999. *China's national minority education: culture, schooling and development*. New York: Falmer Press.
———. ed. 2001. Bilingual education in China. *Chinese Education and Society* 34: 2.
———. ed. 2006. *Education and social change in China: inequality in a market economy*. New York: M.E. Sharpe.
———. 2007. School access in rural Tibet. In *Education and reform in China*, ed. E. Hannum and A. Park. New York: Routledge.
Postiglione, G., Z.Y. Zhu, and Ben Jiao. 2004. From ethnic segregation to impact integration: State schooling and identity construction for rural Tibetans. *Asian Ethnicity* 5, no. 2: 195–217.
Postiglione, G., Ben Jiao, and Sonam Gyatso. 2005. Education in rural Tibet: development, problems, and adaptations. *China: An International Journal* 3, no. 1: 1–23.
———. 2006. Household perspectives on school attendance in rural Tibet. *Educational Review* 58, no. 3: 317–37.
Postiglione, G., Ben Jiao, and 2007. Language in Tibetan education. In *Bilingual education in China: practices, policies and concepts*, ed. A.W. Feng. New York: Multilingual Matters.
Sautman, B., and J.T. Dreyer. 2005. *Contemporary Tibet: politics, development, and society in a disputed region*. New York: M.E. Sharpe.

Sen, A. 2006. *Identity and violence: the illusion of destiny*. New York: W.W. Norton and Company.
Sino-Tibetan Agreement. 1951 reprinted in Pradyumna P. Karan, *The changing face of Tibet*, 89–91. Lexington, KY: The University Press of Kentucky, 1976. http://www.mtholyoke.edu/acad/intrel/sintibet.htm (accessed 10 August 2007).
Spack, R. 2002. *America's second tongue: American Indian education and the ownership of English, 1960–1900*. Lincoln, NB: University of Nebraska Press.
Stites, R. 1999. Writing cultural boundaries: national minority language policy, literacy planning, and bilingual education. In *China's national minority education*, ed. G. Postiglione, 95–130. New York: Falmer Press.
Street, B. ed. 2001. *Literacy and development: ethnographic perspectives*. London: Routledge.
Tibetan Autonomous Region Education Research Institute (TAR ERI). 1999. *Zizang zizhiqu jiaoyu falu fagui xuanbian [A collection of educational guidelines and regulations of the Tibetan Autonomous Region]*. Lhasa: Tibet People's Press.
Tongzhi. 1994. Approved regulations concerning our region's provision of the 'three guarantees'. In *Zizang zizhiqu jiaoyu falu fagui xuanbian [A collection of educational guidelines and regulations of the Tibetan Autonomous Region]*. ed. Tibetan Autonomous Region Education Research Institute, 424–7. Lhasa: Tibet People's Press.
UNESCO. 2000. *Education for all: the year 2000 assessment final country report of China*. cited as EFA 2000 Country Report of China, Section 3.3.3. http://www.2.unesco.org/wef/countryreports/china/contents.html.
Upton, J. 1999. The development of modern school based language education in the PRC. In *China's national minority education: culture, schooling, and development*, ed. G. Postiglione, 281–342. New York: Falmer Press.
Wang, C.J., and Q.H. Zhou. 2003. Minority education in China: from state preferential policies to dislocated Tibetan schools. *Educational Studies* 29, no. 1.
Wang, S.L., and J.W. Lou. 2007. *Public finance in China: reform and growth for a harmonious society*. Washington, DC: World Bank.
Wang, S.Y. 2007. The failure of education in preparing Tibetans for market participation. *Asian Ethnicity* 8, no. 2: 131–48.
Wu, D.G. 1995. *Zhongguo Xizang jiaoyu gaige yu fazhan de lilun yanjiu [A study of educational reform and development in Tibet]*. Kunming: Yunnan Press.
———. 1999. *Xizang zizhiqu jiaoyu keyan lunwen wenxuan pian [Research papers on education the Tibetan Autonomous Region]*. Lhasa: Tibet People's Press.
Wu, Y.J., Duoji Ciren, and Ziwang Junmei. 2006. *Zhongguo Xizang fazhan baogao 2006 [Blue book of Tibet 2006]*. Lhasa: Tibet People's Press.
Xia, Z., J.X. Ha, and A. Abadu. 1999. Xizang Zizhiqu Minzu Jiaoyu 50 Nian [50 years of ethnic education in the Tibetan Autonomous Region]. In *Zhongguo minzu jiaoyu 50 nian [50 years of ethnic education in China]*, 45. Beijing: Hongqi Press.
Ying, F.T. 1984. Ying Fatang tong zhizai zhonggong xizang zizhiqu san jie er ci quan wei kuoda huiyi shang de jianghua [Comrade Ying Fatang's Speech in the Second Enlarged Plenary of All Committee Members of the Third Tibet Autonomous Region Committee of the CPC]. In *Shen shi zizhiqu shaoshu minzu jiaoyu gongzuo wenjian xuanbian 1977– 1990 [Selected documents on ethnic education in provincial, municipal, autonomous regions [1977–1990]*, ed. Guo Fuchang. Chengdu: *Sichuan minzu chuban she* [Sichuan Ethnic Press].
Yu, H.B. 1995. *Shuangyu yanjiu [Research on bilingualism]*. Chengdu: Sichuan University Press.

―――. 2007. *Schooling and identity among the Naxi*. PhD diss., submitted to the University of Hong Kong.
Yu, S.Q., and E. Hannum. 2006. Poverty, health and schooling in rural China. In *Education and social change in China: inequality in a market economy*, ed. G. Postiglione. New York: M.E. Sharpe.
Zheng, P. 2007. Tibet's education in best development phase. http://en.tibet.cn/news/tin/t20070708_268288.htm, July 8 (accessed 12 August 2007).
Zheng, X.R. 2002. *Woguo yiwu jiaoyu jieduan shaoshu minzu wenzi jiaocai jianshe diaocha yanjiu* [*Research on China's ethnic minority language teaching materials development for the compulsory education years of schooling*]. Beijing: Beijing Normal University manuscript, Report to the Ford Foundation Beijing.
Zhou, A.M. 2002. *Xizang jiaoyu* [*Education in Tibet*]. Beijing: Wuzhou Chuanbo Press.
Zhou, M.L., and J. Fishman. 2003. *Multilingualism in China: the politics of writing reforms for minority languages, 1949–2002*. Berlin: Walter de Gruyter.
Zhou, M.L., and H.K. Sun, eds. 2004. *Language policy in the People's Republic of China: theory and practice since 1949*. Norwell, MA: Kluwer Academic Press.
Zhou, Q.S. 2000. *Yuyan yu renlei* [*Language and mankind*]. Beijing: Central University of Nationalities Press.
Zhou, W. 2003. *Xizang de yuyan he shehui* [*Tibetan language and society*]. Beijing: China's Tibetology Publish House.
Zhu, Z.Y. 2007. *State schooling and ethnic identity: the politics of a Tibetan neidi school in China*. New York: Lexington Press.

7 Dislocated Education
The Case of Tibet

As the United Nations Millennium Development Goals deadline for education approaches, boarding schools offer one option for providing access to quality education for children from remote communities.[1] Developing countries already make use of them in rural areas to rationalize costs and concentrate resources, as well as to settle nomadic populations. Boarding schools are viewed as especially suitable for remote areas where populations are dispersed. Yet, boarding schools for indigenous peoples are hardly a new phenomenon. Moreover, their establishment has had as much to do with a civilizing mission as with the aim of providing educational access to under-served communities. As globalization's march continues to homogenize through mass schooling, the last populations are among the most culturally diverse. Efforts to provide education for all are inevitably accompanied by national missions to "civilize" minority peoples through boarding schools that dislocate children from their home communities.

The early nation-building experiences of Australia, Canada, and the United States are marked by the establishment of boarding schools to assimilate indigenous peoples.[2] Such institutional efforts to civilize failed spectacularly, with Australia and Canada having recently apologized for dislocating children from their home communities. Systematic dislocation continues in many parts of the world. Contemporary examples in East Asia include Laos, Vietnam, and China, each with over 50 officially designated ethnic minority groups. China is perhaps the most notable, not only for its boarding school initiative in Yunnan, its most multiethnic province, but also in Tibet and Xinjiang, where an ambitious program dislocates students to schools beyond their regional borders to central China. Starting in 1985, such boarding schools were set up for students from Tibet.[3] This so-called *neidi* (inland or hinterland) school policy continues and has remained popular with parents and students for nearly a quarter century.[4] There is no explanation why China has managed to continue relocating children when many other countries have discontinued the practice, nor is there an understanding of why these schools are viewed as an attractive option for students and their families.

While doing fieldwork on basic education in rural and seminomadic areas in Tibet, I discovered that top achieving primary school graduates headed off to boarding schools in central China. As I began to study these schools, reactions to my topic in North America and Australia tended to evoke what Gita

Steiner-Khamsi and Ines Stolpe (2006, 165) call "horrific associations of cultural alienation and forced assimilation."[5] In contrast, the view in China was that these schools simply provided a base to train talent that most local schools were unable to match. Yet, I was also aware that the unresolved controversy over Tibet played into the educational intentions of these schools. Therefore, I became interested in how *neidi* schools were perceived by students and their parents, how they were supposed to help develop Tibet, to what extent they acculturated Tibetans, and whether they fit the ominous stereotype of cultural alienation and coercion. As this article shows, I came away convinced that Tibetan students acculturated to the Chinese mainstream, but usually on their own terms. That is, they did not become less assertive in their ethnicity, though the paucity of knowledge about Tibetan language and cultural heritage provided by the schools made this a formidable challenge. I also concluded that this experience resonated with that of African Americans who may have acculturated but remained determined to rediscover their ethnic heritages and reconstruct their historical experiences on their own terms. Furthermore, I was aware that China's ability to sustain these boarding schools would inevitably depend on whether they delivered what they promised, namely, a better education and a high-status job.

The sociological study of education has broadened our understanding of how schools act as agencies for social and cultural reproduction as well as resist forms of state-sponsored socialization.[6] Anthropological study has demonstrated how responses to schooling by indigenous ethnic minorities create oppositional cultures founded in folk theories—informal, almost intuitive ways of explaining how the world works around them. Empirical study across both fields has provided a number of explanations for the under-achievement of ethnic minorities.[7] Less attention has been focused on the resiliency and sustainability of policies that dislocate ethnic minorities from their home communities. In the case of Tibet, the official reason for the establishment of nonindigenous boarding schools has been to raise talented people for Tibet's economic development. Tibet is, in fact, the poorest provincial-level entity in China, with a severe lack of qualified secondary school teachers, acutely inadequate educational facilities, and the lowest levels of educational achievement (Postiglione et al. 2005; Keidel 2009).

While boarding programs in Australia, Canada, and the United States largely failed in their missions of cultural assimilation, China continues to sustain boarding schools that follow a national curriculum transmitted by teachers, with the exception of the Tibetan language and literature teachers, who are not Tibetan or have not lived in Tibet. This in itself does not mean that China's *neidi* schools are assimilating Tibetans to become Han Chinese, as some observers suggest.[8] While Tibetan graduates accept a view about the backwardness of their economy, they are less prone to accept one about the inferiority of their native culture. In this sense, there is a fundamental difference between China and the other countries mentioned above. In particular, the cultural distance between the Anglo colonial settlers and native peoples of America, Australia, and Canada was far greater than the one that exists between peoples in the adjacent lands of China and Tibet, who share a Buddhist heritage and have had centuries of contact and interchange. Therefore, cultural distance may be a less useful notion than cultural self-determination in a comparative study of boarding schools for dislocated children. In general, student mobility for secondary education resonates in China, where many students, mostly Han Chinese, are sent away even beyond national borders to secondary schools in developed countries. Moreover, *neidi* schools for Tibetans in the Chinese capital have a history that extends back to the Qing dynasty and republican government eras.[9] Thus, state-sponsored schooling that dislocates Tibetans is plausibly buoyed by a folk theory of success. In pragmatic terms, this theory enables Tibetan students and their families to calculate the value of both mainstream cultural capital and ethnic cultural vitality. Their calculations may reflect a strategy to amass cultural capital from the credentials that the boarding schools offer. However, such calculations remain viable only as long as they conform to a folk theory of success. The basis for such a theory exists in a tradition of religious education whereby a son would leave his family at a very young age for the monastery, a departure that would confer cultural capital on the son and his family.

The themes of reproduction and resistance that find utility in neo-Marxist studies of schooling throughout the world tap into the culturally bound logic of Tibetan households. These families live in a world of limited but highly determinate choices about school access for their children. Despite having their own internal logic, folk theories of success inadequately explain how resistance, sometimes couched in terms of oppositional culture, shapes strategies of capital conversion (Bordieu 1986). Folk theories contain assumptions about these strategies for acquiring mainstream cultural capital, which is then converted into social and economic opportunities. Thus, studies of how boarding school for indigenous minorities is sustained should examine choices made to attend such schools, responses to circumstantial challenges in school, comparative weighing of the education received to the alternative and the outcomes it provides, as well as forms of social resistance and cultural opposition, and the cultural capital trade-offs between minority and mainstream cultures for social status, economic, and community-bound opportunities for leadership.

The next section provides background on the education of ethnic minorities in China, as well as education in Tibet, and is followed by a review of the origin and development of boarding schools for Tibetan students. The rest of the article examines the experiences and reflections of Tibetan students and their families. Data are partially derived from the oral history recollections of Tibetans who graduated from nonindigenous boarding schools. Along with other data about the origin and development of *neidi* schools, the oral histories contribute to an understanding of how the Chinese government continues to sustain these schools, despite the experiences of Western countries.

Background

Indigenous minorities in remote regions of developing countries attain literacy and basic education later than the larger population. Ethnic minority education in developing countries, especially for girls, remains an urgent global challenge.

The cultural dimensions of such education, particularly language and religion, increase the complexity of the task. This is true for China, most particularly in Tibet. Tibetan demands for schools to elevate the status of their culture within the national framework are ubiquitous. Yet, the content of education, especially in boarding schools, reflects the state's view of ethnicity, as represented by Xiaotong Fei's (1989) concept (*duoyuan yiti geju*)—plurality and unity within the configuration of the Chinese nation, which delineates a process for all ethnic group cultures to move toward a unified national culture that is largely defined by Han Chinese culturalism. Thus, schools are saddled with the formidable challenge to conserve ethnic minority cultures within a national context that places a premium on Han Chinese cultural capital.[10] In the case of Tibetans, schools must represent Tibetan cultural heritage by linking the content of schooling to students' values and beliefs, while at the same time socializing them into a Chinese national identity. Moreover, the acquisition of Han cultural capital does not in itself prevent ethnic minorities in China from being marginalized within the national mainstream.

Given China's complex ethnic minority makeup, with 55 culturally unique groups whose total population exceeds the national population of all but 10 countries in the world, the state can hardly respond to minority educational needs as if they were a single entity. Minority educational policies are supposed to account for the unique conditions faced by different regions such as Tibet, Xinjiang, Inner Mongolia, Guanxi, and Ningxia. Practice, however, is another matter, because policies may easily be interpreted to conform with the agendas of regional leaders. The degree of regional autonomy practiced in educational matters is still an issue for research and investigation.

Within the context of a folk theory, China's civilizing project of national schooling in Tibet and other ethnic regions is challenged by cultural resistance to aspects of schooling that encroach on ethnic culture and identity formation and, at the same time, do not yield promised economic rewards. The school's ability to address cultural and economic dimensions of educational access is crucial to its success. John Ogbu and Margaret Gibson's (1991) work in the United States adds nuance to this perspective, noting the distinction between *voluntary minorities*, or those who emigrate out of choice to a new place, and *involuntary minorities*, or those who are indigenous or are forced to reside in or move to a region. The logic is that voluntary minorities are more disposed to accept the new society and its education system, whereas involuntary minorities may resist state schooling and develop an oppositional identity in the face of pressure to assimilate on unequal terms. Resistance will be particularly strong if indigenous minorities view the education system as a way to strip them of their own culture and identity without giving them equal opportunity in the wider society. If, however, indigenous minorities believe that they can use education to achieve success, they will often surmount the obstacles posed by cultural distance. When Tibetans associate boarding school attendance with a high likelihood of economic success—success that might improve their status and power in the national mainstream—then the probability of willing participation increases.

118   *Cultural processes*

Of China's five national autonomous regions, Tibet is the most ethnically homogeneous, intensely religious, geographically remote from Beijing, and economically poor. References to Tibet in this article are to the Tibetan Autonomous Region of the People's Republic of China (PRC), sometimes known as political Tibet, a constitutionally designated territory. Cultural Tibet is about as large as the continental United States and extends beyond the TAR and into four adjoining provinces where most of China's Tibetans live. The TAR covers 1.2 million square kilometers, 12.5 percent of the area of China. Tibetans were 95.5 percent of the TAR's population in 1990 and 92 percent in 2000, and they currently constitute a minority of the population in the capital city of Lhasa.[11] Located a great distance from China's mainstream cultural center, its residents possess a distinctive culture with a complex religious tradition and writing system dating back over a thousand years. Most Tibetans live at extraordinarily high altitudes, predominantly on plateaus averaging 3,600 meters above sea level and surrounded by mountains. Following Tibet's so-called peaceful liberation in 1950, when the Chinese military entered and declared Tibet a part of the PRC, there were few changes to the traditional theocratic structure of government, the organization of monasteries, and traditional forms of landholding (Goldstein 2007). However, political difficulties led to the Dalai Lama's flight to India in 1958, where he remains in residence a half century later. The establishment of the TAR followed his departure, in 1965.

Between 1913 and 1951, as Melvyn Goldstein (1989, 1997) notes, Tibet had a de facto independent polity. Monastery education dominated until 1951, when the Chinese established a school in Tibet and the Seventeen Point Agreement was signed, one provision of which read "the spoken and written language and the school education of the Tibetan nationality shall be developed step by step in accordance with the actual conditions of Tibet" (quoted in Goldstein [1989, 767]). By 1959, shortly after the Dalai Lama fled to India, education in Tibet was brought closer in line with the rest of China. Monastery education, with its emphasis on recitation of scripture, continued to exert a strong influence, although monasteries have become tightly controlled, especially in terms of size. It is impossible to separate Tibetan religion from other aspects of Tibetan culture, and many Tibetan households still aspire to have one of their children enter a monastery. Until recently, monks were often the most literate members of rural and nomadic communities, but a wide cleavage between monastery and school has become pervasive (Nyima 1997; Bass 2008).

After the Dalai Lama fled to India, education for Tibetans was put on the fast track by the Beijing government, though it remained about a decade behind more developed areas of China. The Cultural Revolution, a 10-year political campaign aimed at rekindling revolutionary fervor and purifying the Chinese Communist Party, tore into the fabric of Tibetan life with devastating results, including a massive destruction of temples and the monastic system. Class struggle became the order of the day, and the quality of teaching and learning, already low, worsened. Where they remained open, schools became predominantly an ideological arena for propaganda and self-criticism. Class warfare took precedence over academic affairs, and any mention of cultural heritage became associated with feudalism and was severely criticized. Nevertheless, the later part of the Cultural Revolution in Tibet saw an expansion of school numbers. Catriona Bass (1998) provides figures that show rapid growth in elementary school enrollments from 1965, the year the TAR was established, and a leveling off in 1978, when the emphasis of educational policy shifted from quantity to quality and enrollments began a drastic decline. With the 1981 dissolution of communes that collectivized agriculture and pastoral life, rural and nomadic parents began to withdraw their children from school to labor in the new household economy system. The more open policy after the Cultural Revolution initially led more children to pursue formal education in monasteries instead of the poorly staffed schools that lacked trained teachers. The unintended effect of reform era decentralization was to leave rural schools with fewer resources for school buildings, instructional materials, teacher salaries, and especially the reform and localization of school curriculum. Access to education remained a problem because of Tibet's size, remoteness, and population dispersion. Like other ethnic autonomous regions, the TAR's special status came with educational policies that provided Tibetan-language school textbooks and instruction, boarding schools in nomadic regions, and boarding schools in nonlocal regions.

Origins and Development

The *neidi* schools for Tibetans were established several years after Vice Premier Hu Yaobang's visit to Tibet in 1981.[12] Aside from ordering many Chinese officials to return to China and for those who remained in Tibet to study the Tibetan language, Hu stressed the need to improve education.[13] Visits followed by other high-ranking central government leaders and led to a call for mainland cities to establish schools and classes for Tibetans.[14] Beijing, Lanzhou, and Chengdu established *neidi* schools in 1985, and by the end of 1986 there were 16 such schools. In 1987, the policy was affirmed. Chinese president Jiang Zemin declared in 1990 that *neidi* schools help Tibetans understand the motherland and widen their worldview. A 1993 working group on Tibet called for long-term support for *neidi* boarding school education. The success of the Tibet *neidi* schools led to the establishment of similar schools for students from the Xinjiang Uyghur Nationality Autonomous Region in 2000 (Chen 2008).

In 1985, 20 percent of Tibet's elementary school graduates were dislocated for junior secondary education (Ying 1984).[15] As the secondary school enrollment rates of the TAR continued to grow, the proportion but not the number being dislocated to China decreased.[16] From 1985 to 2005, 25,000 students went to 89 *neidi* schools in 20 provinces and municipalities (Xiangba 2005). The student cohorts that have spanned the 20 plus years since *neidi* schools were established may be usefully periodized into three groups. The first group completed a preparatory year, followed by a standard 3-year junior secondary school education. After graduation, a small number went on to one of the three *neidi* senior secondary schools. Most of the others either returned to Tibet or, after a short visit home, continued their study for another 3 years in *neidi* vocational-technical classes.

The second group had more opportunities to attend a *neidi* senior secondary school after graduating from a *neidi* junior secondary school; a smaller proportion could still opt for *neidi* vocational classes. Only a small portion of regular senior secondary graduates went on to college, though not without preferential admission policies; these were mostly 2- or 3-year colleges. By 1994, there were 5,081 *neidi* junior secondary students, 2,041 students in *neidi* specialized middle-level (senior secondary vocational) schools, 1,062 students in *neidi* middle-level teacher training schools (senior secondary level), 866 in *neidi* regular senior secondary schools, and 563 at *neidi* colleges and universities, mostly in 3-year diploma programs.

As elementary school education in Tibet began to improve, the third group began to skip the *neidi* junior secondary preparatory year. Also, more students completed their junior secondary school in Tibet before being dislocated to a *neidi* senior secondary school. The vast majority of these students were guaranteed preferential admission to a college or university after graduation from senior secondary school. Although many attend 3-year tertiary programs (similar to community colleges or polytechnics), a number were also admitted to 4-year bachelor degree programs, including Tibet University and other universities in China.[17] Thus, the *neidi* program continually upgraded educational opportunities to accommodate the elevated aspirations of Tibetan households as market forces and competition for nonfarm labor jobs increased.

The Social Composition of Dislocated School Graduates

Gender and ethnicity.—*Neidi* schools maintained a fairly even balance in student gender profile. For example, the *neidi* school in Hubei Province admitted 1,046 boys and 1,222 girls between 1985 and 2004 (Liu 2005). Other schools had a similar gender profile. A major portion of *neidi* school graduates join the ranks of Tibet's elementary school teachers, a profession that has become increasingly dominated by women. Since *neidi* schools are designed to serve the TAR, not just TAR Tibetans, other ethnic groups are also admitted. These include not only the indigenous Luoba and Moinba but also Han Chinese, children from mixed ethnic families, and Tibetans from other provinces who are permanent residents of Tibet. In 1995, 120 places were set aside for the children of non-Tibetan cadres, public officials holding an administrative post in party and government. For their children to secure a place, such cadres must serve for 10 years as permanent residents in Tibet, and their children must score over 120 on the entrance exam, above the mark required for Tibetans. City-level cadres in the TAR must have lived and worked in Tibet for 20 years, and their children must achieve an entrance exam score of 110 (110 in Aba and Nackchu, 180 in Lhasa), a measure that reflects the growing demand for access to *neidi* schools on the part of Han Chinese and other groups not satisfied with the quality of the local schools where they serve as cadres.

Language.—*Neidi* schools' first cohort groupings comprised mostly urban children who had attended elementary schools where the medium of instruction was Chinese, though most still needed a preparatory year of language training when they arrived at their *neidi* school. By 1991, of 1,282 new entrants, 997 came from Tibetan-medium elementary schools and 285 from Chinese-medium schools. In 1992, the prestigious Beijing *neidi* school began accepting graduates of Tibetan-medium elementary schools. The Chengdu *neidi* school admitted students from all parts of Tibet who had studied in Chinese-medium elementary schools. By 1993, the number of dislocated students exceeded 10,000, and students were no longer divided according to their language of instruction in elementary school. Their entrance exam contained three subjects: Tibetan, Chinese, and mathematics.

Region.—As the *neidi* school program gained momentum, more attention was paid to the composition of incoming classes. In 1992, Beijing's *neidi* school set an 80 percent quota for rural and nomadic region students from all parts of Tibet. While the early cohorts were dominated by urban children of cadre families, the aim was to shift enrollments in favor of children from rural and nomadic regions. However, students were selected on the basis of examination results, according to quotas set for each district of Tibet. Although there are no reliable figures to assess the outcome of the policy favoring children of families from rural and nomadic regions, my research indicates that at least half of the students were from cadre households. The boarding schools are clearly preparing an elite stratum, with about half of the children already from elite households and the rest aspiring to that category.

Prefectures and counties.—The Tibet government also aims to make school access geographically representative. To this end, each district is allocated a quota. However, it is up to the district to allocate quotas to individual counties under its jurisdiction, and it is not unusual for some counties to have few students scoring high enough to attend *neidi* schools. For example, on a 2007 visit to Nyerong, a nomadic county in northern Tibet, it was discovered that while 70–80 percent of the school teachers were graduates of the *neidi* schools, none were originally from Nyerong. Most *neidi* schools are paired with specific districts in Tibet for the purposes of student selection. Some Tibetan language and literature teachers and some management personnel are also sent to the *neidi* schools from specific districts of Tibet.

Over the first 20 plus years of the *neidi* school policy, many incremental changes occurred. The number of *neidi* schools increased, selection quotas were modified, rural and nomadic student enrollments rose slightly, partnerships between the host city and Tibet's districts were adjusted, the cost of airfares from Tibet to *neidi* schools was left to households, and students who scored below the entrance exam cutoff were permitted to enroll as self-funded students.

The School Environment

Boarding schools are ethnically segregated.[18] In cases in which host city students also attend, classes are segregated despite a common curriculum except for a Tibetan language and literature class. Thus, while the schools aim to integrate

122 Cultural processes

Tibetans into Chinese nationhood, this is not reflected in the composition of the classroom.

Unlike Anglo schools for native peoples, *neidi* schools exhibit ethnic symbols on campus such as mosaics, murals, sculptures, photos, or other representations of cultural artifacts. However, religious symbols are excluded except for the occasional photo on display of the Panchen Lama, the second-highest religious figure in Tibetan Buddhism. There is also an observance of Tibetan New Year with specially prepared meals and visits by Tibetan leaders. Students are required to study the national curriculum, but classes on Tibetan language and literature are also compulsory. Attention to the study of Tibetan language and literature declines rapidly in senior secondary school as preparations are made for the national college and university entrance examinations. Not only does the *neidi* school prepare students ideologically to become citizens of China's Tibet, but it also becomes the formal agent of interpretation for defining Tibet's cultural heritage, values, and traditions. Zhu's research shows that students at nonindigenous boarding schools appropriate the social and psychological "space" that is created between themselves and the school's national socialization program to construct their ethnic identities (Zhu 2007).

Methodology

In order to understand why China's *neidi* boarding school approach succeeds where other countries' attempts have failed, as well as what might make nonindigenous boarding schools ultimately unsustainable, I visited schools and interviewed graduates of *neidi* schools after they returned to Tibet. In 2006-7, recollections were recorded of life before, during, and after dislocation for schooling.

Subjects spoke freely about their experiences before, during, and after the *neidi* school phase of their lives. They were not asked specific questions about their attitudes. In this context, respondents spoke about what was important to them, as well as the specific factors that played a role in their experiences. Each session, lasting 2-3 hours, took place in homes, workplaces, or restaurants. Interrater reliability confirmed that site, time, language, questioning style, gender, and ethnicity of the interviewer and interviewee had no significant effect on response patterns. Understanding such effects was one of the intentions behind the training program for the interview team.[19] I conducted workshops on questioning techniques, accompanied the research teams on selected visits, and conducted interviews on specific points with graduates, parents, and teachers. The interview environments were non-threatening, and subjects, graduates of inland schools that have a relatively high status in Tibet, were self-assured.

The oral histories of 172 graduates were recorded, among whom 46 percent were women and 54 percent were men; 62 percent were from urban areas, 31 percent from rural areas, and 5 percent from nomadic areas (plus 2 percent unclassified). Almost half (49 percent) had grown up in cadre families, more than a quarter (27 percent) came from agricultural or nomadic households, 20 percent were from worker or urban resident households, and the remaining 4 percent were from either business, unemployed, or unclassified households. More than half (60 percent) of the 172 subjects entered *neidi* boarding schools in the first cohort (1985–88), 31 percent in the second cohort (1989–92), and 9 percent in the third cohort (1993–96).

Visits were made to nonindigenous boarding schools to better understand how education was organized and conducted and to observe the learning environment and campus life. While there, students, teachers, and administrators were interviewed. *Neidi* school graduates were difficult to locate because they are scattered throughout Tibet. Graduates interviewed for this study were from cohorts that had already returned to Tibet and had jobs. Most returned to Tibet between 1992 and 1993. Therefore, we were able to explore the schools' long-term effects after graduates returned to Tibet. The first round of oral histories took place in three main population centers: Lhasa, Shigatse, and Nakchu. The second round took place at three lower-level counties of these urban centers: Lhundrup, Penam, and Nyerong. In the first stage, oral histories were gathered in Lhasa (54), Shigatse (58), and Nakchu (60) from a total of 172 *neidi* school graduates. Interview data were also gathered from leaders of units that employed *neidi* school graduates, often school principals. In the second stage, oral histories were conducted of *neidi* school graduates who had been assigned jobs further away from urban centers. These included 18 from Penam and 22 from Lhundrup counties. A handful of oral histories were conducted in townships located between Nakchu and Nyerong counties. Oral histories based on guiding questions were tape-recorded and later transcribed. The files were initially grouped into sets of 10 in the order in which the oral histories were recorded, so that key themes in response patterns could be identified, summarized, and reviewed at workshops with the research team at the Tibet Academy of Social Science and the University of Hong Kong.

Considering Dislocation

Reflections about school and home before going to study outside of Tibet are best understood within context. Tibetan elementary school quality generally pales in comparison to that in the host *neidi* city. There are also large differences between the elementary schools students attended in Tibet. Children from rural or nomadic areas may have attended a 2-year, one-teacher village school before completing the final 4 years of elementary school in a township school, where they boarded from Monday to Friday. Meanwhile, children from a city or county seat may have attended a full six-grade elementary school with better-qualified teachers for the main subjects of mathematics, Tibetan, and Chinese. Regardless, *neidi* school teachers often remark on the inferior academic standards of Tibetans. Home life before dislocation, especially in rural and nomadic areas, is dominated by traditional Tibetan religious values (Postiglione et al. 2005, 2006; Postiglione 2008). Rural and nomadic households—most monogamous though with a fair share of polyandrous and polygamous marriages—have more children, poorer access to health care, higher rates of illiteracy, and less disposable income. Traditional values weighed heavily on life at home, and child development patterns included strict deference to parents.[20] By contrast, urban households had parents with more education and fewer children.[21] Urban households also had higher levels of literacy. From an analysis of the oral history recordings we were able to classify 45.9 percent of *neidi* graduates who had been from an urban family with a literate parent and only 16.9 percent who had been from a rural family with a literate parent. Aside from 11.6 percent of graduates whose oral histories did not include a reference to literacy, the rest were from nonliterate families.

Students from urban schools are also advantaged in that they sometimes move away together with several classmates. In one case, half of the students from an urban elementary school succeeded in the entrance examination and attended the same *neidi* school. In another case, only four students in an elementary school graduating class were eligible to attend a *neidi* school. Although there were district quotas, education authorities had some flexibility in adjusting the cutoff scores for different schools in a district. However, in the remote Nyerong County, most elementary schools did not have even one student qualified to be admitted to a *neidi* school. Thus, there was an effort to recruit to elite schools students whose parents could understand the potential payoff of Chinese schooling and who were more familiar with life in China from news, television, and other sources. Bass (1998) notes apprehension among Tibetan parents in 1984, just as the program of nonindigenous boarding school education began. However, she also points out a change in attitude over time. As the program became more popular, half the intake of secondary students each year went to China (Bass 1998). Both the quality of education offered in China and the experience of their children at boarding schools had much to do with parental and community change in attitudes and perspectives. Initial apprehension about sending a child to a *neidi* school gradually wore off.

Families generally received information about *neidi* schools from classmates, relatives, and friends or were shown photographs and letters by those who had already been to China for education or training. Still, parents were not completely at ease, such as those who worried that their 11-year-old daughter was too young to take care of herself. Other families, especially those who were illiterate or nomadic, did not understand much or had little information about *neidi* schools. Students or graduates who spoke about the decision to attend *neidi* school indicated their parents believed that *neidi* schools offered a good education.

QUESTION: How did you decide at that time to study at a *neidi* school?
ANSWER: I was influenced by my father. He supported my study at a *neidi* school, because he wanted me to eventually go on to attend university, and to him the *neidi* school was the best pathway.
QUESTION: In 1991, before you went to the Tianjin Hongguan middle school, what was the situation at home?

ANSWER: At home, my mother and father were cadres and hoped that I would test well for the *neidi* school entrance, because everything was better there, and after I returned to Tibet, I would have a solid foundation.

Although they had the most to gain in relative terms from a boarding school education, parents in rural and nomadic areas knew less about the *neidi* schools than urban parents. As students graduated and returned to start their own families, the policy became more widely known. In some cases, a local teacher or principal of an elementary school returned students had attended would tell parents about why it was worthwhile to attend a boarding school. Students, whether from cadre or farming families, were persuaded by the possibility of getting a good job after graduation as well as by the living standards and learning conditions at *neidi* schools.

One graduate recalled the envy some students felt toward those attending school in China, and several spoke of their wish to "see the world." Still, at 11 or 12 years of age, permission of their parents was essential if they were to attend a *neidi* school. A substantial number of students were from rural and nomadic regions, where we had encountered the preference of parents to keep children at home to labor in the household economy after primary school rather than send them to the county seat for a junior secondary education of doubtful quality and poor job-related outcomes. However, gaining access to a *neidi* school meant an opportunity to attend an elite school of high quality and with good job prospects.

QUESTION: So there were three children at your home. Was it a consideration of your parents that if you left, there would be a loss of labor, an influence on your family income?
ANSWER: No, I left with my second brother. We were in the same cohort and graduated at the same time. At that time, my parents didn't think about it at all. For them, it was a happy thing that we were able to pass the examination. They said if you go there for school, no matter how poor and how difficult it is at home, you needn't worry about the work at home.
QUESTION: Did your parents know anything about the school where you were sent?
ANSWER: No, we lived in a village, so all they knew was that their children were going to attend a good school and they should go to the school. My parents didn't know anything else. My father had been to *neidi* for training several times when he worked in a factory. He had been there, so he knew *neidi* was a good place. He was happy to let us go, but my mother didn't know about *neidi* at all.

Children who gained access to *neidi* schools attended free; otherwise most families could not have afforded the expense. As the schools gained in popularity, the government continued to bear tuition costs but not students' transportation expenses between Tibet and the schools. Households with children who scored below the required level on the entrance examination could also gain access as fee-paying students.[22] As more information about life and learning in *neidi* schools made its way to Tibet, prospective students and their parents became persuaded of the value of the trade-off of leaving Tibet for several years and returning with a good education.

Data about predislocation suggest that decisions to attend *neidi* schools are less informed by oppositional culture than by a folk theory that calculates gain and risk. Gains in mainstream cultural capital through credentials, potential to expand social capital networks, better job prospects, and quality of education are set against the loss of household labor in the case of agricultural and nomadic families, separation from children for an extended period, and risk of safety. Especially for rural and nomadic-area children, attendance guarantees a link with urban life, not only in China but also when they return to and are allocated a job in Tibet. For Tibetan urban households, social capital is bound up with links to China and the assurance of jobs that can reproduce parental cadre status. The cultural capital gained through knowledge of the Chinese language and mainstream culture grooms students for middleman status in relations between Tibet and the mainland. For both urban and rural parents, there are few alternatives. Their children attend secondary school either in Tibet or in China, the latter offering the higher-quality education.[23] The third alternative, popular even with urban cadre families until government regulations changed in the late 1980s, was to send children to India for secondary school. This alternative, which offered an English-language education and the familiar surroundings of a Tibetan community, is no longer an option. While students could still find their way into India and secondary school with the aid of the exile community, it is highly doubtful that a good job could be found upon return to Tibet. For example, such graduates were once in demand as tour guides owing to their English proficiency. However, this demand has dwindled with the increase in Chinese tour guides who have English as a second language.

Like schools elsewhere in Chinese urban areas, the state-sponsored and ethnically segregated boarding schools for Tibetans have introduced market principles and competition in their recruitment activities. The education bureau arranged a venue where each school representative has a display booth, not unlike boarding school student recruitment fairs run by European and American schools in major Asian cities. Tibet boarding school exhibitors provide colorful school literature, photographs, videos, student essays or art projects, brochures, and statistics about the school. Schools can also display commemorative books that review their many years of operation. Despite its market-oriented appearance, this is a state-sponsored event not unlike others that would fall under the banner of a socialist market economy with Chinese characteristics. The government has increasingly come to encourage competition among schools, including public and private (*minban*) schools and those run by a combination of state and what it calls social forces. The boarding school for Tibetans in each province remained insulated from this sea change in school reform; now there is an effort to move them in the same direction. Secondary schools in the TAR continue to improve their conditions and may recruit teachers from China, including graduates of *neidi* schools. *Neidi* schools also compete, albeit to a small degree at present, with the growing number of private *minban* schools in Chinese cities, some of which will recruit Tibetan students who can pay their high fees.

Dislocating

Climate, low altitude, local foods, and separation from family and friends led to illness for some Tibetan students in the first weeks of school. The adjustment was made easier by older students and teachers who looked after the new students. Some schools group students according to their home regions to help newcomers cope with school life. Some schools provide milk for breakfast, as a substitute staple for the butter tea that Tibetan students were used to drinking at home. Students found some comfort in the stark contrast between Tibet and Chinese urban life, though they also noted that the air was cleaner and clearer in Tibet, and the water tasted differently in their hometowns. However, all agreed that they were able to adjust within a month or two.

Boarding schools for indigenous people in other countries were often located away from major urban areas, but Tibet's *neidi* schools are located in major cities such as Beijing, Shanghai, Wuhan, and Tianjin. Students were generally impressed with urban life in China and conditions associated with the popular meaning of "modern." When students are off campus, they enter a relatively urban part of China, though leaving the school grounds is restricted to a few hours per week, usually on Sundays. While this restriction could be perceived as harsh, Tibetan parents did not object since it ensured a higher level of safety in an urban environment away from home and curtailed the amount of spending by students. When students did spend extended time off campus, it was usually part of a cultural outing or summer tour organized by the school.

Schools placed a strong emphasis on discipline and patriotism. Corporal punishment is frowned on and would not sit well with Tibetan parents, even though it is a common method of discipline in many rural Tibetan schools. Any perception that Han Chinese teachers mistreat Tibetan students at *neidi* schools would have a deleterious effect on the willingness of parents to have their children leave Tibet. Yet, schools did view Tibetan children as coming from a rugged mountain lifestyle and in need of socialization into more "civilized" ways and habits of urban Chinese children, with a stress on hygiene, dress, and Chinese-language skills.

Despite the highly disciplined atmosphere of the *neidi* schools, dislocated students who discussed the atmosphere of teaching and learning found it more liberal than in the TAR, where open approaches by Tibetan teachers risked being construed as subversive. One graduate remarked that writing in *neidi* was all right as long as one did not violate general political principles. In contrast, a slight and unintentional expression in TAR might become a big problem.

While *neidi* school teachers viewed Tibetan ways as needing Chinese-style civilizing, they have better access to learning materials and employ more dynamic methods of teaching than most teachers in the TAR. *Neidi* school graduates who became teachers commented that they would like to treat their own students in the way their *neidi* school teachers treated them. Students expressed the view that they were respected more by their *neidi* school teachers than by teachers in Tibet. However, our research was not able to identify any Tibetan graduates who returned to their old *neidi* school and were hired to teach subjects such as mathematics or science, a situation that casts some doubt on the overall success of the policy after more than 20 years.

Each *neidi* school usually had only one teacher from Tibet to teach Tibetan language and literature. Although these teachers formed a close relationship with their students, they usually lacked the training and teaching methods possessed by their peers. They did not integrate well with the rest of the teaching staff, a situation compounded by their 2-year contractual appointments and cultural distance from mainstream Chinese culture. Most, if not all, of the host city's *neidi* teachers have not been to Tibet. Travel there is not encouraged or included as part of their training. Still, at least nine out of 10 students who spoke about their *neidi* teachers remembered them as caring and responsible.

> It was possible that some of our teachers have never been to Tibet and knew only a little about Tibet. However, they were all excellent and full of a sense of responsibility. They took care of us as if they were our parents when we were ill upon arriving there. They treated us like their own children and taught us carefully in such issues as bathing and cleaning. Some of our girls were beginning to menstruate and needed such things as sanitary napkins and underwear. Our teachers then brought us to the shop and helped us to buy those things after discovering our need.
>
> Our teachers were very good and kind. They treated us as if they were our mothers. Our principal teacher still keeps in touch with us. At the time when I was in *neidi* school, I felt that the teachers were just like mothers. I turned to them when I came across any problem. We had a good relationship with our teachers.

Some schools also had classes for local, mostly Han Chinese, students, but these were separate from Tibetan classes, and local students did not live at school with Tibetan students. Opportunities for interaction between Tibetan and host city students were arranged periodically, usually through sporting competitions, field trips to the theater, or joint academic events. Although contact with host city students was relatively rare, Tibetan students portrayed their Chinese counterparts as hardworking and having good study habits.

Students followed Tibetan culinary customs during Tibetan festivals, such as eating *tugba*, Tibetan-style noodles, and sheep heads. The architecture and environment of *neidi* schools are similar to those of other schools in China, except for the sculptures, murals, ceramic displays, paintings, and photographs of Tibet on the school grounds. *Neidi* schools recognized Tibetan holidays by hosting leaders from Tibet, serving special Tibetan foods, and permitting students to wear traditional dress and sing Tibetan songs. Nevertheless, according to the laws of China, religious practices are not permitted in the schools.[24] Although graduates often commented that they wanted to learn more in school about Tibetan history and culture, they experienced no identity confusion about being a Tibetan. The expression of Tibetan ethnicity was not discouraged by the school authorities, but it was also not encouraged within the pervasive civilizational discourse. Nevertheless, it was impossible for students to escape a territorial identity regularly expressed in the curriculum with the maxim "love Tibet."[25] The school stressed the connection of Tibet to the Chinese motherland and the need for students to return to Tibet after graduation to develop its economy.

Students wrote letters home, initially in the Tibetan language, but later in Chinese to demonstrate their learning. Most parents needed a translator to read the letters in Chinese.[26] Both students and parents refrained from passing on news of a death in the family or sickness at school so as not to alarm the other. In one case, a girl did not learn of her father's death for 3 years.

A main thematic issue and debate surrounding *neidi* schools continues to be the language of instruction. About 70 percent of the first *neidi* school cohort was recruited from elementary schools that used Tibetan as the language of instruction. Chinese language is the main teaching medium in all *neidi* schools, including junior secondary schools. Students are also required to learn a foreign language, which invariably means English.

While most *neidi* schools provide Tibetan language and literature as a subject, there is a lack of will to promote the study of Tibetan language and literature. This situation left students with quite different perspectives. Some did not consider the Tibetan language as a "common tool" of communication in "modern society": "from the point view of social development, the Tibetan language is not going to be mainstream." Another student remarked: "[I] just feel that the Tibetan language is not that useful." However, one graduate recalled a case of a senior secondary school he attended that did not offer adequate Tibetan language classes, and the students reacted to it by refusing to attend classes. Another stated: "I think the Tibetan language class should be put at the same level as the other subject classes. ... Tibetan language class should gain more attention, after all it is part of our ethnic culture. I think Tibetan literacy is part of a very advanced culture, and many things are carried through the Buddhist texts. If one knew [the knowledge in the Buddhist texts], one would possess a different quality. So I think Tibetan literacy is very important. ... I would definitely have my child learn Tibetan well."

Feelings toward the Tibetan language were complex and sometimes contradictory. As a general pattern, studying in *neidi* schools did not result in improved or more extensive study of Tibetan language and literature. In fact, many felt that their Tibetan language ability had been weakened. Some regretted not being able to master Tibetan. In such a case, students demanded that the school give more attention to Tibetan in the curriculum, and in another case, students tried to set up a Tibetan-language library on their own.

Tibetan history and cultural traditions are still not heavily emphasized, despite the 1988 State Education Committee notice that it should be the duty of all levels of schooling in and for Tibet to enable the Tibetan people to inherit and develop their history and cultural traditions as well as learn advanced scientific technology and the cultures of other ethnic groups. The notice suggested that educational content, textbooks, and curriculum design for Tibetan children should not copy indiscriminately the experience of schools in the region where the *neidi* schools are located but rather be informed by Tibetan history, culture, production, and economic life. The 1988 notice also prescribed that *neidi* schools should strengthen instruction of the Tibetan language in terms of curriculum and content. Nevertheless, most *neidi* schools simply followed the standard curriculum of the urban schools of the city where they were located. Consequently, more careful attention to parts of the curriculum concerning Tibetan history, geography, and culture was proposed at the 1993 Work Conference on Educational Support for Tibet. English language did not become a compulsory subject until a few years later.

A major challenge for schools has been how to deal with issues of religion and language. *Neidi* schools attempt to separate education and religion. For example, Tibetan students who studied in Beijing visited a nearby religious site, Yunghegong, a Tibetan Buddhist temple founded by an emperor in the Qing dynasty, as part of a school tour, not as a pilgrimage in the typical Tibetan manner. Most Tibetan families do not worship in temples but rather in their homes, where often one room is dedicated for religious artifacts. Religious items were not permitted in school, and many students grew skeptical of aspects of their religion. Yet, students generally did not look down on their parents' religious views. The schools did not deny that religion was part of the Tibetan cultural tradition, but they did convey the view that religion is a stumbling block to modernization and development.

In the end, *neidi* schools adopt a weak and largely symbolic approach to culturally relevant education for Tibetans. Institutionalizing more meaningful education for Tibetans would be enhanced if school norms in China encouraged a learning environment that recognizes and reflects the ethnic diversity of the nation. While schools in some rural and nomadic areas reflect the ethnic cultures of their students, urban schools reflect mainstream Chinese culture. The *neidi* schools attempted to transmit mainstream Chinese culture while showing a token respect for Tibetan culture. Token respect intersected the discourse on national unity through the prescription "love Tibet."

Ethnic minority culture appears centrally in language and literature classes but not as a thematic feature throughout the curriculum. The *neidi* schools offer a relatively high-quality education and reproduce an elite cadre class in Tibet, but they also foster an oppositional culture as a response to the lack of Tibetan history, language, and literature. It is a weak form of oppositional culture since students are willing to make a cultural sacrifice in order to dedicate their time to preparing for the college and university entrance examinations. From most Tibetan students' point of view, the school can be forgiven for not giving more emphasis to their native language than examination preparation, which is, after all, standardized across China.

Relocating Back to Tibet

Few *neidi* school graduates failed to relocate back to Tibet. Only five out of the first group of 172 subjects we interviewed said they considered staying in other parts of China to work. For the cohorts we interviewed, graduating from a *neidi* school provided a path to stable employment. Some students did not like the weather, missed home, and wanted to return to help Tibet. Others reported that they knew the people and the environment of Tibet better, so they felt it was natural to return home. Fresh graduates came away with the idea that their free education obliged them to work at lessening the development gap between Tibet and China. Nevertheless, the proportion of graduates going on to college has increased in recent years, some continuing their studies in Tibet but many in *neidi* colleges. On school visits, we observed long lists of student names and the colleges they would be attending.

Virtually all graduates internalized the idea from their *neidi* schooling that the purpose of their study was to serve Tibet's future, and many talked about their plans to use the knowledge they learned in China for the betterment of Tibet. This message was emphasized by their teachers, including their Tibetan language teachers. This message was also stressed by visiting Tibetan dignitaries. A *neidi* graduate recalled that the Panchen Lama visited his school in Kunming and told students to study for the "uplifting of Tibet." When oral histories turned to the subject of families, the most commonly expressed sentiment was that graduates wanted to return home to tend to their aging parents, whom they missed and wanted to rejoin. A graduate recollected a sense of belonging to Tibet as a spiritual home. Rarely if ever did graduates express that they felt more at home in *neidi* school than in Tibet. A few noted that their long stay made them feel isolated.

This contrasts with Xinjiang *neidi* school students, mostly Uyghurs, who wish to stay in *neidi* areas after graduation rather than return to their home province (Chen 2008). This may be due to the fact that Uyghurs have been able to integrate in Muslim, especially Hui, communities that exist in urban areas throughout China. Tibetans have no such cultural cushion communities.

In short, few Tibetan graduates looked for jobs in central China. They returned home after graduation, where they experienced a process of readjustment. Several said readjustment took 3–6 months, and a few said it took longer than a year. Those assigned to remote places often said it took time to overcome the physical discomfort of high altitude and Tibetan food, which contains more meat and fewer vegetables. Those assigned to work in Lhasa said it was not very different from a Chinese city, especially in terms of food and clothes. In short, the readjustment process was not a major difficulty. There were very few aspects of life in Tibet that graduates rejected, although some mentioned poor hygiene, excessive use of alcohol, and the conservative views of the older generation toward the outside world.

Tibetan Buddhism is a main part of the cultural identity of Tibetans, and students' attitudes have been influenced by state ideology to discard so-called superstitious dimensions of Tibetan culture. In this respect, the *neidi* schools seem to have made inroads. However, students did not reject Tibetan culture. On the contrary, it seems that the longer they are away from home, the more they grow to love Tibetan culture. While expressing a strong need to do something for Tibet, they also said they loved Tibetan culture and felt proud of it.

Language has been one of the most contested areas in Tibetan education. Before being dislocated for their education, most Tibetans studied at Tibetan-language elementary schools. Progress in learning the Tibetan language at *neidi* secondary school was slow and not of consequence for the college and university entrance examinations. However, after returning to Tibet, graduates came to recognize its importance as a doorway to ethnic heritage:

> If one really wants to learn about it [Tibetan], one must be able to read Tibetan language books. However, my Tibetan language level is not good enough.
>
> After attending *neidi* school, I gave up studying Tibetan, and there are personal reasons and environmental reasons as well. From the point of view of nationality, it is a great loss. ... There is a certain, special cultural background existing in every ethnic nationality. Being a part of one ethnic nationality, I feel I should carry on the culture of this ethnic nationality.

After students arrived in China for secondary school and found themselves immersed in mainstream Chinese culture, their knowledge vacuum became evident. This "vacuum" led to useful insights about the future potential of Tibet:

> Because there was a rise in my knowledge, and I've been more exposed to the outside world, there is a big difference in perspective. ... Some may say that we were on organized tours, sightseeing in *neidi*, and wasted money, but I think it's not so. For example, when one is in China, and sees a table, we know at the moment that we couldn't produce a table like that in Tibet. But, as long as you saw it, you would think about it. As a teacher, you would compare the teaching methods, and see how students are taught there, and how we are taught here. You saw the difference. Now there is globalization ... if a product from Tibet is good enough, the whole world is going to use it.

Upon returning to work in Tibet, *neidi* school graduates were held in high regard by their employers. However, school principals viewed *neidi* policy as favoring schools in China over their own schools in Tibet. Whether or not this led to a concerted effort by principals to improve the quality of education in their schools is another question, though resource limitations in the TAR schools are a formidable challenge. One principal expressed a common view about *neidi* graduates' declining language capabilities: "We were from the 1986 entrance class, or the second of the inland school cohorts to be admitted, and the students of that era had a good foundation, with good Tibetan. But, after that, the emphasis on the Tibetan language declined."

An elementary school principal in Tibet found that graduates from *neidi* schools were unable to teach in the Tibetan language as well as he expected. In Tibet, elementary school teachers are required to be able to teach both Tibetan and Chinese, as well as mathematics. *Neidi* school graduates in this elementary school were unable to teach in Tibetan, nor did they communicate well with the students when instructing them in Chinese. The principal made a suggestion that *neidi* teacher-training programs address these problems and train students to be able to work in rural areas, where Tibetan is the dominant language.

Thus, cultural capital gained through improved capacity in Chinese was offset by a diminished capacity to work with rural people using the Tibetan language. This does not mean that *neidi* graduates were unable to function in rural settings or as rural schoolteachers. I observed a high level of dedication on the part of *neidi* graduates who worked in rural areas. However, their written Tibetan was less than would be expected of a schoolteacher. While they were often the best Chinese speakers in rural communities, their Chinese was by no means equal to that of most urban graduates in China.

The data on relocation show the trade-off between Tibetan language skills that enable closer relationships with the people of Tibet and an education that secures better job prospects. Moreover, many jobs available to earlier cohorts were in urban government departments, where meetings came to be increasingly conducted in Chinese. Urban government jobs have become scarce, and more graduates are employed in counties and at the township level, many as schoolteachers. For the latter group of *neidi* graduates, Tibetan language skills are essential because there are few Chinese speakers in rural and nomadic areas.

Still, the indication is that dislocated students return to Tibet well versed in the curriculum of mainstream China, with its dose of skepticism toward religious beliefs, opportunities for continuing education, and a solid sense of ethnic identity. In this context, the oppositional culture gradually dissipated upon relocation, and the original folk theory of success was reaffirmed except for one aspect. Graduates consistently pointed to the need to learn more about their culture, language, and heritage.

Rate of Capital Returns and Saliency of Ethnic Identity

Boarding schools for indigenous minorities in Australia, Canada, and the United States are legendary for their efforts to erase indigenous cultural memories.[27] Some East Asian countries see boarding schools as a practical means to move toward the United Nations' Millennium Development Goals. As we have seen, since 1985, China has developed and expanded a system of nonindigenous boarding schools, by which urban centers throughout China host Tibetan students for up to 7 years of secondary school education. After 10 years, the Tibet *neidi* school model was institutionalized for the far western province of Xinjiang. The government has been able to sufficiently popularize the policy of board schooling to urban, rural, and nomadic households such that many households perceive a favorable cost-benefit calculation involving cultural capital in the form of language capacity (Chinese and Tibetan), quality of instruction, graduation credentials leading to jobs, and an implicit capacity to build social capital with non-Tibetans in the TAR and beyond. Recollections also reveal a subtext of opposition culture due to a lack of access to knowledge about cultural heritage. However, these dissipate during relocation in the TAR if good jobs, elite status, or further education is accrued but remain a potential subtext if they do not.

In the case of Australia, Canada, and the United States, many parents were coerced to turn over their children to schools that failed to provide any education about ethnic language, oral traditions, cultural artifacts, or literature. Native expression, song, and dance were prohibited. Behavior was controlled through corporal punishment and fear by reference to religious doctrine. The school building and campus environment were often bereft of indigenous architecture and other cultural symbols. Contact with parents and the home ethnic community was minimized or cut off altogether. At best, these schools were portrayed as providing access to basic mainstream knowledge and work skills. At worst, they were portrayed as institutions for cultural genocide. The evidence is thin on how these schools improved the plight of native children within the larger national fabric or even back home within indigenous communities (Buti 2007). In fact, popular resentment toward these educational institutions lingers even to today. One of the most notorious boarding schools is today a museum to remind citizens of past mistakes. Nevertheless, China's nonindigenous boarding schools for Tibetans have existed over a significant amount of time with as yet little popular resentment (Chen and Postiglione 2009). This is not to say that Native Americans always held boarding schools in contempt, as Edward Goodbird's 1914 story recounts: "We Indians have helped you White people. All over this country are corn fields; we Indians gave you seed for your own corn, and we gave you squashes and beans. On the lakes, in your parks are canoes: Indians taught you to make those canoes. ... We Indians think that you are paying us back, when you give us schools and books, and teach us the new way" (quoted in Spack [2002, 140]).

Another difference between this type of boarding school education for indigenous peoples of Tibet and that for indigenous Australians, Canadians, and Americans is that the former were relocated to urban and the latter to rural areas. Tibetan families do not appear to have been coerced to send their children to boarding schools in China. Some families whose children did not score high enough to gain entrance to these schools had the option to pay an extra fee for admission. Tibetan students were offered classes about their language and literature. To some extent, the schools recognized, albeit through their own definitions as the formal agents of interpretation, Tibetan culture through representations of Tibetan art and architecture, music, and observance of holidays. The schools also actively involved children in learning activities incorporating Tibetan painting and story writing. We found no evidence that Han Chinese teachers used corporal punishment, and there appeared to be a close relationship between Tibetan students and their Han Chinese teachers.[28] Such relationships with teachers were not absent from Native American schools. In quoting

Standing Bear, Ruth Spack (2002, 102) notes that he was "ready to do anything" for his beloved teacher and that his father supported his choice and was impressed during his visit to the Carlisle school.

Tibet's boarding school literature is replete with references to moral and political education, with an unmistakable stress on patriotism to shape behavior and national identity (Zhu 2007). Communication with parents is not cut off. Parents are permitted to, and increasingly do, visit the schools. Graduates have so far been able to gain a relatively high status upon returning to Tibet but would have a difficult time if they chose to compete for high-status jobs in the cities where they attended *neidi* schools. While the schools do not prohibit the use of native language on campus, students noted a lack of emphasis on the Tibetan language. It is not surprising that the knowledge and determination to strengthen a sense of Tibetan cultural heritage among their students is absent. Thus, one core component of education, the transmission of cultural heritage from one generation to another, is weak. Some might even argue that the lack of a strong grounding in one's cultural heritage could stunt the capacity for critical and innovative thought.

While this article argues that nonindigenous boarding schools have not spawned much of an opposition culture, they have awakened consciousness about ethnic heritage within the national context, a risk only if graduates return to their homelands and begin to discover that high-status, or at least stable, job opportunities are no longer available to them. It is well known that leaders of national movements in some countries have been those whose ethnic consciousness was awakened by the education they received in schools and universities in more developed nations. However, the more urgent issue for Tibetan graduates of *neidi* schools is whether or not their hinterland education has prepared them for the rough and tumble of market economics. The *neidi* school policy was fashioned during a time when Tibet still had enough of a planned economy to guarantee jobs to returning graduates. Once the folk theories of success that undergird the popularity of boarding schools are undermined by unemployment or underemployment, ethnic consciousness could become more salient as dissatisfied youths seek ways to shore up their self-respect amid an increasingly competitive labor market.

Respondents from the earlier cohorts commented that the difference between themselves and their counterparts who studied in the TAR is that being away from home gave them a broader view of the world and made them more independent, self-reliant, and adaptable to different situations and environments. Although these are useful skills for a market economy, most of these graduates received job assignments through government agencies when they returned to Tibet. Stable jobs that continue to be assigned to graduates are in only two or three sectors, including teaching, which absorbs about half of *neidi* graduates. As the government struggled to popularize 6-year basic education with qualified teachers, *neidi* graduates were assigned as teachers to township-level schools in remote rural and nomadic regions. There were and still are few if any Han Chinese speakers in these regions, and those who accepted the posts have the potential to play a key role in school and community development if their preparation is sufficient.

The future of nonindigenous boarding school education in China and other countries, including new programs that have received international visibility, is challenged by a complex set of costs and benefits (Mathur 1994; Kratli 2001; Manynooch 2008).[29] While they develop the leadership potential of youths from underserved communities, including girls and ethnic minorities, they also remove the best intellectual resources from the local community school systems. While this may prod local schools to become more competitive by improving the quality of instruction, such efforts continue to be hampered by resource limitations. Success of the boarding school policy will eventually be measured by the ability of local schools to match their quality. It will also be measured by the quality of graduates and their ability to gain competitive employment as science teachers in the boarding schools and to take on leadership roles in civic and community development when they return to their home regions. While graduates of boarding schools are expected to remain committed and employ their knowledge and skills to develop their homelands, the measure of the education they receive is also judged by whether it can ensure that they are competitive within the context of national and local labor markets. Finally, boarding schools for ethnic minorities can foster an identity with the larger nation, but their success in doing so over decades can be measured by how long it takes for prominent members of the ethnic minority community to become part of the management team of these schools and to what extent they are staffed on a multiethnic teaching faculty. With the global trend in school privatization, there is also increasing space for ethnic minority communities to run their own schools in developed urban areas of the country, where they might also build surrounding communities with close links to the home communities that could transfer talent and cultural capital in both directions.

Notes

1 For example, much attention has been given in the popular media recently to Oprah Winfrey's boarding school for girls from poor regions of South Africa.
2 See McBeth (1983), Trennert (1988), Adams (1995), Ellis (1996), Miller (1996), Child (1998), Archuleta et al. (2004), Churchill (2004), Lomawaima and McCarty (2006), and Trafzer et al. (2006).
3 By Tibet is meant the Tibetan Autonomous Region (TAR) of the People's Republic of China. The TAR is sometimes referred to as "political Tibet" as distinguished from "ethnic Tibet," a much larger region that includes not only the TAR but also the Tibetan areas of the four adjacent Chinese provinces of Qinghai, Sichuan, Yunnan, and Gansu. Dislocated boarding schools were established for students from Xinjiang in 1999. Xinjiang means the Xinjiang Uyghur Autonomous Region.
4 *Neidi* in Chinese is usually rendered as "inland," a term that refers to the Chinese mainland territory. A *neidi* school generally refers to a school in a major Chinese city such as Shanghai, Beijing, Tianjin, or Qingdao that is staffed largely by Han Chinese teachers and administrators from that host city and follows the national curriculum. China is not unique in the region.

5 Steiner-Khansi and Stolpe drew a different conclusion in their study of boarding schools in Mongolia.
6 See Ogbu and Gibson (1974, 1991), Bordieu (1977), Morrow and Torres (1995), and Ogbu (1995, 2003).
7 These include several explanations, e.g., (1) capital deficiency (Schultz 1963; Becker 1964;Jenks et al. 1979; Bordieu 1986; Fischer et al. 1996); (2) oppositional culture (Ogbu 1978; Suarez-Orosco 1991; Kao and Tienda 1998); (3) stereotype imposition (Steele 1992); (4) peer influence (Sewell et al. 1969; Halliman 1982); (5) social detachment (Tinto 1993; Johnson et al. 2001); (6) ethnic segregation (Steele 1998); (7) social class reproduction (Bowles and Gintis 1976; Willis 1977); (8) school effects (Coleman 1966); and (9) preparation for university (Nettles 1991).
8 The unsubstantiated assertion that these schools "forcibly assimilate" Tibetans is found on an official Web site. See China's impact on Tibetan cultural and linguistic identity at http://www.tibet.net/en/index.php?id= 1601&articletype = flashold& rmenuid = morenews, accessed on April 6, 2009.
9 The Tibetans who attended these schools were largely from ethnic Tibet and specifically the area beyond the present-day TAR—which did not exist as a political entity of China at that time.
10 Han cultural capital refers to the broad array of cultural knowledge of the Chinese language, especially how to write it, the ethnic themes of the Han Chinese found in classical and modern literature, and the credentials from Chinese schools. These become a kind of additive knowledge that is intended to confer social status. Regarding Han Chinese views of minority culture, see, e.g., Heberer (1989), Gladney (1991), Dikotter (1992), Mackerras (1994, 1995), and Harrell (2002).
11 See the chapter on Tibet and the movement of Tibetans in Irendale et al. (2001, 138–39).
12 There has been a great deal of confusion about the translation of *Xizang neidiban* from Chinese to English. The government's former translation of "Tibet inland schools and classes" could give the incorrect impression that these schools and classes are held within Tibet. A more recent government English translation is "hinterland schools." In actuality, the *Xizang neidiban* are largely located in major Chinese cities and are basically Chinese boarding schools; thus a more precise English translation would be "dislocated schools." This article uses the term *neidi* schools instead of *neidiban* to denote that it focuses on the schools in which Tibetans constitute all or a major part of the school population rather than the dispersed vocational classes set up for Tibetans in some largely Han Chinese populated senior secondary schools.
13 Hu led urgent discussion about how to improve the living standards of Tibetans. He criticized Han cadres, reduced their numbers in Tibet, and ordered those who stayed to learn Tibetan. It is claimed he said that money sent to Tibet for education ended up in the Yarlong River and that the amount of funding allocated to one school in Tibet was enough to establish two in China.
14 The main leaders who visited were Hu Qili and Tian Jiyun.
15 Two key documents pertaining to the establishment of the *neidi* schools were *Concerning Attaining the Target of the Formation of Interior Region Tibetan Schools and Classes for Cultivating Talented Students* (Central Government Document no. 22 of 1984) and *Circular Concerning Attaining the Central Implementation Target of Cultivating Tibetan Talent in the Interior Regions* (Document no. 25 of 1984).
16 It should also be pointed out that in the 1980s, and despite government restrictions, many Tibetan officials continued to send their children to India for secondary schooling. The *neidi* schools were also viewed as a way to provide a high-quality alternative.
17 The research in this article refers largely to the first and second cohorts, since they have already returned to Tibet in greater numbers; the later cohorts are only beginning to return to Tibet and will be interviewed in future research.

18 Though there has been some experimentation. Small numbers of academically superior students were sent to neighboring schools to study in integrated classes with Han Chinese students. While this is viewed as a positive step toward mainstreaming, it is also seen by *neidi* school principals as draining off the best talent from the *neidi* schools (in the same way that TAR school principals view *neidi* schools as draining off the best talent from their schools).
19 This was tested by assigning a number to the interviewer and then comparing data patterns.
20 On rural life in the areas where some of the subjects for this research were interviewed, see Goldstein et al. (2003).
21 Xiang level is a designation between a village and county.
22 According to interview L11, the students with a score beyond 170 had a chance to study in *neidiban*, whereas the students who further scored beyond 200 were able to go to *neidiban* in Shanghai.
23 The exception is the Lhasa Number One Secondary School, whose education quality is often preferred to that in *neidi* boarding schools.
24 This rule seems to be more flexible for Uyghurs and some other Muslim groups. Muslim boys and girls are permitted to wear a hijab (for girls) or a doppa (for boys) on their heads in school. They are also provided with a separate cafeteria in which no pork products are used.
25 "Love Tibet" rather than "love Tibetans" encouraged more identification with "political Tibet" and less with "ethnic Tibet." The official title of the boarding schools is Tibet Neidi (Inland) School rather than Tibetan Neidi (Inland) School.
26 Cell phones are used by some students to call home.
27 See Dumont and Wax (1969, 217–26), Wax et al. (1969), Deyhle and Swisher (1997), Reyhner (2001), and Spack (2002).
28 Although the interview atmosphere did lead to students voicing complaints about selected aspects of their education, we did not receive any reports that corporal punishment was used by Han teachers on Tibetan students. Many village teachers in Tibet, usually those who had not received a long period of teacher training, viewed corporal punishment as a necessary part of schooling. However, it is probable that Han teachers in *neidi* schools were told to never use corporal punishment since this would jeopardize the Tibet *neidi* school policy. See, e.g., reports of harsh discipline methods used in Oprah Winfrey's Leadership Academy for Girls, a boarding school for girls in South Africa. Also among the complaints were that parental visits were denied, and there was "a climate of intimidation and fear" (http:// www.tvguide.com/news/oprah-winfrey-scandal-37280.aspx).
29 Also see Viet Nam News, "Co-operation with Laos Continues to Develop," *Viet Nam News Agency,* November 11, 2007 (http://vietnamnews.vnagency.com.vn/showarticle.php?num = 05ECO110707); Viet Nam News Agency, "Ethnic Schools to Include Vocational Training," *ThanhnienNews.com,* January 24, 2008.

References

Adams, David Wallace. 1995. *Education for Extinction: American Indians and the Boarding School Experience, 1875–1928.* Lawrence: University Press of Kansas.
Archuleta, Margaret, Brenda J. Child, and K. Tsianina Lomawaima. 2004. *Away from Home: American Indian Boarding School Experiences, 1879–2000.* Santa Fe, NM: Heard Museum.
Bass, Catriona. 1998. *Education in Tibet: Policy and Practice since 1950.* London: Zed.
Bass, Catriona. 2008. "Tibetan Elementary Curriculum and Its Role in Nation Building." *Educational Review* 60 (1): 39–50.
Becker, Gary S. 1964. *Human Capital: A Theoretical and Empirical Analysis with Special Reference to Education.* New York: Columbia University Press.

Bordieu, Pierre. 1977. "Cultural Reproduction and Social Reproduction." In *Power and Ideology in Education,* ed. Jerome Karabel and A. H. Halsey. New York: Oxford University Press.

Bordieu, Pierre. 1986. "The Forms of Capital." In *Handbook of Theory and Research for the Sociology of Education,* ed. John G. Richardson. New York: Greenwood.

Bowles, Samuel, and Herbert Gintis. 1976. *Schooling in Capitalist America.* New York: Basic Books.

Buti, Tony. 2007. "The Systematic Removal of Indigenous Children from Their Families in Australia and Canada: The History—Similarities and Differences." http://www.newcastle.edu.au/centre/cispr/conferences/land/butipaper.pdf.

Chen, Yangbin. 2008. *Muslim Uyghur Students in a Chinese Boarding School: Social Recapitalization as a Response to Ethnic Integration.* New York: Lexington.

Chen, Yangbin, and Gerard A. Postiglione. 2009. "Muslim Uyghur Students in a Dislocated Chinese Boarding School: Bonding Social Capital as a Response to Ethnic Integration." *Race and Ethnicity: Multidisciplinary Global Contexts* 2 (Spring): 287–309.

Child, Brenda J. 1998. *Boarding School Seasons: American Indian Families, 1900–1940.* Lincoln: University of Nebraska Press.

Churchill, Ward. 2004. *Kill the Indian, Save the Man: The Genocidal Impact of American Indian Residential Schools.* San Francisco: City Lights.

Coleman, James. 1966. *Equality of Educational Opportunity.* Washington, DC: U.S. Government Printing Office.

Deyhle, Donna, and Karen Swisher. 1997. "Research in American Indian and Alaska Native Education: From Assimilation to Self-Determination." *Review of Research in Education* 22: 113–94.

Dikotter, Frank. 1992. *The Discourse of Race in Modern China.* Seattle: University of Washington Press.

Dumont, Robert V., and Murray Wax. 1969. "The Cherokee School and the Intercultural Classroom." *Human Organization* 18 (3): 217–26.

Ellis, Clyde. 1996. *To Change Them Forever: Indian Education at the Rainy Mountain Boarding School, 1893–1920.* Norman: University of Oklahoma Press.

Fei, Xiaotong. 1989. "Zhonghua minzu de duoyuan yiti geju" [Plurality and unity in the configuration of the Chinese nationality]. *Beijing Daxue Xuebao* 4: 1–19.

Fischer, Claude S., Michael Hout, Martin Sanchez Jankowski, Samuel R. Lucas, Ann Swindler, and Kim Voss. 1996. *Inequality by Design: Cracking the Bell Curve Myth.* Princeton, NJ: Princeton University Press.

Gladney, Dru. 1991. *Muslim Chinese: Ethnic Nationalism in the People's Republic.* Cambridge, MA: Council of East Asian Studies.

Goldstein, Melvyn C. 1989. *A History of Modern Tibet, 1913–1951.* Berkeley: University of California Press.

Goldstein, Melvyn C. 1997. *The Snow Lion and the Dragon: China, Tibet, and the Dalai Lama.* Berkeley: University of California Press.

Goldstein, Melvyn C. 2007. *The Calm before the Storm: 1951–1955.* Vol. 2 of *A History of Modern Tibet.* Berkeley: University of California Press.

Goldstein, Melvyn C., Ben Jiao, Cynthia M. Beall, and Phuntsog Tsering. 2003. "Development and Change in Rural Tibet: Problems and Adaptations." *Asian Survey* 43 (5): 758–79.

Halliman, Maureen. 1982. "The Peer Influence Process." *Studies in Educational Evaluation* 7 (3): 285–306.

Harrell, Stevan. 2002. *Ways of Being Ethnic in Southwest China.* Seattle: University of Washington Press.

Heberer, Thomas. 1989. *China and Its National Minorities: Autonomy or Assimilation.* New York: Sharpe.

Irendale, Robyn, Naran Bilik, Wang Su, Fei Guo, and Caroline Hoy, eds. 2001. *Contemporary Minority Migration, Education and Ethnicity.* Cheltenham, UK: Elgar.

Jenks, Christopher, Susan Bartlett, Mary Corcoran, and Greg J. Duncan. 1979. *Who Gets Ahead: The Determinants of Economic Success in America.* New York: Basic Books.

Johnson, Monica Kilpatrick, Robert Crosnoe, and Glen H. Elder Jr. 2001. "Students' Attachment and Academic Engagement: The Role of Race and Ethnicity." *Sociology of Education* 74: 318–40.

Kao, Grace, and Marta Tienda. 1998. "Educational Aspirations among Minority Youth." *American Journal of Education* 106: 349–84.

Keidel, Albert. 2009. "Chinese Regional Inequalities in Income and Well-Being." *Review of Income and Wealth,* forthcoming.

Kratli, Saverio. 2001. *Education Provision to Nomadic Pastoralists.* Brighton, UK: Institute of Development Studies.

Liu, Zhijie. 2005. *Qingxi Xizang weilai, ai rong xueyu xuezi* [Affection is the future of Tibet, love melts the snow region students], Hubei jingzhou Xizangban ban-ban ershi Zhounian jinian (1985–2005) [Hubei Jingzhou Tibet Classes' Twenty Year Anniversary (1985–2005), published in Hubei Jingzhou, August, 65–66].

Lomawaima, K. Tsianina, and T. L. McCarty. 2006. *"To Remain an Indian": Lessons in Democracy from a Century of Native American Education.* New York: Teachers College Press.

Mackerras, Colin. 1994. *China's Minorities: Integration and Modernization in the Twentieth Century.* Hong Kong: Oxford University Press.

Mackerras, Colin. 1995. *China's Minority Cultures: Identities and Integration since 1912.* New York: St. Martin's.

Manynooch, Faming. 2008. "National Integration: Education for Ethnic Minorities in Laos." PhD diss., University of Hong Kong, Sociology Department.

Mathur, N. N. G. 1994. *Problems of Tribal Education.* Udaipur, India: Shiva.

McBeth, Sally J. 1983. *Ethnic Identity and the Boarding School Experience of West Central Oklahoma American Indians.* Lanham, MD: University Press of America.

Miller, J. R. 1996. *Shingwauk's Vision: A History of Native Residential Schools.* Toronto: University of Toronto Press.

Morrow, Raymond Allan, and Carlos Alberto Torres. 1995. *Social Theory and Education: A Critique of Theories of Social and Cultural Reproduction.* Albany: State University of New York Press.

Nettles, Michael T. 1991. "Racial Similarities and Differences in the Predictors of College Student Achievement." In *College: Black and White; African American Studies in Predominantly White and in Historically Black Public Universities,* ed. Walter Allen. Albany: State University of New York Press.

Nyima, Palden (Nima, Badeng). 1997. "The Way Out for Tibetan Education." *Chinese Education and Society* 30 (4): 7–20.

Ogbu, John U. 1978. *Minority Education and Caste: The American System in Cross Cultural Perspective.* New York: Academic Press.

Ogbu, John U. 1995. "Understanding Cultural Diversity and Learning." In *Handbook of Research on Multicultural Education,* ed. James A. Banks and Cherry A. M. Banks. New York: Macmillan.

Ogbu, John U. 2003. *Black American Students in an Affluent Suburb: A Study of Academic Disengagement.* Mahwah, NJ: Erlbaum.
Ogbu, John U., and Margaret Gibson, eds. 1974. *The Next Generation: An Ethnography of Education in an Urban Neighborhood.* New York: Academic Press.
Ogbu, John U., and Margaret Gibson, eds. 1991. *Minority Status and Schooling: A Comparative Study of Immigrant and Involuntary Minorities.* New York: Garland.
Postiglione, Gerard A. 2008. "Making Tibetans in China: Educational Challenges for Harmonious Multiculturalism." *Educational Review* 60 (1): 1–20.
Postiglione, Gerard A., Ben Jiao, and Sonam Gyatso. 2005. "Education in Rural Tibet: Development, Problems, and Adaptations." *China: An International Journal* 3 (1): 1–23.
Postiglione, Gerard A., Ben Jiao, and Sonam Gyatso. 2006. "Household Perspectives on School Attendance in Rural Tibet." *Educational Review* 58 (3): 317–37.
Reyhner, Jon. 2001. "Family, Community, and School Impacts on American Indian and Alaska Native Students' Success." Paper presented at the 32nd National Indian Education Association convention, Billings, MT.
Schultz, Theodore. 1963. *The Economic Value of Education.* New York: Columbia University Press.
Sewell, William H., Archibald O. Haller, and Alexandro Portes. 1969. "The Educational and Early Occupational Attainment Process." *American Sociological Review* 34: 83–92.
Spack, Ruth. 2002. *America's Second Tongue: American Indian Education and the Ownership of English, 1860–1900.* Lincoln: University of Nebraska Press.
Steele, Claude M. 1992. "Race and the Schooling of Black Americans." *Atlantic Monthly* 269 (4): 68–78.
Steele, Claude M. 1998. "A Threat in the Air: How Stereotypes Shape the Intellectual Identities and Performance of Women and African Americans." In *Confronting Racism: The Problem and Its Response,* ed. Jennifer Eberhardt and Susan Fiske. Thousand Oaks, CA: Sage.
Steiner-Khansi, Gita, and Ines Stolpe. 2006. *Educational Import: Local Encounters with Global Forces in Mongolia.* New York: Palgrave Macmillan.
Suarez-Orosco, Marcello M. 1991. "Migration, Minority Status and Education: European Dilemmas and Responses in the 1990s." *Anthropology and Education Quarterly* 22: 99–120.
Tinto, Vincent. 1993. *Leaving College: Rethinking the Causes and Cures of Student Attrition.* 2nd ed. Chicago: University of Chicago Press.
Trafzer, Clifford E., Jean A. Keller, and Lorene Sisquoc. 2006. *Boarding School Blues: Revisiting American Indian Educational Experiences.* Lincoln: University of Nebraska Press.
Trennert, Robert A. 1988. *The Phoenix Indian School.* Norman: University of Oklahoma Press.
Wax, Murray, et al. 1969. *Indian Education in Eastern Oklahoma.* Lawrence: University Press of Kansas.
Willis, Paul. 1977. *Learning to Labor: How Working Class Kids Get Working Class Jobs.* Westmead, UK: Saxon House.
Xiangba, Pingcuo. 2005. *Xizang zizhiqu jiaoyu zhi* [Education annals of the Tibetan autonomous region]. Beijing: Tibetology Press.
Ying, Fating. 1984. "Ying Fatang tong zhizai zhonggong Xizang Zizhiqu san jie er ci quan wei kuoda huiyi shang de jianghua" [Comrade Ying Fatang's speech in the

second enlarged plenary of all committee members of the third Tibet Autonomous Region Committee of the CPC]. In *Shen shi zizhiqu shaoshu minzu jiaoyu gongzuo wenjian xuanbian 1977–1990* [Selected documents on ethnic education in provincial, municipal, autonomous regions, 1977–1990], ed. Guo Fuchang. Chengdu: Sichuan Ethnic Press.

Zhu, Zhiying. 2007. *State Schooling and Ethnic Identity: The Politics of a Tibetan Neidi School in China*. New York: Lexington.

, # Part III
Institutions
Universities under globalization

Part II

8 Maintaining Global Engagement in the Face of National Integration in Hong Kong

The retrocession of Hong Kong to Chinese sovereignty has far-reaching implications for the academic profession in Hong Kong's universities. In recovering sovereignty over Hong Kong in July 1997, the People's Republic of China (PRC) acquired seven universities—three of which are among the top 10 in Asia—with over 5,000 full-time academic staff.[1] At least five are larger than more than 90 percent of China's universities.[2]

Hong Kong universities and their faculty differ in fundamental ways from those on the mainland, especially in their distinct Western academic traditions and autonomy, as well as their organization, governance, finance, and institutional cultures. The greater global integration of academics in Hong Kong is as much a function of technological resources as of academic freedom.[3] Maintaining Hong Kong's universities as they are is a major challenge for the new Special Administrative Region (SAR) government as well as Beijing.

Academics are the driving force in Hong Kong universities. Compared with China's professoriate, Hong Kong's has greater influence on the flow and control of knowledge, as well as on academic policies at the department, school, and institutional levels.[4] This has been due not only to the freedom of Hong Kong society but also to the composition of the professoriate, which includes a high proportion of overseas Chinese (most with foreign passports) and foreign academics (most from Western democracies).[5] Although China's universities have become more open, with larger numbers of academic staff engaged in international exchange, Hong Kong's professionals remain more international in composition.[6] Nevertheless, academic internationalism in Hong Kong usually is associated with links to Australia, Britain, Canada, and the United States, while China's is more globally inclusive.[7]

Hong Kong's recognized position as a key communications hub coupled with unrestricted university access to the internet ensures full participation in global academic discourse.[8] Since the mid-1990s, there has been a great deal of internet traffic, in both English and Chinese, between academics in Hong Kong and mainland China. When this is combined with Beijing's encouragement of closer ties between Hong Kong and Chinese universities, the result is a vibrant academic discourse.[9] At the same time, however, academics in China are subject to restrictions on their internet usage despite this increased access. The academic profession in Hong Kong wrestles with the question of how to preserve academic freedom and institutional autonomy in the face of the retrocession to China and must do so as it deals with issues relating to the increasing student diversity following rapid expansion in the early 1990s, increased pressure to improve standards of research and teaching, and the devolution of responsibility for institutional governance and finance.[10]

The Hong Kong Context and Its Universities

After 35 consecutive years of real increases in gross domestic product, Hong Kong's over 6 million inhabitants (95 percent Cantonese-speaking Chinese) enjoy a living standard higher than some developed countries—including Britain.[11] But despite having had freedom of speech and the rule of law, it only gained a fully elected legislature in 1995, which was replaced on July 1, 1997 with an appointed legislature.[12] Other features include an efficient civil service, effective communications and transportation networks, robust textile and electronics industries, a highly skilled and educated populace, and an internationally oriented university system.

In 1997, the territory became an SAR of the PRC under a "one country/two systems" arrangement, in which the previous education system is expected to remain.[13] The new constitution—the Basic Law—calls for a high degree of autonomy and provides that the people of Hong Kong will rule themselves.[14] The decolonization of higher education has come to mean closer, more frequent contacts with universities in China, declining legitimacy for colonial educational policy, localization of the highest administrative positions, efforts to step up as well as resist the pace of democratization, increased emigration of faculty with return migration of those who have acquired overseas passports, and expanding linkages with adjacent southern China—especially the Pearl River Delta.

As Hong Kong's universities move closer to China they also are becoming increasingly globalized. Until 1990, Hong Kong for years had sent more students overseas for university education—mostly to Australia, Britain, Canada, and the United States—than it admitted to local universities. Even after 1994, when the number of students at local universities surpassed that going overseas,[15] the international character of Hong Kong's universities was underscored by the composition of its academic staff. Of those with doctorates, approximately 90 percent earned them outside Hong Kong.

Hong Kong's academic profession has much to gain or lose in the coming years. It is more closely bound to Western university traditions and practices than elsewhere in Asia, which allows Hong Kong to offer China a unique model of successful East-West academic integration. In addition, given the precarious status of intellectuals in China, Hong Kong's reincorporation could have major implications for academic freedom and institutional autonomy.[16] The academic profession can contribute to a smooth transition as well as serve as a catalyst for change.

Academic freedom was never a major issue in Hong Kong. Within a community dedicated to commercial interests, the academic community historically was small and not very influential, and academics seldom, if ever, challenged the government. Until 1964, there was only one university—the University of Hong Kong—which was staffed mostly by British expatriates and British-educated Chinese and had close ties to government. Most high-level civil servants, even today, are graduates of this university. The Chinese University of Hong Kong, which was established to serve the increasing number of graduates from Chinese medium secondary schools, was staffed by a diverse group of Chinese academics with connections to many different Chinese communities. Although schools in Hong Kong were prohibited from any discussion of politics until after 1989,[17] universities were under no such government ordinance and purges of university staff for their political views were unknown. Nevertheless, by 1990, there were indications that academic self-censorship was on the rise, as it was in the Hong Kong press.[18] After July 1997, the first area of sensitivity would concern publications that advocated, directly or indirectly, two Chinas or one China and Taiwan.[19]

Since 1990, at least the academic profession has been marked by increasingly diverse views. Largely the result of higher education's expansion, this is partly due to the recruitment of more local Chinese as well as non-British-trained academics. A decision to nearly double the number of students admitted to university first-degree studies by 1994–95 was made in October 1989.[20] Referred to in some quarters as crisis management and "too little, too late," the sudden expansion acted as a confidence booster in the wake of increased emigration following the Tiananmen crisis.[21] Nevertheless, it improved the opportunities of secondary school graduates to attend university in Hong Kong, and the mean percentage of the relevant age group admitted increased to 18 percent in 1994–95, when total enrollment reached almost 58,000. An estimated 25,000 or more attend universities overseas (excluding mainland China and Taiwan). The expansion also has been reflected in a drop in the number of overseas student visas issued since 1990.[22]

There are nine degree-granting institutions of higher education in Hong Kong, including seven universities, a tertiary institution, and the Academy of Performing Arts. All but the Open Learning University are fully government funded.[23] Before 1990, most degree courses were offered in two universities. A third university was established in 1991. One polytechnic began offering degree courses in 1983, and the other polytechnic and one tertiary college began to offer degree courses in 1986, representing 42 percent of all first-degree enrollments in the major institutions by 1988–89. The polytechnics and one of the tertiary institutions earned university titles in 1994, while the Open Learning University earned the title in 1997. At least one more tertiary institution is expected to be elevated to university status by 1997–98. The three top-tier research universities—the University of Hong Kong, the Chinese University of Hong Kong, and the Hong Kong University of Science and Technology—each provides a range of programs leading to undergraduate and graduate degrees. They offer research programs in every subject area and allow faculty to undertake consultancy and collaborative projects with industry.[24] The medium of instruction is English except in the Chinese University of Hong Kong, which is bilingual.

The Hong Kong Polytechnic University and the City University of Hong Kong (the former polytechnics) offer courses leading to the awards of diploma, higher certificate, higher diploma, and a bachelor's degree. They also offer a small number of graduate degrees and have some research programs, emphasize the application of knowledge and vocational training, and maintain strong links with industry and employers. The Hong Kong Baptist University (formerly Baptist College) and Lingnan College provide undergraduate courses in the arts, sciences, social sciences, business, and communication. They plan to or already offer a small number of graduate courses, with research programs in some areas. The Open University, known as the Open Learning Institute until 1997, is a distance learning institution based on the British model.

The most influential body in higher education is the University Grants Committee (UGC), which was established in 1965 to advise the government on the facilities, development, and financial needs of universities.[25] In 1996, the body included nine Hong Kong Chinese, six members from the United Kingdom, three Americans (including a professor of Hong Kong Chinese origin), and one Australian. The chief executive of the Hong Kong SAR appoints the members of the UGC, which was expected to include members from mainland China after the return of Chinese sovereignty. The first SAR chief executive named by an election committee in Hong Kong and approved by the National People's Congress in Beijing has targeted education as a priority and appointed the UGC chair as one of his executive counsellors.[26]

Public knowledge of the UGC's recommendations for increased funds to cover massive expansion of higher education led to measures for greater accountability in teaching and research. The international makeup of UGC members resulted in moves to bring Hong Kong's universities, along with their relatively well-salaried academic staff, into the global movement to decentralize financial responsibility. By 1997, universities in Hong Kong faced budget cuts for the first time, even though the economy remained robust.

Although most of their funds come from the government, universities in Hong Kong are autonomous. Decisions about hiring, course content, staff evaluation, academic titling, salaries, and so forth are made by the individual institutions. Nevertheless, there are natural limitations to that autonomy. When the University of Hong Kong decided in 1988 to add a fourth year to its 3-year degree program, the Education Commission of Hong Kong undercut it by mandating that all secondary education had to last 7 rather than 6 years.[27] There are other limitations as well, as noted in a 1996 UGC review of higher education. "We take very much for granted in Hong Kong an adherence to institutional autonomy and academic freedom, as they have served us well in the past. These are not absolutes—there are restrictions—and their survival depends very much on pragmatic considerations of efficiency as on moral and ethical arguments. Nevertheless, there is a strong 'hands off' element in the relations between government (directly or indirectly through the advisory bodies) and higher educational institutions. It is important to maintain it."[28]

This position has opened the door to challenge tenure on pragmatic rather than political grounds. Members of the UGC have noted the debate in the United

States about the viability of tenure over the long-term. Given Hong Kong's economic philosophy, market forces will be welcomed increasingly into the academic arena, leaving open the possibility that tenure and the academic freedom it is supposed to protect will be less secure—a prospect of some concern at the time of the sovereignty transfer.

Institutional autonomy also has necessitated the formation of a committee composed of the heads of the seven higher education institutions that meets periodically to discuss matters of mutual interest and concern, including their common preference to convert to a 4-year system. University heads use these meetings to inform each other of changes within their institutions that may affect the larger system, such as the introduction of a credit unit system or alterations in the system of academic titles.

China's Professoriate

Higher education in China has changed dramatically since the late 1970s as universities have been pressed into the service of economic liberalization and reform. Regular enrollment was expanded by enlarging institutions and setting up new ones, although increased market forces, less government financial support, and expanding student numbers led to a degree of consolidation by the mid-1990s. Large numbers of students and scholars continue to go abroad as more international exchanges have been encouraged. Finally, *minban* (non-state-run, or private) universities and colleges are being established to mobilize more resources for accelerating higher education development.[29]

Chinese institutions are funded and managed according to national regulations, but the government's insistence that universities raise more of their own funds has led to increased managerial autonomy. Unlike Hong Kong where there are no private universities, China has encouraged such institutions. Nevertheless, Hong Kong's universities enjoy an autonomy not found on the mainland.

Even with the consolidation since 1995, China still has more than 1,000 higher education institutions.[30] These are classified by specialization: comprehensive universities, natural science and technology, agriculture, forestry, medicine and pharmacy, teacher training, language and literature, finance and economics, political science and law, physical culture, art, and others. Institutions also are classified by the government department to which they are responsible, including the state education commission, central ministries and agencies, and local authorities (usually the provincial government).[31] Comparing size, we find that only 137 of China's 1,054 institutions have more than 5,000 students, while four of Hong Kong's seven universities exceed 10,000. In short, about half of all Chinese institutions (536) have under 2,000 students, and 69 percent (729) have fewer than 3,000.[32]

The traditionally older professoriate in China has become younger, although the proportion of faculty holding doctorates remains far below their counterparts in Hong Kong. Like Hong Kong, academic titles are heavily weighted at the bottom end of the scale, and the percentage of women faculty remains low (30 percent for China and 25 percent for Hong Kong).[33]

150   *Institutions*

The average age of Hong Kong faculty in 1996 was 43,[34] which is relatively young compared with countries such as Japan, Russia, and Israel, where the average age was 51 in 1993.[35] Most of China's full professors are between 56 and 60. Yet, almost 30 percent of academic staff across ranks equivalent to assistant, associate, and full professor are between 31 and 35.[36] Reasons for this include the expansion of higher education and the return of scholars from abroad who are dissatisfied with their employment prospects outside China.

More than half of Hong Kong academics have doctorates, while staff qualification levels in China resemble those in other developing countries. Within Chinese academia, less than 1 percent have doctorates, 5 percent possess master's degrees, 49 percent have bachelor's degrees, and the rest have lesser qualifications. Among full professors, 1 percent have a doctorate, another 1 percent have a master's, 27 percent have a bachelor's, and the rest have less.[37] The impact of the Cultural Revolution—when formal academic qualifications did not exist—must be considered when viewing these figures, however, as China's universities began to offer doctoral degrees only in the early 1980s, and then only at top universities in selected fields. Stringent standards limit professors, including those with doctorates, to carrying doctoral students only if they and their institutions receive approval of the State Education Commission.

In regard to academic rank, Hong Kong is bottom heavy compared with counterparts overseas. At the University of Hong Kong in 1995, for example, less than 20 percent of the staff were full professors (including professor and reader categories) compared with 40–60 percent at most North American universities.[38] This situation is changing as a system of cross-retitling from British to American systems and upward retitling without pay have been introduced to improve international recruiting efforts as well as to provide incentives for long-standing lower-rank staff. As already noted, the imbalance is even more extreme in China. Of the full-time staff in the top three ranks of China's institutions in 1995, 10 percent were professors, 35 percent were associate professors, and 55 percent were assistant professors (lecturers).[39]

Attributes and Attitudes of Academic Staff at Top Universities in Hong Kong and China

Educational differences resulting from capitalism and socialism are mitigated by many similarities that could be a result of cultural similarities, the dominance of state-funded universities, the economic integration between Hong Kong and the rest of China, market reforms in mainland China, and stepped-up academic exchanges not only between the two systems (the SAR and the rest of the PRC) but also within the larger global academy.[40] The latter has been spurred on by the fact that PRC academics returning home from overseas can visit Hong Kong without a visa.[41] Illustrative comparisons can be made from faculty survey data collected at one of China's top universities (CTU) and Hong Kong's three top universities (HKTU).[42]

The most prominent differences concern qualifications and salaries. Almost three-quarters of the HKTU faculty hold a doctorate compared with 23 percent at CTU. Unlike Hong Kong, where most academics expressed satisfaction with their salaries, only 6 percent of CTU faculty rated their salaries as good or excellent. More than half of CTU faculty say that paid consulting is necessary compared with 7 percent for HKTU, and more than 80 percent of CTU faculty hold other paid positions while less than 4 percent do so at HKTU. This trend is a result of increased educational marketization in China. In Hong Kong, where the cost of living is high, universities easily could lose prominent academics to the private sector if salaries were reduced.

Nevertheless, these surveys indicate a number of similarities regarding views toward student quality, research activity, governance, higher education and society, academic freedom, and international connections. Although more intellectual freedom exists at CTU than at other universities in mainland China, independent critiques of the system are not encouraged. At HKTU, such critiques are sometimes frowned on; the system evolved, after all, as a product of colonialism within a conservative Chinese society to support the status quo. Still, a critical tradition rooted in the Western university nevertheless survives. Western academics could hardly constitute a serious threat because of their generally limited integration into local culture and society.

Student Quality

More than 60 percent of CTU faculty rated their students as good or excellent compared with 45 percent at Hong Kong's three top universities. About 37 percent of CTU faculty disagreed with the statement that "students in their department are better now than 5 years ago," while the figure for HKTU was 44 percent. Student enrollment has risen in both places, but HKTU's more rapid expansion—almost 100 percent between 1989 and 1996—may account for the slightly different views. Nevertheless, higher education in China is likely to expand from 3 percent of the relevant age group in 1994 to 8 percent in 2000, which may well bring CTU faculty views more in line with those of HKTU.

Although Hong Kong faculty gave their students the highest rating in mathematics and quantitative reasoning skills in an international survey of 13 countries and Hong Kong conducted by the Carnegie Foundation for the Advancement of Teaching, CTU faculty rated the preparation of their students even higher than HKTU faculty rated their students. Aside from the fact that CTU students are drawn from a much larger population pool, the CTU mathematics department is one of the country's most distinguished. Few Hong Kong faculty view their students as adequately prepared in written and oral communication skills (giving them among the lowest ratings in the international survey). CTU professors rated the preparation of their students in written and oral communication skills more than twice as high as the Hong Kong figure. This can be accounted for by the fact that Chinese language learning was not given strong emphasis in Hong Kong under the colonial regime. English language education, while emphasized, did not provide most students with strong communication skills. This is due in large part to the fact that 98 percent of the Hong Kong population are Chinese, leaving few opportunities to use English. With the onset of Chinese sovereignty, most secondary schools converted to Chinese language (mostly Cantonese) as the medium of instruction, and the learning of standard Mandarin Chinese became compulsory beginning in primary school.

Research Activity

Views concerning research show the greatest similarities, with 55 percent of CTU faculty and 53 percent of HKTU faculty stating that their interests lie primarily in research rather than teaching. Moreover, 86 percent of CTU and 85 percent of HKTU faculty say that research plays an important role in staff evaluation. When asked if publications used for promotion are just counted and not qualitatively evaluated, approximately half the faculty at CTU and HKTU agreed.

With respect to expectations and pressures to do research, however, CTU faculty report being more challenged. Twenty-eight percent of HKTU faculty agreed that they frequently feel under pressure to do more research than they would actually like, while the figure for CTU is 44 percent. Eighty-five percent of HKTU faculty believe that regular research activity is expected of them, while 49 percent of CTU faculty so indicate. This may be accounted for in part by the shortage of research funds and facilities at CTU compared with HKTU. In fact, 38 percent of HKTU faculty agreed that research funding was easier to get than 5 years earlier, and only 17 percent of CTU faculty agree.

In an authoritarian society, one would expect restrictions on certain types of research publications. In fact, only 38 percent of CTU faculty agreed that there are no political or ideological restrictions on what scholars may publish, while 68 percent of HKTU agreed. Such restrictions apparently do not infringe on academics' connections with international counterparts, however, as 44 percent of HKTU faculty believe that international connections are important in staff evaluations compared with 57 percent of CTU faculty.

University Governance and Academic Freedom

Regarding the degree to which decision making is centralized, HKTU faculty viewed the selection of key administrators in their institutions as only slightly more centralized (78 percent) than CTU staff did (71 percent). Likewise, 56 percent of HKTU faculty indicated that decisions determining budget priorities were centralized compared with 62 percent of CTU faculty. Given China's many years of centralized planning and top-down decision making, that CTU academic staff still view most decisions—including the selection of new faculty, faculty promotions, assignment of teaching loads, approval of new academic programs, and the establishment of admission standards—as more centralized is not surprising.

Faculty influence on academic policies must be understood in the context of a more hierarchical, less open, and more centralized tradition at CTU. Sixty-seven percent of CTU faculty see themselves as very, somewhat, or a little influential at the department level in shaping key academic policies, in contrast to 82 percent for HKTU faculty. This can be viewed within the context of institutional democracy, as HKTU staff elect either their department heads or deans (or both), and agendas and minutes from many committees, including those of the university senate, are circulated to all staff members. In addition, 42 percent of CTU faculty agree that the administration is often autocratic, compared with 57 percent of HKTU faculty. That most HKTU academics received their higher degrees in Western universities where the tradition was more open, less hierarchical, and more decentralized than in Hong Kong might account for certain aspects of their response patterns.

Both HKTU and CTU tout academic freedom as an important value embodied in their university traditions,[43] and while China has a history of clamping down on intellectuals, 65 percent of HKTU (though only 34 percent of faculty at Hong Kong's other four institutions of higher education) and 55 percent of CTU faculty agreed that the administration supports academic freedom.[44] Yet, only half of CTU faculty and even fewer—44 percent—of PKU faculty indicated that they were free to determine the content of the courses they teach, in contrast to 78 percent at HKTU.[45]

Higher Education Priorities

Sixty-three percent of CTU but only 44 percent of HKTU faculty agreed that the government has the responsibility of defining the overall purposes and policies of higher education. Moreover, 33 percent of HKTU faculty believe that the government should provide free tuition to students, while only 12 percent of CTU faculty thought so. However, about 40 percent of both faculty groups believe that there is far too much governmental interference in important academic policies. Relative agreement between the two groups also was displayed in regard to views about the role of business: 91 percent of CTU and 86 percent of HKTU faculty believed that businesses should contribute more to higher education.

At first glance, the CTU responses might seem unexpected in a socialist system. However, the changing context of economic reforms and the introduction of market mechanisms has penetrated the thinking of the academic community. This is not only reflected in activities to supplement their incomes but also in their views toward the financial contribution that students should make toward a university education. In fact, CTU and more than 30 other institutions directly under the State Education Commission introduced tuition fees beginning in 1994.

154 *Institutions*

Table 8.1 Highest Priorities for Higher Education in the Future

Priorities	Hong Kong's Three Top Universities	China's Top Universities
Protect free intellectual inquiry	1	3
Promote scholarship and research	2	2
Strengthen the society's capacity to compete internationally	3	1
Educate students for leadership	4	7
Prepare students for work	5	6
Lifelong learning for adults	6	8
Help to solve basic social problems	7	4
Preserve cultural heritage	8	5

Sources: Data for Hong Kong's three top universities are from the International Survey of the Academic Profession, 1991–93, conducted by the Carnegie Foundation for the Advancement of Teaching. Data for China's top universities are from a survey I conducted in 1994.

Note: Rankings are based on the relative percentage of faculty that believe it should be assigned the highest priority by society. Priorities are ranked 1–8, 1 being the highest, 8 the lowest.

The HKTU and CTU faculty ranked the same three concerns, within a field of eight, as the highest priorities for the future of higher education (see table 8.1), though they differed in the ordering.[46] Global competition is foremost in the minds of both faculties but more so at CTU. Likewise, free intellectual inquiry is seen as significant by both but more so by HKTU faculty. As decolonization proceeds, HKTU faculty place a higher priority on educating students for leadership than on the preservaton of cultural heritage.

International Academic Activity

The CTU academics, more than HKTU faculty, reported that foreign students are enrolled more frequently at their institutions and their own students have studied abroad more frequently. More CTU than HKTU faculty also reported that connections with overseas scholars were very important to their professional work. Eighty-eight percent of CTU academics indicated that they must read books and journals published overseas in order to keep up with developments in their fields, whereas the figure for HKTU academics, all of whom can read English, was 100 percent. Finally, 70 percent and 66 percent of CTU and HKTU academics, respectively, believe the curriculum should be more international in focus.

As expected, views of the faculties of HKTU and CTU differ based on contextual and institutional idiosyncracies. Yet, similarities abound and may very well be attributed not only to the factors mentioned at the beginning of this section but also to their increasingly similar interactions with the global academic community.

Hong Kong's Academics within the Global Academy

Although academics in both Hong Kong and China are young, those in Hong Kong are more credentialed and international in composition. Nevertheless, with the expansion of higher education in China, this situation could change within a decade. For Hong Kong, key issues are the maintenance of the academic profession, preservation of academic freedom, and continued integration into the global academy, in addition to contributing to China's economic development.

Maintenance of the profession will be difficult if academic staff leave in the early period of the SAR. In 1993, 37 percent of academic staff from Hong Kong's top three institutions and 47 percent from the others indicated that they were likely to leave their institutions within 5 years. The figure was 56 percent for overseas appointees and 33 percent for local appointees.[47] The expressed likelihood of academic staff leaving their institutions should be viewed in the context of increased emigration among the larger population prior to 1997 as well as in the generally high mobility rates that exist in Hong Kong across occupations. Also, to be sure, a wide gap may exist between expressed likelihood and a concrete decision to leave one's institution.

By 1996, few had actually left and the turnover rate, including overseas staff, was not abnormally high.[48] By that time, confidence in the future status of Hong Kong had grown as memories of the Tiananmen incident receded. In anticipation of an outflow, Hong Kong's universities had developed strategies to boost their ability to recruit internationally, especially by converting the title system from the British (lecturer, senior lecturer, reader, professor) to the American (assistant, associate, professor) model. Upward retitling without pay also was instituted so that overseas academics could be recruited as associate professors on assistant professor salaries, which generally are higher than associate professor salaries in their country of origin. This measure helped to retain other key faculty who might have left Hong Kong. A further incentive was to offer an early payout of accumulated retirement benefits in lump sum and without loss of tenure to fearful academics. By 1997, Hong Kong's professoriate generally was still intact. Overseas academics in Hong Kong have foreign passports, and although they could be the first to leave if the situation deteriorated, it is the locals who more often go abroad, most just long enough to gain a foreign passport before they return. This practice is facilitated by an unofficial policy of extended leave without pay for valued academic staff.

Regardless of the staff outflow after 1997, the expansion of higher education will necessitate broader faculty recruitment. That surely includes China, despite the mainland's own shortage of doctorates and doctoral programs. This has created a large market for overseas doctoral programs, something that Hong Kong's universities also are tapping into by increasing the proportion of their doctoral students from mainland China. Hong Kong's universities also have begun to employ mainlanders with doctorates from the United States and other countries who have not returned to China.[49]

156   *Institutions*

There also were no overt attacks on academic freedom in Hong Kong as the return of Chinese rule approached. No politically motivated purges of academic staff occurred, with none expected in the short term. Academics with dissenting views—including members of the political party intentionally marginalized by Beijing—could still be found teaching.[50] University shops sold books not approved on the mainland, and university presses published books with dissenting views. Self-censorship was on the rise by 1997, however, in anticipation of change.

Continued integration into the global academy will help to ensure academic freedom as well as improve the quality of education and the standard of research. Such international engagement seems assured with so many faculty from the United Kingdom, Commonwealth countries, and the United States. Although faculty from other parts of the world are far fewer in number, this selective internationalism has served Hong Kong higher education well in many ways, including the maintenance of standards and the nurture of international academic interchange.

The main challenge to Hong Kong's professoriate is to maintain its globalism while fostering the rapid expansion of academic exchange with universities in China. This academic exchange relies on a variety of sources in Hong Kong and the rest of China. The UGC allocation, which alone was 2.5 million Hong Kong dollars for academic exchange with China in 1991–92, jumped to 4.4 million in 1995–96. As more of the academics recruited by Hong Kong are mainland Chinese who earned their doctorates in the United States and other Western countries, they will join their Hong Kong counterparts, serving as a bridge between the Hong Kong and mainland academic communities—unless the recruitment process becomes overly politicized and Hong Kong's academic culture changes radically.

Notes

Part of this research was supported by a grant from the Hong Seng Bank Golden Jubilee Educational Fund administered by the Centre of Asian Studies of the University of Hong Kong, as well as by a research grant from the Sik Sik Yuen Foundation, administered by the Faculty of Education of the University of Hong Kong. I would like to thank Mark Constas, Edward Trickey, and Li-fang Zhang for their useful comments.

1 Those seven universities are the University of Hong Kong, the Chinese University of Hong Kong, the Hong Kong University of Science and Technology, Hong Kong Baptist University, the City University of Hong Kong, the Hong Kong Polytechnic University, and the Open Learning University. Lingnan College will be elevated to university status in due course, and there may be eight universities in Hong Kong by the time this article appears. For figures on the number of academic staff, see data derived from reports of the University Grants Committee of Hong Kong. See also *Asiaweek* 23, no. 20 (May 23, 1997): 34–44.
2 See *Zhongguo jiaoyu tongji nianjian, 1995* (Educational statistics yearbook of China, 1995) (Beijing: People's Education Press, 1996).
3 See Gerard A. Postiglione, "Hong Kong Higher Education within the Global Academy," in *Hong Kong's Reunion with China: The Global Dimensions,* ed. Gerard A. Postiglione and James T. H. Tang (New York: Sharpe, 1997), pp. 239–68.
4 See Ruth Hayhoe, *China's Universities and the Open Door* (New York: Sharpe, 1989).
5 This can be seen in Gerard A. Postiglione, "The Future of Hong Kong's Academic Profession in a Period of Profound Change," in *The International Academic*

Profession: Portraits of Fourteen Countries, ed. Philip Altbach (Princeton, N.J.: Carnegie Foundation for the Advancement of Teaching, 1996), table 5.1.
6 See Weifang Min, "China," in *Asian Higher Education: An International Handbook and Reference Guide,* ed. Gerard A. Postiglione and Grace C. L. Mak (Westport, Conn.: Greenwood, 1997), pp. 37–55.
7 China's academic exchanges encompass Africa and South America as well as Eastern Europe and the Middle East, while Hong Kong's academic relations have had little exchange with these regions and largely ignored Eastern Europe, including Russia, until the 1990s.
8 See Ernest L. Boyer, Philip G. Altbach, and Mary Jean Whitelaw, eds., *The Academic Profession: An International Perspective* (Princeton, N.J.: Carnegie Foundation for the Advancement of Teaching, 1994), fig. 37, p. 53. A higher proportion of the Hong Kong academic staff gave excellent ratings to their computer facilities than academic staff from any of the other 13 countries in this survey.
9 Many universities, including Peking University and Qinghua University in Beijing and Fudan University in Shanghai, have established offices and/or special agreements for academic exchange with universities in Hong Kong and Macau.
10 See University Grants Committee of Hong Kong, *Higher Education in Hong Kong* (Hong Kong: Government Printer, 1996).
11 See Donald Tsang, *Hong Kong Economic Outlook, 1997* (Hong Kong: Government Printer, 1997).
12 The Hong Kong Provisional Legislature, composed of appointed members confirmed by Beijing, reversed civil liberties legislation enacted by Hong Kong's fully elected Legislative Council, which it replaced on July 1, 1997.
13 See Gerard A. Postiglione, "From Capitalism to Socialism: Hong Kong Education within a Transitional Society," *Comparative Education Review* 35, no. 4 (November 1991): 627–49, and "The Decolonization of Hong Kong Education," in *The Hong Kong Reader: Transfer to Chinese Sovereignty,* ed. Ming K. Chan and Gerard A. Postiglione (New York: Sharpe, 1997), pp. 98–123.
14 See *The Basic Law of the Special Administrative Region of Hong Kong of the People's Republic of China* (Hong Kong: Consultative Committee of the Basic Law, 1990).
15 Todd M. Davis, ed., *Open Doors, 1994–1995, Report on International Educational Exchanges* (New York: Institute of International Education, 1995).
16 See, e.g., Merle Goldman, with Timothy Creek and Carol Lee Hamrin, eds., *China's Intellectuals and the State: In Search of a New Relationship,* Harvard Contemporary China Series no. 3, Council on East Asian Studies (Cambridge, Mass.: Harvard University Press, 1987); Richard Madsen, "The Spiritual Crisis of China's Intellectuals," in *Chinese Society on the Eve of Tiananmen: The Impact of Reform,* eds. Deborah Davis and Ezra Vogel, Harvard Contemporary China Series no. 7, Council on East Asian Studies (Cambridge, Mass.: Harvard University Press, 1990), pp. 243–60; and Merle Goldman, "The Intellectuals in the Deng Xiaoping Era," in *State and Society in China: The Consequences of Reform,* ed. Arthur Lewis Rosenbaum (Boulder, Colo.: Westview, 1992), pp. 193–218.
17 In 1971, an Education Department ordinance stated, "No instruction, education, entertainment, recreation or propaganda or activity of any kind which, in the opinion of the Director, is in *any way of a political or partly political nature and* prejudicial to the public interest or the welfare of the pupils or of education generally or contrary to the approved syllabus, shall be permitted upon the occasion of any school activity" (see Education Department, *Education Regulations* [Hong Kong: Government Printer, 1971], chap. 279, sec. 84). The italicized text was deleted in 1990. See also "Call to End Ban on Politics in Schools," *South China Morning Post* (June 7, 1989).
18 See letter of December 7, 1993, from the Dean, Faculty of Law, Registry of the University of Hong Kong, Annex N, University Senate Minutes, item no. 24, March 1, 1994.

158   *Institutions*

19 This was made clear by the director of the Hong Kong and Macau office of the State Council of the People's Republic of China.
20 See the reprint of the annual address by Governor David Wilson to the Legislative Council, October 11, 1989, in *Hong Kong, 1990: A Review of 1989*, ed. David Roberts (Hong Kong: Government Printer, 1990), pp. 4–22. See also University Grants Committee Secretariat, *University Grants Committee of Hong Kong, Facts and Figures, 1994* (Hong Kong: University Grants Committee Secretariat, April 1995). The figure of 58,000 refers only to the number of students in the seven institutions of higher education under the University Grants Committee and includes undergraduate and graduate, as well as subdegree students.
21 "Academic Hits Out at Crisis Intervention," *South China Morning Post* (November 5, 1989).
22 University Grants Committee of Hong Kong, *Getting Ready for Tertiary Education*, abridged version, 4th ed. (May 1996), p. VIII-5. This is a study commissioned by the University Grants Committee.
23 Hugh Witt, ed., *Hong Kong Yearbook, 1993: A Review of 1992* (Hong Kong: Government Printer, 1993). The seven universities and tertiary college are funded through the University Grants Committee as well as the Hong Kong Institute of Education, while the Academy of Performing Arts is funded through the recreation and culture branch of the government. Hong Kong has a postsecondary institution, Shue Yan College, which is privately funded.
24 See the University Grants Committee of Hong Kong's "Appendix L," in their *Report for July 1991 to June 1995* (Hong Kong: Government Printer, May 1996), pp. 69–72.
25 See the University Grants Committee website, http://www.ugc.edu.hk.
26 *Basic Law of the Special Administrative Region of Hong Kong*. Also, see the speech by the chief executive, the Honorable Tung Chee Hwa, at the July 1, 1997, ceremony to celebrate the establishment of the Hong Kong SAR of the PRC, where he stated: "Education is the key to the future of Hong Kong. ... It should encourage diversification and combine the strength of the east and west. We shall draw up a comprehensive plan to improve the quality of education and inject sufficient resources to achieve this goal" (http://www.info.gov.HK.HK1997.handover.ecele.html).
27 *Education Commission Report Number 3* (Hong Kong: Government Printer, 1988).
28 University Grants Committee of Hong Kong, *Higher Education in Hong Kong*, chap. 43, par. 3 (n. 10 above).
29 Min (n. 6 above); also see Ka-ho Mok, *Chinese Intellectuals and the State in Post-Mao China* (London: Macmillan, in press); and Feng Wei, *Zhongguo zhishijie: Dazhendang—Shanghai chenfuzhongde Zhongguo zhishifenzi saomiao* (The great tremors in Chinese intellectual circles: An overview of intellectuals floundering in the sea of commercialism) (Beijing: Zhongguo shehui chubanshe, 1993).
30 *Zhongguo jiaoyu tongji nianjian, 1995* (Educational statistics yearbook of China, 1995 [n. 2 above]) lists 1,054 institutions of higher education. See also Gerard A. Postiglione and Liu Fang, eds., "Higher Education in 1994: Selections from China Education News," *Chinese Education and Society* 28, no. 6 (November-December 1995): 1–91.
31 See Min.
32 *Zhongguo jiaoyu tongji nianjian, 1995* (Educational statistics yearbook of China, 1995), p. 16. The majority of institutions in China have small numbers of students: 68 have 4,001–5,000 students; 120 have 3,001–4,000 students; 193 have 2,001–3,000 students; 167 have 1,500–2,000 students; 184 have 1,001–1,499 students; 142 have 501–1,000 students; 24 have 300–999 students; and 10 have fewer than 300 students.
33 Ibid.
34 University Grants Committee of Hong Kong, *Higher Education in Hong Kong* (n. 10 above).

35 See Boyer et al., fig. 2, p. 35 (n. 8 above).
36 *Zhongguo jiaoyu tongji nianjian, 1995* (Educational statistics yearbook of China, 1995), p. 28.
37 Ibid.
38 Calculations are from K. W. Ng's "Staff Ranks" (University of Hong Kong, Statistics Department, February 2,1996), fig. 1: "Comparison of Academic Staff between the University of Hong Kong and North American Universities."
39 *Zhongguojiaoyu tongji nianjian, 1995* (Educational statistics yearbook of China, 1995), p. 28.
40 See Ingmar Fagerlind and Lawrence J. Saha, "Education and Development under Capitalism and Socialism," in their *Education and National Development: A Comparative Perspective* (Oxford: Pergamon, 1983), pp. 195–233; see also Burton Clark, *The Higher Education System: Academic Organization in Cross- National Perspective* (Berkeley: University of California Press, 1983).
41 Academics coming direcdy from China to Hong Kong must apply for a visa, a process that averages 3 to 4 months, more time than it takes to acquire a visa to visit the United States.
42 In Hong Kong, 222 academic staff from the University of Hong Kong, the Chinese University of Hong Kong, and the Hong Kong University of Science and Technology (collectively identified here as HKTU) were questioned in May 1993 as part of a survey of academic staff across all seven University Grants Committee institutions. The surveys sampled across academic ranks within all departments and similar academic units. A staff list from each institution was used. After selection of a random number, every third person was sampled across departmental listing arranged by rank. The University and Polytechnic Grants Committee figure for total academic staff across institutions in 1993–94 was 3,562. The sampling process using staff lists yielded 1,247 names, approximately 35 percent of the population. After selection of a random number, every third person was selected across departmental listings arranged by rank. There were 472 respondents for an approximately 37 percent response rate, which accounts for about 13 percent of the total population. Completed surveys were returned either to the General Post Office or to one of the institutional monitors. In China, 278 academic staff from CTU were surveyed in fall 1994. A total of 1,040 questionnaires were sent to CTU, which accounts for one-third of the total faculty. There was an approximately 27 percent response rate, which accounts for 11 percent of the total population. After selection of a random number, every third person on the staff list arranged by department by age was chosen. Questionnaires were mailed individualy with a stamped preaddressed envelope.
43 See "Mission Statement of the University of Hong Kong," available from http://www.hku.hk.
44 Of the CTU respondents, 7.2 percent did not answer this question, and 11.5 percent indicated that they did not know.
45 Of the CTU respondents, 5.8 percent did not answer the question, and 2.9 percent indicated that they did not know.
46 Represented as the proportion of staff that indicated an issue should be the highest priority.
47 Overseas appointees may remain in Hong Kong for less time than it takes to earn tenure. Overseas terms usually include better housing accommodations and travel allowances, along with other benefits in some cases. Eligibility is based on overseas residency, however, because Hong Kong is an emigrant, as well as an immigrant, society, and there are many Chinese (including those originating from Hong Kong, Taiwan, other parts of Southeast Asia, and Western countries and mainland Chinese who come via long periods of study in the United States and other places) as well as non-Chinese employed on overseas terms. Moreover, local appointees are not solely

160 *Institutions*

composed of those who are ethnic Chinese; there are also a few individuals, usually long-term residents of Hong Kong who are "Westerners," included in this category. The differences between local and overseas terms gradually disappear with promotion to higher rank. Nevertheless, the appointment itself is still classified as local or overseas. Since the survey was completed, universities have taken measures to dismantle differences between local and overseas terms.

48 Interviews were conducted with the director of personnel of one HKTU institution and the vice director of personnel at another HKTU institution in early 1996. The former stated that no mass exodus of staff was expected, that resignation levels remained normal, and that if resignation levels increased, these individuals would probably be locals without foreign passports rather than overseas appointees. The latter stated that the turnover rate for tenured staff that year was 5.19 percent.

49 See Hyaeweol Choi, *An International Scientific Community: Asian Scholars in the United States* (Westport, Conn.: Greenwood, 1995).

50 On August 4, 1997, two universities in Hong Kong defended freedom of expression after a legislator from the Beijing-appointed Hong Kong Provisional Legislature wrote to the senior administration of two universities saying that two faculty members were unfit to receive public funding because they criticized his views on patriotic education. On July 17, 1997, new regulations on outside practice were issued at another university requiring staff to seek approval before giving interviews and preparing manuscripts for books and journals. See May Sin-Mi Hon, "Academic Freedom Roar over Clamp," and Shirley Kwok, "Colleges Defend Right to Criticize," both in *South China Morning Post* (August 5, 1997), p. 3. Although officials claim that the regulations are intended to restrict staff from engaging in outside work to earn extra income, faculty are demanding a written memorandum clarifying the regulations. See B. Sung, "Put 'Restrictive' New Rules in Writing, Staff Tells University," *Hong Kong Standard* (August 7, 1997), p. 1. On June 5, 1997, another university in Hong Kong permitted students to display a sculpture for 2 months that commemorates the Tiananmen tragedy of June 4, 1989.

9 Anchoring globalization in Hong Kong's research universities

Network agents, institutional arrangements, and brain circulation

Introduction

Research universities are expected to play a greater role in anchoring globalization into national development. By anchoring globalization we mean the capacity to access global networks of economic, scientific, technological, cultural and human resources. Developing economies view their futures as being significantly enhanced by a strategically nested flagship university in an internationally networked city (Altbach and Salmi 2011). Universities are becoming judged on the extent to which their research can drive the kind of innovation that will provide a competitive edge for their region (Dill and Van Vught 2010). Effective management of knowledge networks is prerequisite to raising the status of a research university in the global rankings. Among the key resources are: amphibious entrepreneurs who act as agents for knowledge networks by carrying practices and assumptions across disparate social domains (Powell and Sandholtz 2012); institutional arrangements that differentiate research universities from one another within a larger system (Mohrman, Ma and Baker 2008); and, brain circulation that capitalizes on non-local talent to build a transnational community of scholars and scientists (Saxenian 2005). This article examines the case of Hong Kong, a former British colony and now a Special Administrative Region of the People's Republic of China, and the manner and model in which its research universities have come to anchor globalization through a specific configuration of network agents, institutional arrangements, and brain circulation.

Although long known for its entrepreneurial prowess as an international hub for competitive business practices and global trade, Hong Kong used these same characteristics in its evolving aim to become a center for the reception, translation and diffusion of knowledge. Under the Basic Law of the Hong Kong Administrative Region, Hong Kong's system is distinct from that of the Chinese mainland in its social, political, and educational practices. Moreover, its universities have capitalized on this one-country and two-systems arrangement by remaining closely integrated with the global academy, while at the same time reaping benefit from its long-held mission to support the modernization of the Chinese mainland. Its universities have always valued Hong Kong's special bond with the Chinese motherland, yet they remain intellectually and academically free to use books and ideas banned on the Chinese mainland. Hong Kong's open borders, official policy of bilingualism, and first-class information technology, media, and communication infrastructure help it sustain global linkages for the reception and dissemination of knowledge and information. The international profile of its academic profession, most of whom are ethnic Chinese recruited with advanced degrees from overseas, makes it an ideal center for translation and interpretation of ideas between China and the rest of the world. In short, the constitution of its university sector permits unencumbered knowledge networks – a core feature of the role of its universities in anchoring globalization, and brain circulation facilitated by network agents that help research universities anchor globalization (Saxenian 2005).

This article examines the role of Hong Kong's universities in anchoring globalization through a particular network format for the exchange of ideas in research, and highlights the role played by network brokers and amphibious entrepreneurs who, as key agents, shape an enabling environment to help spark innovation in research. The resulting high velocity of brain circulation provides Hong Kong with the capacity to access and disseminate scientific knowledge around the world. Despite measures by government to facilitate institutional collaborations among its own universities, Hong Kong's research universities are as closely linked with their counterparts overseas and on the Chinese mainland as they are with one another. Other government initiatives also promote the kind of knowledge exchange intended to resolve the tension between global and local culture. While Hong Kong's research universities draw most of their talent from overseas, the long-term success and stability of the university system is viewed as requiring the preparation and promotion of highly talented, localized academic leadership.

Thus, an understanding of Hong Kong's network format and agency is essential for capturing the story about the rise of its research universities to world-class status amid the forces of global convergence and divergence. The process of configuring the network rather than the configuration itself can provide a useful case study for emergent global cities with rising expectations for how their research universities can anchor globalization in ways that contribute to, rather than detract from, their development. Yet, network layouts for the exchange of ideas in research and innovation continue to evolve with the shifting patterns of globalization. In the case of Hong Kong, that evolution is also increasingly affected by the alignment of policies and plans for research and development by the Chinese nation of which Hong Kong has become an integral part.

From tiger to dragon

Much managerial discourse in Hong Kong higher education prescribes that it is imperative to ensure globalization works for, rather than against, research productivity and innovation. With a scarcity of natural resources and manufacturing industries, Hong Kong is left to rely almost solely upon its human resources. Its school system produces a very high caliber of achievement in mathematics and science (Organization for Economic Cooperation and Development [OECD] 2012). Its higher education system, which has responded to calls from industrialists and civil society alike to encourage more creativity and innovation by intensifying a liberal studies curriculum, continues to place a heavy emphasis on performance measurement and quality indicators (Postiglione and Wang 2011). Hong Kong has the highest proportion of globally ranked research universities in one place, viewed in part due to its strategic management of knowledge networks (Postiglione 2011).

Yet, this was not the case 30 years ago when Hong Kong was a low- to mid-level income economy, surrounded by regional poverty, with only two universities that focused on undergraduate teaching. Hong Kong's rise was accompanied (though not always led) by the expansion of higher education and establishment of research universities. Thirty years later, research universities are expected to drive the economy and exchange knowledge with the surrounding society. This is facilitated by conditions that included a high degree of internationalism, a highly valued but self-defined Chinese cultural heritage, bilingual and bicultural adaptability, capacity to attract talented scientists, technology that permits a close integration with the global academy, open borders and easy mobility, stern protection of academic freedom, a lively intellectual climate, and the adjacent mainland of China with its policy of economic reforms and opening to the outside world (Postiglione 2006, 2007; Altbach and Postiglione 2012). In themselves, these basic conditions constitute an enabling environment for research universities. However, they alone do not drive research output and innovation. This is also determined to a great extent by the government's macro-steering and the strategic management of specific institutional and organizational circumstances in each university.

In simple terms, the government steers the system but provides universities with a high level of autonomy. Each institution' s research portfolio has the responsibility to attract and manage funds, persuade funding bodies, plan strategic research themes and areas of excellence, monitor and evaluate research and publications, disseminate and publicize (and sometimes commercialize) research breakthroughs, as well as provide research teams and their doctoral students with a supportive and dynamic environment to increase academic research output and innovative science.

This article begins with a contextual overview of the past three decades in order to provide an understanding of the character and evolution of the environment that enables research universities to develop their own strategies for managing academic knowledge networks and research output. Data is also provided on the trends in research collaboration of Hong Kong academics in comparative perspective. Finally, an institutional case study is presented to better illustrate styles of managing research networks and academic output in Hong Kong. In this way, the article presents a story of how a developing economy with few natural resources or manufacturing industries, and with only one or two undergraduate universities, made the transition to a system of mass higher education with three to four globally ranked research universities.

The evolution of an enabling environment

In 1980, Hong Kong was ensconced within a region of Asia surrounded by a great deal of poverty. In Asia, only Japan managed to upscale its economy to compete internationally. In its wake, four smaller economies (Hong Kong, Singapore, South Korea, Taiwan) began to forge ahead based on export trade and semi-skill-based manufacturing. By the early 1980s (until the 1997 Asian economic crisis), the four Asian tigers posted impressive growth rates (Chen 1979, 1983, 1994, 1997). With only a pair of universities, Hong Kong prospered through trade, re-export, small manufacturing enterprises, and financial services backed up by an independent legal system (Youngson 1982). Its economy remained relatively unencumbered by government bureaucracy and its civil service earned a reputation for the highest level of integrity in the region (Burns 2004). It also managed to rid itself of corruption, while remaining unscathed by the rising tide of global terrorism (Lee 1981). Its greatest challenge was to overcome the Asian economic crisis that began in 1997 and lingered through the SARS epidemic of 2003 (So and Chan 2002; Loh 2004).

Thirty years ago Hong Kong only had two small universities. It managed until 1963 with only one university, the English-medium University of Hong Kong (established in 1911), with students from Chinese families in Hong Kong and Malaysia (Chan and Kunich 2002; Kunich 2012). By the late 1930s, Hong Kong experienced a series of disruptions that included the Japanese occupation and China's civil war that led to the establishment of the People's Republic of China (PRC) in 1949. The trade embargo during the Korean War (1950–51) led to the establishment of the textile industry, during which migration from the Chinese mainland ballooned the Hong Kong population. As basic education became popularized, a second university (the Chinese University of Hong Kong) was established in 1963, from a collection of missionary and other Chinese colleges, to absorb the growing number of graduates from the Chinese-medium secondary schools (Sweeting 2004).

When the Chinese mainland initiated its policy of economic reform and opening to the world in December 1978, Hong Kong's two undergraduate universities together admitted only 2% of the relevant age group into degree programs. Throughout the 1980s Hong Kong shared similarities with Singapore, another ex-British colony with an elite system of higher education that severely limited access to degree places. The low access rates were possible because their English-medium schools broadened students' opportunity to enter university overseas. For the same reason Taiwan and Korea, without a large English-medium sector, had to absorb more of the demand domestically for university education. The Hong Kong colonial government preferred elite higher education without a substantial amount of research funding, and it was not until the late 1990s that international development agencies espoused the potential of more higher education to build a knowledge economy.

Since universities need a critical mass of undergraduates to establish viable graduate schools, the rise of research universities in Hong Kong gained traction after the Tiananmen incident (1989), when the government decided to double university enrolments in the wake of an exodus of talent. Before 1990, most degree courses were offered in two universities. A third university, the Hong Kong University of Science and Technology, was established in 1991. One polytechnic began offering degree courses in 1983 and another polytechnic and one tertiary college began to offer degree courses in 1986. The polytechnics and one of the tertiary institutions earned university titles in 1994. Another was elevated to university status by late 1999.

The three top-tier research universities – the University of Hong Kong, the Chinese University of Hong Kong, and the Hong Kong University of Science and Technology – each provide a range of programs that lead to undergraduate and graduate qualifications. Both the Hong Kong Polytechnic University and the City University of Hong Kong (the former polytechnics) offer a number of graduate degrees and have research programs in selected areas. They have a strong emphasis on the application of knowledge and vocational training, and maintain strong links with industry and employers. The Hong Kong Baptist University (formerly Baptist College) and Lingnan University (formerly Lingnan College) together provide undergraduate courses in the arts, sciences, social sciences, business, and communication studies, but also offer graduate degrees, with research programs in selected subjects. The Hong Kong Institute of Education offers degrees at all levels and has moved toward a more comprehensive profile of academic programs in anticipation of gaining university status (University Grants Committee [UGC] 1996, 1999, 2000, 2002, 2004a, b, 2009). The other degree-granting institutions are Shue Yan University, the first private university, the Open University of Hong Kong (government established but financially independent) that offers distance education, and the Hong Kong Academy of Performing Arts under the government's Home Affairs Bureau of Government.

The funding of eight degree-granting institutions is largely determined by the recommendations of the UGC, an influential group of local and international leaders in academia, business, and society. It is composed of a near equal proportion of local and international appointments, and provides a global network of advisory services that steer the overall format for the management of the knowledge networks of research universities.

As Hong Kong began to rapidly expand its universities in the 1990s, it also began to diverge from the other Asian tigers. Learning from Japan's success, the governments of the other three tigers (Singapore, South Korea and Taiwan) ratcheted up their high-tech industries, but Hong Kong's non-interventionist government refused to do so. Hong Kong's colonial end-date of 1997, and the tendency of investors to think in the short- rather than long-term, led to an abbreviated vision for high-tech industries. Instead, the Hong Kong government chose to focus on infrastructure, which also came to include the establishment of a University of Science and Technology (officially opened in 1991). This became a test of the viability of a science and technology (S&T) university because the proportion of the government budget for research and development (R&D)

was amongst the lowest in the world for an economy with average personal income levels that rivaled those in the UK. Allocation for R&D was 0.7% of GDP, placing Hong Kong in the fiftieth position in global rankings for this indicator (Ng and Poon 2004; World Bank 2012).

Hong Kong took advantage of the sunset years of a colonial administration to nest an American-style research university within the British colonial system of higher education. This added a dynamic element to the duality of an English-medium (HKU) and Chinese-medium (CUHK) university. The new University of Science and Technology (HKUST) distinguished itself from the status quo by putting research on an equal footing with teaching, and elevating an entrepreneurial approach to university development. In the American format, the new university appointed rather than elected Deans, and required students to enroll in social science and humanities courses outside of their science and technology specialization (Postiglione 2011).

Although Hong Kong's budget for R&D remains low, the 1988 decision to establish a Research Grants Council (RGC), during the planning stage of HKUST, was pivotal for the transition to a system of research universities (UGC 2000, 11). As part of the UGC, the RGC provided a template for large-scale research funding and further refined the global network of advisory services that steers the format for the management of the knowledge networks. The RGC made competitive research grants available to all academic staff. As the primary source of research funds, the RGC nudged Hong Kong's traditionally teaching-focused universities toward a heavier research orientation.

The more entrepreneurial HKUST was quick off the starting blocks and its share of research funding gradually rose to levels comparable with the other two leading research universities. It remains ahead of them in the proportion of competitive RGC grants received. For example, in 2009 its application success rate was 47%, ahead of the 36% for the other two top research universities. The amount awarded per faculty member is almost twice as much as at any other university. Thus, the RGC and HKUST were important catalysts for Hong Kong's research productivity. Yet, the government's resistance to invest heavily in high-tech industrialization limited the potential role of Hong Kong's research universities as a catalyst for that sector. The powerful property and real estate sectors, as well as the second-tier civil servants who were perched to lead Hong Kong after its handover in 1997, did little to support Hong Kong's development as a center of high technology, driving that opportunity northward where Shanghai became the proactive benefactor.

In summary, Hong Kong took a calculated risk at a critical turning point in its history. The odds were stacked against Hong Kong by a lack of natural resources, a small manufacturing sector, a minuscule budget for R&D, and an uncertain future. With mainland China's economic reform less than a decade old, Hong Kong took steps to expand higher education and decided before the end of the 1980s to establish a Research Grants Council and an American-style university of science and technology. This was indeed a shrewd gamble. However, the choice was taken with little debate.

Thus, Hong Kong's research network and knowledge exchange system of today had its trajectory set by 1990. The burst of university funding was also fed in part by a concern about a possible brain drain following the Tiananmen incident. However, the stakeholders in government, business, and higher education decided to move forward to build confidence as Hong Kong's capitalist system prepared to come under the umbrella of a socialist China under reform. The confidence-building exercise included construction of one of the world's major airports, as well as sustained protection of academic freedom. The expansion of research universities was also driven by aspirations for global excellence in higher education and the recognition by international development agencies such as the World Bank that economic survival would increasingly depend upon the capacity of universities to support a knowledge economy.

The decade of the 1990s would see the elevation of several colleges and polytechnics to university status. However, certain issues remained unsettled. For example, a debate about changing the length of university education from a three-year to a four-year structure, which began in 1988, was stifled until 2013 by a variety of factors, as was the issue of merging universities to improve resource efficiency. A review of the higher education system (UGC [Sutherland Report] 2002) suggested that new economic realities called for concentrating resources in fewer institutions. While the matter met with much debate, it was resisted by the academic profession in the two universities that were to be merged. Nevertheless, the basic format was set for the organization and administration of universities, though they remained under continual review, with increased top-slicing of university budgets for reallocation that would support initiatives and incentives to strengthen research capacity, including ways to better manage research networks and academic output.

Government steering and institutional autonomy

Through the UGC and RGC, the government steers the direction of the higher education sector through prioritized funding and performance guidelines. Yet, each university is an autonomous body with its own ordinance and governing council. Universities control curricula and standards, staff and student recruitment, research, and internal allocation of resources. The UGC, as a non-statutory body, often mediates between universities and government because it not only has the responsibility to ensure academic freedom and institutional autonomy, but also to ensure that taxpayers' moneys are spent well. The UGC offers advice to, and receives advice from, government and universities and is expected to take on a role in promoting quality, especially regarding international standards, through peer reviews and initiatives to monitor and enhance the academic standards. It has a stated aim to make Hong Kong a regional education hub.

The UGC carries out a Research Assessment Exercise (RAE), which follows, if not two steps behind, the framework used in the UK. Based on the RAE result, it adjusts the distribution of the research portion of block grants to each university. In this way, it aims to hold universities accountable and drive improvements in research output. The bean-counting quality of the RAE has withstood criticism in Hong Kong more than elsewhere, for reasons mentioned later in this article. The membership of the UGC is comprised of academics and university heads, many of whom can be considered amphibious entrepreneurs since they include eminent academics from outside of Hong Kong who are also part of the local community of leaders in business and commerce that sit on university councils and help set the course of higher education.

The RGC, established in 1988, operates under the umbrella of the UGC, and advises on research matters. Like the UGC, the RGC is a non-statutory advisory group that is responsible to government for advice about research undertaken by academic staff of UGC institutions. As an international knowledge network of global leaders in academia and business, the UGC and RGC are expected to encourage initiatives that better use knowledge networks to increase academic productivity and drive innovation. Some of this is accomplished through special grants that support cross-institutional collaboration, such as the Collaborative Research Fund (CRF). In 2012/13, the RGC increased the CRF by 50% to $80 million, from $53 million, in 2011/12, in an effort to fund more high-quality collaborative research projects. The RGC sets out an aim to fund out-of-the-box cross-disciplinary projects. Project teams are expected to engage in inter–disciplinary, collaborative research by crossing departmental and institutional borders. In assessing proposals, the RGC is supposed to put an emphasis on capacity building and the potential of a research topic to develop into an area of excellence that distinguishes Hong Kong from other research hubs.

Hong Kong's UGC uses a development strategy in which resources are distributed competitively but it does not set out to concentrate resources in one institution at the expense of others. Its view is that Hong Kong's research universities should complement one another and thereby strengthen the entire system's research capacity:

> by developing an interlocking system where the whole higher education sector is viewed as one force ... values a role-driven yet deeply collaborative system of higher education ... committed to extensive collaboration with other institutions.
>
> (UGC 2009)

In sum, the government, through the UGC/RGC, aims to drive collaboration among academics across Hong Kong's universities. The international composition of the UGC/RGC committees symbolizes a commitment to building knowledge networks throughout the global academy. The members act as network brokers and conduits between Hong Kong and the rest of the developed world, including top-ranked universities. Moreover, as new members are appointed, they act as fillers of network holes. Some of the local appointees of the UGC are from the business and industrial community. Though local by residence, they are internationally connected and act as amphibious entrepreneurs across a number of sectors, including higher education (Saskin 2004). As Hong

Kong local stakeholders, the appointees are also key advocates for excellence. This has led to a heavier reliance on quantification as part of quality assurance mechanisms, and though controversial to an extent, is tolerated to some degree by comparing it to the alternative that plagued efforts elsewhere in China.

Still, some credit this, at least in part, for why three of Hong Kong's eight universities are ranked in the top 10 in Asia *(THE* 2012). However, within a system of autonomous universities, the UGC's role is limited. There has even been discussion in academic circles as to whether the UGC has outlived its role, especially as universities have to generate a larger and larger amount of their own funding. The bulk of the work of building and managing domestic and international knowledge networks is handled by each university, to which we will turn in a later section.

Patterns of research collaboration

The template of institutional arrangements, network agents, and brain circulation for anchoring globalization in Hong Kong's universities facilitates a high amount of research collaboration, both domestic and international, by Hong Kong academics. The level of collaboration has significantly risen in the past two decades according to surveys of the academic profession by the Carnegie Foundation for the Advancement of Teaching and the Changing Academic Profession project (Table 9.1) (Postiglione 1997; Postiglione and Wang 2011). The post-colonial era of research collaboration has retained the traditional collaboration networks with academics in Western Europe, Australia, and North America, but has widened to include more collaboration not only with mainland Chinese academics but also with counterparts in many parts of the world, including Japan and South Korea, Eastern Europe and the Republics of former Soviet Union, South Asia, Africa and Latin America. Moreover, as Southeast Asian countries have expanded their universities, and Australia has internationalized theirs, more regional collaboration has become possible.

Table 9.1 Research collaboration among Hong Kong (PRC) academics

	1993 (%)	*2007 (%)*
Are you working independently on any of your research projects?	284 (74.2)	349 (50.7)
Do you have collaborations in any of your research projects?	301 (78.6)	578 (83.9)
Do you collaborate with international colleagues?	92 (35.1)	415 (60.2)
n	471 (100.0)	689 (100.0)

Source: 1993 data: Boyer, E.L., P.G Altbach, and M. Whitelaw. 1994. The Academic Profession: An International Perspective. Princeton: Carnegie Foundation for the Advancement of Teaching, Figures from Table 9.1 from unpublished tabulations of the Hong Kong portion of the database for the International Survey of the Academic Profession. 2007 data: International Survey of the Changing Academic Profession (ISCAP). 2007. Data source for tables 9.1 from unpublished tabulations of the Hong Kong portion of the ISCAP data base.

Note: %, proportion of 'yes' respondents in each question.

Three-quarters of Hong Kong academics were working on independent research projects in 1993 but only half had at least one such project in 2007. While only 79% of academics were collaborating on a research project in 1993, that figure had risen to 84% in 2007. The most prominent change among Hong Kong academics concerned their international collaboration on research projects, which jumped from 35% in 1993 to 60% in 2007. This change is more pronounced among the most productive 20% of academics, 84% of whom indicated they collaborate, while 95% indicated they collaborate internationally on research projects (Table 9.2). Moreover, Hong Kong academics are more collaborative than their Asian counterparts, though they are less competitive in this respect when compared to their counterparts elsewhere in the world (Table 9.3).

A higher degree of international collaboration is not surprising for Hong Kong (Table 9.4). Hong Kong academics are most international in citizenship of all 19 systems (except Australia) that participated in the international survey, and 75% of Hong Kong academics earned an overseas doctorate at a university, usually in the USA or the UK. This may also help to explain why Hong Kong academics have a relatively low level of identification with their universities when compared to their counterparts in other university systems.

While the rise of Asian economies has led to more regional collaboration and cross-border partnerships in research, data from the Web of Science make it clear that Asian research patterns are still closely wed to universities in western countries (Table 9.5) (Chapman, Cummings, and Postiglione 2010). For example, Asian academics from Hong Kong, Indonesia, Malaysia, Singapore, the Philippines and Vietnam collaborate often with counterparts in the USA, Australia, and England. Within Asia, Japan has spent many years trying to build research networks in Southeast Asia. The large size of China and India makes them emerging partners for knowledge networks with other Asian partners. Finally, knowledge networks in the natural sciences, medicine and engineering

Table 9.2 Research collaboration among top 20% most productive Hong Kong (PRC) academics, 1993 and 2007

	1993 (%)	2007 (%)
Are you working independently on any of your research projects?	58 (81.7)	64 (46.7)
Do you have collaborations in any of your research projects?	61 (85.9)	131 (95.6)
Do you collaborate with international colleagues?	45 (59.2)	116 (84.7)
n	76 (100.0)	137 (100.0)

Source: 1993 data: Boyer, E.L., P.G Altbach, and M. Whitelaw. 1994. The Academic Profession: An International Perspective. Princeton: Carnegie Foundation for the Advancement of Teaching, Figures from Table 9.2 from unpublished tabulations of the Hong Kong portion of the database for the International Survey of the Academic Profession. 2007 data: International Survey of the Changing Academic Profession (ISCAP). 2007. Data source for tables 9.2 from unpublished tabulations of the Hong Kong portion of the ISCAP data base.

Note: %, proportion of 'yes' respondents in each question.

Table 9.3 Collaboration among academics from 19 higher education systems 2007–8 (%)

	Collaboration	Domestic collaboration	International collaboration
Canada	84	69	64
USA	78	61	33
Finland	88	69	70
Germany	68	64	50
Italy	82	77	59
Netherlands	88	64	63
Norway	82	60	66
Portugal	63	69	54
UK	82	67	61
Australia	89	67	59
Japan	62	52	24
Korea	75	65	30
Hong Kong, China	*84*	*55*	*60*
China	73	37	13
Malaysia	85	55	32
Argentina	88	69	47
Brazil	58	45	28
Mexico	66	47	35
South Africa	54	45	41

Source: International Survey of the Changing Academic Profession (ISCAP). 2007. Data source for tables 9.3 from unpublished tabulations of the Hong Kong portion of the ISCAP data base.

Note: %, proportion of 'yes' respondents in each question.
Research collaboration: Do you have collaborators in any of your research projects?

Table 9.4 Research collaboration for academics in Asian systems of higher education, 2007–8

	Japan (%)	Korea (%)	Hong Kong PRC (%)	China (%)	Malaysia (%)
International collaboration	24	30	60	13	32
Co-authored with foreign colleagues	31	28	49	3	27
Published in a foreign country	42	53	86	28	49

Source: International Survey of the Changing Academic Profession (ISCAP). 2007. Data source for tables 9.4 from unpublished tabulations of the Hong Kong portion of the ISCAP data base.
- International collaboration: Do you collaborate with international colleagues?
- Co-authored with foreign colleagues: Have you ever published co-authored paper with colleagues located in other (foreign) countries in the last three years?
- Published in a foreign country: Have you ever published paper in a foreign country in the last three years?

Note: %, proportion of 'yes' respondents in each question.

still predominate (Table 9.6). This is the case throughout Asia. However, Hong Kong academics in the humanities and social sciences have a greater outreach, due again to internationalism and academic freedom, to collaborate with counterparts in other parts of the world.

Table 9.5 Collaboration on co-authored journal publications in six Asian countries

	Hong Kong	Indonesia	Malaysia	Singapore	Philippines	Vietnam
Number of articles (Total)	10,542	1,129	7,749	9,426	940	1,409
Number of authors (Total)	31,721	4,363	20,715	29,791	3,939	5,768
Number of authors (domestic)	Hong Kong (15,439)	Indonesia (1,563)	Malaysia (12,665)	Singapore (14,890)	Philippines (1,310)	Vietnam (1,959)
Number of co-authors from abroad	China (7,578)	Japan (555)	England (650)	USA (3,709)	USA (580)	USA (449)
	USA (2,724)	USA (323)	India (639)	China (2,426)	Japan (262)	Japan (379)
	Australia (815)	Australia (276)	Australia (632)	Australia (1,155)	Australia (144)	South Korea (332)
	England (615)	Malaysia (259)	USA (576)	England (854)	England (128)	France (259)
	Canada (504)	Netherlands (175)	Japan (525)	Germany (586)	South Korea (119)	Italy (241)
	Taiwan (473)	Germany (130)	Iran (524)	Japan (552)	Germany (107)	Germany (216)
	Singapore (376)	England (117)	Saudi Arabia (315)	France (537)	China (97)	England (165)

Source: Web of Knowledge, 2011.
Unit: Number of co-authors.

Table 9.6 Research publication by discipline

Hong Kong	Indonesia	Malaysia	Singapore	Philippines	Vietnam
Engineering (1,935)	Engineering (128)	Engineering (1,205)	Engineering (1,808)	Agriculture (149)	Mathematics (189)
Physics (1,097)	Chemistry (112)	Chemistry (837)	Chemistry (1,589)	Plant Sciences (70)	Physics (175)
Chemistry (1,070)	Environmental Sciences & Ecology (106)	Crystallography (772)	Physics (1,535)	Environmental Sciences & Ecology (67)	Chemistry (172)
Computer Science (929)	Physics (75)	Materials Science (735)	Materials Science (1,270)	Life Sciences & Biomedicine (45)	Engineering (124)
Materials Science (924)	Materials Science (60)	Physics (493)	Computer Science (692)	Chemistry (40) Engineering (40)	Materials Science (101)
10,542	1,129	7,749	9,426	940	1,409

Source: Web of knowledge, 2011.
Unit: Number of articles.

Table 9.7 Academic perspectives in Asia about performance-based management

		China	Hong Kong	Japan	Korea	Malaysia
A strong performance orientation	Sample	60.1	65.4	52.3	62.8	56.6
	Top 10%	69.5	67.9	61.7	64.8	58.6
	Bottom 10%	56.5	63.9	40.0	59.9	59.7
Performance-based allocation of resources to academic units	Sample	49.6	58.3	31.2	34.1	34.9
	Top 10%	52.9	56.6	39.6	40.7	50.0
	Bottom 10%	49.6	57.0	23.4	33.1	33.1
Considering the research quality when making personnel decisions	Sample	56.3	69.3	59.7	33.0	39.8
	Top 10%	58.0	72.8	62.4	36.6	50.0
	Bottom 10%	52.9	71.3	53.5	22.4	40.6

Source: CAP, 2007.
- At my institution, there is a strong performance orientation.
- To what extent does your institution emphasize the following practices? Performance-based allocation of resources to academic units.
- To what extent does your institution emphasize the following practices? Considering the research quality when making personnel decisions.

Unit: % of 'strongly agree' and 'agree' in five-point Likert scale.

In sum, the data from the international surveys of the academic profession and the Web of Knowledge both indicate the globally collaborative nature of the academic profession in Hong Kong. Recruitment of academic staff is competitive internationally and institutional management provides ample opportunity for short- and long-term visits by distinguished academics involved in collaborative projects. Institutional management facilitates academic productivity by providing advantages for building international knowledge networks and for publishing research findings overseas. At the same time, performance measures bite with a vengeance as they drive academic productivity. Hong Kong academics agree more than those from most other systems that performance measures are used to make personnel decisions and also decisions about the allocation of resources in their universities (Table 9.7). While there is a downside to the overuse of quantitative measures, especially in stifling creativity, the Hong Kong system can absorb this due to the composition of the academic profession, many from the UK where these measures were developed, and returnees from mainland China who view it in comparative perspective. It also placates the members of university councils who remember the days of colonial universities and who are now in government and industry where performance measures are common. While the measures have been found to increase stress on academics, it also raises their level of job satisfaction, presumably knowing that institutional decisions are relatively fair and less politicized (Postiglione and Wang 2011).

Establishing knowledge networks

Hong Kong's universities seemed to catch on quickly to the new demands of managing knowledge networks, partly due to their close integration with the global academy, but also due to appointing university presidents who were prominent in leading universities overseas. For example, the president of the

University of Hong Kong is a world-renowned geneticist. The Chinese University of Hong Kong has had presidents who were awarded the Nobel Prize for fiber optics, and named 'Asian Hero' by *Time* magazine for work on SARS. The president of the Hong Kong University of Science and Technology distinguished himself in the US National Science Foundation, in charge of the Mathematical and Physical Sciences Directorate.

It was apparent by the turn of the century that global competition, especially for low-resource economies, would hinge on knowledge networks. As the cost of higher education began to rise, the community in Hong Kong began to question expenditures. University councils composed of leaders in business and commerce began to engage more in the discussions about the running of universities. University presidents began to take a greater role in attracting donations, leaving the running of the academic side of the university to its provosts. With the professionalization of management, and the increased sophistication of information technology, universities in Hong Kong were expected to function more efficiently, though not always aligned with the values of the academic profession. The increased demand by the academy for research funds in an economy that allocated little of gross domestic product (GDP) to R&D made it more important for universities to appeal to local entrepreneurs, foundations and alumni. As the walls of the elite university era were drawn down and the door opened wider to the larger community, the demand also grew for networks that permitted more exchange of knowledge between university and society.

Case studies can be used to illustrate how network agents, institutional arrangements, and brain circulation drive a research university that operates in a highly resilient enabling environment of a globally ensconced civil society. A particularly illustrative case of how Hong Kong research universities have anchored globalization concerns the relatively recent establishment and development of the Hong Kong University of Science and Technology (HKUST). Within the context of the enabling environment cited earlier in this article, that is provided to Hong Kong's universities, HKUST's network format and agency worked in favor of its rise amid the forces of global convergence and divergence. The process of configuring its network was shaped by rising expectations about Hong Kong approaching post-colonial status and China's economic reform and opening to the outside world. The network layout for the exchange of ideas in research and innovation continued to evolve without assaulting the traditions of Hong Kong higher education. That evolution is also increasingly affected by the alignment of policies and plans for research and development of the nation of which Hong Kong is part.

The case of HKUST's institutional management of research capacity

Managing the take-off phase

Although established in 1991, HKUST became an internationally ranked research university within a decade. Its rapid rise illustrates how a new research university builds and activates academic capital for research collaboration in global knowledge networks, even in the context of a system that had accumulated a certain amount of inertia. A critical factor in its take-off was the planning of the first-tier faculty recruitment. This was done by its first president, a renowned physicist with significant access to knowledge networks of leading scientists. Born in Shanghai, and schooled in Hong Kong and Taiwan, Woo Chia-wei became the first Chinese president of a leading university in the United States. As a member of the planning team during a period of time when recruitment was encumbered by troubling events on the mainland in 1989, and then as president beginning in 1991, he managed to project the saliency of HKUST's uniqueness, and strategically settle it into the already existing system of higher education. Aside from being an accomplished scientist who helped reinforce the idea of liberal arts education for preparing scientists and engineers in Hong Kong's higher education system, he was also very much in the mold of an amphibious entrepreneur, by being able to situate himself in multiple worlds on both sides of the Pacific. No doubt this helped him to build trust and persuade many of the most accomplished American scientists of Taiwan origin to leave academia in the USA and take up a post in what would soon be a special zone of the PRC.

Elevating knowledge networks

HKUST and its management of knowledge networks continued to evolve after its first 10 years when the second president, Paul Chu, also a world-renowned scientist, took office, when Hong Kong was still suffering the effects of both the Asian economic crisis and was soon embattled by the SARS crisis. Yet, he managed to establish an Institute of Advanced Study (IAS) modeled after that at Princeton University, where noted scientists from around the world visit, think, and conduct workshops. The IAS, with an international advisory board composed of 12 Nobel Laureates, promoted collaborative projects across disciplines and institutions, and forged relationships with academic, business, community, and government leaders, all with the aim to transform Hong Kong and the Greater China region into a global source of creative and intellectual power. For example, visitors included Aaron Ciechanover, Nobel Laureate in Chemistry, and Eric Maskin, Nobel Laureate in Economics. It also recruited 'star scholars' as permanent Institute Faculty Members and honors each with a named professorship, which provides salary enhancement and additional research funding. Another 60 named fellowships are available for young and promising scholars who join IAS as postdoctoral fellows to work closely with the permanent Institute Faculty.

Managing funds for research in a new donor culture

Research funding available to HKUST steadily increased, except during the Asian financial crisis. Donations for research by such groups as the Hong Kong Telecom and the Hong Kong Jockey Club Charities Trust were helpful to the research profile of HKUST, especially for biotechnology. HKUST's research fund as of June 2008 included Hong Kong private funds (28.2%), non-Hong Kong sources (1.9%), RGC funds (35.7%), UGC funds (24.1%), and other Hong Kong Government funds, mostly from the Innovation and Technology Commission (10.1%). The total includes R&D projects administered by R&D corporations (HKUST 2009). The high-impact areas of research have been identified as Nano-Science and Nano-Technology, Biological Sciences and Biotechnology, Electronics, Wireless and Information Technology, Environment and Sustainable Development, and Management Education and Research. Aside from their scientific significance, they are viewed as adding value to the social and economic development of the region, including Hong Kong and the surrounding Pearl River Delta.

Starting off as the only university in Hong Kong without an alumni sector, HKUST looked for ways to take advantage of the timely rise of Chinese philanthropy. The government facilitated the donation culture by providing matching grants. Donations in the early phase of development came from a variety of local business and family foundations. During its tenth anniversary, HKUST noted that it received contributions from 18 foundations and 19 corporations, as well as seven individual and family donors.

Collaborations, partnerships, and internationalization

HKUST's collaborations, partnerships, and internationalization have also played a significant role in anchoring globalization. Under the Hong Kong Area of Excellence scheme in research, HKUST has collaborative projects with other universities in Hong Kong in the following areas: Chinese Medicine: Research and Further Development (with CUHK), Institute of Molecular Technology for Drug Discovery (with HKU), Centre for Marine Environmental Research and Innovation Technology (with CUHK), Developmental Genomics and Skeletal Research (with HKU), and Control of Pandemic and Inter-Pandemic Influenza (with HKU).

HKUST also has a Research and Development Corporation (RDC) for partnerships and knowledge transfers with industry. Moreover, RDC partnerships and other HKUST academic partnerships extend beyond Hong Kong to commercial high-tech research products. For example, HKUST, Peking University, and the Shenzhen Municipal government established a tripartite cooperative institution that engages in production, study and research. HKUST scientists are expected to be globally networked and are accountable for knowledge products that drive their fields of research expertise.

Accessing social and cultural capital

Each university draws upon special conditions to establish knowledge networks. For example, HKUST has accessed social and cultural capital to recruit many overseas Chinese scientists who were embedded in mainstream research university knowledge hubs. The first president of HKUST drew upon his extensive social networks of scientists that spanned the Pacific. The approaching date of Hong Kong's return to China was a source of cultural capital for those overseas Chinese scientists who would not have come to Hong Kong were it not for the end of the colonial era and the Chinese mainland's reform policies. In short, HKUST capitalized upon advantageous conditions such as institutional autonomy and the provision of capital resources. Yet, its success was also ensured by strategically proactive recruitment and a form of governance of its academic faculty that was initially unique in Hong Kong higher education.

This set of conditions, as well as the timing of its establishment and take-off, also contributed to situating itself relatively quickly within global networks of knowledge production and output. The first president of HKUST characterized those he recruited as having shared purpose and relentless drive to support his university's rise into the ranks of the so-called 'world-class' research universities (Woo 2006).

Planning, risk-taking and governance

Management of knowledge networks by a new research university requires risk taking and shrewd decision making in order to take advantage of the context within which the institution is established, including an economy on the rise, industrial restructuring, a shifting emphasis in higher education toward more applied research and commercialization, an already existing local system of higher education, and the intensification of the global discourse on knowledge economics. In the case of HKUST, it was also essential for the planning committee to be adroit enough to establish a new international university without assaulting the already existing *governing traditions* in the university system.

At the very least, the HKUST case emphasizes the centrality of local advocates in government and society, such as S.Y. Chung, who led the planning for the new university, as well as amphibious entrepreneurs in the academic world who easily crossed the geographical spheres of knowledge networks in the Chinese mainland, Taiwan, Hong Kong, Canada and the USA. The macro-enabling environment for the HKUST project permitted a new pattern of brain circulation that not only gave a strong emphasis to the research enterprise, but also to the commercialization of research. HKUST's Business Faculty played a key role in ratcheting up the entrepreneurial capacity of the institution.

Recruiting and sustaining talent

Although many factors can be seen to support the design and trajectory of the research output enterprise, of the key decisions made by the university leadership there was none more crucial for the establishment of an internationally recognized research university than initial faculty recruitment. This set in motion a platform with a top layer of academic talent that could be used to draw upon, establish, nurture, and initiate new knowledge networks. Although managing top academic and scientific talent from around the world is a process that cannot be controlled or predicted, access on a personal level to a defined network of noted scientists, and the ability to persuade academic leaders of the wisdom of trading a secure position at one top university for the opportunity to begin a second life as part of a new enterprise, are indispensable traits for a university president or vice-presidents with the research portfolio. Recruitment for HKUST involved geographically expansive interviewing of prospective faculty. Moreover, the HKUST case demonstrates that competitive salaries, though helpful, may only be of limited benefit to recruitment efforts. Salary was not the main factor in persuading already established top talent to dislocate their selves. Many were already highly paid in American universities and a move to Hong Kong meant a major trim in their living space, often affecting their family routines and children's education.

After a new research university has gotten off to a strong start in its first phase of development, the next challenge becomes how to retain an academic profession that remains committed over a long period, not only to maintaining a high caliber of research but also to building a purposeful engagement with the society and country within which the university is situated. In the second phase of development of a new research university, that began by recruiting overseas talent, the issue of how to ensure that knowledge networks take root in the local society, in this case, Hong Kong, becomes crucial to sustained success. This means the reproduction of a high enough threshold of academic leadership that is culturally, civically, and emotionally rooted in the host city.

The HKUST case shows a gradual trajectory to a more localized academic leadership that is able to keep the university globally networked, actively involved, and leading in selected fields of knowledge. Thus, for any newly established research university that rapidly achieves success and status within the larger international network of research universities, it is important to plan ways to sustain the gains of the initial developmental stage. While HKUST experienced good timing and some luck, its focus remained the same: emphasize research and hire the best scientists. Nevertheless, while one can recruit the top scientists from the outside at the initial phase, continuity cannot be sustained unless a certain indigenization takes hold in the next phase.

A large sector of the next generation of young scholars had to make Hong Kong a centerpiece of their academic lives. In short, sustaining a rise has to move forward with the preparation of a generation of local scientists who will serve and become leaders for the surrounding region, in this case, for South China as it develops in the decades to come. In fact, building knowledge networks for Hong Kong researchers in the Chinese mainland may have different challenges and requirements than building the same networks elsewhere.

HKUST facilitated the creation of a model of a global research university with a scholarly community adjoining a globally emergent and reformist China (Mohrman, Ma, and Baker 2008). In this sense, HKUST identified a niche within the Hong Kong system, by establishing a new international university and projecting its vision far beyond that system and into the Chinese mainland, especially signified by the new Southern University of Science and Technology under planning in the adjacent Shenzhen Special Economic Zone. It identified a niche, not only in the field of science and technology but also in delivering a research-focused university culture, and encapsulated it into an institutional vision that stressed uniqueness. The central factor underlying its success was the substantial recruitment from two generations of overseas networked Chinese scholars, many of whom had emotional attachment to their cultural heritage and intense commitment to China's development. By providing them and other local and international faculty with a unique historical opportunity and a scholarly work environment that was adequately resourced, HKUST sustained its creation of a robust scholarly community.

Conclusion: anchoring globalization

Regardless of their level of development, research universities remain nested within regional civilizations. It is all the better if they are situated within global cities and endowed with amphibious agents that act as globally linked conduits who help format a template to facilitate research collaboration and drive innovation through open borders and brain circulation. The management of institutional research networks is enhanced by stakeholders who have the means to mediate the clash of civilizations. This is especially important for stakeholders who can help universities maintain the balance between being instruments of international competition, as well as being instruments of peace.

In this respect, an important development shaping the future of research and knowledge networks is an initiative ushered in by the Central Government of China. Since Hong Kong's funding for research and development is only 0.7% of GDP, the rise of its research universities has much to do with international collaboration. Scientists who came from overseas or were networked through previous study overseas to large projects were enabled by the institutional conditions to take advantage of such knowledge networks to improve collaboration.

Meanwhile, the proportion of Hong Kong academics that collaborates with colleagues at universities on the Chinese mainland has risen rapidly. This was originally due to the calculation that research budgets in Hong Kong could take advantage of the low salaries on the Chinese mainland. Later, the environment of research had improved and many more scholars were returning to mainland universities after overseas study, and others were attaching themselves there through special programs. By 2010, the Chinese mainland was increasing its budget for R&D by about 20% per year and the door was opening to Hong Kong scientists to apply for large funds. This is only the case in science and technology fields where they can partner with what are designated as state key laboratories. Partner laboratories in Hong Kong can receive up to 1.2 million dollars of support for five-year projects. In the case of the adjoining region of Guangdong province, the seven strategic industries include:

- Energy saving and environmental protection (clean energy technology);
- Next generation IT (modernization of the country's telecommunications infrastructure);

- Bio-technology (pharma and vaccine manufacturers);
- High end equipment (airplanes, satellites, manufacturing technology);
- New energy (nuclear, wind, solar);
- New materials (rare earths);
- New energy cars (electric and hybrid cars, batteries).

Nevertheless, while increased collaboration with scientists on the Chinese mainland will provide another major source of research funding, scientific research there is still considered relatively weak, and as Bai Chunli, President of the Chinese Academy of Sciences, stated on a 2012 visit to Hong Kong, 'There are still many negative elements hindering the birth of scientific discovery.'

In an Asian region which aims to become the global driver of the world economy by mid century, there is an emerging discourse about the urgent need for a commitment to be reflective about how to bring the western academic model into the service of the local and regional communities. The president of the Hong Kong Institute of Education made reference to this as it concerns developing countries in Asia: 'Will Asia be just producing more of the same of the Western-originated contemporary higher education model, or will it be able to unleash a more critical understanding and practice in higher education, a cultural and epistemological reflection on the role of universities as venues of higher learning' (Cheung 2013).

In short, world-class research universities in Asian developing countries also have to be regionally focused with national positioning and global impact that does not just move in lock-step with the western model. The focus has to be on the selection of fields and specialties so that there can be an efficient employment of resources to address regional growth challenges. Governance needs to support an organization and system that is innovative and unique, that promotes a sense of ownership among academic staff, that protects the academic research atmosphere, and that is international without assaulting local or national traditions.

Hong Kong's two-pronged development strategy was resilient enough to provide HKUST and other research universities in Hong Kong with the autonomy to sustain their uniqueness even during economic recession. The one time that a consolidation of universities which would have created a remix of local knowledge networks was considered, it was almost unanimously opposed by academic staff and alumni. Hong Kong's universities have been able to distinguish themselves from one another in a system largely financed by government but provided by law with a high degree of autonomy.

The Hong Kong model, though not easily duplicated due to a specific set of historical conditions that existed during the establishment and development of its research universities, still provides a useful case of research university institutionalization. Much of the enabling environment referred to above can be duplicated. However, for some research university systems, changing the medium of instruction to English could be fraught with difficulties. That has not stopped leading universities in Japan and Germany, for example, but it has handicapped the rise of universities in Malaysia and Korea. Hong Kong was also in a unique position in being able to draw on both the Chinese diaspora and its adjacency to the Chinese mainland during an era of economic reform and opening to the outside world. Nevertheless, research universities in developing counties may be able to duplicate some aspects. They can recruit from the diaspora in countries on their continents and plan to calibrate more closely with the development of their global cities as they stand in relationship to their hinterlands. Finally, there is the role for network brokers who can help fill holes in knowledge networks. As local agents, they can act as network conduits, advocates and stakeholders from government and the business community. As global agents and committed stakeholders they become amphibious entrepreneurs. Their ability to work together becomes pivotal for building and maintaining a framework for managing an effective network layout that facilitates brain circulation and knowledge translation, adaptation, transmission and innovation.

Selective aspects of the Hong Kong model can be employed where suitable for the particular economic, political and social context in specific developing countries. The model has already had an influence in mainland China. For example, the new South China University of Science and Technology has been more heavily influenced by HKUST than by any other university outside of China. While the Chinese mainland may still look more toward Harvard than Hong Kong, the advantage of the latter model is that it succeeded in a cultural setting that resonates with that in the Chinese mainland. At the same time, the Hong Kong model continually fine tunes itself to the rise of top universities in Beijing and Shanghai, and elsewhere in Asia.

In short, the Hong Kong model anchors globalization by realizing that research universities in a global age play a central role as both infrastructure and as confidence builders. Its development model is best viewed more as a process than a product model, especially in its ability to recognize opportunities and take calculated risks in planning and implementation at different phases of development. It has also been able to keep corruption at bay better than most systems in Asia, while resisting an overly rapid privatization of higher education. While enabling entrepreneurialism in its research universities, it has also nurtured a culture of philanthropy in partnership with government, which provided matching grants on donations. While its budget for research and development is modest, it looks highly upon academic staff with extensive national and/or international knowledge networks that attract external research funds. The turnover rate and mobility of academic staff are viewed as contributing to the international linkages that help sustain knowledge networks. Yet, some would point to a stultifying assessment environment that helps maintain quality and productivity while increasing work stress and opportunities for fresh thinking.

Research universities in developing countries can better anchor globalization in national economies through a cosmopolitan format as exemplified in the Hong Kong model. That model rests on an enabling environment of institutional arrangements, amphibious agents as staunch stakeholders, and a deft engagement with brain circulation. Above all else, the Hong Kong model is one that places an emphasis on the establishment, protection, and elaboration of knowledge networks. For developing countries, that means a model that takes strategic advantage of economic globalization by nesting its research universities in a cosmopolitan center where it can more easily access regional and international scholar hubs. It also means enlisting amphibious entrepreneurs who have a stake in the local community, a willingness to take a role in facilitating brain circulation, and the agility to bridge academia, industry and government, all the while standing forth to support an enabling environment of academic freedom and mobility.

Acknowledgements

Thanks to Philip Altbach, Gili Drori, Jisun Jung, Anatoly Oleksiyenko, David Zweig, David Palmer, and Jung C. Shin for comments and suggestions on an early draft. An earlier draft of this paper was presented for the OECD Program on Innovation, Higher Education, Research and Development at the Center for International Higher Education, Boston College, 10–13 October 2012.

References

Altbach, P.A., and G.A. Postiglione. 2012. Hong Kong's academic advantage. *Peking University Education Review.*

Altbach, P.A., and J. Salmi, eds. 2011. *The road to academic excellence: Emerging research universities in developing and transition countries.* Washington, DC: The World Bank.

Boyer, E.L., P.G. Altbach, and M. Whitelaw. 1994. The Academic Profession: An International Perspective. Princeton: Carnegie Foundation for the Advancement of Teaching.

Burns, J.P. 2004. *Government capacity and the Hong Kong Civil Service.* Oxford: Oxford University Press.

Chan, L.K.C., and P. Cunich. 2002. *An impossible dream: Hong Kong University from foundation to re-establishment, 1910–1950.* New York: Oxford University Press.

Chapman, D.W., W.K. Cummings, and G.A. Postiglione. 2010. *Crossing borders in East Asian higher education.* Hong Kong: Springer Press and the Comparative Education Research Centre of the University of Hong Kong.

Chen, E.K.Y. 1979. *Hypergrowth in Asian economies: A comparative study of Hong Kong, Japan, Korea, Singapore and Taiwan.* New York: Macmillan.

Chen, E.K.Y. 1983. *The new multinationals.* New York: John Wiley.

Chen, E.K.Y. 1994. *Transnational corporations and technology transfer in developing countries.* London: Routledge.

Chen, E.K.Y. 1997. *Asia's borderless economy: The emergence of sub-regional economic zones.* New York: Allen & Unwin.

Cheung, B.L. 2013. Higher education in Asia: Challenges from and contributions to globalization. *International Journal of Chinese Education,* in press.

Dill, David D., and Frans A. van Vught. 2010. *National innovation and the academic research enterprise: Public policy in global perspective.* Baltimore: Johns Hopkins University Press.

HKUST. Hong Kong University of Science and Technology. 2009. Technology Transfer. http://www.vprg.ust.hk/kt.html (accessed 26 February 2010).

ISCAP. International Survey of the Changing Academic Profession. 2007. Data source for tables 9.1–4, and 7 from unpublished tabulations of the Hong Kong portion of the data base.

Lee, R.P.L. 1981. *Corruption and its control in Hong Kong*. Hong Kong: Chinese University of Hong Kong Press.

Loh, Christine. 2004. *At the epicentre: Hong Kong and the SARS outbreak*. Hong Kong: Hong Kong University Press.

Mohrman, K., W.H. Ma, and D. Baker. 2008. The university in transition: The emerging global model. *Higher Education Policy* 21: 5–27.

Ng, S.H., and C.Y.W. Poon. 2004. *Business restructuring in Hong Kong: Strengths and limits of post-industrial capitalism in Hong Kong*. New York: Oxford University Press.

Organization for Economic Cooperation and Development (OECD). 2012. Hong Kong's success in PISA. http://oecdeducationtoday.blogspot.hk/2012/05/hong-kongs-success-in-and-pisa-one.html (accessed 30 September 2012).

Postiglione, G.A. 1997. The academic profession in Hong Kong higher education within a period of profound change. In *The academic profession: Studies from 14 countries*, ed. P.A. Altbach, 193–230. Princeton: Carnegie Foundation for the Advancement of Teaching.

Postiglione, G.A. 2006. The Hong Kong Special Administrative Region of the People's Republic of China: Context, higher education, and a changing academia. In *Quality, relevance and governance in a changing academia: International perspectives*, ed. Huang Futao, 97–114. Hiroshima: Research Institute for Higher Education, Number 20, COE Publication Series. September.

Postiglione, G.A. 2007. Hong Kong: Expansion, reunion with China, and the transformation of academic culture. In *The changing conditions for academic work and careers in selected countries*, ed. William Locke and Ulrich Tischler, 57–76. Kassel: International Centre for Higher Education Research.

Postiglione, G.A. 2011. The rise of research universities: The case of the Hong Kong University of Science and Technology. In *The road to academic excellence: Emerging research universities in developing and transition countries*, ed. P.A. Altbach and J. Salmi. Washington, DC: The World Bank.

Postiglione, G.A., and S.R. Wang. 2011. Governance of the academy in Hong Kong. In *Changing governance and management in higher education*, ed. William Locke, W.K. Cummings and D. Fisher. Dordrecht: Springer.

Powell, Walter W., and Kurt W. Sandholtz. 2012. Amphibious entrepreneurs and the emergence of organizational forms. *Strategic Entrepreneurship Journal* 6, no. 2: 94–115.

Saskin, S. 2004. Local actors in global politics. *Current Sociology* 52, no. 4: 649–70.

Saxenian, AnnaLee. 2005. From brain drain to brain circulation: Transnational communities and regional upgrading in India and China. *Studies in Comparative Development* 40, no. 2: 35–61.

So, A., and Ming K. Chan. 2002. *Crisis and transformation in China's Hong Kong*. New York: M.E. Sharpe.

Sweeting, A. 2004. *Education in Hong Kong, 1941 to 2001: Visions and revisions*. Hong Kong: Hong Kong University Press.

THE. Times Higher Education. 2012. World University Rankings. http://www.timeshigheredu-cation.co.uk/world-university-rankings/2012–13/world-ranking/region/asia (accessed 26 February 2013).

University Grants Committee. 1996. *Higher education in Hong Kong*. Hong Kong: Government Printer.

University Grants Committee. 1999. *Higher education in Hong Kong – A report by the University Grants Committee*, Supplement (May) Hong Kong: Government Printer.

University Grants Committee. 2000. *Facts and Figures,* 31. Hong Kong: Government Printer.
University Grants Committee. 2002. Higher education in Hong Kong (Sutherland Report), March. Hong Kong: Government Printer.
University Grants Committee. 2004a. *Hong Kong higher education: To make a difference, to move with the times,* January. Hong Kong: Government Printer.
University Grants Committee. 2004b. *Integration matters,* March. Hong Kong: Government Printer.
University Grants Committee. 2009. http://www.ugc.edu.hk/eng/ugc/policy/policy.htm.
Web of Knowledge. 2011. http://apps.webofknowledge.com/UA_GeneralSearch_input.do?product=UA&search_mode=GeneralSearch&SID=X1B42CPj2PDcLD2apok&preferences-Saved=
Woo, C.W. 2006. *Jointly creating the Hong Kong University of Science and Technology.* Hong Kong SAR, China: Commercial Press.
World Bank. 2012. Research and development expenditure (as % of GDP). http://data.worldbank.org/indicator/GB.XPD.RSDV.GD.ZS (accessed 25 September 2012).
Youngson, A.J. 1982. *Hong Kong economic growth and policy.* Hong Kong: Oxford University Press.

10 The Rise of Research Universities
The Hong Kong University of Science and Technology

"Rome wasn't built in a day."

Before the end of the 19th century, the president of Harvard University, Charles Eliot, counseled John D. Rockefeller that US$50 million (about US$5 billion in today's currency) and 200 years would be required to create a research university (Altbach 2003). After the turn of the century, and with Rockefeller's more than US$50 million, the University of Chicago needed only 20 years to attain top standing. In Asia just before the turn of this century, the newly established Hong Kong University of Science and Technology (HKUST) took only 10 years and less than a tenth of Eliot's figure to become one of Asia's top 10 research universities.[1]

Globalization has quickened the establishment of a research university and shortened the time that nations with rapidly rising economies are willing to wait for such an achievement. For this reason, the current models of world-class research universities have in part shifted away from those institutions that took a century or more to mature toward those that accomplished the feat in a shorter period and within the new rough-and-tumble era of competitive knowledge economics. Even in the "post-American" world with the rise of the rest—notably India and China, where ancient civilizations and extensive national histories are treasured—it seems that a century is far too long to wait for a new research university to ripen (Zakaria 2009). Thus, nations have come to consider establishing new research universities while at the same time strengthening the research capacity of traditional national flagship universities. As this chapter will show, a two-pronged strategy is more sensible for an economy on the move rather than a conventional approach that concentrates resources in already established flagship institutions (Ding 2004; Altbach and Balan 2007; Salmi 2009).

This chapter examines a case in Hong Kong SAR, China, in higher education—the establishment and development of HKUST and its unprecedented achievement of becoming an internationally ranked research university within a decade of its establishment in 1991. This university's rapid rise hinges on a number of factors. Although impossible to duplicate elsewhere, such an array of factors is worthy of detailed consideration. These examples illustrate how a successful research university can be established if the institution is accurate in its perception of opportunity within a rapidly changing economic and political environment; proactive in its approach to capitalizing on potential support and overcoming potential hurdles in society; and skillful in planning first-tier faculty recruitment, highlighting its uniqueness, and devising a way to settle into the existing system of higher education. Selected patterns in this case study will resonate with conditions in other emerging economies. Nevertheless, the complex and interwoven nature and process within a changing environment will make any effort to set out specific conditions for establishing world-class research universities a fruitless endeavor. After identifying the main factors surrounding the establishment and development of HKUST, the chapter provides further discussion about the larger issue of establishing research universities.

Key Factors for HKUST

HKUST took advantage of the sunset years of a colonial administration to nest a U.S. research university culture within the British colonial system of higher education. As Hong Kong's other universities remained wedded to their institutional ethos and heritage, this university distinguished itself from the status quo with foresight about the potential role of a science and technology university in the forthcoming Hong Kong SAR, China. It launched several measures that would eventually be seen in other universities. These measures include putting research on an equal footing with teaching, relying on an entrepreneurial approach to development, appointing rather than electing deans, and requiring students to enroll in social science and humanities courses outside their science and technology specialization.[2] In fact, this policy occurred as part of the general trend of globalization in higher education.

The university's establishment coincided with the founding of the Hong Kong Research Grants Council, which provided funds to strengthen research capacity at colleges and universities in Hong Kong (UGC 2000) Today, the Research Grants Council remains the primary source of research funds, which has nudged the traditionally teaching-focused universities of Hong Kong SAR, China, toward more research. Yet, HKUST had a faster launch. The amount of funding it received gradually rose to award levels comparable with other universities and today remains ahead in the proportion of successful grant applications. For example, in 2009 its application success rate was 47 percent, ahead of 36 percent for the other two top research universities. The amount awarded per faculty member is almost twice as much as that at any other university. Thus, with the establishment of the Research Grants Council, the timing of HKUST's establishment as a research university was ideal.

As the 1990s approached, the four Asian "tigers" (Hong Kong; the Republic of Korea; Singapore; and Taiwan, China) were bleeding manufacturing to nearby Asian countries with lower production costs. With increasingly educated populations, the tigers upgraded their domestic industries toward more value-added production. During this industrial upgrading, the governments of Singapore; Korea; and Taiwan, China set the course for high-technology-intensive industries. Although labor-intensive industries from Hong Kong began moving across the border to the Chinese hinterlands, the government eschewed publicly funded high-technology initiatives, choosing instead to rely on market economics as the driving force. It limited itself to the support of infrastructural investment, including a university of science and technology, which quickly made HKUST a symbolic centerpiece of Hong Kong's high-technology upgrading. Its focus on science and technology in a rising Asia resonated with the popular vision of knowledge transfer for a modern China. That vision was enhanced by HKUST's faculty of business and management in a commercial city like Hong Kong. Unfortunately, the government's reliance on market forces failed to make Hong Kong a high-technology center and thereby limited the potential role of the new university to be a catalyst for Hong Kong's rise in that sector. The powerful property and real estate sectors as well as the second-tier civil servants who were perched to lead Hong Kong after the handover to China in 1997 did little to support Hong Kong's development as a center of high technology, thereby driving that opportunity northward where Shanghai became the proactive benefactor.[3]

HKUST's rapid rise was also assisted by the timing of its establishment, shortly after the government's decision in November 1989 to double enrollments in degree-place higher education. This decision occurred in the wake of the Tiananmen Square event when many potential scientists, who would have studied at this university when it opened in 1991, headed instead for overseas universities to further their study. When annual emigration from Hong Kong began to increase during the 1990s, reaching a high in one year of about 65,000, including highly educated residents, the government moved to double university enrollments. This expansion of higher education enrollments would have been more difficult to achieve without the university's establishment in 1991. Return migration rates of these Hong Kong residents increased in the mid-to late 1990s as they felt secure enough to return, with or without overseas residency or passports.[4]

HKUST's most important success factor was the recruitment of outstandingly talented scholars and scientists. All faculty members had doctorates, and 80 percent received doctorates from or were employed at 24 of the top universities in the world. The university recruits this caliber of academic staff from among the senior scholar generation of the Chinese diaspora. The generation of Chinese scholars who left China for Taiwan, China, and then studied overseas, usually in the United States, was riveted on the changes taking place in China during its first decade of economic reform and the opening to the outside world that began in December 1978. The growing number of China's overseas scholars at U.S. universities reached a tipping point. HKUST recruited heavily from this vast pool of talented academics born in Taiwan, China, or mainland China and trained overseas mostly at U.S. universities, something that the other universities in Hong Kong were less inclined to do at that time.

Woo Chia-wei, the university's first president, was a member of this unique generation of Chinese academics. A physicist by training, Woo had also been president of a major research university in the United States. In fact, he was the first ethnic Chinese person to head a major U.S. university. He was also part of an extensive network of Chinese research scientists in the United States. It was highly significant for HKUST that a senior generation of scientists who had attained international reputations in their fields of expertise felt secure enough in their careers to leave their established posts and move to Hong Kong. This shift indicated a certain faith in President Woo, who not only oversaw the establishment and early development of HKUST, but also was instrumental in assembling an outstanding and internationally renowned academic faculty. As HKUST's first president, Woo set the pace for the next two presidents.

To continue its trajectory toward becoming the premier university of science and technology in Asia, HKUST chose Paul Ching-Wu Chu as its second president. Chu was a pioneer in the field of high-temperature superconductivity. While the T. L. L. Temple Chair of Science at the University of Houston and founding director of the Texas Center for Superconductivity, he also served as a consultant and a visiting staff member at Bell Laboratories, Los Alamos National Laboratory, the Marshall Space Flight Center, Argonne National Laboratory, and DuPont. Chu received the 1988 National Medal of Science, the highest honor for a scientist in the United States, was named Best Researcher in the United States by *U.S. News and World Report* in 1990, and was appointed by the White House to be one of 12 distinguished scientists to evaluate the National Medal of Science nominees. One of his major contributions to HKUST was the establishment of the Institute for Advanced Study. Succeeding Paul Ching-Wu Chu, who retired in late 2009, was Tony Chan, who had been assistant director of the U.S. National Science Foundation in charge of the mathematical and physical sciences directorate. In that position, he guided and managed research funding of almost HK$10 billion (US$ 1.29 billion) a year in astronomy, physics, chemistry, mathematical science, material science, and multidisciplinary activities. Although he is just beginning his term as president of HKUST, he is expected to combine his skills as a preeminent scholar and scientist and a world-class administrator.

A key consideration for potential recruits to HKUST in the mid to late 1990s was the surge of prosperity in the economy, as investment from China pushed the economy to record levels. This development helped HKUST gain a fair amount of financial resources from the government, although the amount would still pale in comparison to that of top research universities in the United States. Like other universities in Hong Kong, HKUST received a regular injection of funds on a triennial basis from the University Grants Committee and research funding from the newly established Research Grants Council. However, unlike the other universities, HKUST did not have alumni who could support the university with private donations.

Academic salaries reached levels compatible with those offered in other developed countries, which made the decision of recruited staff to relocate to Hong Kong easier, though salary was not the key factor in the equation for top-rung recruitment. For many distinguished academics, relocation meant moving from a spacious U.S.-style house to smaller apartment-style living quarters in Hong Kong, plus a separation from family studying or working nearby.

The approaching date for sovereignty retrocession represented an important and historical turning point for Chinese academics that intensified their emotional attachment to China. The scientific talent that was stored by Taiwan, China, for three decades and that led the economy's successful drive in high technology production was for the first time being focused on Hong Kong's development, specifically in expanding its higher education system. For Chinese-American academics, this change in focus signified an important opportunity to make a significant contribution to U.S.-China relations.

In short, scholars with a strong emotional attachment to China were elated by the increased openness and economic progress of the country. For them, this progress provided an opportunity to take part in a significant event and play a role in China's modernization. In this sense, timing was crucial for staff recruitment. If HKUST had been established a decade earlier, when it was not yet clear that the colonial status of Hong Kong would end in 1997, then most of that university's Chinese academics would not have chosen to work in Hong Kong. An important factor to these scholars, HKUST ensured a degree of academic freedom as yet unavailable in mainland China.

Thus, HKUST created a valuable niche, which it projected through its institutional vision and supported by recruiting two generations of overseas-based Chinese scholars. It presented a unique historical opportunity to work in a dynamic economy and rapidly expanding university system. It established a robust scholarly climate adjoining a globally emergent and reformist China, coinciding with the systematic upgrading of publicly funded research in Hong Kong's universities.

Although the speed in launching a new research university can be hastened by such key factors, some are not easily duplicated elsewhere. Factors such as a dynamic economy, academic freedom, and proximity to the Chinese mainland contributed to the common development of the entire system of higher education in Hong Kong. Each higher education system has unique conditions, some of which can be turned into opportunities for the establishment of research universities. A world-class research university cannot be created in a vacuum. HKUST is nested in a system in which it identified a niche, but projects its vision far beyond Hong Kong's academy.

Although universities in Hong Kong SAR, China, currently are financed by the government, their autonomy is protected by law.[5] In the late 20th century, competition among the top three research universities (the University of Hong Kong, the Chinese University of Hong Kong, and HKUST) for financial support and academic status from the same government coffers also created a new dynamic in higher education in Hong Kong SAR, China. To some extent, this approach contributed to the rise of the economy's entire university system. After HKUST was established, the government's funding allocation pie resource was enlarged. Yet, these funds were still disbursed on a competitive basis. Rather than using a conventional strategy of concentrating resources in one or more already established flagship institutions, Hong Kong used a two-pronged development strategy in which resources were not concentrated in one institution at the expense of others. It uses a strategy for creating research universities in which, at least in theory, the universities complement one another and thereby strengthen the entire system's research capacity. The University Grants Committee asserts a systemwide approach

> developing an interlocking system where the whole higher education sector is viewed as one force... values a role-driven yet deeply collaborative system of higher education... committed to extensive collaboration with other institutions.
>
> (UGC 2010b)

The extent to which this approach is realized in practice is certainly open to debate. Still, some observers credit this strategy, at least in part, for the reason that four of the eight universities in Hong Kong SAR, China, are ranked in the top 10 in Asia (Times Higher Education 2008). The rest of this chapter examines the HKUST case in more detail. The factors unique to its establishment and development receive the most attention, and the chapter concludes with a reassertion of the conditions for the establishment of research universities in emergent economies.

The HKUST Context

New universities, whether public or private, are part of a society and its higher education system. HKUST was established in a highly mobile society, with a system that had not yet made the transition from elite to mass higher education. Hong Kong SAR, China, remains a relatively small region of 422 square miles with some of the most densely populated areas in the world. The ethos of higher education was shaped by its history as a British colony from 1842 to 1997, after which it returned to China in a one-country-two-system arrangement (So and Chan 2002). Although most research is conducted in English, there are two official languages: Chinese (Cantonese dialect) and English. The University of Hong Kong was established in 1911 and the Chinese University of Hong Kong in 1963.[6] The proportion of the age cohort that had access to higher education was 2 percent in 1981 and 8 percent by 1989, when an executive decision was made to double enrollment to 16 percent by 1994 (UGC 1996). During that period, four colleges and polytechnics were upgraded to university status, and by end-1997, Hong Kong SAR, China, had seven universities (UGC 1999). The Asian financial crisis that began in 1998 crippled any discussion about further expansion. When expansion finally occurred, it was largely through privately funded two-year associate-degree programs at community colleges (Postiglione 2008, 2009). The universities have since upgraded research capacity, preserved academic freedom, and converted from a three-to a four-year bachelor-degree program, thus bringing the system into line with the two main trading partners of Hong Kong SAR, China—mainland China and the United States (UGC 2002a, 2004a, 2004b). The four-year system permits HKUST to deepen its original initiative, set in 1991, of providing all students with a significant amount of humanities and social sciences, more than had been offered at the other comprehensive universities in Hong Kong SAR, China.

Basic Characteristics of HKUST

The following describes the fundamental attributes of HKUST: its placement in several of the global rankings of universities; and its roles, goals, and objectives.

Global Rankings

Because this book focuses on the establishment of world-class research universities, it is notable that HKUST has achieved an impressive score on several international league tables (HKUST 2010d): (a) number 35 of the world's top 200 universities in 2009; (b) number 26 of the world's top 100 universities in engineering and information technology in 2008 and in technology in 2008 (Times Higher Education 2008); (c) number 2 of the world's top 200 Asian universities in 2010; (d) number 39 of the world's top 100 universities in engineering and technology and computer sciences (number 1 in "Greater China") in 2010; and (e) number 52–75 of the world's top 100 universities in social sciences (number 1 in "Greater China") in 2010.[7]

HKUST's Roles, Goals, and Objectives

The Hong Kong University of Science and Technology (a) provides a range of programs leading to the award of First Degrees and postgraduate qualifications; (b) includes professional schools, particularly in the fields of science, technology, engineering, and business; (c) offers courses in humanities and social sciences only at a level sufficient to provide intellectual breadth, contextual background, and communication skills to an otherwise scientific or technological curriculum and for limited postgraduate work; (d) offers research programs for a significant number of students in every subject area; and (e) provides scope for academic staff members to undertake consultancy and collaborative projects with industry in areas where they have special expertise. (UGC 2008)

HKUST emphasized the importance of being unique at a time when Hong Kong SAR, China still viewed its universities as elite institutions. HKUST professed to become a "leading force in higher education," "a global academic leader," "an agent of change," and "a catalyst for significant progress in science and technology research and education in Hong Kong, and the Mainland" (HKUST 2010e). This focus supports Jamil Salmi's assertion that a world-class research university "should be based on a forward-looking vision that is genuinely innovative" (Salmi 2009, 57). Nevertheless, some of HKUST's goals echo those of research universities around the world:

- Give all students, undergraduate and postgraduate alike, a broadly based university experience that includes superior training in their chosen fields of study; a well-rounded education that enhances the development of their creativity, critical thinking, global outlook, and cultural awareness; and a campus life that prepares them to be community leaders and lifelong learners.
- Provide a dynamic and supportive working environment in which faculty and staff may continually develop intellectually and professionally.
- Provide an open environment and atmosphere conducive to the exchange of knowledge, views, and innovative ideas among students, faculty and staff members, and visiting scholars.
- Be a leading institution for research and postgraduate study, pursuing knowledge in both fundamental and applied areas and collaborating closely with business and industry in promoting technological innovation and economic development.
- Promote and assist in the economic and social development of Hong Kong SAR, China, and enrich its culture (HKUST 2010b).

Students and Academic Staff Members

The initial student recruitment in 1991 for the newly established university was one of HKUST's most crucial activities, because in the eyes of the public, it had yet to gain a reputation. In this respect, it adopted a proactive approach focused on bringing the university into direct contact with many sectors of the population. It opened itself to the community by taking advantage of its spectacular campus and facilitating access and visits, especially by potential students and their families. Its newly designed campus with impressive architecture and a panoramic view of the surrounding mountains and seaside was a major attraction. About 250 secondary schools were invited to each send two student representatives on the day the new university's foundation stone was laid.

Aside from opening the campus to the public, the university arranged exhibitions throughout Hong Kong. Professors met prospective students on an individual basis to provide general information, though these exhibitions did not include recruitment. Students were formally selected through a Hong Kong-wide recruitment system that came to be known as the Joint University Programmes Admissions System. This main route assisted senior secondary school students with the results of their Hong Kong Advanced Level Examinations to apply for admission to the bachelor's degree programs offered by the seven public universities and the Hong Kong Institute of Education.

Before HKUST opened, it developed a plan for the number of students allocated to the three major faculties: science students would constitute 25 percent, engineering 40 percent, and business administration 35 percent. Also, 20 percent of all students would be postgraduate students (Kung 2002, 5). These proportions remained stable through 2009 (see table 10.1). However, the student body of the university remains below 10,000. Initial impressions suggest that this figure is in keeping with an economy of scale and helps retain a particular institutional ethos. However, faculty numbers can confound the picture (see table 10.2). In 1991, the University Grants Committee resourced HKUST to enroll 7,000 students, even while the other two research universities grew to 12,000 students. During the administration of HKUST's second president, student numbers grew toward 10,000 based on a government promise to support a student-faculty ratio of 12 to 1.[8] The government's promise went unfulfilled while student numbers continued to rise. The unfulfilled promise stifled the planned proportionate rise in the student-faculty ratio, thereby adding to the burden on faculty. Such a disproportionate rise reduced faculty research time and was detrimental to faculty morale.[9] When the ratio rose to 19 to 1, it had a significantly adverse effect on research productivity. HKUST operated with a relatively high student-faculty ratio and a lean professoriat. However, HKUST's currently diversified student population of full-time undergraduates, fulltime research postgraduates, and full-time and part-time postgraduates, requires a significant number of adjunct faculty members. This development, in turn, has moved the student-faculty ratio in the direction of 15 to 1 or even 14 to 1.

Table 10.1 Students at Hong Kong University of Science and Technology, 2010

Program or area of study	Undergraduate	Postgraduate	Total
Science	1,431	476	1,907
Engineering	2,310	1,489	3,799
Business and management	2,132	1,189	3,321
Humanities and social sciences	—	280	280
HKUST Fok Ying Tung Graduate School	—	2	2
Interdisciplinary programs	137	69	206
Total (as at January 2010)	6,010	3,505	9,515

Source: Reprinted by permission from Hong Kong University of Science and Technology.
Note: — = not available.

Table 10.2 Faculty of Hong Kong University of Science and Technology, 2009

Program or area of study	Regular	Visiting	Total
Science	100	19	119
Engineering	149	15	164
Business and management	126	12	138
Humanities and social sciences	54	6	60
Division of Environment[a]	7	1	8
Total (as at January 2009)	436	53	489

Source: Reprinted by permission from Hong Kong University of Science and Technology.
a. The Division of Environment is under the Interdisciplinary Programs Office.

The top three research universities in Hong Kong SAR, China, draw their largest grants from the same public source. Thus, a rapid expansion in the numbers of faculty members and students at one institution over another would be unlikely. Likewise, faculty-student ratios would be proportionate across research universities. Universities in Hong Kong SAR, China, receive block grants that can be allocated with a degree of flexibility. Although fund allocation formulae within specific institutions may vary, student admission numbers and faculty hiring usually adhere to what was promised in proposals to the University Grants Committee. In short, maintaining stability in the proportionate rise of students and faculty across institutions is seemingly in the best interest of a public system of research universities.

This stability could be considered a strategic factor in the establishment of a research university within a group of public universities. Yet, private research universities generally set their own targets for staff and student recruitment. Rather than block grants, their main sources of income are student tuition, alumni funding, other donations, and research grants from government and corporate sponsorship. In the United States, top public research institutions still draw a significant amount of their main public funding from government budgets. Therefore, such allocations are usually made in the context of preserving the state's system of research universities. Those arrangements could also work in reverse—such as when a state legislature closes a local undergraduate college in its system, but the top research universities in the system usually survive.

The same adverse effects held true for Hong Kong in the early years of HKUST, when an action that seemed equitable in a systemwide context worked against the mission of a research university. In the case of HKUST, its planning committee chair has stated in retrospect:

> Regrettably, the University Grants Committee has since strayed from the principle of giving priority to needs and values, but instead, allocated funds "equitably" to all the varsities. Consequently, UST was not able to offer more places at the postgraduate level in past years as its mission stipulated. This, to me, is unfortunate and a retrograde policy that has caused Hong Kong to lag behind the competition in advanced science and technology.
>
> (Chung 2001, 54)

HKUST's Inauguration and Commencement

Appreciation of HKUST's ascent into the research university stratosphere rests heavily on understanding its preestablishment plan and takeoff (Woo 2006). In 1984, the Sino-British Joint Declaration[10] on Hong Kong's future was signed, and China established the adjacent Shenzhen Special Economic Zone. As the border began to blur and Hong Kong's manufacturing and investment flowed into the Shenzhen zone, Sir Edward Youde, governor at the time, saw this new symbiosis with China as leading to an economic and technological transformation that would continue to relocate Hong Kong's manufacturing industries to south China. The governor expressed a new vision in which Hong Kong would become technologically upgraded. In September 1985, he asked the University and Polytechnic Grants Committee to explore the feasibility of a third university that would augment the existing setup of two low enrollment universities, two polytechnics, and two colleges. At a meeting of the governor's Executive Council in March 1986, the committee responded positively, confirming that the new university would focus on science and technology, management, and postgraduate training (Chung 2001, 148–58).

Planning and Construction

A planning committee was established in 1986, chaired by Sir Chung Sze-yuen of the governor's Executive Council. Its terms of reference included building a campus with a funding allocation from the Royal Hong Kong Jockey Club.[11] The first enrollments were planned for 1994. However, the new campus opened on October 2, 1991, with 600 students. Nine years later, HKUST was ranked seventh in Asia according to *Asia Week*. In 2001, the HKUST business school was ranked the best in Asia by the *Financial Times* and 48th in the world. By 2010, the *Financial Times* ranked the HKUST master of business administration program ninth in the world, tied with the University of Chicago Booth School of Business. This ranking also becomes significant for understanding HKUST's extensive collaboration with business and industry, as noted later in this chapter.

In 1987, the Royal Hong Kong Jockey Club, a nonprofit community organization, pledged HK$1.50 billion (US$192 million) for a project estimated to cost HK$1.93 billion (US$247 million), inflation included (Flahavin 1991). The figure was based on unit costs from the then recent building of the urban campus of the City Polytechnic of Hong Kong. Although this estimate was useful, the fact remained that City Polytechnic was advantaged by its urban environment—unlike HKUST, which was built in a rural area lacking basic infrastructure such as utilities and sewage as well as specific requirements for conducting research in fields such as microelectronics and biotechnology laboratories.

Nevertheless, cost-overrun concerns were raised on May 4, 1988, when HKUST came before the Legislative Council for approval. Because funds for the campus came from the Jockey Club, supplemented by the government, a review by the legislature was required before approval. The government's initial cost estimate for capital construction was conservative and was made public. As campus construction proceeded and was put on a fast track to permit an earlier opening date, building engineers recognized the project's complexity and consulted with the government and the Jockey Club. The exchange of views led to a common understanding of the gap between the originally publicized estimate and the project's cost increase because of both inflation and faster pace of construction. In this context, the new president and his team noted inadequacies in laboratory facilities and building area. The University and

Polytechnic Grants Committee expanded the area of the campus, and by June 1990, the budget was increased to HK$3.548 billion (US$455 million), a figure approved by the Legislative Council without objections (Chung 2001, 157). Phases I and II of the construction were completed on schedule in 1993 for HK$3.224 billion (US$413 million), 8.6 percent less than the estimate without overruns (Walker 1994).

In general, the establishment and development of new research universities in developing societies can periodically be plagued by cost overrun issues because of the vast sums required to build a research university. If not handled correctly, these issues can affect the public's view of a new institution. In the case of HKUST, the effort to speed the building process in the interest of facilitating the overall expansion of access to higher education in Hong Kong was overshadowed for a time by building costs. Such cost issues are often quite detailed, and their complexities are not easily presented to the public. Thus, a country's system of governance, especially its legal system and accounting transparency, is critical when establishing a new research university. Today, a developed society like Hong Kong SAR, China—with its vigorous legal and financial accounting systems held in high regard by the international community—commonly has extensive oversight on such large government projects. With the freest press media in Asia, Hong Kong SAR, China, has a literate public kept informed during every step of the process about any questions in the cost of large public projects. Yet, the financial issues surrounding such a large enterprise are often open to multiple interpretations by the media and can become convoluted by the politics of a particular era. Nevertheless, a high degree of transparency is essential for establishing a new research university despite the risks of multiple interpretations. Although the public continues to question major expenditures, past and planned—including a cyberport, a Disneyland, and a high-speed railway—this association of ideas does not include HKUST.

Presidential Search

The name of the university was chosen in 1986 and was officially proposed in the first report of the planning committee in September 1987. HKUST was formally incorporated in April 1988 and immediately sponsored the first meeting of its University Council. After a global search, the first president was appointed in November 1988. Forty-four applications were received, and 47 other names were put forward. More than half came from England (25 applications and 35 names put forward); nine applications from the United States and Canada plus seven other names put forward; two applications from Australia plus one other name put forward; five applications from Hong Kong with seven other names put forward; and three applications from other countries with three other names put forward. Of these, 14 applicants were interviewed, and five of them (from Australia, Hong Kong, the United Kingdom, and the United States) were selected for final consideration (Kung 2002, 5). Though selection committee members, Chung Sze-yuen and Lee Quo-wei, suggested the new president be a person of Chinese descent, the governor would agree only that the final choice must be a candidate who was president of a top Western university. The final choice, put forward and reported to the governor on September 21, 1987, was Woo Chia-wei, a distinguished theoretical physicist and president of San Francisco State University (which had 25,000 students). The choice was approved on October 10, 1987, and publicly announced on November 5. He was well-known in Hong Kong and spoke the commonly used Cantonese dialect as well as the national language of Mandarin. It was highly significant that Woo Chia-wei was the first person of Chinese descent to head a major university in the United States. This distinction would translate as a tremendous boost to the HKUST recruitment of academic staff, a key factor in its rapidly won success.

The government provided HKUST and its new president with an initial vision statement:

> To advance learning and knowledge through teaching and research, particularly: (i) in science, technology, engineering, management and business studies; and (ii) at the postgraduate level; and to assist the economic and social development of Hong Kong.
>
> (HKUST 2010)

President Woo appreciated that this vision generally provided the proper guidance and was worded loosely enough to allow the founding faculty to interpret it more forcefully. When he assumed the presidency, he requested that the university be allocated a larger percentage of graduate students. Although this request was not granted, he nevertheless succeeded, on the basis of the words "social development," to upgrade the university's General Education Centre into a School of Humanities and Social Sciences that granted master and PhD degrees.

Elements of HKUST

Language of Instruction

Instruction at HKUST was to be delivered in English. The University of Hong Kong had always adhered to the principle that all instruction be delivered in English, though the campus life of students reflected the bilingual nature of society.[12] The Chinese University of Hong Kong permitted its teachers to use either Chinese (Cantonese or Mandarin) or English as their instructional language. The new university's orientation toward science and technology contributed to this uncontroversial decision to adhere to English-language instruction, despite the upcoming reunion of Hong Kong with China. Most senior professors had been accustomed to teaching in English, and most could not lecture in Cantonese, which was the lingua franca of Hong Kong.

The global university rankings indicate that the language of instruction does not automatically determine the ranking of a research university. For example, Tokyo and Kyoto universities (Japan), where much funding is allocated to translation of

English-language journals, are among the world's top-rated Asian universities. There are other top universities, but the issue of language of instruction in world-class universities is complex and has been discussed elsewhere. For example, Jamil Salmi (2009, 61) mentions 11 non-native-speaking higher education systems where some graduate programs are offered in English. Although Hong Kong SAR, China, where most graduate programs are in English, is not mentioned within this group, its higher education system receives a special distinction within China and has two official languages, Chinese and English. Although some of mainland China's top universities use English in selected courses and programs, the only examples of English-language universities on the mainland are relatively new joint ventures: the University of Nottingham Ningbo, China; Xi'an Jiaotong-Liverpool University in Suzhou; and United International College (Hong Kong Baptist University and Beijing Normal University) in the Zhuhai Special Economic Zone adjoining Hong Kong SAR, China.

The language of instruction has implications for HKUST's aim to internationalize its student recruitment, which already extends far beyond Hong Kong SAR, China—including mainland China and overseas. In fact, HKUST has the highest percentage of nonlocal students among its counterparts (UGC 2010a). Although the figures for students from overseas and other parts of Asia are comparable to those at other universities, the percentage of students from the Chinese mainland surpasses other universities, which will probably have a long-term effect of strengthening future partnerships and collaborations. Although most graduate students are from the mainland, the proportion of undergraduate students from the mainland matches that at other universities and will continue to do so as HKUST adopts a four-year university system—in 2012—similar to that on the Chinese mainland.

Innovations in Governance

A key innovation of HKUST that contributes to its maxim "be unique and not duplicate" is the manner in which administrators are chosen. All deans are appointed by recommendations from search committees, and the search committees are dominated by faculty members, rather than appointed by the administration or elected from within a school or faculty, as was the case in the universities of Hong Kong at the time. This process was innovative within the context of Hong Kong, which had a system that adhered closely to the British model of higher education. The HKUST system was a U.S. model in terms of academic field appointments and reflected the U.S. corporate system in which faculty governed the academic part of the university. HKUST also triggered a change at other universities in Hong Kong away from traditional academic titles (lecturer, senior lecturer, and reader and professor) to those used in the United States and elsewhere (assistant professor, associate professor, and professor). Similarly, the current customary administrative titles in universities in Hong Kong SAR, China (vice-chancellor, deputy vice-chancellor, and pro-vice-chancellor) are also undergoing some change with increased use of the titles president, provost, and vice president.

A potentially valuable advantage is created when (a) a new research university is to be established and nested within a particular model of higher education and (b) the system provides enough autonomy for it to develop a particular edge over other long-established institutions of the system by innovating its governance or academic structure in accordance with a unique vision. This project also represents a system to speed up the process of introducing reforms in other top institutions, among which ethos and long history prevent any radical changes that would be risky to the identity and long-established brand of the university.

This type of innovation is a potential advantage in the establishment of research universities. HKUST was established during the sunset years of the British administration and at a time when the United States and mainland China were Hong Kong's major trading partners. Not only were most major universities in the world located in the United States, but the higher education system in mainland China also operated more closely to the U.S. model of higher education, and most of China's prospective academics who studied overseas did so in the United States. This situation gave HKUST a tremendous advantage. HKUST's adaptation of innovations from the U.S. university system made it unique. Meanwhile, the British style of higher education in other institutions, although well established and successful, had more inertia toward change than a newly established university. Thus, the timing of HKUST's establishment, something that "may be difficult to duplicate elsewhere," contributed a great deal to its rapid rise (Wong 2010).

Another factor contributing to HKUST's innovative character was the relatively autonomous nature of higher education in Hong Kong at the time. Although HKUST has been a public institution from the beginning, it possessed a high degree of autonomy in most respects and could freely innovate in academic research and instructional delivery. Though it did not have to await approval by government or the University Grants Committee, it adhered to several basic conventions followed by the other two government research universities, especially in terms of student recruitment. Beginning in 2012, all universities in Hong Kong SAR, China, will move to a standard four-year undergraduate program and will begin to recruit from "senior secondary form six."

Academic Staff—Key to the Academic Kingdom

Although there is a global trend toward recruiting part-time academic staff, HKUST instead sought full-time academic staff, as was the case in Hong Kong's university system. The initial planning of academic staff followed a distinct strategy for faculty: (a) 214 engineering faculty members—21 professors, 54 associate professors, and 139 assistant professors; (b) 171 science faculty members—17 professors, 43 associate professors, and 111 assistant professors; and (c) 160 business administration faculty members—16 professors, 40 associate professors, and 104 assistant professors.[13] This structure differed from the single professor chair system used by departments in Hong Kong's other universities at the time (Chung 2001, 5–6).

HKUST recruited practically all academic staff from outside Hong Kong, most of whom were born in China. If the staff had been recruited largely from the traditional expatriate and local academic pools, that practice would have detracted from the uniqueness of HKUST. This is another point worthy of consideration by universities in a developing country that have a large contingency of students and scholars who study overseas for doctorates but have yet to return home in great numbers. Jamil Salmi (2009, 61) considers this issue but does not mention that Hong Kong SAR, China, probably has the largest proportion of returned diaspora academic staff members, though many are originally from other parts of China. Korea, for example, has been able to attract back a significant number of its overseas academics, though they largely populate second-tier universities. However, Mongolia has not yet been successful in luring them home. The establishment of a new and well-endowed research university can be an attraction. For example, if Mongolia's newly discovered precious mineral deposits tip its economy forward as predicted for future years, it may be able to consider such an initiative. There are other potential examples from the ranks of developing countries.

Another distinguishing characteristic of HKUST concerns the qualifications of its academic staff and the academic centers from which faculty are recruited. Not only do all of HKUST's faculty members possess doctorates from universities around the world, but at least 80 percent also have worked or earned doctorates at renowned research universities—such as California Institute of Technology; Carnegie Mellon University; Columbia University; Cornell University; Harvard University; Imperial College London; Massachusetts Institute of Technology; Northwestern University; Princeton University; Purdue University; Stanford University; University of British Columbia; University of California, Berkeley; University of California, Los Angeles; University of Cambridge; University of Chicago; University of Illinois; University of London; University of Michigan; University of Oxford; University of Toronto; University of Wisconsin-Madison; and Yale University. These qualifications are not only an indication of the caliber of academic staff, but also represent a wellspring of academic capital that is used to build transnational research collaborations among networks of scholars from similar institutions.

Working Environments: The Best of Both Worlds

The adage about Hong Kong SAR, China, being a meeting point between East and West turns out to be more than a cliche for the academic born in China and trained as a scholar and scientist in the West. The Hong Kong SAR, China, work environment carries many advantages not available elsewhere for some Chinese academics. These advantages include living in a Chinese society and working in an English-language university, teaching in English to Chinese students, conducting research with methods learned in the West and applying them to China's development, publishing in Western academic journals and attaining international recognition, and having their work translated into Chinese for a much larger audience. It also means avoiding the glass ceiling sometimes experienced by Chinese academics overseas and avoiding the restrictions on academic freedom on the mainland. Hong Kong SAR, China, represents a relatively easy adjustment to both academic and societal culture and provides a unique and advantageous environment for innovative academic work. Moreover, a large number of academic staff members at HKUST and at other universities in Hong Kong SAR, China, are foreign nationals, some of whom have Chinese heritage though they may have been born or naturalized overseas. The United Kingdom, for example, has a high proportion (27 percent) of foreign-national academic staff (Salmi 2009, 61). However, in a recent international survey, Hong Kong SAR, China, ranked second (after Australia) in the proportion of foreign nationals.

Multigenerational Recruitment from the Top Down

As mentioned earlier, the first president of HKUST took a major role in recruitment and is quoted as saying: "You've got to start from the top because only first-class people can attract other first-class people. In fast-moving fields like science, engineering, and management, you are either first class or without class" (Course 2001, 8). The academic pillars of HKUST began with those age 50 or younger who were born on the mainland; whose families left for Taiwan, China, in the 1940s; and who had gone to the United States for study and had remained there to start families. Although many became naturalized U.S. citizens and worked in the United States for decades, their aspirations included making a contribution to their homeland. According to Woo: "They had talent, they had ability, but in the end, what brought them here was their hearts" (Course 2001, 9).

Academics of that generation included Jay-Chung Chen, an aeronautics expert recruited from the Jet Propulsion Laboratory at the California Institute of Technology. Chih-Yung Chien was a top experimental physicist from Johns Hopkins University who had conducted his research on the world's largest high-energy accelerator at the European Organization for Nuclear Research. Shain-Dow Kung, a specialist in biotechnology and acting provost at the University of Maryland Biotechnology Institute, became the dean of science in 1991. Other recruits during the first decade included Leroy Chang, a world-renowned experimental physicist from International Business Machines (IBM), and fivefold national academy member in the United States and China. Another internationally noted HKUST scholar was Ping Ko, who came from the University of California, Berkeley, and was director of the microfabrication laboratory. Otto C. C. Lin, who was dean of the School of Engineering at Tsing Hua University and director of the world-famous Industrial Technology Research Institute (ITRI) in Taiwan, China, became HKUST's vice president for research and development. Other notable scientists included Eugene Wong, who had been recruited by the U.S. White House to be associate director of the Office of Science and Technology Policy and who came to HKUST from the chair of electrical engineering and computer science at the University of California, Berkeley, where he developed the theory that provides the statistical foundation for processing images and other multidimensional data.

The younger generation of recruits comprised those in their late 30s and early 40s, including Chan Yuk-Shee, who was the Justin Dart Professor of Finance at the University of Southern California and became the founding dean of the HKUST School of Business and Management. They were mandated to "establish a leading business school in Asia by the end of the century" (Course 2001; Kung 2002).

A striking theme among top recruits was the idea of making a new beginning with a vision that HKUST could become a world-class research university. The caliber of these scholars and scientists in turn attracted other senior academics, including many non-Chinese, from North America, Asia, and Europe. Peter Dobson, first HKUST's director of planning and coordination and later its associate vice president for academic affairs, was recruited from the University of Hawaii. Thomas Stelson was executive vice president of the Georgia Institute of Technology and became vice president for research and development. Gregory James came from the University of Exeter to become the director of the HKUST Language Center.

Recruitment is one of the most strategic aspects in the rapid establishment of internationally recognized universities. Although this recruitment requires finding already-established leaders in their fields, a good portion of these scholars may be close to retirement and will lead their departments in the new university for only a few years. Thus, their value may be more in attracting top younger scholars than in contributing over the long run at the new university. They could also become influential emeritus professors if they reside in the university's region and maintain close contact after retirement, which is less likely if they were originally recruited from overseas. Moreover, in any new recruitment exercise, a certain degree of attrition of top scholars is not unexpected, something that factor must be built into all recruitment plans.

Finally, although salaries may not be a singular attraction for some scholars, their salaries at the new university will be viewed as an indication of their status and can signal to other scholars in their home university that their departure is not one of downward mobility. In short, a new university must be prepared to provide attractive salaries to distinguished scholars while viewing their motive for joining the university as not merely financial.

Timing

Although salaries were clearly not the most essential attraction for the original group of leading HKUST scholars, the economic growth rate in Hong Kong at the time permitted academic salaries to approach levels compatible with those overseas, thus making relocation easier. Nevertheless, for academics based at U.S. universities, relocating often meant a transition from spacious houses to modest apartments. Although Hong Kong academic salary levels had generally been lower than their counterparts in U.S. universities, this situation began to change. The five-year period from 1988 to 1993 saw a doubling of salaries. By 1998, the increases were 2.7 times more than in 1988.

In the 1990s, academic salary scales were linked to those of the civil service and rose steadily, though academic salaries have since been unlinked from those of the civil service.[14] Although some government officials had opposed the rise in academic salaries, the approaching date of sovereignty retrocession had caused some concern about a possible brain drain. HKUST recruited 120 faculty members each year, averaging about 10 recruits per month, 80 percent of whom had received their PhDs in North America.

Timing contributed to HKUST's success in several other ways. It acted as a confidence booster to a society in transition from a colony to a new system within China. As stated earlier, many of HKUST's Chinese academics would probably not have accepted an offer to work at HKUST a decade earlier when it was not clear that the colonial status of Hong Kong would end. Other timely factors were the expansion of Hong Kong's degree enrollment from 8 percent to 16 percent of the relevant age group between 1989 and 1995 and the increasing availability of research funds from the newly established Hong Kong Research Grants Council.

Governance Structure

HKUST established itself as a new international university without assaulting the governing traditions of the United Kingdom in Hong Kong. The governance structure now consists of a court, council, and senate.[15] The court, established in May 1994, meets once per academic year for several hours, is an advisory body on general policy, and considers presidential and council reports. However, it plays no actual role in the governance of the university.[16]

The council is the supreme governing and executive body of the university. It is responsible for investments, contracts, property, appointments of presidents and vice presidents, budget, finances, and statutes; and it confers honorary degrees and academic awards. It consists of up to three public officers appointed by the chief executive of Hong Kong SAR, China; up to 18 external members who are not public officers or employees of the university; and 12 internal members of the university including the president, vice presidents, deans of schools, and academic members nominated by the senate. It is presided over by a lay chair (that is, a non-HKUST employee). The council may meet several times per year. However, an executive committee, known as the standing committee of the council, meets regularly. This body promotes the university's interests in local, regional, and international spheres, and some of its members volunteer to raise funds.

The senate sets academic policies. Members are employees and students, including the president; vice presidents; deans of schools; heads of academic departments, units, and centers; academic staff members elected by their peers; and student representatives. It has a maximum of 54 members, of whom 32 hold academic offices or department positions, while 19 are elected or co-opted from the academic staff and three are student representatives. Its work covers academic planning and development; management of facilities for residence, teaching, learning, and research (libraries, laboratories, and so forth); and provision of student welfare. Finally, boards of the four schools (science, engineering, business and management, and humanities and social science) and the newly named HKUST Fok Ying Tung Graduate School are responsible to the senate for teaching and other work of the schools.

The top governance layers of the government-funded universities of Hong Kong SAR, China, generally manage with some uniformity. They provide a certain amount of integrity with the elite leadership strata of Hong Kong SAR, China, as reflected in the membership of the court and council. This uniformity does not mean that government university relations are always smooth. For example, despite the University Grants Committee being a buffer between government and universities, the HKUST planning stage was not without controversy. The chair of the planning committee's view was that the University and Polytechnic Grants Committee (now the University Grants Committee) stifled its development by allocating places "equitably" rather than according to "needs and values" (Chung 2001, 155). However, in general the government has not interfered directly with the universities in Hong Kong SAR, China. This situation is reflected in Jamil Salmi (2009, 59) quoting Ruth Simmons: "Great universities are not only useful in their own time, but in preparing for future times. What allows a great university to do that is as little interference from the state as possible." However, the amount of interference by government can be interpreted in various ways. Although government interference may not be direct, it does have ways to steer the path of universities—making its interference more subtle. Chung Sze-yuen interpreted what he thought were limits placed on HKUST's postgraduate expansion, and a more recent University Grants Committee report supported the secretary of education's preference that HKUST and the Chinese University of Hong Kong consider a merger. In fact, the University Grants Committee's role in university development in general and in HKUST's development in particular cannot be overlooked. For example, the committee sees itself as key for proactively helping universities make Hong Kong SAR, China, Asia's world city and the education hub of the region, particularly with mainland China. However, the University Grants Committee has not been proactive in helping the universities fend off efforts by government to interfere in their development. Clearly, some debate exists about the committee's role. Its supposed proactive role extends into "strategic planning and policy development to advise and steer the higher education sector," which is to be done with incentives and other mechanisms that "assist institutions to perform at an internationally competitive level in their respective roles" (UGC 2010b). These mechanisms include the Teaching and Learning Quality Process Reviews, Research Assessment Exercise, and Management Reviews, which are mandated for HKUST and other institutions. HKUST submitted a Self-Evaluation Document in July 2002 and successfully completed the Teaching and Learning Quality Process Reviews in 2003. These were its second set of such reviews. It also successfully completed management reviews in 1998 and 2002. The Research Assessment Exercise, a mechanism borrowed from the United Kingdom, was still used in Hong Kong SAR, China, in 2006. Yet, the perceived value of these and related University Grants Committee exercises, by the administration of HKUST and other universities, has not been evident.

Research Funding and Donations

HKUST remains a young university, and its governance structure continues to evolve. In 2009, HKUST's second president, Paul Ching-Wu Chu, completed his term, and Tony Chan began his presidency. President Chu, a world-renowned scientist, took office during difficult times—when Hong Kong SAR, China, still suffered the effects of both the Asian economic crisis and the SARS (severe acute respiratory syndrome) crisis. He still managed to establish an Institute for Advanced Study, modeled after the one at Princeton University. The institute provides a center for noted scientists from around the world to visit, think, and conduct workshops.

The Institute for Advanced Study of HKUST champions collaborative projects across disciplines and institutions. It forges relationships with academic, business, community, and government leaders for helping to transform Hong Kong SAR, China, and the greater Chinese region into a global source of creative and intellectual power. Its visiting members included Aaron Ciechanover, Nobel Prize winner in chemistry in 2004. Eric Maskin, Nobel laureate in economics in 2007, visited on March 17, 2010. The Institute for Advanced Study also has a highly distinguished international advisory board, comprising 12 Nobel laureates. It is also recruiting 10 "star scholars" as permanent institute faculty members and will honor each with a named professorship (each with an endowment of HK$30 million [US$3.87 million]), which provides salary enhancement and additional research funding. Another 60 named fellowships (each with an endowment of HK$10 million [US$1.29 million]) are available for young and promising scholars who join the institute as postdoctoral fellows to work closely with the permanent institute faculty.

The research and development (R&D) budget for Hong Kong SAR, China, is only 0.7 percent of gross domestic product, placing it 50th in global rankings for this indicator. Thus, the amount of research funds available to HKUST might be considered as quite substantial, until compared with the counterpart universities from which the first generation of its leading scientists were recruited. Though modest by comparison, research funding available to HKUST has steadily increased except around the time of the Asian economic crisis. Donations for research by such groups as Hong Kong Telecom of about HK$10 million (US$1.3 million) and the donation by the Hong Kong Jockey Club of HK$130 million (US$17 million) for biotechnology were also helpful to the research profile of HKUST.

As of June 2008, the HK$350.9 million (US$4.5 million) research fund included Hong Kong SAR, China, private funds of HK$98.8 million (US$12.66 million; 28.2 percent); non-Hong Kong SAR, China, sources of HK$6.5 million (US$832, 860; 1.9 percent); Research Grants Council funds of HK$125.3 million (US$16.05; 35.7 percent); University Grants Committee funds of HK$84.7 million (US$10.85 million; 24.1 percent); and other Hong Kong SAR, China, government funds (mostly from the Innovation and Technology Commission) of HK$35.5 million (US$4.55 million; 10.1 percent).[17] The total includes R&D projects administered by R&D corporations (HKUST R and D Corporation Ltd 2010). The high-impact areas of research are nanoscience and nanotechnology, electronics, wireless and information technology, environment and sustainable development, and management education and research. Aside from their scientific significance, these areas are viewed as adding value to the social and economic development of the region, including Hong Kong SAR, China, and the surrounding Pearl River Delta.

Donations have come to play an increasingly important role in the finance and development of higher education in Hong Kong SAR, China. Starting off as the only university in Hong Kong without an alumni sector, HKUST was keen to find ways to offset this condition and took advantage of the timely rise of Chinese philanthropy. The Hong Kong government facilitated the donation culture by providing matching grants to donations made to universities. Selected donations included Sino Group HK$20 million (US$2.56 million), Kerry Group HK$20 million (US$2.56 million), Shun Hing Group HK$10 million (US$1.28 million), Shui On Group HK$25 million (US$3.20 million), and Hang Lung Group HK$20 million (US$2.56 million).[18] By agreement, the donation amounts from the following donors were not disclosed: Hang Seng Bank, Hysan Trust Fund, and Li Wing Tat Family. IBM and JEOL (Japan Electron Optics Laboratory) also donated equipment. The Croucher Foundation made continuous donations to various projects of the university. All these donations were made during HKUST's early development stage. During its 10th anniversary, HKUST noted that it had received contributions from 18 foundations and 19 corporations, as well as seven individual and family donors. There has been a continuous stream of donations too extensive to list here.

Collaborations and Partnerships

HKUST's collaborations and partnerships have contributed to its success (Ji 2009). The university has taken specific measures to address one of its major goals, stated earlier in the chapter, to collaborate closely with business and industry in promoting technological innovation and economic development. When declared, this goal set HKUST apart from the other two leading research universities of the time. Its major innovation in this respect was to establish a wholly owned company known as the Research and Development Corporation (RDC), a unit that serves as the business arm of the university to commercialize research. RDC is the signatory for contracts and contract administration carried out by all university departments.

To further develop its collaborations and partnerships with the private and public sectors in Hong Kong SAR, China, and the region, RDC has established a number of subsidiaries and joint ventures and has extended its reach into the Pearl

River Delta and beyond. It has increased its presence on mainland China, where it offers services that meet specific market requirements. For example, RDC develops collaborations with public and private sectors within the adjoining Pearl River Delta in Guangdong Province and elsewhere in China, including Beijing. The corporation has a partnership with Peking University and the Shenzhen municipal government in a tripartite cooperative institution that engages in production, study, and research. The institution helps to commercialize high-technology research products. HKUST also has a partnership in Beijing's financial district under a tripartite agreement to establish an International Financial Education and Training Center in Beijing with Beijing Street Holding Company, Ltd., and Beijing International Financial Center (Liu and Zweig 2010).

RDC works closely with the university's technology transfer office to market intellectual property that has been created by the university. In this way, it acts as a technology transfer point between HKUST and both public and private sectors. It handles licensing for commercial collaboration in biotechnology, computer engineering, information technology, and 10 other areas.

As part of RDC, the university also established an Entrepreneurship Center. Opened in 2000, the center seeks to encourage participation of university academic staff members and students in the commercialization of new technology. The Entrepreneurship Center provides them with workspace, business consultation services, and incubation facilities. It also helps introduce venture capitalists to academic staff members and students, resulting in more than 20 spin-off and seven start-up companies, one of which is listed on the Hong Kong Stock Exchange.

In July 2010, HKUST submitted a Knowledge Transfer Report to the University Grants Committee (HKUST 2010a), in which it proposed a five-year strategy to establish a knowledge transfer platform to strengthen entrepreneurship, generate funding for innovation, and create new business opportunities.

Conclusion

Universities are nested within regional civilizations, each of which provides unique conditions that can be drawn upon to establish outstanding research universities. HKUST has drawn upon both Chinese and Western civilizations for talent and innovation and has capitalized on advantageous conditions such as institutional autonomy and the provision of capital resources. Yet its success was ensured by a strategically proactive recruitment that yielded an academic faculty with global recognition, shared purpose, and relentless drive, which taken together supported HKUST's rapidly unprecedented rise within one decade into the ranks of the so-called world-class research universities.

Establishment and Planning

A planning committee for a new research university needs to know how to take advantage of the context within which the institution will be established, including an economy on the rise, industrial restructuring, a shifting emphasis in higher education toward more research, an existing local system of distinguished research universities, and the intensification of the global discourse of knowledge economics. A planning committee also must be skillful enough to establish a new international university without assaulting the existing governing traditions, in this case the British academic model of Hong Kong.

In short, the HKUST case emphasizes the centrality of a skillfully executed establishment phase. The caliber of the individuals who design and carry forth the planning during the preparatory phase has a profound influence on the initial trajectory of a research university and can make or break its takeoff period. Among the many key decisions made by a preparatory committee is the selection of a university leadership that can drive the recruitment of the top layer of academic talent. Clearly, there is no more crucial activity for the establishment of an internationally recognized research university than initial faculty recruitment.

Recruitment

Undoubtedly, access to top talent from around the world is a process that cannot be fully controlled. However, access on a personal level to defined networks of noted scientists and the ability to persuade academic leaders to trade a secure position at a top university for the opportunity to join a new enterprise in a country of their ethnic heritage are indispensible traits for a founding university president. In the case of HKUST, that recruitment process involved geographically expansive interviewing of prospective faculty, in one case conducting interviews in nine cities within seven days. Moreover, the HKUST case demonstrates that competitive salaries, though helpful, may be of only limited benefit to recruitment efforts. This issue holds true especially for recruitment of academics who can drive a university beyond its opening day and remain committed over time not only to maintain a high caliber of research, but also to build a purposeful engagement with the society and country where the university is situated. For HKUST, salary was not the main factor in persuading already-established top talent to move. Many recruits were already highly paid in U.S. universities, and relocation to HKUST meant a significant decrease in their living space, often affecting their family's routines and children's educations. Given the risks, distinguished scientists at top U.S. universities would have been unlikely to relocate to a new but unknown university if ethnic and emotional attachments to China had not been as much a factor as competitive salaries.

Sustainability

For any newly established university rapidly achieving success and status within the larger international network of research universities, the long-term aim is to sustain the gains of the initial developmental stage. As HKUST's vice president for research remarked, "eighteen years is not a long time" (Chin 2009). Therefore, the focus must remain on the areas of strength in terms of faculties and their programs. The areas identified by the founders continue to remain central to the institution. However, certain aspects of globalization have made universities, including HKUST, modify the type of emphasis on courses and specialized areas of research. For example, disciplines of study have maintained their integrity; but as discussed earlier, a strategic shift toward multidisciplinarity had to occur (Chin 2009). The need for depth remains, but the interactivity across fields on campus has increased. It is more widely recognized that the problems facing the region require solutions not focused on disciplinary boundaries. Whether it is gene-sequencing and community health policy, civil engineering and climate change, or life sciences and global communication, students increasingly need to look ahead and be prepared to solve problems across a spectrum of areas.

Models

Research universities are also sensitive to models. HKUST has remained cognizant of the Massachusetts Institute of Technology and Stanford University models. HKUST has already had to make modifications as the limitations of the original models arose. Although it experienced good timing and some luck, its focus remains the same: emphasize research, and hire the best scientists. Nevertheless, a shift has occurred. While the university can recruit top scientists from the outside initially, continuity cannot be sustained unless a certain indigenization takes hold in the next phase. The next generation of young scholars was more easily able to make Hong Kong SAR, China, a centerpiece of their academic lives. In short, the university went forward with the preparation of a generation of local scientists who will serve and become leaders for the surrounding region of south China as it develops in the decades to come.

Context: Institutions and Systems

Several sections of this chapter highlight how a new research university nests itself within a larger system of existing research universities. It can draw strength from other research universities as well as become a catalyst for those universities' reforms. Although this development requires a new university to identify with other research universities as part of a system, it also benefits the new institution to stand apart with enough vision and vitality to clearly project the institution's uniqueness. This balance can become upset from intrasystem recruitment during the establishment phase. Therefore, it is important for university leaders to reach an informal consensus on such matters. University heads in Hong Kong SAR, China, have channels for communication and meet periodically, not by government proclamation but as a group of university presidents with common interests. Registrars and other university officers at different levels also have informal networks of communication. For example, although each university is currently developing its new first-year general education curriculum and each is free to design and develop in its own way, informal opportunities exist to periodically share experiences and outcomes at forums or other academic events.

HKUST and other research universities in the Hong Kong SAR, China, system share basic characteristics at the institutional level that are common to research universities everywhere. However, these research universities share the challenge to justify their existence within a bustling Asian business center whose lifeline is global competition in business, trade, and commerce and whose institutional and academic conventions were largely born from colonial transplants. It was within that system that HKUST had to distinguish itself from the other colonial institutions of the time. It did so by establishing a highly entrepreneurial research-culture university without assaulting local governing traditions. It also anticipated the postcolonial context from the beginning.

Thus, this case provides knowledge about lessons for the way a new research university nests itself within a larger system of research universities. In each phase, from planning to establishment to daily operations, the new institution must enhance rather than tip the balance in the larger system. For HKUST to succeed, there needed to be an existing system of respected and well-established institutions that viewed the massive investment of resources in a new institution not as a loss for themselves but as a win-win situation for the system as a whole. This cooperation will not diminish the competitive discourse among the institutions in the system. If anything, it sharpens it. The new research university draws strength, stands apart, and becomes a catalyst for change. Such system change would have been inevitable, but weighty traditions in long-established universities can resist change without the needed catalyst.

Yet it is useful to point out certain systemwide conditions for the successful establishment and development of a new research university that were then present in Hong Kong and for which a new institution cannot be a catalyst. Academic ethics and a corruption-free environment were in place before HKUST joined the larger system and have been sustained since then.

In a small system of less than 10 universities, it is easier to form and present a coherent identity across borders. Sharing core commitments such as intellectual freedom, knowledge exchange, ethnic equality, and other factors, which all help wed institutions to a larger system, facilitates this collaboration. The University Grants Committee also plays a role here in articulating the differences in institutional roles within the larger system and reinforces these differences in the way it finances institutions.

Financing Research

If Hong Kong SAR, China, had not moved to innovations in competitive financing, there would be less vitality in the system and less of a platform for a new university to have a compelling presence within a larger system. Within that framework, there is also a built-in collaborative element. Competitive research grants are administered by the Research Grants Council of Hong Kong. These research grants, though not on a scale compatible with major universities in the United States, have generally led to effective outcomes in terms of research productivity. For example, in 2002, a decade into HKUST's development, a portion (less than 15 percent) of these grants was directly allocated to HKUST and other universities to support small-scale research projects. HKUST administered these grants through internal competition. However, the major portion (more than 80 percent) was allocated for competitive bids from individuals or groups of academic staff members from all universities. The remaining portion (about 5 percent) placed an emphasis on collaboration across institutions and disciplines—"allocated in response to bids from the institutions for major research facilities/equipment or library collections to support collaborative research involving two or more institutions, or group research activities that operate across disciplines and/or normal institutional boundaries" (UGC 2002b). HKUST has established collaborative projects at other universities within Hong Kong SAR, China. These projects cover a number of areas, including Chinese Medicine Research and Further Development (with the Chinese University of Hong Kong), the Institute of Molecular Technology for Drug Discovery and Synthesis (with the University of Hong Kong), the Centre for Marine Environmental Research and Innovation Technology (with the City University of Hong Kong), Developmental Genomics and Skeletal Research (with the University of Hong Kong), and Control of Pandemic and Inter-Pandemic Influenza (with the University of Hong Kong). Nevertheless, the depth of collaboration may be shallow in certain areas, because this scheme was a top-down initiative by the University Grants Committee.

The Research Grants Council of Hong Kong's competitive bidding occurs on the basis of evaluations by specialized academic referees in Hong Kong SAR, China, and overseas. Overseas assessment, though expensive on a large scale, is crucial because of a limited number of assessors in particular fields within Hong Kong SAR, China. Another factor distinguishing HKUST from other universities is that during the early phase of development, many of its scientists already had experience with major research grants from their previous academic appointments at U.S. universities.

In sum, the crucial factors learned from this case study illustrate that purpose must include a shared vision. HKUST's founding president summed up these crucial factors: (a) vision—shared vision, clear mission, zeal; (b) goals—regional preference, national positioning, global impact in selected specialties; (c) focus—selection of fields and specialties, focusing of resources; (d) governance—organization and system; (e) adaptation—internationalization without an assault on the dual traditions; (f) heart—brains, muscles, spirit, mind, strength; and (g) soul—faculty as the soul of the university, shared purpose, and relentless drive. In this formula, the goal is to become the preferred regional university, with national positioning and global impact in selected academic research specialties. The focus must be on the selection of fields and specialties for an efficient focusing of resources. Governance needs to support an organization and system that is innovative and unique, promotes a sense of ownership among academic staff, protects the academic research atmosphere, and is international without assaulting local or national traditions. Finally, the heart of a research university is always a faculty that is not only talented, but also has a shared purpose, proactive spirit, and relentless drive.

HKUST facilitated the creation of a robust scholarly community adjoining a globally emergent and reformist China. In this sense, HKUST identified a niche within the Hong Kong system—by establishing a new international university and projecting its vision far beyond that system and into mainland China—especially signified by the new Southern University of Science and Technology under planning in the adjacent Shenzhen Special Economic Zone.

HKUST identified a niche not only in the field of science and technology, but also in delivery of a research-focused university culture, and it encapsulated that niche into an institutional vision that stressed its entrepreneurial uniqueness. The central factor underlying its success was the substantial recruitment from two generations of overseas-based Chinese scholars. By providing them and other local and international faculty members with a unique historical opportunity and a scholarly work environment that was adequately resourced, HKUST sustained its creation of a robust scholarly community.

Hong Kong's two-pronged development strategy was resilient enough to provide HKUST with the autonomy to sustain its uniqueness even during economic recession. When a consolidation of HKUST with one of the other top two universities was considered, the initiative was unanimously opposed by HKUST's faculty and staff members, students, and alumni and was eventually buried. HKUST was able to successfully distinguish itself from other local institutions in a system largely financed by government that guarantees a high degree of autonomy for innovation.

Notes

1 In 1900, US$50 million was roughly equivalent to US$3 billion in 2000.
2 HKUST's first president, Woo Chia-wei, was influenced by his time as a postdoctoral fellow in physics at the University of California, San Diego, and 11 years later as its provost, when its Revelle College required science and technology students to take 40 percent of their coursework in the humanities and social sciences.
3 The government's later support for establishment of a cyberport, conceived in 1999 and modeled on Silicon Valley, failed miserably as the technology stock bubble began to deflate. The cyberport became viewed more as a high-end real estate development rather than a setting where technology companies would fuel the leap of Hong Kong SAR, China, into the 21st century.
4 Because of the Tiananmen Square event, some Chinese mainland academics studying overseas at the time were granted automatic residency in the United States, and a few of them later sought employment in the Hong Kong academe. Nevertheless, most of the first tier of senior academic leaders recruited by HKUST from the United States had originally studied in Taiwan, China.
5 These universities include Chinese University of Hong Kong, City University of Hong Kong, Hong Kong Baptist University, Hong Kong Polytechnic University, Hong Kong University of Science and Technology, Lingnan University, and the University of Hong Kong. The only exception is the recent decision to bestow university status to Shue Yan College, the first private university in Hong Kong. The Open University

214 Institutions

of Hong Kong is not included because it was initially financed by the government before moving toward a self-financing model.

6. The Chinese University of Hong Kong was also, to some extent, American in character because of its U.S. missionary heritage, four-year curriculum, and high proportion of academic staff with degrees from universities in the United States. However, it was established when the colonial government was in a dominant position, whereas HKUST was established in the last years of the colonial government when its legitimacy was more open to question.

7. The data in a, b, c, and d are from the Academic Ranking of World Universities in Shanghai. The category rank for social science (e) results from the methodology of these Shanghai rankings in which the data distribution for the various indicators used is examined for any significant distorting effect and standard statistical techniques are used to adjust the indicator. See http://www.arwu.org/ and also http://www.arwu.org/FieldSOC2010.jsp.

8. President Paul Chin-Wu Chu led HKUST from the beginning of 2001 to August 2009.

9. Faculty and student numbers were to rise proportionately, but the third phase of the expansion plan did not take place, leaving faculty numbers below their planned expansion number.

10. See Joint Declaration of the Government of the United Kingdom of Great Britain and Northern Ireland and the Government of the People's Republic of China on the Question of Hong Kong, December 1984, Ministry of Foreign Affairs, China. http://www.fmprc.gov.cn/eng/ljzg/3566/t25956.htm.

11. The Hong Kong Jockey Club is the largest single taxpayer in Hong Kong SAR, China—HK$12, 976 million (US$1, 666 million) in 2008–09 or about 6.8 percent of all taxes collected by the government's Inland Revenue Department. (By 1997, "Royal" had been dropped from the club's name.) A unique feature of the club is its nonprofit business model whereby its surplus goes to charity. Over the past decade, the club has donated an average of HK$1 billion (US$0.13 billion) (rate effective January 1, 2008) every year to hundreds of charities and community projects, such as HKUST. The club ranks alongside organizations such as the Rockefeller Foundation as one of the largest charity donors in the world. It is also one of the largest employers in Hong Kong SAR, China, with about 5,300 full-time and 21,000 part-time staff members.

12. The only exception is for those students who major in the study of Chinese language and literature. The language of campus life moved from bilingual (English and Cantonese) to trilingual as the number of students from the Chinese mainland increased, along with the international rise in popularity of Mandarin.

13. It is useful to note that the total figure in the original staff planning scheme, without the faculty of humanities and social sciences, was 525, while the figure for all academic staff was only 483 as of 2009 (see table 10.2).

14. Since then, academic salaries have been reduced more than once because of market forces and the economic recessions.

15. Information on the governance structure of HKUST is drawn from the detailed regulations found in the university calendar and replicated on its website. http://www.ust.hk/.

16. It consists of one immediate and two honorary chairs, eight ex officio members, and up to 44 appointed members, plus a maximum of 100 honorary members. Currently appointed members include 40 business and community leaders appointed by the council or by the chancellor (chief executive of the government of Hong Kong SAR, China), in addition to four representatives of the university senate appointed by the council. Members hold office for three years from the date of their appointment and are eligible for reappointment.

17. These amounts were converted using the rate effective June 1, 2008.

18. These amounts were converted using the rate effective June 1, 2008.

References

Altbach, Philip G. 2003. "The Costs and Benefits of World-Class Universities." *International Higher Education* 33 (6): 5–8.
Altbach, Philip G., and Jorge Balan. 2007. *World Class Worldwide: Transforming Research Universities in Asia and Latin America*. Baltimore: Johns Hopkins University Press.
Chin, Roland. 2009. Personal interview, Hong Kong University of Science and Technology, Hong Kong SAR, China, October 28.
Chung, Sze-yuen. 2001. *Hong Kong's Journey to Reunification*. Hong Kong SAR, China: Chinese University of Hong Kong Press.
Course, Sally. 2001. *HKUST Soars: The First Decade*. Hong Kong SAR, China: Office of University Development and Public Affairs and the Publishing Technology Center, Hong Kong University of Science and Technology.
Ding, Xueliang. 2004. *On University Reform and Development*. Beijing: Peking University Press.
Flahavin, Paulette. 1991. *Building a University: The Story of the Hong Kong University of Science and Technology*. Hong Kong: Office of Public Affairs, Hong Kong University of Science and Technology.
HKUST (Hong Kong University of Science and Technology). 2010a. "Knowledge Transfer Annual Report 2009–10." Report to the University Grants Committee, HKUST, Hong Kong SAR, China. http://www.ugc.edu.hk/eng/doc/ugc/activity/kt/HKUST.pdf. Accessed November 10, 2010.
———. 2010b. "Mission and Vision." HKUST, Hong Kong SAR, China. http://www.ust.hk/eng/about/mission_vision.htm. Accessed August 23, 2010.
———. 2010c. "Our Mission." Postgraduate Programs, HKUST, Hong Kong SAR, China. http://publish.ust.hk/pgstudies/.
———. 2010d. "Rankings and Awards." HKUST, Hong Kong SAR, China. http://www.ust.hk/eng/about/ranking.htm. Accessed August 23, 2010.
———. 2010e. "Strategy." HKUST, Hong Kong SAR, China. http://www.ust.hk/strategy/e_2.html.
HKUST R and D Corporation Ltd. 2010. "Policy and Procedures." Hong Kong University of Science and Technology, Hong Kong SAR, China. http://rdc.ust.hk/eng/policy.html. Accessed June 10, 2011.
Ji, Shuoming. 2009. "Taking Aim at Hong Kong's Science and Technology: Fuse China with International Power." *International Chinese Weekly* (May 24): 24–31.
Kung, Shain-Dow. 2002. *My Ten Years at the Hong Kong University of Science and Technology*. Hong Kong SAR, China: Hong Kong Joint Publishing Company.
Liu, Amy, and David Zweig. 2010. "Training a New Generation of Mainland Students: The Role of Hong Kong." Paper prepared for submission to *Asian Survey*. http://www.cctr.ust.hk/about/pdf/David_CV_2010.pdf.
Postiglione, Gerard A. 2008. "Transformations in Transnational Higher Education." *Journal of Higher Education* 29 (October): 21–31.
———. 2009. "Community Colleges in China's Two Systems." In *Community College Models: Globalization and Higher Education Reform*, ed. Rosalind Latiner Raby and Edward J. Valeau, 157–71. Amsterdam: Springer.
Salmi, Jamil. 2009. *The Challenge of Establishing World-Class Universities*. Washington, DC: World Bank.
So, Alvin, and Ming K. Chan. 2002. *Crisis and Transformation in China's Hong Kong*. New York: M. E. Sharpe.

Times Higher Education Supplement. 2008. http://www.topuniversities.com/world universityrankings/results/2008/overall_rankings/fullrankings/.
UGC (University Grants Committee). 1996. *Higher Education in Hong Kong: A Report by the University Grants Committee.* Hong Kong: UGC. http://www.ugc.hk/eng/ugc/publication/report/hervw/ugcreport.htm.
———. 1999. *Higher Education in Hong Kong: A Report by the University Grants Committee: Supplement.* Hong Kong: UGC. http://www.ugc.hk/eng/ugc/publication/report/hervw_s/content.htm.
———. 2000. *Facts and Figures.* Hong Kong SAR, China: UGC.
———. 2002a. *Higher Education in Hong Kong: Report of the University Grants Committee,* Report for UGC prepared by Stewart R. Sutherland. Hong Kong SAR, China: UGC. http://www.ugc.edu.hk/eng/ugc/publication/report/her/ her.htm.
———. 2002b. "Overview." UGC, Hong Kong SAR, China. http://www.ugc.edu.hk/english/documents/figures/eng/overview2.html. Accessed November 10, 2010.
———. 2004a. "Hong Kong Higher Education: To Make a Difference, To Move with the Times." UGC, Hong Kong SAR, China. http://www.ugc.edu.hk/eng/doc/ugc/publication/report/policy_document_e.pdf.
———. 2004b. "Integration Matters." UGC, Hong Kong SAR, China. http://www.ugc.edu.hk/eng/doc/ugc/publication/report/report_integration_matters_e.pdf.
———. 2008. "Role Statements of UGC-funded Institutions, Annex IV." UGC, Hong Kong SAR, China. http://www.ugc.edu.hk/english/documents/figures/pdf/A4_Eng.pdf. Accessed August 23, 2010.
———. 2010a. "Statistics." UGC, Hong Kong SAR, China. http://cdcf.ugc.edu.hk/cdcf/statIndex.do. Accessed June 10, 2011.
———. 2010b. "UGC Policy." UGC, Hong Kong SAR, China. http://www.ugc.edu.hk/eng/ugc/policy/policy.htm.
Walker, Anthony. 1994. *Building the Future: The Controversial Construction of the Campus of the Hong Kong University of Science and Technology.* Hong Kong: Longman.
Wong, Yuk Shan. 2010. Personal interview, University of Hong Kong, Hong Kong SAR, China, December 21.
Woo, Chia-wei. 2006. *Jointly Creating the Hong Kong University of Science and Technology.* Hong Kong SAR, China: Commercial Press.
Zakaria, Fareed. 2009. *The Post-American World: And the Rise of the Rest.* London: Penguin.

11 Research universities for national rejuvenation and global influence
China's search for a balanced model

Balancing quantity and quality in teaching and research

Thirty-five years after the launch of its economic reform and opening to the outside world, China finds itself inching closer to become the world's largest economy (Jacques 2009; Beardson 2013; Telegraph 2014). To sustain the pace of economic growth, higher education is increasingly expected to play a more powerful role in China's rise (Postiglione 2011a). It already has the largest system of higher education and more scientific publications than any other country except the USA (University World News 2007; Guardian 2011; Royal Society 2011). Moreover, it bodes well for the university systems that secondary school students in the largest city outperformed their counterparts in the 60 countries involved in the Program for International Student Assessment of mathematics and science achievement (OECD 2013). Yet, the search continues for a Chinese research university model that can balance quality and quantity in research and teaching (Liu 2010; Kirby 2014). This paper argues that finding one depends upon deepening internationalization, defining national sovereignty, and expanding university autonomy. The paper does this by examining selected aspects in the development of the research university systems of the Chinese mainland and China's Hong Kong, especially with respect to the governance of research and teaching.

A unique China model?

Beyond the race to excel on international indicators of success is the longstanding aim of national rejuvenation and restoration of China's status in the world. China has long sought to learn how to effectively borrow and adapt, not copy, from advanced systems without muting the influence of its ancient culture. Interest never ceases about how indigenous ideas and principles can guide university education. It is common to credit scholars of the classical era, such as Confucius and Mencius, Sunzi and Mozi, and later Wang Yangming and Zhu Xi. In the modern era, Hu Shi is well known, but others such as Cai Yuanpei, Liang Shuming, Ye Yangchu, Mei Yiqi, Jiang Bailing, Yan Fu, Tao Xingzhi, and Pan Guangdan remain influential (Yang 2003; Hayhoe 1996). Educational leaders like Cai Yuanpei, an early president of Peking University, understood the

German, French, and English traditions of higher education and considered how these could be brought together with the spirit of Confucianism and other historical traditions. In short, there is a lingering concern that university education has not been sufficiently shaped by indigenous ideas (Yang 2013).

For this reason, China's emergent role on the world stage comes with a concern about what principles and ideas should drive a delicate balance between quality and quantity in research universities. This is echoed in a question posed by a Hong Kong Chinese scholar: "Will Asia be just producing more of the same of the Western-originated contemporary higher education model, or will it be able to unleash a more critical understanding and practice of higher education, a cultural and epistemological reflection of the role of universities as venues of higher learning?" (Cheung 2012: 186).

Many agree that China forged a unique model of economic development (Ramo 2004; Huang 2011; Williamson 2012). But unlike economic institutions that make financial gain an end itself, the success of research universities is measured by the creation and transmission of knowledge, not the accumulation of wealth. Nevertheless, Marginson (2011) sees a China model with a strong nation-state, an inclination toward universal higher education, national examination that drives competition and family commitment, and government determination to invest in research. Altbach (2011) believes that China has not, and will not in the near future, develop a university model to challenge the international status quo model.

An indigenous model would be rooted in the Chinese academy, the UK *shu yuan,* which predates the four historically sacrosanct Western institutions of higher learning, namely Bologna, Oxford, Cambridge, and the Sorbonne (Hayhoe 1996). Yet, investiture of such a hallowed tradition in the contemporary university can be enormously complicated for China. While it is questionable how it would boost global competitiveness, it may enliven the intellectual climate, especially as it aligns, however ambiguously, with the growing experimentation with liberal studies curriculum borrowed and adapted from Harvard and other overseas universities. It may be wishful thinking but as Harvard's Vogel (2003) observes: "The result of China's opening and reform for higher education has been an intellectual vitality that may be as broad and deep as the Western Renaissance."

At the end of the day, China does not yet possess a unique university model that challenges the so-called Western one. As the international popularity of the university ranking framework developed by the Shanghai Jiaotong University makes clear, China's universities are almost singularly focused on racing toward, rather than away from the Western model as they aspire to match the technological superiority of the West.

Transition to mass higher education and building research universities

The economic reforms and opening to the outside world that began in 1979 led to a recovery in higher education. Intellectuals were rehabilitated and "sent-down youth," formerly at school before the cultural revolution, began to return to urban areas. University entrance examinations were reintroduced, and academic standards were strengthened. By 1985, there were 1,016 institutions of higher education and about 2% of the 18–22 age groups attended university. There was also a shift in the direction of overseas study as capitalist economies in Europe and North America became favored study destinations.

Expansion of all forms of higher education

Between 1985 and 1998, the Ministry of Education was upgraded to an Education Commission, and universities were given some autonomy in matters of curriculum, staffing, and student selection. Enrollments grew little though and after the period of student demonstrations in 1986 and 1989. By the late 1990s, economic globalization put China on a course of unprecedented expansion of university enrollments. By the end of the twentieth century, a knowledge economy discourse signaled a determined shift from elite to mass higher education. While only about 4% of the 18–22 age group was involved in higher education in 1995, the 2005 figure had surpassed 20% (NCEDR 2000–2009).

The Asian economic crisis in the late 1990s led to faster expansion of higher education as a way of delaying entry of secondary school graduates into the labor market, and as an economic stimulant—families willingly opened their bank accounts and spent more money on university fees and expenses. By 2010, about 30% of 18–22 year olds—roughly 30 million students—were enrolled in 2,263 colleges and universities, including 1,079 universities and 1,184 higher vocational and junior colleges (Cheng et al. 2011). The largest city had a gross enrollment ratio exceeding 60% (Shen 2003). Between 2010 and 2020, the gross enrollment rate of higher education was set to exceed 40%, and from 2021 to 2050 to reach at least 50%.

The reform of research universities

One of the boldest efforts to reform research universities was the so-called Peking University Personnel Reform (Rosen 2004, 2005). This reform of the faculty appointment system aroused strong feelings on and off campus and became a controversial social issue. It called for external competition in hiring and a "last ranked, first fired" practice for academic staff. In the mid-1990s, salaries of Hong Kong university staff were said to be nearly 99 times that at Peking University. From 1982 to 2000, salaries grew by 101%. Thus, to maintain academic quality, the income of university teacher salaries in higher education was sharply increased. The average university teacher salary was said to be higher than that of other professions. Yet academic salaries in 2010 remained the lowest of the BRIC countries.

Expectations were raised for establishing a system of world-class universities in 1998 when President Jiang Zemen addressed the audience, me included, at the Great Hall of the People to mark the 100th anniversary of Peking University. Government support, as indicated in the so-called 211 and 985 initiatives, provided major financial backing to top institutions with high levels of academic promise (Zhou 2006: 36–46). Enormous attention was directed at both the international rankings of top universities and the questions of how to establish and maintain a world-class university. Under the so-called "211" and "985" projects, Beijing pumped investment into the elite, with the aim of creating internationally competitive universities. The 211 project provides extra financial support for 112 universities selected to spearhead national economic development, while the 985 project aims to transform 40 top institutions into world-class universities.

Flagship institutions—such as Peking and Tsinghua in Beijing, and Fudan and Jiaotong in Shanghai—jockey for position in world university rankings. In 2010, two mainland Chinese universities were ranked in the top 200 globally in the Shanghai Jiaotong AWRU ranking, and six in the Times Higher Education ranking (AWRU 2013; THE 2013).

Chinese universities climbed the global ranks by boosting their presence in scientific publications. In 2008, they published 204,000 papers in peer-reviewed journals, raising their share from 4.4% in 1999 to 10.2% in 2008 (Royal Society 2011). Only the USA had a higher share. China's proportion of GDP for research and development grew from 0.7%, 1998, to 1.5%, 2005, and has since risen to almost 2.0%, making it the third largest R&D spender worldwide (in purchasing power parity terms) after the USA and Japan. By 2010, it spent nearly 10% of the world total (Hu 2011: 95–120, OECD 2012). However, the high numbers of scientific publications cannot mask the fact that quality remains a problem. This is reflected in the low frequency with which the world's scientists cite China's scientific publications—only 4% of the time compared to 30% for the USA, placing China sixth in the rankings. Research funding has rapidly increased, but most goes to projects proposed by senior members of a department or those who are politically connected.

Research universities began to change as they deepened their international engagement. By the end of the first decade of the twenty-first century, some research universities became unrecognizable from their former selves. Hardware infrastructure began to rival research universities in advanced countries. Yet, the software side remains weak as they struggle to improve the quality of teaching and research, and address problems such as academic corruption, and relevance of university graduates for a rapidly changing workplace.

Balancing institutional autonomy, state sovereignty, and internationalization

At the very least, national rejuvenation is bringing the global academy more understanding of historical legacy, one that goes beyond a preoccupation with the imperial examination system, and the accompanying view that it still shapes a style of learning anathema to drive creativity and innovation (Kissinger 2011; Vogel 2013; Hu 2011). Scholarship about historical struggles, developmental experiences, and institutional renovation may also be seen as a creative resistance of Western domination (Jacques 2009; Schell and DeLury 2013; Shambaugh 2013). However, to avoid this kind of scholarship becoming superficial will require a feisty defense of academic freedom and institutional autonomy. Otherwise, it risks floundering as official lip service to nationalism without a critical intellectual bite.

As the research universities continue to deepen their engagement with overseas counterparts, an array of possibility opens. Already, international cooperation has led to new curriculum models, funding formulas, personnel reforms, performance measures, instructional technologies, institution building strategies, and innovative experiments in learning, all of which have led toward a more open, though still "quality catch-up" learning environment.

The top-tier universities are increasingly coming to resemble their OECD counterparts, but they are more than state universities or state-steered. State governance of the academic system finds itself caught between the goals of internationalization and safeguarding national sovereignty. Government encourages Sino-foreign cooperation along with stern warnings of its dangers.

Meanwhile, the leadership wholeheartedly supports the race for world-class universities. With capital expenditure that is the envy of other university systems in developing (and some developed) countries, national leaders expect to shortcut the process of a few hundred years that other leading international universities underwent. And to some extent, the leadership may be correct. Globalization has compressed time scales. China's Hong Kong University of Science and Technology (HKUST) managed to rocket up the global rankings in a decade (Postiglione 2011b). Yet, as the case of the Chinese mainland's fledgling South China University of Science and Technology has shown, the lack of institutional autonomy from government stifles vision and innovation (Xin 2012).

Amid the transition to mass higher education and the aim to improve quality, the call continued for more international cooperation in higher education. By 2013, there were 1,060 approved Sino-foreign joint ventures in higher education with 450,000 students involved. Since 2003, there have been 1,050,000 from higher education institutions (Lin 2013). Sino-foreign cooperation in higher education comes with stern warning about risks to Chinese sovereignty, as a minister of education remarked: "Tough tasks lie ahead for China to safeguard its educational sovereignty as it involves our fundamental political, cultural, and economic interests and every sovereign nation must protect them from being harmed" (Chen 2002, p. 5).

The 2003 law on educational joint ventures opened the floodgates to hundreds of partnerships between Chinese and foreign universities. Reforms are underway at top Chinese colleges to copy, adapt, and innovate on models of liberal higher education customary abroad. Attention is building about whether foreign-partnership campuses can have a significant impact on China's current higher education system. These collaborations and partnerships constitute one type of laboratory for innovative formats in higher learning. While the jury remains out on long-term sustainability of cross-border campuses, both host and guest universities will learn a great deal from cooperation in the running of partnered colleges and universities (Wildavsky 2012).

The majority of international university programs are taught and run by foreign academics, at a substantial premium, within Chinese universities. They are popular with middle-class parents because they give their children the cachet of a foreign education without the cost of studying abroad. In a few cases, foreign universities have gone one step further and set up full campuses with Chinese universities. Nottingham University has a campus in Ningbo; Shanghai Jiaotong and the University of Michigan run an engineering institute in Shanghai; and Xi'an Jiaotong and Liverpool University have established an independent university in Suzhou. In 2013, New York University, which already has overseas study programs in 10 countries, opened a new campus in Shanghai with East China Normal University. It will conduct integrated classes in humanities and social sciences, with an equal number of Chinese and foreign students. Duke University has also established a campus in Kunshan in partnership with Wuhan University (Redden 2014a).

Others American universities with similar aspirations include Keane University and University of Montana (Redden 2014b).

The rise in Sino-foreign joint ventures has led to more discussion about sovereignty in higher education (Postiglione 2009). An influential scholar of Chinese higher education cautions that permitting foreign entities to hold a majority (more than 51%) of institutional ownership can lead to an "infiltration of Western values and cultures at odds with current Chinese circumstances" (Pan 2009: 90). The Vice-Director of Shanghai Education Commission, Zhang Minxuan, makes it clear that a Sino-foreign venture in running an educational institute has to "make sure China's sovereignty and public interests are not harmed" (Zhang 2009b: 33). To do so, at least half of its board of directors have to be Chinese citizens. Zhang Li of the Ministry of Education points out that China's commitment to provide access to its educational market is larger than any other developing country, and therefore, "we must safeguard China's educational sovereignty, protect national security, and guide such programs in the right direction" (Zhang 2009a: 19).

The sovereignty issue has obvious implications for the governance and institution of a Sino-foreign campus on Chinese soil. A different model is offered by the recently established South China University of Science and Technology (SCUST). Headed by Zhu Qingshi, past president of the China University of Science and Technology, SCUST aimed to be the first university on the Chinese mainland to secure independence from the higher education bureaucracy—although the result thus far has not been as expected (Science 2012). SCUST is not a Sino-foreign campus but it has tried to follow the lead of the Hong Kong University of Science and Technology which became world ranked within a decade of its establishment (Postiglione 2011a, b). SCUST enrolls students not only on the basis of the national college and university examination—a terrifying exercise in rote learning and regurgitation known as the *gaokao*—but also on the basis of their creativity and passion for learning. SCUST faculty members are not given administrative ranks, in the hope that professors will concentrate on teaching and research rather than climbing the greasy pole (Li 2011). These experiments in new educational models are encouraging, but do not seem to have led to larger reforms in Chinese higher education. Meanwhile, Sino-foreign ventures continue to be fringe experiments.

Thus, the debate about the establishment of universities with Chinese characteristics is embedded within an unambiguous paradox, namely the incompatibility of three elements within its university system: internationalization, institutional autonomy, and educational sovereignty. While any two are achievable, handling and attaining all three simultaneously remain a work in progress. To get a fuller picture, a perspective on the reform era and transition to mass higher education is useful.

The main challenge: Make research and teaching drive creativity and innovation

Despite having the world's second largest economy, there is widespread concern that universities produce fewer independent thinkers than their competitors (McFarlan et al. 2014). As the labor cost advantage is lost, maintaining the country's economic ascent depends on boosting the quality of its higher education system. Generating new products and services will require universities to foster creative and innovative thinking, in addition to carrying out cutting edge research. China's higher education system has expanded to widen student access, but the focus is turning to the reform of university governance, enlivening academic culture, and better aligning university teaching to the needs of the workplace.

A major challenge is to raise the quality of higher learning after the expansion that began in the late 1990s, when China shifted from elite to mass higher education. While the top tier of 76 universities are administered by the State Ministry of Education, most higher education institutions are under local government control (MOE 2014). Teaching is still relatively weak, and universities have a poor record of producing employable graduates. Before graduation in May 2013, only about half of the seven million graduates to be had signed job contracts.

Economic globalization has led to concern about the current system's ability to compete. As Richard Levin, president of Yale University and frequent visitor to China, stated what is increasingly driving higher education: "As never before, universities become instruments of national competition as well as instruments of peace" (Levin 2006). Chinese businessmen and scientists alike bemoan a lack of entrepreneurial spirit among graduates. Qian Xuesen, the father of Chinese rocket science, sees universities as failing to encourage creativity, multidisciplinary breadth, and innovative thinking: "…none of our institutions of higher learning is running in the right direction of cultivating excellent talent and is innovative enough" (Zhao and Hao 2010).

Meanwhile, both domestic and foreign firms are ratcheting up demand for more broad-based skills than those provided by narrowly focused degree courses. Critics also included former premiers Zhu Rongji and Wen Jiabao, who acknowledge that the ability of the higher education system to enhance economic competiveness will depend on fostering more creative, independent thinking (SCMP 2011a, b). I heard a similar comment from Jack Ma of Alibaba, when I facilitated a discussion for the Clinton Global Initiative in Hong Kong in 2008. Lee Kai-fu, former head of Google China, said "The Chinese education system isn't as well connected to the marketplace. So if you take a college student and drop him into a start-up, there are so many errors he could make, whereas people in the US, they are more independent thinkers who are able to solve problems on the fly and are more suitable as entrepreneurs" (SCMP 2013).

Several top research universities responded to these criticisms. Peking University's Yuanpei program is an experiment with liberal arts education, modeled on Harvard's. It aims to foster creativity, multidisciplinary thinking, and leadership. Tsinghua University intensified the degree of student engagement in learning by introducing classes in group problem solving as well as improving the quality of communication between students and teachers (Hennock 2010).

Other top-tier institutions are experimenting with models of learning that break away from the lecture, textbook, memorization, and exam cycle that is still so common in many universities. Below the top tier of 985 and 211 universities, most colleges and universities still operate with fewer resources, less qualified academic staff, and less attention from the central government. Policy levers without financial support are less effective for improving the responsiveness of the larger higher education system.

The expansion was so rapid and extensive that policy makers become consumed with handling the burgeoning numbers of students without a sufficient reform of teaching and learning. The promulgated National Outline for Medium and Long-term Education Reform and Development (2010–2020) targets a higher education enrollment rate of 40% by 2020, by which time 20% of the working-age population should have university degrees (MOE 2011). Given the demographic profile, the country must spend the rest of the decade fostering talent in the shrinking proportion of youth who will have to support an increasingly aging population in the future. That should mean shaking up the current system and encouraging greater independence among both professors and students. A national evaluation of undergraduate teaching was undertaken, but it is driven by the Ministry of Education in a typically top-down manner. This contrasts with the best international universities, which have the autonomy to design, implement, and take the major responsibility for their own success or failure (Jiang 2009; Ross and Cen 2000).

Tendencies for standardization sometimes stifle the dynamism that can emerge naturally out of diversity. The basic government-university relationship has loosened somewhat but the practice of autonomy remains in its infancy. There is far less autonomy than is found among counterparts in developed economies. Rigidity in the system sometimes prevents the free flow of information, essential for world-class universities. As Jamil Salmi of the World Bank noted: "[The] rule of law, political stability and the respect of basic freedoms are important dimensions of the political context into which high quality universities operate" (Salmi 2011: 339).

Government is aware that over-administration is an obstacle to achieve greatness in higher education, and it has committed itself to relieve universities of some of their bureaucratic load. But there are many doubts about the extent to which this can be achieved. It is not only a matter of the state granting autonomy to universities: To improve the quality of higher learning, universities have to be ready and willing to take greater responsibility for their own governance. Many university chiefs maintain a close relationship with government, and many remain more interested in retaining their civil servant rank than breaking the pedagogical mold.

China has most of the essential ingredients to build great research universities: the aspiration, plenty of brain power, and sufficient government support. The cultural tradition values education, and academic staff are increasingly qualified enough to improve the quality of learning on campus. But university governance needs an overhaul whether China is to obtain a better balance of quality and quantity in research and teaching. With academic tenure and promotion now dependent on churning out strings of articles, teaching plays second fiddle to often dubious research. The pressure to produce has also fueled a wave of academic corruption: Plagiarism is rife. The quality of much teaching and research will remain an issue for some time.

Yet, there may be good reason to be optimistic about the future array of possibility open to higher education in the Chinese mainland. China's Hong Kong, with a population of 7 million, has more top-ranked universities than any city in Asia. The reasons may yield useful insights for the future of research universities in the Chinese mainland and also for Sino-foreign cooperation in creating improved environments for balancing research, teaching, and learning.

China's second system: inverted academic culture and governance

Thirty-five years ago, Hong Kong was relatively poor with two undergraduate institutions, and a reputation for trade, small manufacturing, and commerce, but not for higher education. The Research Grants Council was only established in 1991 with funds totaling HK $100 million (US$25 million), but twenty years later, it increased to HK$1 billion. Hong Kong had only two universities until the mid-1990s. It now has three universities ranked among Asia's top ten and the world's top 50 (23, 33, and 40) (QS 2012). All eight universities are academically sound and highly respectable, and five of the top eight are in the top hundred worldwide (QS 2012). Among the reasons, Altbach and Postiglone (2012) proposed academic culture and governance as well as their major instructional language (English), internationalization, leadership of administrators, and the qualification of academic profession of research universities in Hong Kong.

Steering and autonomy Hong Kong's government, through the Research Grants Council and the University Grants Committee, provides overall direction to the higher education sector; prioritized funding, combined with performance guidelines, shapes university policy. At the same time, the universities have almost complete internal autonomy and self-management.

Effective governance The University of Hong Kong stems from the British academic tradition, and the Chinese University brought American missionary and Chinese traditions into Hong Kong's colonial framework. The Hong Kong University of Science and Technology added the American research university model and academic governance to the mix, without assaulting the status quo. All three have strong international governance arrangements that emphasize control by the academics, while at the same time strong administrative leadership. The universities do not get bogged down in endless academic bickering, nor are they ruled autocratically.

Integrated scholarship is valued Aside from research productivity, Hong Kong's academic profession places a relatively high priority on teaching in comparison with counterparts in countries with advanced university systems (CAP 2007). Performance reviews combine teaching, research, and knowledge exchange dimensions. Moreover, the Universities Grants Committee requires Teaching and Learning Quality Process Reviews. All reviews are made public and include possible effects about funding to ensure follow-up by institutions.

Two systems of academic governance of teaching and research at research universities

Finally, with respect to university governance and academic culture, the picture painted above of Hong Kong's advantages, although widely accepted, is not reflected in the views of its academics on the basis of empirical data from the international survey of the Changing Academic Profession (2007).

The results confirm that university governance is far more top down in the Chinese mainland and bottom up in Hong Kong. When asked who has primary influence on approving new academic programs, evaluating teaching, setting internal research priorities, evaluating research, and establishing international linkages, the results are consistent with few exceptions. Hong Kong academics generally see primary influence ascending (government, institutional management, academic unit, faculty committee, and faculty member), while for Chinese academics, the direction is inverted. Yet, academics on the Chinese mainland do not appear to be as troubled by their top-down form of university governance to the same extent as their Hong Kong counterparts (Figs. 11.1, 11.2, 11.3, 11.4, 11.5). Mainland academics are surprisingly less prone than Hong Kong academics to view their universities as more top down in management style. They also indicate, more so than their Hong Kong counterparts, that there is better communication between academics and management, and more collegiality in decision making at their universities (Table 11.1). Likewise, they indicate that their university administrators have a more supportive attitude toward their teaching and research activities, and a less cumbersome administrative process (Table 11.2). Even more surprising, mainland Chinese academics view themselves as more influential than their Hong Kong counterparts. Despite a high degree of transparency in operations at Hong Kong's research universities, academics feel less informed about what is going on at their institutions and less prone to view administrators as providing competent leadership.

Research universities for national rejuvenation 227

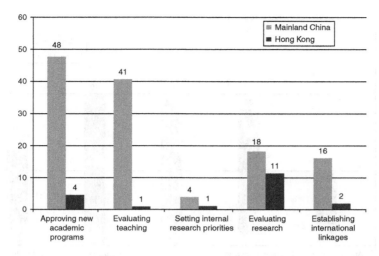

Figure 11.1 Percentage of academics agreeing that government has the primary influence. At your institution, which actor has the primary influence on each of the following decisions? (%)

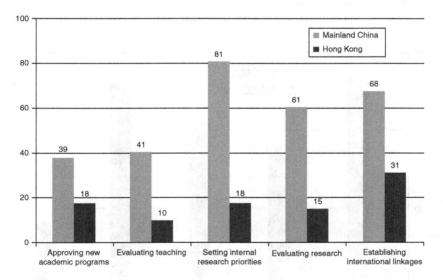

Figure 11.2 Percentage agreeing that the institutional management has the primary influence.
Source: The Changing Academic Profession, 2007.

Yet, Hong Kong academics view their universities as having a stronger performance orientation. This confirms that Hong Kong has a far more efficient and meritocratic system of research universities. Mainland universities would be hard pressed to institute a Hong Kong system of academic performance reviews when

228 Institutions

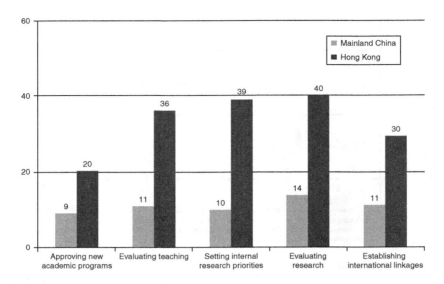

Figure 11.3 Percentage agreeing that the academic unit managers have the primary influence.
Source: The Changing Academic Profession, 2007.

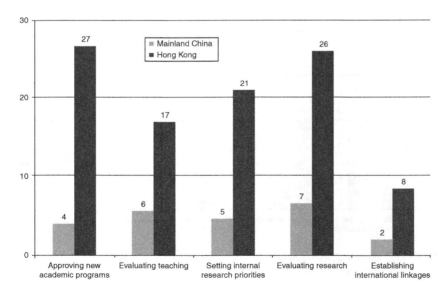

Figure 11.4 Percentage agreeing that the faculty committees have the primary influence.
Source: The Changing Academic Profession, 2007.

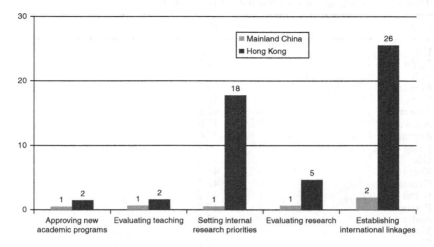

Figure 11.5 Percentage agreeing that the individual faculty member has the primary influence.
Source: The Changing Academic Profession, 2007.

Table 11.1 Views about institutional management and administration: % agreeing or strongly agreeing

	Mainland China	Hong Kong, China
A top-down management style	46	74
A strong performance orientation	60	65
Cumbersome administrative processes	54	62

Source: The Changing Academic Profession, 2007.

Table 11.2 Views about institutional management and administration: % agreeing or strongly agreeing

	Mainland China	Hong Kong, China
Good communication between management and academics	34	25
Collegiality in decision-making processes	36	23
I am kept informed about what is going on at this institution	44	36
Lack of faculty involvement is a real problem	52	40

Source: The Changing Academic Profession, 2007.

Table 11.3 Average age of academic staff in 17 jurisdictions

Country	Average age
US	51.8
Japan	51.7
Italy	49.6
Mexico	48.2
Canada	47.4
Australia	47.1
Norway	47.0
Argentina	47.0
Hong Kong	46.4
UK	46.3
Korea	46.1
Germany	45.3
Brazil	44.3
Portugal	43.4
Finland	43.3
Malaysia	39.5
China	38.8
Total	45.5

Source: The Changing Academic Profession, 2007.

only about 15% of academics in higher education have a doctorate. While universities on the Chinese mainland search for an indigenous model that can balance quantity and quality in teaching and research, it will be difficult at the current stage of development. This is not to say that the bulk of the academic profession on the Chinese mainland would be willing to go full throttle to embrace the Hong Kong model, especially if salaries and conditions matched international standards for research universities in advanced economies. However, the resistance of academic staff to the Peking University Personnel Reform Plan indicates—otherwise—that the Western model for academic personnel was highly unpopular.

Conclusion

For there to be a renaissance in Chinese research universities, the viewpoint of the academic community must reach a critical mass toward a change in governance and academic culture. This does not seem to be the case at present. The slow, though growing, trickle of returnees from overseas has only slightly fostered change. A more significant factor may be found in the demography of China's academic profession. It is younger than many other leading academic professions around the world (Table 11.3). Growing up in a market economy, young academics find their salaries inadequate for their academic lifestyles. They see many others with far less education become more prosperous. In fact, China's academic salaries are lowest among other BRIC countries, and many academics have taken second jobs to raise their income (Altbach et al. 2012). This may be one reason why mainland academics indicate that a lack of faculty involvement at their universities is a real problem.

Unlike the Chinese mainland, Hong Kong has managed thus far to successfully attain three key elements: a high degree of university autonomy, a high degree of internationalization, and the preservation of Chinese sovereignty as set out in the Basic Law of the Hong Kong Administrative Region of the PRC (Postiglione 2013). The Hong Kong case indicates what inhibits the potential of the Chinese mainland's research university system. While the latter's investment in the facilities and world-class hardware in its top research universities has been highly impressive, the soft elements of the academic system, namely institutional governance and academic culture, are less able to drive a better balance between quality and quality in research and teaching.

References

Altbach, P. G. (2011). *Reconsideration of world order in higher education*. Seminar delivered to the Community of Higher Education Research, University of Hong Kong, October 20.

Altbach, P. G., & Postiglone, G. A. (2012). Hong Kong's academic advantage. *Peking University Education Review*, October.

Altbach, P. G., Reisberg, L., Yudkevich, M., Androushchak, G., & Pacheco, I. (Eds.). (2012). *Paying the professoriate: A global comparison of compensation and contracts*. New York: Routledge.

AWRU Academic World Ranking of Universities. (2013). Retrieved on 30 June 2014. http://www.shanghairanking.com/.

Beardson, T. (2013). *Stumbling giant: The threats to China's future*. New Haven: Yale University Press.

Chen, Z. L. (2002). The impact of WTO on china's educational enterprise and related policies. *People's Education, 3*, 4–7.

Cheng, F. P., Liu, I. G. & Wu, H. (2011). 2009 blue book of education: China on the eve of tremendous changes. In *The China education development yearbook* (Vol. 3, pp. 1–36). Boston: Brill Press.

Cheung, B. L. (2012). Higher education in Asia: Challenges from and contributions to globalization. *International Journal of Chinese Education, 1*, 177–195.

Guardian. (2011). *China poised to overhaul US as biggest publisher of scientific papers*. March 28. Retrieved 30 June 2014. http://www.theguardian.com/science/2011/mar/28/china-us-publisher-scientific-papers.

Hayhoe, R. (1996). *China's universities 1895–1995: A century of cultural conflict* (2nd ed.). Hong Kong: Comparative Education Research Centre, University of Hong Kong.

Hennock, M. (2010). With new survey, Chinese colleges ask students what they really think. *Chronicle of Higher Education*. August 9.

Hu, A. G. (2011). *China in 2020: A new type of superpower*. New York: Harper-Collins.

Huang, Y. S. (2011). Rethinking the Beijing Consensus, *Asia Policy*, January.

Jacques, M. (2009). *When China rules the world: The rise of the middle kingdom and the end of the western world*. London: Allen Lane.

Jiang, K. (2009). Chinese evaluation of undergraduate teaching. *Chinese Education and Society, 42*(2), 3–6.

Kirby, W. C. (2014). The Chinese century? The challenges of higher education. *Deadalus*.

Kissinger, H. (2011). *On China*. London: Allen Lane.

Levin, R. (2006). Universities Branch Out, *Newsweek*, Aug. 21–28, 2006. Retrieved 30 June 2014. http://www.law.yale.edu/documents/pdf/Public_Affairs/President LevinArticle.pdf.

Li, R. (2011). Radical university reformer forced to take a step back. *South China Morning Post.* March 13. p. A7.

Lin, J. H. (2013). Sino-Foreign Cooperation and Hong Kong-Mainland Coopersation in Education. Seminar of the Wah Ching Centre of Research on Education in China, March 28.

Liu, D. Y. (2010). *Zhongguo gaoxiao zhican. The Shame of Chinese higher education* 高校之殇. Wuhan: Hubei People's Press.

Marginson, S. (2011). Higher education in East Asia and Singapore: Rise of the Confucian model. Manuscript.

McFarlan, F. W., Kirby, W. C., & Abrami, R. (2014). *Can China lead: Reaching the limits of power and growth.* Cambridge: Harvard Business School Press.

MOE Ministry of Education. (2003). *Law of the People's Republic of China on the Promotion of Private Schools.* Retrieved 10 June 2014. http://www.moe.gov.cn/publicfiles/business/htmlfiles/moe/moe_619/200407/1317.html.

MOE Ministry of Education. (2011). China's new national plan for medium- and long-term education reform and development (2010–2020). Retrieved 30 June 2014. http://www.moe.edu.cn/publicfiles/business/htmlfiles/moe/s3501/index.html.

NCERD (National Center for Educational Development Research). (2000–2009) *Green paper on education in China.* Beijing: Educational Science Publishing House.

OECD. (2012). *Main science and technology indicators.* Retrieved 30 June 2014. http://www.oecd.org/sti/inno/msti.htm.

OECD. (2013). *Asian countries top OECD's latest PISA survey on state of global education.* December 3. Retrieved 30 June 2014. http://www.oecd.org/education/asian countries-top-oecd-s-latest-pisa-survey-on-state-of-global-education.htm.

Pan, M. Y. (2009). An analytical differentiation of the relationship between education sovereignty and education rights. *Chinese Education and Society, 42*(4), 88–96.

Postiglione, G. A. (2009). China's international partnerships and cross-border cooperation. Editor's Introduction to *Chinese Education and Society, 42*(4), 3–10.

Postiglione, G. A. (2011a). Higher education: University challenge. *China Economic Quarterly, 15*(2), 22–25.

Postiglione, G. A. (2011b). The rise of research universities: The Hong Kong University of Science and Technology. In P. G. Altbach & J. Salmi (Eds.), *The road to academic excellence: The making of world class universities.* Washington DC: The World Bank.

Postiglione, G. A. (2013). Anchoring globalization in Hong Kong's Research Universities: Network agents, institutional arrangements and brain circulation. *Studies in Higher Education, 38*(3), 345–366.

QS. (2012). http://www.topuniversities.com/university-rankings/world-university-rankings/2012. Top universities worldwide.

Ramo, J. C. (2004). The Beijing consensus. The Foreign Policy Centre. May. Retrieved 28 January 2014.

Redden, E. (2014a). Phantom Campus in China. *Inside higher education.* Febuary 12. Retrieved 30 June 2014. http://www.insidehighered.com/news/2008/02/12/china#sthash.XjQmRUiI.dpbs.

Redden, E. (2014b). Bucking the Branch Campus. *Inside higher education.* March 12. Retrieved 30 June 2014. http://www.insidehighered.com/news/2014/03/12/amid branch-campus-building-boom-some-universities-reject-model#ixzz34fcVHp8L.

Rosen, S. (2004). The Beida reforms I. *Chinese Education and Society.* New York: M.E. Sharpe.

Rosen, S. (2005). The Beida Reforms II. *Chinese Education and Society*. New York: M.E. Sharpe.
Ross, H., & Cen, Y. H. (2000). Chinese higher education and evaluation in context. *Chinese Education and Society*, 42(1), 3–7.
Royal Society. (2011). *New countries emerge as major players in scientific world*. March 28. https://royalsociety.org/news/2011/new-science-countries/.
Salmi, J. (2011). The road to academic excellence: Lessons of experience. In P. G. Altbach & J. Salmi (Eds.), *The road to academic excellence: The making of world class research universities* (p. 339). Washington, DC: The World Bank.
Schell, O., & DeLury, J. (2013). *Wealth and power: China's long march to the twenty-first century*. London: Little Brown.
Science. (2012). With eye to innovation, China revamps its universities. *31 August*. Retrieved 30 June 2014. www.sciencemag.org August 31.
SCMP South China Morning Post. (2011a). *Zhu Rongji resurfaces to criticise education reforms*. April 23. Retrieved 30 June 2014. http://www.scmp.com/article/965804/zhu-rongji-resurfaces-criticise-education-reforms.
SCMP South China Morning Post. (2011b). *Wen in renewed plea for wider political reforms*. April 29: 1. Retrieved 30 June 2014. http://www.scmp.com/article/966328/wen-renewed-plea-wider-political-reforms.
SCMP South China Morning Post. (2013) Former Google China head Lee Kai-fu sows seeds of change, August 8. Retrieved 30 June 2014. http://www.scmp.com/news/china/article/1295061/lee-kai-fu-nurtures-start-ups-and-hopes-better-china.
Shambaugh, D. (2013). *China goes global: The partial power*. Oxford: Oxford University Press.
Shen, Z. (2003). Shanghai jiang shuaixian shixian gaodeng jiaoyu puji hua: 2002 nian gaodeng jiaoyu maoruxuelu yida 51%, 5 nianhou jiangda 60% yishang (Shanghai will take the lead in the massification of higher education: Gross enrolment rate reaches 51% in 2002 and set to move beyond 60% in five years). *China Education Daily*, February 17, 2003. Retrieved December 23, 2007 from http://www.jyb.com.cn/gb/2003/02/17/zy/jryw/1.htm.
Telegraph. (2014) *China 'to overtake America by 2016'*, April 26. Retrieved 30 June 2014. http://www.telegraph.co.uk/finance/china-business/9947825/China-to-overtake-America-by-2016.html.
THE *Times Higher Education World University Rankings* (2013). http://www.timeshighereducation.co.uk/world-university-rankings/.
University World News. (2007) UK: China the next higher education superpower, 25 November. Issue No. 7. Retrieved 30 June 2014. http://www.universityworldnews.com/article.php?story=20071123120347861.
Vogel, E. (2003) China's intellectual renaissance. *Washington Post*, Dec 5, 2003.
Vogel, E. (2013). *Deng Xiaoping and the transformation of China*. Cambridge: Harvard University Press.
Wildavsky, B. (2012). *The great brain race: How global universities are reshaping the world*. Princeton: Princeton University Press.
Williamson, J. (2012). Is the "Beijing Consensus" now dominant? *Asia Policy*. January.
Xin, H. (2012). With eye to innovation, China revamps. *Science*, 337, 634–645. August 10. www.sciencemag.org.
Yang, D. P. (Ed.). (2003). *Daxue jingshen*. Beijing: Wenhui. The Spirit of Higher Education.

Yang, R. (2013). Indigenizing the western concept of the university: Chinese Experience. *Asia Pacific Education Review, 14*(1), 85–92.

Zhang, L. (2009a). Policy direction and development trends for Sino-Foreign partnership schools. *Chinese Education and Society, 42*(4), 11–22.

Zhang, M. X. (2009b). New era. New policy: Cross-border education and Sino-Foreign cooperation in running schools in the eyes of fence-sitter. *Chinese Education and Society, 42*(4), 23–40.

Zhao, L. T., & Hao, J. J. (2010). China's higher education reform: What has not been changed? *East Asian Policy, 2*(4). Singapore: World Scientific. Retrieved 30 June 2014. http://www.eai.nus.edu.sg/Vol2No4_ZhaoLitao&ZhuJinjing.pdf.

Zhou, J. (2006). *Higher education in China*. Singapore: Thomson.

12 Global recession and higher education in eastern Asia

China, Mongolia and Vietnam

Overview

During the 1980s, countries in Asia that borrowed from the World Bank and the International Monetary Fund (IMF) were instructed to cut back on government spending, including that for higher education. Likewise, during the late 1990s, many Asian colleges and universities became casualties of the financial crisis. The effects still linger in some countries. However, the global recession of 2008 runs counter to this trend. The response of developed nations has been less about cutting back and more about the rebuilding and strengthening of colleges and universities. At the same time, there is a growing consensus among scholars of Asian higher education that the financial architecture and governance of higher education needs reforming (Lee 2004; Mok 2006, 2008; Tilak 2004). Therefore, asking developing countries in Asia to cut back on their knowledge infrastructure is difficult to justify as developed countries do the opposite. Although there is no way to escape the difficulties of the global recession, the answer for the developing nations of Asia is not to undo the gains in higher education of the last 20 or 30 years.

Past economic shocks in Asia have also generally limited the capacity of their colleges and universities to serve vulnerable populations. These populations vary somewhat among countries, but, at one time or another, have encompassed the urban poor, newly unemployed households of the lower middle class, recently unemployed urban workers, and rural migrants in manufacturing and related sectors, as well as rural populations of women and ethnic minorities, including those with basic education. Although government responses are formulated, sometimes on the advice of donor agencies, recessions share the essential result of intensifying poverty among the poor and augmenting vulnerable populations through a massive increase in unemployment. However, the global recession differs in fundamental ways; not so much in its source or intensity, but in the rapidly changing context of regional development in eastern Asia. The environment of the global recession is that of an eastern Asia far more economically integrated than during past economic shocks, with more unified aspirations about becoming globally competitive and socially responsible as it moves toward the center of the world economic system (ADB 2008a; UNESCO 2003). It follows that past assumptions about higher education and its function in national development need be reconsidered to enable effective responses from government and the private sector.

Looking back to see ahead

From the 1970s, international development agencies began to take a conservative view of the expansion of higher education in the developing world. Contending that the rates of return were much higher for basic education, they advised countries of the risks of expanding university education. This led to a neglect of higher education and left "higher education in a perilous state" (World Bank 2002). Universities in the developed world took advantage of this period as many top students from Asia and elsewhere looked to Europe and North America for university degrees. By the late 1990s, many developing economies in Asia began to expand higher education (Postiglione 2005; Lee and Healy 2006). However, governments preferred to focus their funds on the state supported flagship institutions (Altbach and Umakoshi 2004; Altbach and Balan 2007). In the meantime, privatization was used to satisfy the increased demand that resulted from the successful implementation of basic education and a growing middle class that could afford to spend more on their children's education. The detrimental effects of rapid privatization on educational quality are well-known and government has acknowledged the need to develop regulatory frameworks and increase monitoring and evaluation. The Asian economic crisis of the late 1990s wreaked havoc on their fledgling systems of higher education, both public and private. Some financial resources were culled back and re-appropriated to basic education. However, the crisis was of paramount importance as it required more public and private universities to engage in collaboration and partnerships in order to ensure their survival and sustain their programs. It also led cash strapped government to permit more financial independence and institutional autonomy in higher education. By the time the world economic crisis hit in 2008, higher education systems in eastern Asia were already less dependent on government and more attuned to economic climate changes and challenges, and at least slightly more adept at creating ways to weather an economic downturn. Since this was a global recession and not an economic crisis created in Asia, the response in higher education was a growing consensus to maintain the gains of past years. Before the global recession, many Asian universities had begun to take note of how their own and neighboring universities were inching their way forward in the increasing ubiquitous global league tables. Charting the upward trajectory of Asian universities contributed to a view that increased global economic competitiveness cannot be attained by scaling back the development of higher education.

The effects of the Asian financial crisis of 1997–1998 and the response by governments tell an interesting story. In the case of Southeast Asia, the intensity of the crisis' effects varied somewhat across countries depending on their economies, share of public and private institutions, and college enrollment rates in domestic and international institutions. However, governments shared a number of response patterns.

Indonesia shifted the share of education resources toward basic and away from higher education. As Purwadi (2001: 71) noted, "the crisis simply prevented pupils of low economic status from affording even the least costly university education." Applications declined at elite private colleges and universities, but some households were able to shift over to less expensive public colleges and universities, while youth from poor households were more likely to drop out. Economic subsidies from the government were reduced even while some institutions endeavored to cut or eliminate tuition fees for selected poor students. Institutions were differentially affected and some gained more financial independence and autonomy as they were forced to find alternative ways to mobilize resources.

In Malaysia, the middle class was particularly hard hit. When funds for overseas study were drastically reduced, enrollments at public institutions shot up even while the government instituted austerity measures that cut operating and development expenditures by 18% (Hassan 2001). Low-income *Bumiputra*[1] were hard-pressed to continue in higher education. The pressure increased as public universities were corporatized and many established foundations and subsidiaries to mobilize funds. The government responded with a National Higher Education Fund to help students afford study fees. Malaysian students overseas returned home and public-private higher education franchising developed further.

Thailand's higher education budget declined during the economic crisis. Investment expenditure was halved. Student loans were made available on a wider scale. However, the number of students applying for places declined by 30–60% and private vocational colleges could only meet a third of their targets (Varghese 2001). Dropout rates increased as children helped support their households. When enrollments began to increase again, it was in the public sector, with a 23% rise. Also, similar to Malaysia, fellowships to study overseas were canceled.

Similar effects were apparent in the Philippines, where the economic crisis initially stalled higher education enrollments, particularly in the private sector, and where quality remained a key concern. Philippine households cut expenditures on nonessential goods, and education's share of the total household budget increased slightly from 10.0 to 10.3% on average between 1997 and 1998. The government provided scholarships on a limited scale. The focus was on wider social-protection strategies supported by international donors (Ablett and Slengesol 2001).

Across developing countries in Southeast Asia, college and university budgets were sacrificed in favor of school budgets. The switch from private to public institutions increased, while government subsidies or loans helped alleviate some of the hardships. More domestic study—rather than overseas study—refocused the goals of higher education. Private institutions suffered, but in some countries they formed franchises with public institutions. Public institutions became less dependent and more autonomous, and in some cases became corporatized. Twinning opportunities with overseas institutions increased. The biggest victim was quality, as investment components and governance reforms were delayed in favor of merely sustaining recurrent expenditures for minimal survival.

One worthwhile effect was that institutions gained more autonomy and responsibility for fund raising and a more entrepreneurial spirit. However, sustained reforms in governance were minimal and the quality of instruction and relevance of research remained among an assortment of areas in higher education in need of reform. As the effects of the global recession linger, there is good reason to consider how to foster innovative reforms.

Among developing countries, China capitalized on the Asian financial crisis by expanding higher education when job markets weakened but household savings and family values were substantial enough to support enrollment fees. While expansion occurred largely in the state sector, China also encouraged non-government colleges to expand, thus providing more opportunities to those from previously underserved populations. Meanwhile, it consolidated resources to attain economies of scale, introduced reforms in personnel administration, strengthened its assessment of the quality of instruction, and still managed to support the development of world-class universities.

In general, Asian colleges and universities have a checkered past in weathering recession and economic shock, especially as they impact on particular income groups, regions, and sectors of the labor market. Inadequate government responses may be due to anachronistic assumptions about the role of higher education in development. This paper argues that any further delay of substantial reforms in the governance of higher education during recession runs the risk of a long-term handicap to global competitiveness and sustained hardships for underserved vulnerable populations. Mongolia and Vietnam are two examples of nations that are facing important decisions as to how to proceed in the reform of higher education during the global recession.

Recessions, regional integration, and higher education expansion

A common viewpoint is that the Asian economic crisis was caused by a rapid withdrawal of investment funding to the region and the global recession emanated from the United States, slowed consumption there, and affected export economies in Asia (Pomfret 2010). Moreover, the shock to the export economies was cushioned by the vitality of the larger regional economy in Asia, something which reinforced the logic of regional collaboration. The Asian economic crisis is usually viewed as beginning with the floating of the Thai baht. This led to a major devaluation and expanded the slowdown to South Korea, and across ASEAN, especially Malaysia and Indonesia. High rates of economic growth were no longer possible as GDP growth rates flat-lined or dropped, until 1999 when early indication of growth began to appear. The crisis highlighted the role of major players in the world economy, including a rising Chinese economy. However, the Asian economies had begun to initiate financial sector reforms in the 1990s, which unfortunately were only partially completed. This meant the Asian economies were carrying increasingly fragile financial systems, and as (Radelet et al. 1998: 3) pointed out: "growing short-term foreign debt, rapidly expanding bank credit, and inadequate regulation and supervision of financial institutions." As panic set in, it was further intensified by governments and the IMF, whose disregard to the root problem imposed additional costs on Asia's recovery prospects and their higher education systems.

Since then, however, eastern Asia's movement toward regional integration became increasingly evident. With few formal free trade agreements or regional institutions until the late 1990 s, the region forged ahead quickly with inter-state cooperation in finance and trade (Katada and Solis 2008). Regionalism in eastern Asia has become a key feature of the global political economy. This was also due to the slow process of liberalization under the WTO, and the enlargements of the EU and growing Pan-American moves to increase free trade arrangements. However, a major reason was that the Asian financial crisis of 1997–98 demonstrated the risk of contagion and investors' perception of the region as a single market. Although many Asian leaders had studied in the US, they lost much trust in the US and international institutions for protection. This propelled the search for home-grown means to protect against unpredictable global money markets (Feinberg 2000).

While Asian regionalism remains contentious in some respects, the core actors are ASEAN + 3, with China, Japan, and South Korea competing to seek initiatives within the process of regionalism. They have joined together in a number of agreements, such as a network of currency swap arrangements, and there has been some discussion about an Asian Monetary Fund and common currency baskets. Thus, Asian economies are more integrated than ever before and the demand for human resources is growing rapidly.

The global financial recession affected growth in selected sectors, and higher education could still become a potential casualty (World Bank 2009a). When the region weathered an economic shock in 1997–1998, the experience provided insights for the global recession's implications for higher education and the rising social and economic demand (Lee and Rhee 1999). Sharp shifts in international finance promise to remain an occasional reality of the economic landscape for higher education as Asia drives toward the center of the global economy. Yet, such shifts need not deter reforms in Asian higher education as it expands access to more diverse populations and sustains Asia's knowledge transfer and economic growth. A recession is an opportune time for higher education to continue reforming institutional governance while it resists marginalizing populations from poorer regions and those who become vulnerable during major economic downturns (Varghese 2001).

Economic globalization has transformed the role of colleges and universities in the Asian region. Rapid expansion has been fueled by an increased demand for higher education that has been fostered by the successful popularization of basic education, rising household expectations, government subscription to the discourse of knowledge economics, human resource needs, and increased availability of distance programs, and private for-profit programs (Postiglione and Tan 2007). From institutions that prepare an elite stratum, colleges and universities are becoming institutions serving multiple stakeholders. Enrollment in higher education is expected to double in 5 years and triple in 10 years in many developing countries in this region (ADB 2008b). Among the challenges will be improving knowledge transfer to poor communities, preparation of vulnerable youth for an increasingly competitive labor market, and confidence by households to send a child to college or university. Institutions of higher education are also becoming symbols of national ambition during times of growth as well as recession.

During past economic crises, higher education budgets have been secondary to those for basic education. However, the global recession requires different measures, including a shift toward cost sharing among different levels of the education system, a trend that is increasing in many parts of the world (Johnston 2004; Woodhall 2007). For these and other reasons, development agencies are shifting their educational funding toward regular and higher vocational education (Sarvi 2008).

Topics worthy of examination in developing regions of Asia include the effects of the economic shift on student access and retention, changes in household perspectives and strategic decision making, innovation and resilience in institutional governance, the quality and relevance of knowledge and skills transmission, cost-sharing arrangements and the sustainability of private higher education, trends in international student mobility and transnational academic collaboration, the mobility of the academic profession, the shrinkage of the graduate employment market, and funding for research (in science, technology, and medicine) that aids poor communities (Chapman and Austin 2002; Fegan and Field 2009; Chapman et al. 2010; Huang 2006; Sakamoto and Chapman 2011). While the scope of this paper does not permit addressing these aspects in detail, it is possible to review selected literature and data regarding the experience of higher education in selected developing countries of Asia during financial slowdowns. Government policies to ameliorate negative impacts on higher education during economic crises can be reviewed and assessed for their effectiveness.

Economic shocks and higher education reform: China, Mongolia, and Vietnam

This section cites three cases of transitional economies in eastern Asia that are on the move to rapid reforms in higher education. Each introduced market forces into their economies at different times and degrees, and at a different pace. China, the largest country in the world, began a gradual reform in December 1978. It has since become the second leading economy after the United States, with the world's largest higher education system. Massive and landlocked with a sparse population, Mongolia made the most radical transition to market economics, triggered by the fall of the Soviet Union in 1989. It has since seen its East European orientation matched by a tilt back toward Asia. Vietnam's economic liberalization was gradual but it is rapidly becoming engaged in major university reforms. Developments in higher education in each country, not all necessitated by regional or global economic shocks, are reviewed below. However, there are indications that global recession and regional integration are growing forces that shape higher education reform and development in each country.

China

The global recession also took its toll in China. Even in China, where government stimulus measures have been effective in easing the effects of the recession, up to 41 million workers lost their jobs (40% of total global layoffs), and 23 million remained out of work as of October 2009 (Cai et al. 2010). However, China is adhering to its human resource blueprint (that by 2020 young people will average 12.8 years of education), which means that enrollment in higher education will not be cut back (6 million were admitted last year), despite the fact that expansion has resulted in increased unemployment among college and university graduates. By July 2009, 68% of 6.11 million university graduates had found jobs, leaving nearly two million still unemployed.

Measures have been instituted to expand opportunities and find work for graduates. There is also a renewed focus on postsecondary-level vocational and technical colleges, especially as more households drop the traditional emphasis on academic higher education. This is occurring as vocational-technical and community colleges align themselves more closely with the needs of the labor market. In China's case, as well as for other countries in Asia, demography has become a key factor in higher education planning. By 2020, the number of students in primary and junior secondary education will drop by 18 million. With a rising aging population and a decline in the school-age population, a shift of resources toward basic education and away from higher education could have unfavorable long-term implications.

Between 1999 and 2004, enrollment nearly quadrupled. In 1999, enrollment in higher education stood at 1.6 million, and in 2004, enrollment was 4.473 million. According to 2007 Ministry of Education statistics, in 1990, less than 4% of the 18–22 age group was enrolled as students in higher education compared to 22 percent in 2005. About 5 million students are admitted annually. China's higher education institutions expanded rapidly beginning in 1999 as a way to delay entrance into the labor market of large numbers of youth when the Asian economic crisis affected job opportunities. Expansion of paid university places was also a way to get households to spend at a time when the economy needed more of a stimulus. Universities resorted to banks for loans to support capital construction costs, resulting in high levels of debt. Rapid expansion also compromised the quality of higher education. Low quality in turn contributed to graduate unemployment. According to one report, only about 7% of the students about to graduate in July 2009 had managed to secure jobs by March 2009. This is down about 50% from the same period the year before. In fact, the demand for graduates seems to have dipped by 20%, due largely to the global economic slowdown (Qiwen 2009). The China Ministry of Education reported in 2009 that the number of graduates had topped 6 million, a figure far beyond the 1.45 million who graduated in 2002.

The global recession has not alleviated the pressure on the close to 2 million graduates who still need jobs (Zhou and Lin 2009). In January 2010, Chinese Premier Wen Jiabao warned that university graduates face a grim job market as the global slowdown takes hold of the economy (Reuters 2010). More recent reforms aimed to raise the quality of undergraduate education while broadening the curriculum to foster more creatively minded graduates who could promote the innovation needed to sustain China's economic rise. There is an increasingly popular view that graduates in China simply lack certain skills that are relevant to the needs of the labor market (Roberts 2010). For example, international companies often complain about the lack of appropriately skilled Chinese graduates. Companies have to invest in training their new college-educated staff in order to bring them up to par with the standards required for international companies. It is not only foreign companies that struggle to find skilled graduates. At a job fair in Beijing, local employers expressed concern about the quality of graduates (Patton 2009). Domestic companies often indicate a mismatch between their needs and what graduates possess. The global slowdown has put pressure on Beijing to address the shrinking number of jobs available for young graduates.

With the aim of raising quality, China has moved quickly to capitalize on Sino-foreign collaboration in higher education and propagated a law on Sino-foreign cooperation in education in 2003. While one of the major reasons for Sino-foreign partnerships has been to raise the quality of education in China, many believe that educational quality has remained unsatisfactory because partnerships are driven more by commercial benefits than academic motives. The lack of internal governance and quality monitoring by partners has not helped to alleviate the problem. Yet the view remains that to cut transnational partnerships in higher education would be a profound mistake, especially in anticipation of the global economic recovery (Hvistendahl 2009). For countries like China, the view is that higher education has become more important because of the global financial crisis.

Due to its size, reliance on export, low wages, predominance of state owned enterprises, and economic strategy of protecting its markets, China did not experience the Asian economic crisis in the way that many of its neighbors did. Its higher education expansion and development were not curtailed by the crisis. To the contrary, it was able to continue expanding access with the vision of a knowledge economy and logic that households would view it as an investment good that would augment the circulation of capital by the middle class who would pay the rising amount of tuition at public universities and private colleges.

At the same time, China began to attract large numbers of students from throughout Asia, especially from developed countries such as Korea and Japan, who could afford to pay the fees required by Chinese universities, but also students from Southeast Asia, including large numbers of overseas Chinese and others who rely on China's foreign assistance. Thus, China's higher education expansion was not affected in the same way as other countries, something that did not go unnoticed in other university systems of Asia. However, the global economic recession meant a slowdown in job creation for graduates and claims that the expansion might have been too rapid.

The effects of the global recession were also eased somewhat by the cross-border mobility of Chinese university graduates. Many began to work or take up post graduate study in Japan, Singapore, Hong Kong and elsewhere in the region. The rapid expansion in the teaching of Chinese at Confucian Institutes throughout the world also took some of the burden off employment. As the population ages and the younger generation takes on a larger labor burden to sustain the economy, China could very well find itself attracting labor and high level talent from other parts of Asia where facility in Chinese language will have increased with the number of Confucian institutes. Countries like Singapore that have slowing population growth have begun to take advantage of China's talent by establishing boarding schools for young talented students from China who would go to university in Singapore, join the labor market after graduation, and become more easily integrated into Singaporean society. A similar situation has occurred in Hong Kong. An increasing number of students from China can be found working or studying in most Asian countries.

Mongolia

Despite the global recession, Mongolia is determined to move ahead in restructuring its higher education system (Postiglione 2010). Selected key education indicators rival those of its neighbors in northeast Asia—China, the Republic of Korea (hereafter Korea), and Japan. It has a literate population, a popularized school system, and a higher education enrollment rate that has ballooned within a few short years to nearly 80%. This enrollment rate includes a thriving sector of vocational-technical higher education. Since 1990, when the country moved from a planned to a market economy, the private higher education sector has grown to encompass a third of all enrollments. Most colleges and universities are in the capital city, where 40% of the national population resides. The rest of the population, also literate and schooled, adheres to a nomadic lifestyle. English has replaced Russian as the official second language of this land of 2.8 million people, the largest landlocked country in the world. Historical circumstance has made Mongolia the most Europeanized state in East Asia. However, its people retained the Asian value of acquiring as much education as possible.

Despite the global recession, Mongolia ranked seventh internationally in the share of GDP (9.0%) allocated to education, and its education law guarantees that at least 20% of the government budget is spent on education (Government of Mongolia 2006). Yet higher education receives only 12% of that amount. This made sense for a developing country in transition. However, the time is ripe for a rethink of the higher education system, including its funding structure. State universities obtain government funds for heating and lighting, but little else. One university leader pointed out that 80% of academic staff salaries come from student fees. A national fund for higher education provides coverage to one child from each civil servant's family, and support is also provided for outstanding students from poor families. However, there is also a view that higher education is a source of poverty because two-thirds of the personal loans taken by countryside cattle-rancher families is spent on the higher education of their children.

With such high literacy, school attendance, and higher education enrollment rates, as well as a sustained Asian value toward education, Mongolia would seem to be in a good position to provide equitable access to higher education and restructure the system to bring the standard of teaching and research up to internationally recognized levels. Nevertheless, the global recession has created severe limits on reform for the time being.

Mongolia faces several daunting challenges during global economic shocks. First, government spending on higher education is severely limited in comparison to other regional players. For example, the two economies of Malaysia and Hong Kong, China overshadow most Asian countries with respect to per student expenditure as a share of GDP. Mongolia's transition to a market-oriented system included introducing fees for higher education. However, unlike governments in China, Japan, or Korea, Mongolia's cannot make the same investment in its top universities. The evidence suggests that the amount of government investment in higher education does matter, not only to the quality of teaching and research but also to ensuring access to all who meet the criteria for admission. Hong Kong spends about 30% of its education budget on higher education and has the highest concentration of top-rated universities, all government funded, in one city in Asia. Moreover, government ensures that loans are available to university students that need them. While there are also some Asian governments that allocate a smaller slice of the pie to higher education, improving access for poor populations and raising the quality are difficult to achieve with a 12% slice of the education budget for higher education.

Second, like China and Vietnam, the quality of private higher education has yet to surpass that of public institutions. Despite their short history, some private institutions are catching up and offer a few competitive programs. One view is that state institutions receive such a small amount of funding that they actually operate with state titles but in private mode. Heads of private sector institutions would like more support from the government. Some would approve of placing a third of students in state institutions with the private institutions enrolling the rest. In Indonesia, Japan, Korea, Philippines, and Taiwan, private universities enroll the majority of students—in some cases more than 80%. Mongolia's private institutions enroll 34% of all students.

Third, there are also far too many institutions of higher education. With 162 institutions, the average number of students at each is about 900; a figure that does not permit attaining an economy of scale. Consolidation has been used to address this problem elsewhere. For example, the average number of students in China's institutions was 3,112 in 1990, up from 1,919 in 1980, when about 80% of higher education institutions had fewer than 4,000 students and 60% had fewer than 3,000 students. However, by 2000, 612 colleges and universities were consolidated into 250, and several universities now have over 50,000 students. Other countries are dealing with similar problems, especially at the outset of privatization when many small colleges—sometimes with poor quality instruction—were established. After the initial phase of privatization, the need for quality assurance often ends in the closure and consolidation of many institutions.

Mongolia is a developing country that aspires, as do its neighbors in northeast Asia (China, Japan, and South Korea), to have internationally recognized research universities. The intention to establish highly recognized research universities has to be matched by a national budget that does not skimp on funds for research and development. Some continue to argue that making a direct association between R&D budgets and research productivity is risky. (The research and development R&D budget for Hong Kong is only 0.7% of GDP, but the economy has a very high per capita rate of research output.) Regardless, Mongolia's R&D budget of 0.28% of GDP places it 70th in the world (Hong Kong ranks 50th). Colleges and universities in Mongolia spend about 1.5% of their institutional funds on research. Those in the United Kingdom spend about 7–10%. Therefore, Mongolia's research universities will remain hard pressed without a larger national R&D budget.

With the discovery of massive mineral deposits, Mongolia has a promising economic future. The global recession has put most higher education reform on hold. In the meantime, the economy is too weak to support its large number of university graduates and many seek employment elsewhere. The reason has a great deal to do with the quality of higher education, where major reforms are critically needed. If the above challenges facing higher education are urgently addressed, Mongolia will find itself better prepared to take advantage of the opportunities on its horizon.

Mongolia's higher education has been affected severely by both economic shocks, as well as by national politics. Highly vulnerable to international markets, it expanded higher education throughout each shock. Even as late as the global economic crisis, which had a major effect on education in general, one candidate for president promised to eliminate fees for higher education. After decades of looking West, Mongolia is reestablishing its position within a far more integrated eastern Asian region. For example, its universities have established scientific partnerships with top institutions in Asia, including Yonsei University in Korea, Keio University in Japan, and Tsinghua University in China, as well as elsewhere in Asia. Mongolia's mining companies, predicted to remake the economy of Mongolia, as well as providing a major source of natural resources for the energy needs of Asia's regional economies, have become listed on the Hang Seng Index, Hong Kong's internationally influential stock exchange. The governments of the Republic of Mongolia and the Hong Kong Special Administrative Region of China have established visa-free access for citizens of both, greatly increasing opportunities for academic interchanges.

Vietnam

Since 1989, Vietnam has had one of the fastest-growing economies in the world, with access to education increasing at all levels. This includes growth in primary and junior secondary education, with a renewed focus on ethnic minority-populated areas. Vietnam's General Statistics Office indicated in 2008 that GDP had passed US $1,000 per capita. Although low within the Association of Southeast Asian Nations (ASEAN), incomes have risen almost fourfold since 1989. Those living on less than US$1 per day have fallen from 60% to below 12% (World

Bank 2008). Vietnam experienced two decades of rapid economic growth at an average of 7.4% a year between 1989 and 2008. However, export growth slowed as the global recession took hold and inward investment declined (Picus 2009).

Rural populations, particularly women and minorities, were the first victims of the economic downturn with a rise in jobless rates. Over 20% of migrant workers have returned to their home provinces since the beginning of 2009, having lost their jobs in industrialized areas. The country implemented an economic stimulus package of more than US $8 billion to address the crisis. With many migrant workers and extensive remote regions populated by ethnic minority groups, more support for basic education and pipeline programs that widen the pathways to higher education for these groups continue to be needed.

The recession is an opportunity for Vietnam to focus more intensively on the socioeconomic development of its poor and vulnerable populations. The rapid period of economic development that preceded the global recession saw increased educational opportunities across diverse populations. The recession threatens a setback in socioeconomic development and in access to higher education at a time when Vietnam has been working to improve the quality of its higher education system (Harman et al. 2010).

Vietnam aims to continue in its aim to reach the Millennium Development Goal of Education for All by 2015. However, it also plans to move ahead with its bold plans for higher education. This includes a major upgrading of the quality of its universities, which it sees as central to its economic rise and regional integration. As Huong and Fry (2004: 301) note: "The country's success in realizing its intellectual potential will depend on improving both the quality and efficiency of its university system." Vietnam has rapidly expanded an indigenous system of higher education that aims to strengthen a knowledge economy with graduates that can adapt to new technologies and flexible labor markets (Lee and Healy 2006). The continued reform and development of universities in Vietnam is essential for it to become "a major player on the world scene economically, culturally, and intellectually" (Huong and Fry 2004: 329).

The highest proportion of university graduates, over 70 percent, are employed in technical and professional occupations (Sakellariou 2010). In transition economies like Vietnam, occupation premiums increase over time along with the emphasis on skills of the new expanding labor markets. It is still possible for the labor market to absorb university graduates even though making university education more relevant to the workplace remains a work in progress. Yet, like elsewhere in Southeast Asia's rapidly expanding higher education sector, quality is a problem, especially in terms of how a university education aligns with the needs of the labor market. For example, a World Bank blog from an age 21 unemployed new graduate with a bachelor's degree recounts what is increasingly common: "I expected to find a job easily since I have a degree in computers. But, after going to multiple interviews, I found out that firms are hesitant to hire me because despite my degree, they have to train me to meet their work requirements. It is easier for these firms to hire a graduate with a couple of years of experience instead" (Jimenez 2010).

Vietnam plans to open a new science university in 2010. The Hanoi University of Science and Technology (HUST) aims to have a 10% intake of foreign students, a good number from the Asian region. The recruitment of academic staff will include half of whom can be considered as having attained an international standard of excellence, as indicated by the publication of research papers in top international journals. HUST would be part of a national plan to establish four world-class research universities by 2020. The other three universities include the Vietnam-Germany University, opened in 2008 in Ho Chi Minh City, and two other institutions, including the planned American International University (Down 2009, World Bank 2009b).

The Higher Education Development Policy Program, along with the Second Higher Education Project and the New-Model Universities Project, supports the Government's Socio-Economic Development Plan 2006–2010 and its Higher Education Reform Agenda. These programs aim to strengthen governance, rationalize financing, improve the quality of teaching and research, improve accountability for performance, and enhance transparency in financial management within the higher education sector (World Bank 2009c).

Vietnam also has a thriving sector of vocational-technical education. This growth in postsecondary education not only includes universities. Vietnam has established a network of community colleges that provide a vocational and technical education within a flexible structure of instructional service. Such institutions tend to be more resilient during a recession. Reforms in higher education that involve the establishment of a system of community colleges helped expand opportunities to bring educational progress and jobs to poor communities. As Dang and Nguyen (2009: 97) point out with respect to community colleges: "This ensures a social balance in education—training that helps the poor, especially talented poor students in socio-economically-backward localities, who find opportunities to access higher education." An important measure of socioeconomic success for Vietnam's higher education system will be the ability of its community college system to encompass poor rural populations, including women and minorities, and urban poor who become increasingly vulnerable during recessions due to the rise in jobless rates.

Vietnam is an example of a country determined to develop higher education throughout the global economic crisis, even though it still has a way to go for basic education development. It sees itself in a strong position to develop rapidly in higher education and has moved toward a gradual acceptance of private higher education and public-private partnerships. It has also taken an increasing role in the regional integration and hosted the China-ASEAN Forum on Social Development and Poverty Reduction in 2009. In higher education, Vietnam has participated in the harmonization activities underway across eastern Asia. Among the multiple organizations promoting cross-border harmonization efforts are the ASEAN University Network (AUN), the Asia Pacific Quality Network (APQN) and South East Asia Ministers of Education Organization's Regional Center for Higher Education and Development (SEAMEO-REHID). The themes that cut across these efforts generally include promoting collaboration around issues of teaching, research, student and staff mobility, and quality assurance (Chapman et al. 2010). Within Asia, its partnerships in higher education have continued to grow, including the Okayama-Hue International Master's program in Sustainability of Rural and Environmental Systems between Hue University and Okayama University. This venture is one of the pioneering joint-training programs in the field of environment and agriculture both in Japan and in Vietnam. The students pay a fee to study for 1 year at Hue University and if they pass end-of-course examinations, they will be funded for their 1 year at Okayama University and conferred an MS degree by both Okayama and Hue University.

A national perspective on higher education during recessions

A higher education system is a national endeavor that strengthens capacity to participate effectively in an increasingly competitive global knowledge economy. It is also an enterprise that works best when it marshals talent and fosters leadership and commitment from all sectors of the national population (Task Force 2000). A financial crisis slices into the heart of this national endeavor by heightening the conditions that marginalize selected populations (ILO 1998). The poor remain affected, while the ranks of the vulnerable population grow larger as more citizens suddenly find themselves bereft of the financial wherewithal to cope. Moreover, economic crises and recessions have generally damaged the competitive edge of higher education in Asia. Rather than viewing such times as opportunities to proactively push ahead with major reforms that over the long term will sustain the dynamic rise of Asian higher education within the global system, there is less emphasis on long-term planning than on short-term measures to attain financial buffering and minor management reorganization.

Despite the recent trend toward classification in higher education, students from poor and vulnerable populations in the developing countries of the Asian region are less prone to enter and complete a tertiary education during a recession, and their absence diminishes the representation of national diversity in colleges and universities (Altbach and Umakoshi 2004). Moreover, when poor populations do manage to attend and graduate, they are less likely to locate employment in a depressed labor market. Other populations become more vulnerable and cannot afford private higher education. They are limited in seeking higher education overseas and governments are more likely to reduce scholarships for overseas study.

For poor and vulnerable populations, household finance affects decisions about whether to attend regular or vocational colleges, or to defer a higher education. Economic hardships experienced by households during a recession can affect the ability of students to complete their studies. It becomes more difficult for some households to pay education fees and their children may not be able to repay loans, especially when they are unable to locate employment after graduation. Some households may decide to defer higher education opportunities or select more practical alternatives to an academic track. While household savings and the value that families place on education help sustain access rates in some countries, the choice of what postsecondary institution to attend and what major subject to study becomes of increasing concern to students and their families.

Students from poor and vulnerable populations often attend institutions more likely to experience a drop in the quality of instruction during a recession, thus further decreasing student competitiveness after graduation in an already tightly stretched labor market.

Finally, cutbacks in higher education due to recession also have the potential to affect the amount of funding available for research in the fields of medicine, science, and technology that help poor communities overcome health threats, increase food production, and improve conditions associated with development.

To be sure, the development issues and challenges will differ across the countries of the region. Whatever the case, ministries of education and college and university administrators will be confronted with more complex situations that require increasing strategic governance capabilities (Postiglione 2006). While there were generally major declines in university budgets during the Asian economic crisis of the late 1990s, some places soon began to expand enrollments. Enrollments rose in many of China's universities. Public universities diversified and increased their offerings of market-driven courses. However, this expansion took its toll on the quality of instruction. In countries with large private sectors of higher education, like Indonesia and the Philippines, many households with children in private higher education or in overseas colleges and universities moved them to public universities in the home country, where the fees were less and subsidies were more readily available. This substitution effect from private to public higher education affected the management of academic staffing, but it also initiated higher levels of management autonomy and stricter measures of financial accountability. Public and private colleges and universities tried to twin with overseas institutions to lower costs, and some tried to team up with banks to foster offers of long-term, low-interest loans to students.

The one constant challenge to higher education in any recession is bound to be the rising unemployment rate among graduates. Unfortunately, this was already an emerging issue as a result of the sudden regional massification of higher education that grew at the turn of the century. Still, patterns differ across countries. For example, unemployment of tertiary education graduates in some countries has been far worse than in others. Moreover, the patterns of unemployment may differ among graduates of public or private institutions, as they do among graduates of regular or vocational-professional institutions of higher education (Postiglione 2009a, b, c, d).

Income groups disproportionately affected

Unlike the global recession, the Asian crisis of 1997–1998 resulted from overambitious private sector investment. The declining value of currencies led to crises in banking and manufacturing that eventually resulted in a loss of jobs and a decline in household income. The root cause was not public sector inefficiency but rather the unrestricted inflow of private capital and its sudden withdrawal. Private domestic investment and human capital still drive growth in most places in Asia. Since private colleges and universities in Asia also outnumber public ones in most countries, public confidence can more easily be shaken during a recession if higher education access and quality experience a setback.

Aside from the poor, the rising middle class—the main clients of higher education—were seriously affected. While there was an expectation after the economic shock of 1997–1998 that enrollment would be significantly affected, this was not the case in all countries. Part of the reason was that many Asian economies differed from developed economies that had large government sectors. Large public sectors would naturally be required to make severe cutbacks but the late 1990s Asian recession was a matter of private sector collapse. Therefore, employment in the public sector was not severely affected and this included public higher education. However, the emergent middle class was hard hit with job losses. Still, its demand for higher education did not change. Government institutions of higher education continued to operate and represented hope for the future to a class that associated its rising status with the dual pillars of wealth and education.

Since the publics' sectors were small and not deeply affected, higher education was not devastated on the same scale as the private sector. Private higher education revealed its fragility and lack of stamina within a financial meltdown. Although the massification of higher education had not started at the time of the 1997–1998 crisis, a large proportion of the colleges and universities in Indonesia and the Philippines were private institutions. China, Malaysia, and Mongolia had also begun to establish private colleges and universities but they represented a small proportion of the total. Vietnam led the way in the privatization of higher education in country and among its neighboring economies of Cambodia and the Lao People's Democratic Republic. The two major urban centers of East and Southeast Asia with market economies—Singapore and Hong Kong, China—had not strayed from a public sector-dominated system, though they have begun to do so since then. In most cases, the 1997–1998 crisis caused a decline in employment and household income that led to a steady divestment of income elasticity, which affected enrollments in private higher education.

Those households with substantial savings were willing to expend part of it for educational purposes. Where household savings are substantial, this Asian pattern exhibits itself in many cases. China expanded its higher education at the end of the twentieth century, which would have been impossible without the amount of household savings that families were readily willing to make available for study costs. There are similarities in the global recession in other Asian countries. Even when household savings are low, Asian families are willing to borrow and take out loans for their children's education (as noted for Mongolian cattle-rancher households, above).

In short, the 1997–1998 crisis did not shake the strong commitment to higher education of poor and vulnerable populations. However, attendance was weakened in selected institutional sectors by financial hardships. When household savings were low, decisions about education costs were made on more pragmatic grounds. The quality and relevance of education during economic setbacks becomes increasingly important. Since the recession of the late 1990s, quality assurance measures in Asian higher education have been increasingly promoted by the ASEAN University Network, an organization under the auspices of the Association of Southeast Asian Nations (ASEAN) (UNESCO 2004). The Internet has also become important for households as a source of information for making decisions about higher education in some countries, but in others there is still a need to improve the availability of both the information for decision making, and reliable and inexpensive counseling services for prospective students.

Perspectives on responding to economic crises

A time of recession also offers opportunities to take higher education reform forward in Asia's developing countries. Rather than conceive of responses to the recession as life boats to bring the system back to safety, responses can best be viewed as a way of exploring growth strategies to stimulate college and university reform beyond restoring past levels of access to poor and potentially vulnerable populations. Therefore, there is good reason at this critical juncture to gain a deeper understanding of trends during past and present slowdowns of public expenditure for higher education, effects of slowdowns on labor markets, and their implications for poor and vulnerable populations. While the origins, characteristics, and paths to recovery of the 1997–1998 crisis differ in fundamental ways from the global slowdown, many of the deleterious effects are the same.

As the recession recedes, the challenges of access to and relevance of higher education in developing countries in this region will not disappear. Even developed countries at the height of their economic prowess must constantly be vigilant about how to ensure that opportunities for a higher education are not reserved for privileged groups in society. However, developed countries have been far more successful in putting the mechanisms in place, including improved governance, that effectively deal with problems of access and relevance.

Therefore, the manner in which the global economic situation is addressed in Asia has long-term implications for the reform of higher education. In short, colleges and universities are essential for national development and in times of economic crisis, and it is mistaken to consider them as parts of the education system that can be sacrificed. They not only offer hope and confidence to poor and vulnerable populations, but also make contributions that are invaluable to national development. It is in times of recession that the opportunity arises to fine-tune institutional governance and policies.

Some common responses in higher education during the 1997–1998 crisis were budget cuts, staff reduction, less hiring, wage freezes, delays in building, tightly regulated utilities and maintenance, postponed library purchases, and canceled travel grants for international conferences. Declining household incomes were met with policy responses that increased the availability of subsidies for higher education. During that crisis, cuts in higher education were more on investment budgets than recurrent budgets. In response to students dropping out, student support systems were provided, including grants, loans, and scholarships. In some cases, they worked. However, results varied across countries and income groups. Private colleges and universities were strongly affected by drops in enrollment and diminished stock portfolios exacerbated the problem and required austerity measures that affected quality. Some families made a switch from fee-paying private higher education to less expensive public institutions.

Countries such as China and Malaysia had large numbers of students studying overseas. Countries that had as much as a fifth of students studying overseas inevitably had to reduce fellowships and scholarships to study overseas. Although some countries tried to maintain overseas study fellowships, a more useful response was to establish a credit transfer arrangement that provided an opportunity for students to return from expensive overseas study and continue their education at home institutions.

Such responses to the global recession provided colleges and universities with more autonomy from government, financially or otherwise. This was an encouragement to the private sector and some new universities resulted. Since Western countries were less affected by the Asian crisis but increasingly affected by competition for students and the pressure to internationalize, representatives from many of them came to Asia to recruit students and fostered an increase in twinning programs.

Wealthy countries of the region could provide innovative financial support to students of higher education, despite the economic crunch, because of their access to resources, both institutional and technological. Students could be provided with graduate retraining at public expense. Colleges and universities offered courses in information technology, life sciences, and generic skills to make their graduates more marketable. Poorer countries had to cut back on their educational budgets and resorted to staff retrenchment. This led to creative policy approaches like enhancing university autonomy and strengthening the capacity of these institutions to cope with sudden resource cuts.

The 1997–1998 crisis demonstrated that existing safety net systems were inadequate. Government responses were limited and only minor reform in higher education resulted from the experience. That is not to say that the experience was not useful. More than anything else, it appears that the global recession provides more of an opportunity to consider reforms in several areas, including policy and regulatory frameworks, governance and management of higher education institutions, and equitable access and support for disadvantaged students. At the same time, better regional cross-border collaboration among developing and developed economies in the eastern Asian region holds promise for new forms of resource and cost-sharing arrangements. This also extends beyond the region to transnational collaboration and cost-sharing with colleges and universities in other parts of the world. Finally, aspirations within Asia for the region to become more globally competitive, not only as a knowledge economy but also as an area with more world-class universities, mean that research and innovation in science and technology need to be sustained during a recession.

The 1997–1998 crisis also confirmed the usefulness of periodic policy forums and other occasions where policymakers, scholars, and academics can come together to design systematic strategies for the development and improvement of higher education. Regional perspectives and consultations are needed. For example, Singapore avoided the 1997–1998 crisis by having invested in higher education; so did China to some extent (Postiglione 2005).

Lessons of the global recession

Students from poor and vulnerable populations are not only less likely to find ways to cover their course fees, but are more likely to make decisions about their education based on limited knowledge of the quality of courses of study and their relevance to rapidly shifting labor markets. During this recession, a downward spiral in labor markets makes students and their families less convinced about the return rate for their investments in higher learning. This is also why their willingness to further their education beyond secondary school becomes more tenuous during recessions. The quality of vocational higher education and community colleges that have closer ties to the labor market will be a more important consideration. Those that do enter postsecondary institutions are more likely to drop out than other students. Whatever the case, the recession must not result in a situation that provides an unfair advantage for better-off groups that have escaped the worst excesses of an economic crisis.

Another response from the 1997–1998 crisis was the caution and concern about underfunding basic and senior secondary education. For example, sudden and large shifts of government financing to higher education in countries with developing market economies can be perceived as placing adequate financing for basic and secondary education at risk. Some evidence shows that on average, low-income countries spend as much as 14 times more on higher education as on a secondary school student and 34 times more than on a primary school student (ADB 2008b; Glewwe and Kremer 2006). This disparity is a risk at the best of times, and an even greater risk during a recession. Therefore, a recession calls for urgent action, in particular the kind of cost-sharing and partnerships that will reduce the risk of widening disparities and ensure sustainable financing for all sectors.

The tendency for governments to protect basic and secondary education budgets during a recession, while understandable, can be short sighted. It is inevitable that higher education per student costs will remain well above other levels within the system. Yet countenancing inequity in higher education during a recession can have disastrous implications over the long term. Aside from the obvious loss of talent and the marginalizing of the poor, there is also a loss in the knowledge and skills available to serve in the social and economic development of poor communities.

During recessions, the sense of corporate responsibility becomes less robust and compromised by financial constraints (Salmi and Bassett 2009). Foundations and alumni may cut back on contributions aimed at helping poor students. Other private funding sources for university research that focuses on the plight of poor and vulnerable communities may be affected. The private sector and civil society need to respond by maintaining loans, scholarships, and deferred payback periods. Moreover, private institutions need to respond by providing students from poor and vulnerable populations with better information about course choices and labor markets. International groups that establish higher education programs in Asia need to avoid exploiting poor and vulnerable students for economic gain. Also, international foundations that support scholarships for students from poor regions need to ensure that these students are supported to study in programs that will aid community development in the regions from which the students come.

Selected recommendations

Tuition assistance, subsidies for poor and vulnerable students, and loans

One of the useful lessons of the 1997–1998 crisis was the key role played by emergency subsidies to poor students. Though limited, these measures were essential for sustaining access to education and education completion rates. Nevertheless, the amounts and the means of selection and distribution of subsidies require greater transparency. No capable student should be prevented from continuing his or her education due to poverty.

Part of the answer would seem to be a national system of loans, rather than free education. The experience of developing countries with respect to student loan schemes is varied. Those developing countries which do not have the infrastructure needed to institute a comprehensive loan scheme are cautioned about abruptly starting one. Small countries such as the Lao People's Democratic Republic and Mongolia have different management challenges for implementation of a comprehensive system of student loans than large countries such as China or Vietnam. Measures need to be developed to ensure that loans do not become misdirected by recipients, whose families may be facing strong transitory financial crisis.

One way to address such challenges is to involve the institutions directly, though this may add to costs of maintaining records on the part of the institutions. In this respect, a proper balanced scheme should be reached. The aim in all cases should be to eventually launch a viable system of nationwide student loans for higher education, one that can survive amid future economic shocks and also guarantee a high degree of cost recovery.

Can current conditions support a more sophisticated system of recession proof student loans? The experience of developing countries with student loans was encapsulated in a World Bank paper (2009b). It is useful to examine the best practices in the different student loan systems of developing countries. Sarvi (2008) has taken note of studies by Ziderman (2004) and Woodhall (2007) that assessed the implementation of student loan schemes in five Asian countries. The study revealed weaknesses in areas such as "financial appraisal, forward planning, monitoring and evaluation, inadequate targeting, and inefficiency in collection" (Sarvi 2008: 10).

Information and guidance for students from poor and vulnerable populations

Students, especially those from the first generation in their family to attend college or university, need guidance and protection from substandard higher education. This is especially needed during recessions when resource cutbacks may decrease the quality of instruction in higher education. It is already clear in the global recession that many households are concerned about the quality of higher education. However, the decision on which institution to attend should still be a personal decision. Students who are willing to pay full fees and not get tuition support should be able to attend the academic programs they choose. Especially for students who receive tuition assistance, there is a need for government protection and a guarantee that they are receiving a quality education that has a good possibility of leading to productive employment.

Labor markets and community-based vocational and technical higher education

As higher education has rapidly expanded in many Asian countries, the number of students unable to locate appropriate employment opportunities after graduation has greatly increased in some countries. The recession has intensified this problem. While massification of higher education provides more opportunities to poor and vulnerable populations, it also comes with higher fees for tuition, accommodations, books and other supplies. While the status of regular higher education has remained consistent and rooted in traditional values, there are increasing signs that households are expecting greater relevance of higher learning for the labor market.

Several developing countries in the region are responding to the pressure for greater relevance by placing more emphasis on higher vocational and technical education. However, there is a need to intensify the support for community-based vocational and technical education that can react quickly to rapid changes in the job markets and shorten the time to complete diplomas and degrees. These institutions also need to focus on generic skills, including communication, problem solving, and creative thinking that will help graduates adjust to future economic shifts that could cause restructuring of labor markets. These institutions also need to stay socially relevant to match local community development trends. As community college models have become disseminated across an increasing number of countries, they have demonstrated a high degree of flexibility in the

256 Institutions

delivery of instructional services, especially for underserved populations, and have helped students address the rapidly changing economic landscape.

Performance-based measures

Quality indicators related to performance can decline during a recession. The emphasis given to performance indicators across higher education systems in the eastern Asian region differs significantly. A recent study revealed that academic staff in developing countries like China and Malaysia saw less of a performance orientation in their institutions compared to academic staff in more developed economies like Hong Kong, China and the Republic of Korea (Postiglione and Wang forthcoming). There is a general need to narrow the gap in the use of performance indicators and provide transparent standards for judgment about quality for prospective students and their families. With respect to instructional quality, there is a great deal that can be done to identify and reward competent teachers. The extent to which a system of career incentives can be arranged to develop and retain high quality college and university academic staff during recessions is still an area in which developing countries can make a key part of their long-term planning.

Quality teaching has invaluable downstream benefits to a society experiencing an economic downturn. Quality instructional resources need to be recognized and should match with the provision of physical and social infrastructure that support continued professional development of academic staff.

Cost sharing

There is less reason to compartmentalize the financing of tertiary education such that it becomes an automatic transfer source of funds for basic education during a recession. It makes greater sense to take a more system-wide approach toward cost sharing among different levels of the education system based on present conditions and forward planning (SEAMEO 2005).

One of the positive lessons of the 1997–1998 crisis was the provision of more autonomy for public institutions to enter into new financial arrangements for joint academic programs with private institutions. Therefore, it is worth while to continue to examine a range of cost-sharing alternatives that involve public-private financing partnerships, and to more closely scrutinize legal and social policy issues that determine the success of cost-sharing reforms.

Institutions should be able to make choices from a wide range of policy options that can be adopted to ensure partnerships. More innovative financing mechanisms should be directed at improving both greater access for poor and vulnerable populations and greater quality assurance in higher education.

Public-private partnership models, including those that involve transnational collaboration, have a role in improving the external efficiency of higher education by creating innovative ways to offer new programs at reasonable costs. In some cases, governments provide land and infrastructure, with management and teaching handled by the private sector. Through such cost-sharing, colleges and universities can recover costs and ensure sufficient salaries to attract high-quality faculty members. In other cases, governments provided autonomy to private endeavors but set the upper limit on fees charged to students and ensured minimum standards. Whatever the case, possibilities of expanding private initiatives—consistent with public objectives—can be further explored. In some countries, public support remains essential where other actors are not available and where philanthropic initiatives can supplement the government-planned expansion of higher education.

Diversification and differentiation of institutions

System and institutional diversification is on the rise, as public higher education has to respond to a more complex set of socioeconomic development challenges. Diversification is seen not only among traditional colleges and universities, undergraduate education-focused institutions, and research universities, but also community-driven vocational and technical higher education, as well as tertiary distance education. As program needs become more differentiated, there is a need to examine a wider variety of cross-institutional articulation and funding options between public and private, domestic and cross-national, providers (Postiglione 2008).

Philanthropic ventures

Economic success in Asia has given birth to a spirit of generosity rooted in traditional values. The last decade has seen an exponential rise in the culture of philanthropy, and a significant part of this has been for the benefit of higher education. This has been the case more in some countries than others but the trend is unmistakable. There is a need to provide an environment of confidence about philanthropic partnerships by regulations that encourage involvement, provide accountability, and increase transparency, in order to help identify niches where fresh philanthropic partnership approaches can be launched to address needs in teaching, research, and service functions of colleges and universities.

Upgrading of research

Much of tomorrow's socioeconomic development will be inextricably tied to higher education, including funding for university research laboratories (Postiglione 2009e). This funding can be used to support research in science, technology, and medicine that aids poor communities, as well as research focused on the effects of climate change on the Asian environment (ecological, economic, social, etc.). The number and quality of research universities will increase. However, there is a need to consider strategic possibilities in an Asia-wide context. Research universities are the most expensive component of higher education, and their outputs are not always measurable in the short term. However, well-established research universities will become an indispensible part of regional integration into the global economy with important long-term contributions for facilitating innovation.

Regional strategies to attract international students

For many years, Asia has contributed the largest number of foreign students to colleges and universities in the United States, United Kingdom, continental Europe, Canada, and Australia (Raychaudhuri and De 2007). In anticipation of future recessions, countries in Asia can be more proactive in attracting international students from outside the region. Along with increased trade and economic cooperation, Asian countries can foster a flourishing trade in educational services. Intraregional mobility of students is increasing and forecast to expand further with rising levels of science and technology. One study of intraregional mobility revealed that "as East Asian markets have been experiencing increasing enrolments from other East Asian countries throughout this decade, some traditional destinations have experienced noticeable declines in enrolments from some major East Asian markets or a flattening of demand" (JWT Education 2008: 11). Universities in eastern Asia are now very active in recruiting international students (Table 12.1). Intraregional student mobility in eastern Asia over the medium to long term will continue to increase as the rate of student flows to Western countries slows. Tuition fees are between a quarter and a fifth of those in developed countries. Regional cooperation in this respect has advantages and collectively, Asian countries may be able to mitigate some of the impact of global recessions on their populations.

Conclusion

The global economic crisis has accelerated the need for Asian universities to engage internationally, and to create regional mechanisms through which students and faculty members can move more easily from one country to another. The reform of higher education is central to continued internationalization for economic and social development. Although the global recession has hit some Asian countries harder than others, the downturn constitutes an opportunity to move

Table 12.1 Outlook of international higher education students

Country	No. of students					Growth rate (%)
	2000	2005[a]	2010[b]	2020[b]	2025[b]	
China, People's Rep. of	218,437	437,109	760,103	1,937,129	2,973,287	11.0
Korea, Rep. of	81,370	96,681	114,269	155,737	172,671	3.1
India	76,908	141,691	271,193	502,237	629,080	8.8
Japan	66,097	65,872	68,544	71,974	73,665	0.4
Greece	60,486	68,285	75,339	84,608	89,903	1.6

Source: Bohm et al. (2004).
Top five source countries
[a] Estimated
[b] Forecast

forward with measures that will sustain the region's development. Moreover, as global universities continue to shape the world of higher education, regional partnerships among universities within eastern Asia constitute a potentially pivotal development (Wildavsky 2010). In this respect, some nations have already taken the lead. Among them are Singapore, Malaysia, Vietnam, China and others, covering the spectrum of developed and developing countries. In short, almost all are increasingly engaged in cross-border partnerships in higher education (Chapman et al. 2010). There has also been a gradual tilting of those more in the direction of regional partnerships among universities, although those with developed economies in the West still play a major role. However, such partnerships, whether East–West or regional, only moderately increased the access of poor and vulnerable populations to higher education, including during economic shocks.

Higher education in the eastern Asian region is approaching a historical moment in the sense that economic integration has reached a tipping point. The global recession provides an opportunity unlike any in the past 40 years to address the capacity of colleges and universities to serve poor and vulnerable populations. A measure of success in the next 40 years will be the extension of relevant higher-learning opportunities for all populations, especially those in the most remote ethnic communities of developing countries.

The global recession presents an opportunity to continue urgent reforms (Kuroda 2009). As the knowledge production and knowledge transfer systems of the region become as integrated as their economies, a highly collaborative layer of colleges and universities can promote high quality, international recognition and global competitiveness. Governments and international organizations can help identify a series of centers in the region that excel in particular aspects of higher education and that have the capacity to respond to the demands from across the region. However, it is also important to anticipate future Asia-wide challenges.

This paper highlights the importance of the global recession as an opportunity for new thinking about comprehensive reform in education. The longer that colleges and universities continue to underperform, the greater will be the negative impact on the economies in Asia. In fact, underperformance will only compound the effect of this and any future financial recession. The OECD has demonstrated that underperforming education systems can have disastrous consequences and significant negative impacts on national growth (ADB 2008b).

In the wake of the global recession and a return to a more stable financial environment, government responses that simply restore previous funding patterns for education will find limited improvement in outcomes. This was the case with OECD countries and there is little reason to assume this will not be the case in Asia (OECD 2009). Comprehensive policy and structural reforms in education can better ensure improved educational outcomes. Yet social protection measures remain important in the short run.

In the long term, however, broad based inclusiveness in education systems for the underserved populations, including basic, vocational-technical, and higher education, both regular and vocational-technical, is necessary to make a significantly positive impact on economic growth. This impact can be accomplished by identifying underserved, disadvantaged, and vulnerable populations, and by creating a link that allocates financial aid directly to specific cohorts, such that these cohorts maximize their learning potential, avoid the waste of talent in these populations, and build knowledge and skills capacity for a human resource base that improves social and economic development across Asian countries.

The global economy will continue to encounter and transverse recessions, each with a unique set of characteristics. Such economic shocks reveal the fragility of colleges and universities to serve poor and vulnerable populations. While we are becoming increasingly familiar with the causes of economic crises and recessions, there has been a relative paucity of effective ideas about how to move forward, especially for colleges and universities to build up institutional resilience in time to face future global or regional recessions.

The manner in which each economic shock affects capacity is constantly evolving, with differing and numerous features. This complicates the challenge of building capacity. It is an opportune time to establish one or more regional institutes to bring together practitioners from the public, private, and academic sectors on a regular basis to analyze patterns and connect theory and practice. The aim would be to anticipate, as much as possible; to analyze the implications of potential economic downswings; and to shape new thinking about preparations, responses, and strategies to sustain the capacity of colleges and universities for serving their increasingly diverse populations equitably with relevant and high-quality higher learning.

There is a new urgency to identify and remedy deficiencies with fresh approaches and innovative policy options that embed resilience in the region's rapidly expanding system of colleges and universities. While it will not be easy to find ways to insulate higher education capacity from future economic shocks, colleges and universities must remain free to carry out their mission, encourage new partnerships, and pool ingenuity to innovate while trying to stay one step ahead in the competitive environment of knowledge production and transfer. In short, the goal is to ensure that colleges and universities can cope with future uncertain economic times and flourish within them.

Open Access This article is distributed under the terms of the Creative Commons Attribution Noncommercial License which permits any noncommercial use, distribution, and reproduction in any medium, provided the original author(s) and source are credited.

Note

1 Bumiputras means princes of the Earth and embraces ethnic Malays and other indigenous ethnic groups in Malaysia, where Bumiputra laws are designed to provide opportunity for the majority ethnic Malay population to balance the economic dominance of Malaysia's Chinese population.

References

Ablett, J., & Slengesol, I.-A. (2001). Education in crisis: The impact and lessons of the East Asian financial shock 1997–99. Originally presented at the United Nations Educational, Scientific and Cultural Organization (UNESCO) World Education Forum, Dakar, 26–28 April 2000. Education for All 2000 Assessment, Thematic Studies coordinated by the World Bank. Paris: UNESCO.

ADB. (2008a). *Emerging Asian regionalism: A partnership of shared prosperity*. Manila: ADB. http://aric.adb.org/emergingasianregionalism/.

ADB. (2008b). *Education and skills. Strategies for accelerated development in Asia and the Pacific*. Manila: ADB. http://www.adb.org/Documents/Studies/Education-Skills-Strategies-Development/Education-Skills-Strategies-Development.pdf.

Altbach, P. A., & Balan, J. (Eds.). (2007). *World class worldwide: Transformaing research universities in Asia and Latin America*. Baltimore: Johns Hopkins University Press.

Altbach, P. A., & Umakoshi, T. (2004). *Asian universities: Historical perspectives and contemporary challenges*. Baltimore, MD: Johns Hopkins University Press.

Bohm, A., et al. (2004). *Forecasting international student mobility: A UK perspective*. London: British Council.

Cai, F., Wang, M. Y., & Wang, D. W. (2010). *The China and population and labor yearbook* (Vol. 2). Boston: Brill Academic Publishers.

Chapman, D. W., & Austin, A. E. (Eds.). (2002). *Higher education in developing countries: Changing contexts and institutional responses*. Westport: Greenwood Press.

Chapman, D. W., Cummings, W. K., & Postiglione, G. A., (Eds.). (2010). *Crossing borders in East Asian higher education*. Springer, Berlin.

Down, D. (2009). Vietnam: Transforming higher education. University World News, March 22. http://www.universityworldnews.com/article.php?story=20090320100538501 (Accessed on February 20, 2010).

Fegan, J., & Field, M. H. (2009). *Education across borders: Politics, policy and legislative action*. Berlin: Springer.

Feinberg, R. (2000). "Asians Seek Their 'Made-in Asia' Solutions," Seoul: Korea Herald, July 5, 2000, (http://www.koreaherald.co.kr).

Glewwe, P., & Kremer, M. (2006). Schools, teachers, and education outcomes in developing countries. In E. Hanushek & F. Welch (Eds.), *Handbook of the economics of education* (Vol. 2). Amsterdam: North-Holland.

Government of Mongolia. (2006). *Master plan to develop education in Mongolia in 2006–2015*. Ulaanbaatar: Government of Mongolia.

Harman, G., Hayden, M., & Nghi, P. T., (Eds.). (2010). *Reforming higher education in Vietnam: Challenges and promises*. Dordrecht: Springer Press.

Hassan, A. (2001). Impact of the economic crisis on Malaysia. In N. V. Varghese (Ed.), *Implications of the economic crisis on higher education in East Asia: Country experiences*. Paris: International Institute for Educational Planning (IIEP)/UNESCO.

Huang, F. (2006). *Transnational higher education in Asia and the Pacific*. Hiroshima, Japan: Research Institute for Higher Education.

Huong, P. L., & Fry, G. W. (2004). Universities in Vietnam: Legacies, challenges and prospects. In P. A. Altbach & T. Umakoshi (Eds.), *Asian Universities: Historical perspectives and contemporary challenges*. Baltimore, MD: Johns Hopkins University Press.

Hvistendahl, M. (2009). Presidents of Asian Universities call for more international partnerships. *The Chronicle of Higher Education, 55*(34), 22.

International Labor Organization (ILO). (1998). The social impact of the Asian financial crisis. Technical report for discussion at the high-level tripartite meeting on social responses to the financial crisis in East and South-East Asian Countries, ILO Regional Office for Asia and the Pacific Bangkok, Bangkok, 22–24 April.

Jimenez, E. (2010). Higher education graduates in East Asia: Too few? Too many? Retrieved 16th, November, 2010, from https://blogs.worldbank.org/eastasiapacific/node/2898.

Johnston, D. B. (2004). The Economics and politics of cost sharing in higher education: Comparative perspective. *Economics of Education Review, 23*(4), 403–410.

JWT Education. (2008). International student mobility in East Asia. British Council, February. http://www.britishcouncil.org/eumd-information-research-east-asia-student-mobility.htm (accessed on February 20, 2010).

Katada, S. N., & Solis, M. (2008). Permeated regionalism in East Asia: Cross-regional trade agreements in theory and Practice. In S. N. Katada & M. Solis (Eds.), *Cross regional trade agreements: Understanding permeated regionalism in East Asia* (pp. 1–26). Dordrecht: Springer Science+Business Media.

Kuroda, H. (2009). Time to make Asian regionalism a reality. *The Straits Times* (Singapore). 12 September.

Lee, J.-W., & Rhee, C. (1999). Social impacts of the Asian crisis. http://ideas.repec.org/p/snu/ioerwp/no2.html (accessed February 20, 2010).

Lee, M. (2004). *Restructuring higher education in Malaysia*. Penang: Universiti Sains Malaysia, School of Education.

Lee, M., & Healy, S. (2006). *Higher education in Southeast Asia: An overview in higher education in Southeast Asia*. Bangkok: UNESCO.

Mok, K.-h. (2006). *Educational reform and educational policy in East Asia*. London: Taylor and Francis.

Mok, K.-h. (2008). *Changing governance and public policy in East Asia*. London: Routledge.

Organisation for Economic Co-operation and Development (OECD). (2009). *Education at a glance*. Paris: OECD. www.oecd.org/dataoecd/32/34/43541373.pdf (accessed 20 February 2010).

Patton, D. (2009). China: Pressure to improve graduate job skills. *University World News*. 5 July (Issue 0083). http://www.universityworldnews.com/article.php?story=20090702190256276 (accessed February 18, 2010).

Picus, J. (2009). Vietnam: Sustaining growth in difficult times. ASEAN Economic Bulletin. April. http://findarticles.com/p/articles/mi_hb020/is_1_26/ai_n32149050/pg_10/?tag=content;col1 (accessed February 20, 2010).

Pomfret, R. (2010). Regionalism in East Asia: Why has it flourished since 2000 and how far will it go? (World Scientific Publishers).

Postiglione, G. (2005). Higher Education in China: Perils and promises for a new century. *Harvard China Review*. Spring: 138–43.

Postiglione, G. (2006). Finance and governance in Southeast Asian higher education. In B. C. Sanyal & M. Martin (Eds.), *Higher education in the world, 2006: The financing of universities*. New York, NY: Palgrave.

Postiglione, G. (2008). 亚洲跨径高等教育转型 [Transformations in Transnational Higher Education]. 高等教育學會,第29卷,第21-31頁 [*Journal of Higher Education* 29: 21-31].

Postiglione, G. (2009a). *China's International Partnerships and Cross-Border Cooperation. Chinese Education and Society. Volume 42. Number 4, pp. 3–10.* New York, NY: M.E. Sharpe Publishers.

Postiglione, G. (2009b). Community Colleges in China's Two Systems. In R. L. Raby & E. Valeau (Eds.), *Community College Models: Globalization and Higher Education Reform.* Amsterdam: Springer Press.

Postiglione, G. (2009c). Institutionalizing the Community College Associate Degree in Hong Kong, with Stephen Kwok. In P. A. Elsner (Ed.), *A global survey of community colleges, technical colleges, and further education in different regions of the world.* Washington, DC: American Association of Community Colleges Press.

Postiglione, G. (2009d). China's community colleges: Remolding a model to meet transitional challenges, with D. Watkins and L. Wang. In P. A. Elsner (Ed.), *A global survey of community colleges, technical colleges, and further education in different regions of the world.* Washington, DC: American Association of Community Colleges Press.

Postiglione, G. (2009e). Establishing a research university: The case of the Hong Kong university of science and technology. Presentation at The Third International Conference on World Class Universities, Shanghai Jiaotong University, Shanghai, China, 1–5 November.

Postiglione, G. (2010). Mongolia's challenge: Becoming Asian in higher education. *International Higher Education.* Chestnut Hill, MA: Boston College Center for International Higher Education, No. 60: 20–21.

Postiglione, G., & Tan, J. (2007). *Going to school in East Asia.* New York, NY: Greenwood Press.

Postiglione, G., & Wang, S. R. (Forthcoming). Governance of the academy in Hong Kong. In: Locke, W., & Cummings, W. (Eds.), *The changing academic profession.* New York: Springer Press.

Purwadi, A. (2001). Impact of the economic crisis on Indonesia. In N. V. Varghese (Ed.), *Implications of the economic crisis on higher education in East Asia: Country experiences.* Paris: IIEP/UNESCO.

Qiwen, L. (2009). Most college students in Guangdong still await offers. *China Daily.* 20 March.

Radelet, S., J. D. Sachs, R. N. Cooper, B. P. Bosworth (1998). The East Asian financial crisis: diagnosis, remedies, prospects. Brookings Papers on Economic Activity, Vol. 1998, No. 1. (1998), pp. 1–90. Stable URL: http://links.jstor.org/sici?sici=0007–230 3%281998%291998%3A1%3C1%3ATEAFCD%3E2.0.CO%3B2–5).

Raychaudhuri, A., & De, P. (2007). Assessing barriers to trade in education services in developing Asia—Pacific Countries: An empirical exercise. Asia-Pacific Research and Training Network on Trade (ARTNeT) Working Paper 34. Toronto: ARTNeT, an initiative of UNESCAP and IDRC, Canada.

Reuters. (2010). http://www.reuters.com/article/idUSTRE5062AD20090107 accessed February 17, 2010.

Roberts, D. (2010). A dearth of work for China's college grads more than a quarter of the Class of 2010 has yet to find work, Bloomberg Businessweek.

Sakamoto, R., & Chapman, D. W. (2011). *Cross-border partnerships in higher education: Strategies and lessons.* New York and London: Routledge Press.

Sakellariou, C. (2010). Labor market outcomes of higher education in East Asia. From http://siteresources.worldbank.org/INTEASTASIAPACIFIC/Resources/EastAsia-LaborMarketOutcomesofHE.pdf.

Salmi, J., & Bassett, R. M. (2009). *Impact of the financial crisis.* Washington, DC: The World Bank. September 9.

Sarvi, J. (2008). Higher education in Asia and the Pacific region: Issues of financing and partnerships, particularly from the perspective of access, equity, quality, and diversity of higher education. Paper presented at the Asia-Pacific Subregional Preparatory Conference for the 2009 World Conference on higher education, Macau, China, 24–26 September.

Southeast Asian Ministers of Education Organization (SEAMEO). (2005). *Long range planning for higher education.* Bangkok: SEAMEO Regional Center for Higher Education and Development.

Task Force on Higher Education and Society. (2000). *Higher education in developing countries: Perils and promise.* Washington, DC: The World Bank.

Tilak, J. B. G. (2004). Absence of policy and perspective in higher education. *Economics and Political Weekly, 39*(21), 59–64.

UNESCO. (2003). *Higher education in Asia and the Pacific 1998–2003: Regional progress on implementing the recommendations of the 1998 World Conference on higher education.* Paris: UNESCO Asia and the Pacific Regional Bureau for Education.

UNESCO. (2004). *Indicators of quality and facilitating academic mobility through quality assurance agencies in the Asia-Pacific Region.* Bangkok: UNESCO and Thailand National Accreditation Council.

Varghese, N. V. (2001). *Implications of the economic crisis on higher education in East Asia: Country experiences.* Paris: IIEP/UNESCO.

Wildavsky, B. (2010). The great brain race: How global universities are reshaping the world. Princeton: Princeton University Press.

Woodhall, M. (2007). *Funding higher education: The contribution of economic thinking to debate and policy development. World Bank Working Paper Series 8.* Washington, DC: World Bank.

World Bank. (2002). *Constructing knowledge societies.* Washington DC: World Bank.

World Bank. (2008). World development indicators. www.worldbank.org/data (accessed February 27, 2010).

World Bank. (2009a). *Battling the forces of global recession. East Asia and Pacific Update. April.* Washington, DC: World Bank.

World Bank (2009b). Vietnam new-model universities project. http://web.worldbank.org/external/projects/main?Projectid=P110693&Type=News&theSitePK=40941&pagePK=64308295&menuPK=64282138& piPK=64309265 (accessed October 13).

World Bank (2009c). *Higher education development policy program project information document P104694.* Washington, DC: World Bank. http://www.wds.worldbank.org/external/default/WDSContentServer/WDSP/IB/2009/03/07/000104615_20090309100532/Rendered/PDF/HEDPP0PID0Appraisal.pdf (accessed September 10, 2009).

Zhou, M., & Lin, J. (2009). Chinese graduates' employment: the impact of the financial crisis. *International Higher Education* (55) Spring.

Ziderman, A. (2004). *Policy options for student loan schemes: Lessons from five Asian countries.* Bangkok: UNESCO and Paris: IIEP.

Index

academic corruption 45, 160n50, 220, 225
academic freedom: China vs. Hong Kong 152–3, 156, 202; governance and 152–3; Hong Kong and 146–8; protection of 6, 190, 191
academic staff: attracting back 188, 200–1; attributes/attitudes 150–4; China vs. Hong Kong 150–4; HKUST 193–5, 200–1, 214n13; salaries 214n14; as success factor 212–13
Academy of Performing Arts 147, 165
adaptation 212
Africa 169
African Americans 82, 115
alternative strategies 62–3
American International University 247
amphibious entrepreneurs: benefit to research universities 180, 182–3; Woo, Chie-wei 176; Chung, S.Y. 178; as key resource 161, 162; UGC membership 168
ASEAN University Network (AUN) 247, 251
Asian Development Bank 3, 7
Asian financial crisis 44, 236–9; *see also* economy
Asian Monetary Fund 239
Asian Tigers 62, 164, 165, 187
Asia Pacific Quality Network (APQN) 247
Asia Week 196
assimilationist theory 88; *see also* processes, pluralism and assimilation
attracting back staff 188, 200–1
Australia: academic internationalism 145; boarding schools 4, 114–15, 133–4; emotions evoked 114–15; international students 258; presidential search 197; receiving international students 146;

research collaboration 169, 170; UGC membership 148
autonomy: balancing 220–1, 223; China vs. Hong Kong 149; committee formation 149; debate over 43; education and HK future 13; ethnic minority culture transmission 70, 107–8; expanding 217, 219; global recession impact 252; government steering and 167–9, 225; HKUST 178, 190, 200, 208; Hong Kong 51, 146; infancy state 224; inverted academic culture and governance 225; national rejuvenation and global influence 220–3; natural limitations 148; policy intervention points 14; preserving 145–6; protected by law 18, 43, 69, 146, 181, 190; reform outline 45; regional, educational matters 117; research universities 167–9; SAR 51; Taiwan 52; taking responsibility 225; universities 145–6, 148–9, 163

Bai, Chunli 181
balance 7, 217–31
Baptist College *see* Hong Kong Baptist University
Beijing International Financial Center 208
Beijing Normal University 77, 86, 199
Beijing University 28
"be unique and not duplicate" 199
boarding schools: ethnicity elimination 4; gender and ethnicity 120–1; historical background 4; indigenous people 127; origin and development 119–33; policy of 4; Tibet 101–6, 114–15; Uyghur students 85; Xinjiang 85, 119, 131
boys *see* gender
brain circulation 161–2, 169, 175, 178, 180–3; *see also* globalization

brain drain 167, 204
brain power 225
Britain 17, 20, 57, 107, 145–6
Brunei 49, 57–8
Buddhism 55, 122, 131
Bumputra 237, 260n1
Burns, John 24

Cai, Yuanpei 217
Cambodia 49, 59, 250
Canada: academic internationalism 145; boarding schools 4, 114–15, 133–4; HKUST case 178; international students 258; knowledge networks 178; presidential search 197; receiving international students 146
Cantonese *see* medium of instruction
capitalism to socialism *see* Hong Kong education, transitional society
Carnegie Foundation 169
cattle-rancher households 243, 250
Central China University of Nationalities 86
Centre for Marine Environmental Research and Innovation Technology collaboration 177, 212
Cha, Louis 31n3
Chan, Yuk-Shee 202
challenges: knowledge networks 6; multiculturalism 89; professoriate 5–6, 179; religion and language 130; research universities 223–5; Tibet, cultural heritage 95; unemployment rate 249
Chan, Tony 189
Chan, Yuk-Shee 203
Chang, Leroy 202
Changing Academic Profession project 7, 169
Chen, Jay-Chung 202
Chien, Chih-Yung 202
China: attracting students 242; challenges, harmonious multiculturalism 94–110; economic crisis response 238, 241–3; education of ethnic minority groups 69–77; education system 49, 51, 55, 60–2; ethnic minority identity and educational outcomes 82–9; global recession 240, 241–3; higher education 44–6, 240, 241–3; as model 51; nation-building education strategy 15; partnerships 259; primary and secondary schools 38–9; research universities 217–18, 225–30; "ripening" universities 186, 190; second system 225–30; underachievement 75; unemployment 241–3; unity 3, 82, 108, 117
China, search for balanced model: challenges 223–5; China's second system 225–30; conclusion 230–1; governance 226–30; higher education expansion 219; institutional autonomy 220–3; internationalization 220–3; inverted culture and governance 225–30; overview 7; quality and quantity balance 217; reform 219–20; research and teaching as driver 223–5; state sovereignty 220–3; transitioning 218–20; unique model 217–18
China's National Minority Education: Culture, Schooling and Development 4–5
Chinese Education and Society 84
Chinese Medicine collaborations 177, 212
Chineseness, dual identity 16
Chinese University of Hong Kong: background 147; collaborations 177, 205; HKUST comparison 214n6; language of instruction 198–9; as top-tier research university 165
"Chinglish" 25
Christian influence 4, 55, 56, 74
Chu, Paul 175, 189, 206, 214n8
Chung, S.Y. 178, 196, 197, 205
Ciechanover, Aaron 176, 206
City Polytechnic of Hong Kong 196
City University of Hong Kong 148, 165
civics education 15
civilizing mission, education as 29, 74, 94, 107, 114, 127–8
Code of Aid 19
collaborations: anchoring globalization 180–1; balancing 221; cross-border type 252; expanding 236, 238; government facilitation of 162–3; grants for 168; HKUST 175, 191–2, 205, 207–8; patterns 169–74; promotions 247; regional type 238; research capacity management 177; Sino-foreign 242; transnational 240, 252, 256; Vietnam 247–8
Collaborative Research Fund (CRF) 168
colonial heritage impact 51–2
commencement, HKUST 195–8
community-based educational needs: global recession and higher education 255
Comparative Education Review 1, 5
competition 126–7, 175, 223

Index

compulsory education 41, 51, 53, 60, 62, 72, 97–8
Confucianism 29–30, 35, 52, 55, 217–18; *see also* religion
construction, HKUST 196–7
contexts: culture and identity 29–30; decolonization 20–2; democratization 22–3; education 35–46; ethnic minority groups 42–4; HKUST 191–2, 210–11; Hong Kong 13–34, 191–2; interdependence 27–9; localization 24–6; overview 1–2; processes 20–30; reforms 49–63; social classes structuralization 26–7; transitional society 13–34
contradictions resolution 17
Control of Pandemic and Inter-Pandemic Influenza collaboration 177, 208
corporal punishment 104, 127, 134
corporate responsibilities 242, 254
cost overruns 196–7
cost-sharing 256–7
counties *see* prefectures and counties
creativity, fostering 37, 45, 163, 174, 193, 220, 222–5
credentials 155–6
Croucher Foundation 207
cultural backwardness: educational attainment 44; negative perception of 74; saliency 75; state education policies 73; underachievement, myth of 70, 107
Cultural Revolution 16, 36, 88, 96, 118–19, 150
Cultural Tibet 118
culture: contextual processes 29–30; inverted 225–30; research capacity management 177–8
curriculum: broadening for liberal thinking 45; changes 15; political consciousness 23
cyberport establishment 197, 213n3
Cyrillic alphabet 55, 100

Dalai Lama 96, 118
death 129
decentralization 119
Decision of the State Council to Further Strengthen Education in Rural Areas 42
decolonization processes 13–14, 20–2, 146, 154
degree-o-cratic society 53
Democratic People's Republic of Korea (DPRK) 54
democratization 14, 17, 22–3, 45, 146

Deng, Xiaoping 1, 36, 88
Developmental Genomics and Skeletal Research collaboration 177, 212
Dewey, John 36
Director of Education 18–19, 24
dislocated education: background 116–19; considerations 123–7; development and origins 119–33; dislocating 127–30; ethnicity 120; gender 120; language 121; methodology 122–3; overview 4–5, 114–16; prefectures and counties 121; preferential education policies 101–6; rate of capital returns 133–6; region 121; relocating back to Tibet 131–3; saliency of ethnic identity 133–6; school environment 121–2; social composition of graduates 120–1
diversification and differentiation 257
Dobson, Peter 203
donations *see* funding and donations
donor culture 176–7
drop-out rates: ethnic minority education 72, 84; junior secondary school 95; labouring at home 97; plurality of reasons 62; rural-urban gap 40–1, 44; and school violence 54; Thailand 237; Tibetans 75, 95
Duke University 222
duoyuan yiti geju 3, 88, 117

East Asia 46–63; *see also specific country*
East China Normal University 222
economy and economic shocks/crises: capacity limitations on education 235; China, Mongolia, and Vietnam 8, 235–60; effects of 236–8; global recession and higher education 240–8; and higher education 219, 251–4; interdependence 27–8; lessons learned 253–4; overview 7; social class structuralization 26–7; surge in prosperity 189
education: China *vs.* Hong Kong priorities 153–4; conclusion 46; expansion of opportunities 37; higher education 44–6; historical developments 35–8; inequalities in system 36; overview 2, 35; primary schools 38–9; rural-urban divide 39–42; secondary schools 38–9
education, ethnic minority groups: basic situation 71–2; concepts 72–3; contexts 42–4; cultural processes, pluralism and assimilation 69–77; harmonious

multiculturalism 77; journals 77; overview 3, 69–71; policies 72–3; research on 74–7
educational challenges, multiculturalism 3–4, 94–110
educational policy 17–30
Educational Review 4
Education and Social Change in China: Inequality in a Market Economy 2
Education Commission's Report Number Three 21
elites 18, 30, 70, 87
Elliot, Charles 186
enabling environment 164–7
endowments 206
England 107, 170, 197
English language *see* medium of instruction
enrollments 5, 97, 244
entrepreneurial spirit 178, 183, 223–4, 238
Entrepreneurship Center 208
environment, working 201–2
equalizer, schooling as 50–1
establishment, HKUST 186–7, 188, 208–9
ethnic autonomous areas 5; *see also* autonomy
ethnicity: boarding schools 4, 120–1; dislocated education 120, 133–6; minority groups *(shaoshu minzu)* 71; *minzu vs. zucun* 83
ethnic minority groups, education: basic situation 71–2; concepts 72–3; contexts 42–4; cultural processes, pluralism and assimilation 69–77; harmonious multiculturalism 77; number of 117; overview 3, 69–71; policies 72–3; research literature review 74–7
ethnic minority groups, identity and educational outcomes: case studies 84–7; conclusion 89; education policy 83; introduction 3, 82–3; pluralism 87–9; sociology of 83–4
ethnic symbols 122
Europe: events in Eastern 13; ideals 30; international students 219, 236, 258; Ireland 70, 107; literacy level 56; research collaboration 169
expansion, higher education: China 44–6; global recession and higher education 238–40; multiple polarities 37–8; national rejuvenation and global influence 219; nation-building educational strategy 15

faculty/student ratio 194–5; *see also* academic staff
family: background tied to school achievement 27; communication with 129, 135; view of education 35
Fei, Xiaotong 3, 73, 76, 88, 117
females *see* gender
Financial Times 196
focus 212
Fok Ying Tung Graduate School 205
foodstuffs 27, 42, 98, 128
"forcible assimilation" 115, 137n8
foreign nationals 24, 202
four- *vs.* three-year system 20–1, 167, 191–2, 199–200
freedom *see* academic freedom
freedom of expression 160n50
Fudan University 45, 220
funding and donations: degree-granting institutions 165; government allocation 190–1; HKUST 187, 206–7, 211–13; management of 176–7
future outlook 13–14

gaokao 222
gender: boarding schools 120–1; Cambodia 59; China *vs.* Hong Kong 149; dislocated education 120; disparities in regions 72; Timor Leste 58; urban-rural education divide 39–42
Genghis Kahn 54–5
Germany 181
gifted students 38–9
Gini coefficient 26, 83
Gird coefficient 52
girls *see* gender
glass ceiling 202
global engagement, national integration: academic staff attributes/attitudes 150–4; China's professoriate 149–50; context 146–9; governance and academic freedom 152–3; higher education priorities 153–4; Hong Kong context and 146–9; Hong Kong *vs.* global academy 155–6; international academic activity 154; overview 5–6, 145–6; research activity 152; student quality 151–2; universities 146–54
globalization, anchoring in research universities: collaborations 169–74, 177; conclusions 180–3; culture capital access 177–8; enabling environment 164–7; funds management in donor culture

176–7; governance 167–9, 178; growth 162–3; institutional autonomy 167–9; internationalization 177; introduction 6, 161–2; knowledge networks 174–6; partnerships 177; planning 178; research capacity management 175–80; risk-taking 178; social capital access 177–8; take-off phase 175–6; talent, recruiting and sustaining 178–80
global rankings *see* rankings
global recession and higher education: China 240, 241–3; community-based educational needs 255; conclusions 258–60; cost-sharing 256–7; diversification and differentiation 257; economic crises response 251–4; economic shocks 240–8; expansion 238–40; income groups disproportionately affected 249–51; information and guidance 255; international students, attracting 258; labor markets 255; lessons learned 253–4; loans 254–5; Mongolia 240, 243–5; overview 7–8, 235; performance-based measures 256; philanthropic ventures 257; recessions 238–40, 248–51; recommendations 254–5; reform 240–8; regional integration 238–40; subsidies for students 254–5; tuition assistance 254–5; upgrading of research 257; Vietnam 240, 245–8
goals and objectives, HKUST 192–3, 212
"Gong Ren Zhi Gong" 17
Goodbird, Edward 134
governance: and academic freedom 152–3; Changing Academic Profession project 7; China *vs.* Hong Kong 152–3; factor of success 212; HKUST 199–200, 204–6; innovations in 199–200; inverted academic culture 225–30; national rejuvenation and global influence 226–30; over-administration 224–5; research capacity management 178
government steering 163, 167–9, 225
graduates: dislocated education 120–1; lack of skills 242; unemployment 16, 45, 71, 241–3, 249
Great Leap period 96
Guangdong province 74, 180, 208
Guanxi 117
guarantees: compulsory education 41; freedom of religion 89; government budget 243; jobs in Tibet 105, 126, 135; preferential education policies 98–9, 120; productive employment 255; "three guarantees" 98–9, 109n10

Habibie 58
Hang Lung Group donations 207
Hang Seng Bank 207
Hang Seng Index 245
Hanoi University of Science and Technology (HUST) 247
hardware elements 220, 231
harmonious multiculturalism *see* multiculturalism
heart 212–13
hegemony *vs.* self-determination 60–1
higher education: global recession 219, 238–40; national rejuvenation and global influence 219; priorities 153–4; reform 240–8; *see also specific area*
Higher Education 7, 8
Hinterland Schools 109n9, 114
historical antecedents 96–7
HKUST (Hong Kong University of Science and Technology): academic staff 193–5, 200–1; characteristics of 192–3; collaborations 207–8; conclusions 207–9; construction 196–7; context 191–2, 210–11; donations and funding 195, 206–7, 211–13; elements of 198–208; establishment 208–9; global rankings 192; goals and objectives 192–3; governance 199–200, 204–6; inauguration and commencement 195–8; innovations in governance 199–200; internationalization 207–8; inverted academic culture and governance 226; key factors 187–91; language of instruction 191, 198–9; models 210; multigenerational recruitment 202–3; overview 6, 165, 186–7; partnerships 207–8; planning 196–7, 208–9; presidential search 197–8; rankings 192, 198–9; recruitment 202–3, 209; research funding 206–7, 211–13; roles 192–3; students 193–5; sustainability 209–10; timing 203–4; working environment 201–2
Hong Kong: education system of 49; knowledge networks 178; medium of instruction 181–2; political system 14–15; research collaboration 170; values and traditional practices 50

Hong Kong, global engagement and national integration: academic staff attributes/attitudes 150–4; China's professoriate 149–50; context 146–9; governance and academic freedom 152–3; higher education priorities 153–4; Hong Kong vs. global academy 155–6; international academic activity 154; overview 5–6, 145–60; research activity 152; student quality 151–2; universities 146–54

Hong Kong, research universities and globalization: collaborations 169–74, 177; conclusions 180–3; culture capital access 177–8; enabling environment 164–7; funds management in donor culture 176–7; governance 167–9, 178; growth 162–3; institutional autonomy 167–9; internationalization 177; introduction 6, 161–2; knowledge networks 174–6; partnerships 177; planning 178; research capacity management 175–80; risk-taking 178; social capital access 177–8; take-off phase 175–6; talent, recruiting and sustaining 178–80

Hong Kong Academy of Performing Arts 147, 165

Hong Kong Baptist University 148, 165, 199

Hong Kong education, transitional society: contextual processes 20–30; contradictions resolution 17; culture 29–30; decolonization 20–2; democratization 22–3; educational policy 17–30; future outlook 13–14; identity 29–30; interdependence 27–9; legitimacy 18–19; localization 24–6; overview 1, 13; policy intervention, transfer of power 14–15; Sino-British Declaration 17–19; social classes structuralization 26–7

"Hongkongeseness," dual identity 16

Hong Kong Institute of Education 165

Hong Kong JC see Jockey Club charities

Hong Kong Polytechnic University 148

Hong Kong Telecom 176, 206

Hong Kong University 21, 147, 165, 177, 219

household savings 250

Hu, Qili 101, 137

Hue University 248

humanities requirement 187, 192

Hysan Trust Fund 207

IBM donations 207

identity: oppositional 74; saliency 133–6; Xinjing 89

identity, contextual processes 29–30

inauguration, HKUST 195–8

inclusive education 38–9

income groups disproportionately affected 249–51

India: Dalai Lama 118; dislocation 126; education system 55; globalization impact 186; international students 96; knowledge networks 170; research collaboration 170; "ripening" universities 186, 190; tertiary education 20

indigenous people 127, 133–6; see also specific country

Indonesia: context and reform 46; economic crisis response 237, 238; education system 55, 58; medium of instruction 59; private universities 244, 250; public universities 249; research collaboration 170

Inner Mongolia 55, 86, 117

Inner Mongolia Normal University 86

Innovation and Technology Commission 177, 207

innovations in governance 199–200

innovative thinking, fostering 45

Institute Faculty Members (permanent) 176, 206

Institute of Advanced Study (IAS) 176, 189, 206

Institute of Molecular Technology for Drug Discovery and Synthesis collaboration 177, 212

institutional arrangements see globalization

institutional autonomy see autonomy

institutional diversification 257

integrated scholarship 226

interdependence 27–9

international academic activity 154

International Financial Education and Training Center 208

internationalization: HKUST 207–8; national rejuvenation and global influence 220–3; research capacity management 177

international students, attracting 258; see also students

Internet 145, 251

inverted culture and governance 225–30

involuntary minorities 117
Ireland 70, 107
Islam 55, 57–8

James, Gregory 203
Japan: education system 49, 52–3, 60–2; medium of instruction 181; private universities enrollment 244; rankings 49; research collaboration 169, 170; values and traditional practices 50
JC *see* Jockey Club charities
JEOL donations 207
Jiang, Zemin 106, 219
Jiaotong University 45, 199, 218, 220, 222
Jockey Club charities 176, 196, 206, 214n11
Joint Declaration 23, 24
Joint University Programs Admission System (JUPAS) 193
Journal of Research on Ethnic Minority Education 76, 84

Keane University 222
Keio University 245
Kenya 20
Kerry Group donations 207
Khmer Rouge rule 59
knowledge networks: anchoring globalization 180–2; building 179; challenges 6; elevation 176; emerging partners for 170; establishment 174–5, 177; HKUST 176–9; initiatives 168; international 169, 174; management of 161–3, 165–6; network brokers 162, 168, 182; unencumbered 162
Knowledge Transfer Report 208
knowledge transmission *vs.* wealth 218
Korea and Koreans: attracting back staff 201; case studies 85; education system 60–2; enabling environment 164; medium of instruction 181; model minority 87; private universities enrollment 244; values and traditional practices 50, 53; *see also* South Korea
Kublai Khan 55
Kung, Shain-Dow 202
Kyoto University 198

labor markets *see* markets
language: boarding schools 121; as contested area 132–3; dislocated education 121; exception 214n12; HKUST context 191, 198–9; *see also* medium of instruction

Laos 49, 59
Latin America 169
launching new universities 186, 190
Lee, Chu Ming 31n3
Lee, Kai-fu 224
Lee, Q.W. 197
left-behind children *(liushou ertong)* 40–2
"Leftist School Leavers Gain Acceptance" 31n15
legitimacy 18–19, 26
lessons learned 253–4
Levin, Richard 223
liberal arts 6, 176
Lin, Otto C.C. 202
Lingnan College/University 148, 165
liushou ertong 40–1
Liverpool University 199, 222
Li Wing Tat Family 207
loans 254–5
localization 24–6
"Love Tibet" 129–30, 138n25
Luoba ethnic group 109n3

Ma, Jack 224
Ma, Rong 76
Macao 50, 52, 106
Malaysia: colonial heritage 52; economic crisis response 237, 238; education system 55, 57; enabling environment 164; medium of instruction 181; partnerships 259; research collaboration 170
males *see* gender
Management Reviews 205
Manchu Era 87, 107
Mandarin 25–6, 36; *see also* medium of instruction
Mao Zedong 36, 51
markets: annual recalibration 2; global recession and higher education 255; management of 37; overlapping and shifting demands 37, 72–3
Maskin, Eric 176, 206
massification 45, 49, 255
medium of instruction: boarding schools 121; changing, difficulties of 181; China *vs.* Hong Kong 152; civil service recruitment 25; education system 56; HKUST 191, 198–9; policies 25–6; preferential education policies 99–101; Tibet 95, 99–101; Timor Leste 59; universities 147
meritocratic ideology 27
migrants, children of 40–2

military, lack of 15
miniban see private *(miniban)* schools/ colleges
Minzu jiaoyu yanjiu 76, 84
mobility, academic staff 182
models 210
Moinba ethnic group 109n3
monasteries 55, 75, 96, 116, 118–19
Mongol Era 87, 107
Mongolia: attracting back staff 201; case studies 85–6; "decorated," marginalized culture 86; education system of 49, 54–5; global recession response 240, 243–5; minority educational policies 117; private universities enrollment 244
multiculturalism, harmonious: challenges 89; dislocated education 101–6; education, ethnic minority groups 77; historical antecedents 96–7; introduction 94, 108n1; medium of instruction 99–101; policies and practices 3; preferential education policies 97–106; targets 96–7; three guarantees 98–9; Tibetan civilization 106–8; urgency of basic education 94–7
multi-generational recruitment 202–3
Mushkat, Myron 24
Muslim *see* Islam
Myanmar 49

National Outline for Medium- and Long-term Education Reform and Development 35, 38, 45, 224
natural resources, lack of 166
Naxis 3, 74, 85–7
neidi schools *see* boarding schools
Nepal 83
network agents *see* globalization
network brokers 162, 168, 182
New Culture Movement 36
New-Model Universities Project 247
New York University 222
Ningxia 117
nomadic regions 95
noninterventionism 15
North Korea 49, 53, 54
nutrition 42, 98

objectives, HKUST 192–3
Ogbu, John 4, 76
Okayama University 248
one-country, two-system arrangement 13, 16, 30, 146, 161, 191

Open Learning University 147, 148, 165
Opium Wars 20, 35
oppositional identities 74
Oprah Winfrey's Leadership Academy for Girls 136n1, 138n28
oral histories, graduates of *neidi* schools 122–33

Panchen Lama 122
parents *see* family
partnerships 177, 207–8, 259
passports 24–5, 145–6, 155, 188
Pearl River Delta 146, 177, 207–8
Peking University 45, 177, 208, 217–19, 220, 224
performance-based measures 256
philanthropic ventures 257
Philippines: economic crisis response 237; education system 55, 56; private universities enrollment 244; research collaboration 170
Ping Ko 202
plagiarism 225
planned economy 38, 45, 56, 73, 135
planning 178, 196–7, 208–9
plurality: Hong Kong schools 17; important as harmony 69; "pluralism within unity" 3, 108, 117; social context 73; *see also* processes, pluralism and assimilation
policies and politics: centralized/decentralized system 19; education, ethnic minority groups 72–3; educational 17–30; Hong Kong's future 14–15; intervention, transfer of power 14–15
PRC (People's Republic of China): academic staff 150; Chia-wei Woo influence 176; China Dream promotion 7; establishment 164; ethnic autonomous areas 5; one country/two-system arrangement 145; political Tibet 118; universities acquisition 145
prefectures and counties: appointments 72; boarding schools 121; dislocated education 121
preferential policies: dislocated education 101–6; ethnic minorities 71; ethnic minority education 83; harmonious multiculturalism 97–106; Mongol students 86; overview 7
presidential search, HKUST 197–8
principal, absolute power 19

private capital as root cause 250
Private Education Promotion Law 39
private *(miniban)* schools/colleges 39, 45, 126
processes, pluralism and assimilation: dislocated education 114–38; education, ethnic minority groups 69–77; ethnic minority identity and educational outcomes 82–9; overview 2–5; Tibet 114–38
professoriate: autonomy 5; challenges 5–6, 179; global engagement, national integration 149–50; student/faculty ratio 194–5
professorship, named 206
Projects: 211 and 985 45, 220, 224; Changing Academic Profession 7, 169; New-Model Universities 247; Second Higher Education 247
provincial level 72
Provisional Council of Academic Accreditation 16
Putonghua see Mandarin

Qian, Xuesen 223
Qing Dynasty 7, 35–6, 51, 130
Qinghua University 28
qualifications, faculty 151
quality and quantity balance 217–18
quality indicators 256

rankings: framework popularity 218; globalization 7, 46, 214n7; HKUST 192, 198–9, 221; international attention of 220; management of knowledge networks 161; research & development budget 166, 206; stereotype education 49
rate of capital returns 133–6
rate of return 95
recession: historical developments 236–8; impact on higher education 248–51; integration and higher education expansion 238–40; stifling national initiatives 7–8; *see also* economy and economic shocks/crises
recommendations 254–5
recruitment 188, 202–3, 209; *see also* talent
reforms: China, ethnic pluralism 88–9; core-periphery relevance 2, 60–3; decentralization 119; explanatory frameworks 60–3; global recession and higher education 240–8; national rejuvenation and global influence 219–20; opportunities for comprehensive 259; overview 2, 49–60
regional integration 238–40
religion 74, 89, 118, 129–30; *see also specific religion*
republics of former Soviet Union 169
research activities: China *vs.* Hong Kong 152; as driver 223–5; on ethnic minority education 76–7; HKUST management 175–80; Hong Kong universities 152; upgrading of 191, 257
Research and Development Corporation (RDC) 207–8
Research and Further Development collaboration 177
Research Assessment Exercise (RAE) 167–8, 205
research capacity management: collaborations 177; culture capital access 177–8; funding, HKUST 206–7, 211–13; funds management in donor culture 176–7; governance 178; internationalization 177; knowledge networks elevation 176; partnerships 177; planning 178; risk-taking 178; social capital access 177–8; take-off phase 175–6; talent, recruiting and sustaining 178–80
research universities, anchoring globalization in: collaborations 169–74, 177; conclusions 180–3; culture capital access 177–8; enabling environment 164–7; funds management in donor culture 176–7; governance 167–9, 178; growth 162–3; institutional autonomy 167–9; internationalization 177; introduction 6, 161–2; knowledge networks 174–6; partnerships 177; planning 178; research capacity management 175–80; risk-taking 178; social capital access 177–8; take-off phase 175–6; talent, recruiting and sustaining 178–80
research universities, national rejuvenation and global influence: challenges 223–5; China model 217–18; China's second system 225–30; conclusion 230–1; governance 226–30; higher education expansion 219; institutional autonomy 220–3; internationalization 220–3; inverted culture and governance 225–30; overview 7; quality and

quantity balance 217; reform 219–20; research and teaching as driver 223–5; state sovereignty 220–3; transitioning 218–20
return migration rates 188
RGC (Research Grants Council): financing research 211–12; funding and donations 177, 206; government steering and autonomy 167–9; HKUST planning stage 166; inverted academic culture and governance 225; key factor for HKUST 187
"ripening" universities 186, 190
risk-taking 178
Rockefeller, John D. 186
roles, HKUST 192–3
Royal Hong Kong Jockey Club *see* Jockey Club charities
rural-urban education divide 39–42

safety net systems 252
salaries: anchoring globalization 180; comparisons 219; competitive, limited benefit 179; cost sharing 263; decentralization 114; decisions about 148; HKUST 6, 203–4, 214n14; inadequacy 230; international standards 230; levels 189; prominent differences 151; reform 219; retitling without pay 155; rising 41; student fees 243; timing 203–4; withheld 97
SAR (Special Administrative Region) government: education and Hong Kong's future 13, 18; maintaining Hong Kong's universities 145; studying overseas 106
scholarship, integrated 226
schools and schooling: cultural genocide 134; dislocated education 121–2; as equalizer 50–1; participation improvements 75–6
Second Higher Education Project 247
self-determination *vs.* hegemony 60–1
self-esteem, loss 75
Self-Evaluation Document (HKUST) 205
Seventeen Point agreement 96, 118
shaoshu minzu 71
shehui liliang 39
Shellfare 58
Shenzhen Special Economic Zone (SEZ) 179, 195, 199, 213
Shue Yan University 165
Shui On Group donations 207

Shun Hing Group donations 207
Singapore: collaboration 170; colonial heritage 52; education system 49, 55–7, 253; enabling environment 164; global recession effects 242; high-tech industries 165; manufacturing 187; mathematics and science achievement 8, 49; medium of instruction 52; partnerships 259; potential development 259; public sector-dominated system 250; research collaboration 170; slowing population growth 243
Sino-British Declaration on the Question of Hong Kong: education and Hong Kong's future 13, 17–19; HUST kick-off 195; localization 24; policy intervention 14
Sino Group donations 207
slave experience 82
social capital access 177–8
social class structuralization 26–7
social composition, dislocated students 120–1
social order 29
social sciences requirement 187, 192
soft/software elements 220
Song Dynasty 7, 51
Songsten Gampo 100
soul 212
South China University of Science and Technology (SCUST) 222
South East Asia Ministers of Education Organization 247
Southern University of Science and Technology 213
South Korea: economic crisis response 238; education system 49; globalization 53; rankings 49; research collaboration 169; *see also* Korea
sovereignty *see* state sovereignty
Special Economic Zone (SEZ) 179, 195, 199, 213
special needs students 38–9
staff outflow 155–6
state schools, function 73
state sovereignty 7, 220–3
steering, government 163, 167–9, 225
Stelson, Thomas 203
straight line assimilation theory 5
student/faculty ratio 194–5
students: attracting 242; faculty salaries from fees 243; faculty/student ratio 194; gifted 38–9; HKUST 193–5;

international students 146, 199, 219, 236, 258; quality 151–2; social composition, dislocated students 120–1; special needs students 38–9; study-abroad trend 54; subsidies for 254–5; Tibet boarding schools 101–6, 114–15; underachieving, Tibet 75; Uyghur boarding schools 85; *see also* international students
subsidies 16, 27–8, 83, 254–5
sudden withdrawal, private capital 250
Suharto 58
Sukarno 58
"sunset years," colonial administration 166, 187, 200
sustainability, HKUST 209–10
system diversification 257
Szeto, Wah 19, 31n3

Taiwan: autonomy 52; Confucian values 52; education system of 49; enabling environment 164; HKUST case 178; knowledge networks 178; private universities enrollment 244; scientific talent 188–90; values and traditional practices 50
take-off phase 175–6
talent, recruiting and sustaining 178–80
Tang Dynasty 53, 54
targets, multiculturalism 96–7
teachers: boarding schools 128; rural-urban education divide 41; unqualified discontinued 95; *see also* professoriate
Teaching and Learning Quality Process Reviews (TLQPR) 205
teaching as driver 223–5
Thailand 55, 60, 237
three guarantees 98–9, 109n10
three- *vs.* four-year system 20–1, 167, 191–2
Tian, Jiyun 101, 137
Tiananmen event 155, 160n50, 165, 188, 213n4
Tibet: boarding schools 101–6, 114–15, 127–30; case studies 84–5; challenges, harmonious multiculturalism 94–110; Cultural Tibet 118; curriculum 129–30; dislocated education 114–38; economy backwardness *vs.* culture inferiority 115; education 89, 94; historical antecedents 96–7; language skills deterioration 105; literacy rates 97; medium of instruction 95, 99–101; minority educational policies 117; overview 3–5; relocating back to 131–3; research 84; school access 97; social stability 89; targets 96–7; underachieving students 75; urgency of education 94–7
Tibetan Autonomous Region (TAR): educational policy 75; establishment in Tibet 75, 136n3; overview 3, 108n1; political Tibet 118; preferential policies 97–8
Tibet inland *(neidi)* schools *see* boarding schools
"tiger to dragon" 162–3
Times Higher Education 9, 58–9
timing 6, 188, 203–4
Timor Leste 49, 58, 59
Tokugawa Era 53
Toyko University 198
transparency 197
trilingual capacity 95–6
tripartite agreement 177, 208
Tsinghua University 45, 220, 224, 245
tuition assistance 254–5; *see also* subsidies
turnover rate, staff 182

UGC (University Grants Committee): "equitable" allocation 195, 205; funding and donations 177, 191, 206; government steering and autonomy 167–9; HKUST 166, 194, 200, 205; inverted academic culture and governance 225–6; Knowledge Transfer Report 208; membership 148; roles 211; system-wide approach 191
Understanding Chinese Society 2
unemployment 16, 45, 71, 241–3, 249
United International College 199
United Kingdom: academic internationalism 145; as an educational model 19; democratization 22; foreign nationals 202; foreign students 258; governance structure 204; "insurance" passports 24–5; international engagement 156; international students 258; localization 24; presidential search 197; RAE 205; research collaboration 170; research spending 245; UGC membership 148
United Nations Development Programme 3
United States: academic internationalism 145; boarding schools 4, 114–15, 133–4; completing degree studies in 16, 155; education, staunchly patriotic

82–3; emotions evoked 114–15; foreign students 146, 258, 260; global center 61; global recession 238; HK trading partner 192, 200; HKUST case 178; innovations in governance 199–200; international engagement 156; knowledge networks 178; Korean cultural predispositions 87; nation-building experience 114; oppositional identities 74; presidential search 197; receiving international students 146; research collaboration 170; structuralization, social classes 26; Tibet, size of 85, 118; voluntary migrants *vs.* indigenous 82; voluntary *vs.* involuntary minorities 117; Woo, Chia-wei 175, 177–8, 188–9, 198, 202, 213n2
universities, Hong Kong: academic staff attributes/attitudes 150–4; governance and academic freedom 152–3; higher education priorities 153–4; Hong Kong context and 146–9; international academic activity 154; research activity 152; student quality 151–2
Universities and Polytechnics Grants Committee 19, 196–7, 205
universities under globalization: anchoring globalization in 161–83; global engagement, national integration 145–60; global recession and higher education 235–60; national rejuvenation and global influence 217–31; overview 5–8; rise of 186–214
University Grants Committee *see* UGC
University of Chicago 186
University of Hong Kong 147, 165
University of Michigan 222
University of Montana 222
University of Nottingham 199, 222
unrestricted inflow, private capital 250
upgrading of research 257
urban-rural education divide 39–42
urgency 94–7, 186–7, 260
Uyghurs 85, 131

Vietnam: Confucianism 55; education system of 49, 55–6; global recession and higher education 240, 245–8; partnerships 259; research collaboration 170; values and traditional practices 50
Vietnam-Germany University 247
visas 147, 150, 159n41, 245
vision 192–3, 212–13
voluntary minorities 117
voting 22

wealth *vs.* knowledge transmission 218
Weberian approach 2
Wen, Jiabao 223, 241
Winfrey, Oprah 136n1, 138n28
Winter fungus, impact on schooling 98–9
Wong, Eugene 202
Woo, Chia-wei 175, 177–8, 188–9, 198, 202, 213n2
working environment, HKUST 201–2
Wuhan University 222
Wu Jiawei *see* Woo, Chia-wei

Xiang level 138n21
Xinhua News Agency 20
Xinjiang: boarding schools 85, 119, 131; dislocated education 114, 117; education and social stability 89; minority educational policies 117; national identity 89; rate of capital return 133; state schooling 73
Xinjiang Uyghur Nationality Autonomous Region 102
Xizang neidiban 109n9, 137n12

"yiguo, Lianzhi" *see* one-country, two-system arrangement
Yonsei University 245
Youde, Sir Edward 195
youxiu minzu 70
Yuanpei program 224
Yung Dynasty 54–5
Yunnan 114

Zhang, Li 222
Zhang, Minxuan 222
zhonghua minzu wenhua 73
Zhu, Qingshi 222
Zhu, Rongji 223
Zhuhai Special Economic Zone 199